HDL Programming

VHDL and Verilog

HDL PROGRAMMING

VHDL AND VERILOG

NAZEIH BOTROS

Da Vinci

Published by:

dreamtech PRESS

This edition has been published by arrangement with the **Charles River Media Inc., USA** and published in India by **Dreamtech Press, 19-A, Ansari Road, Daryaganj, New Delhi-110002.**

Reprint Edition: 2008

Printed at: Himal Impressions. Delhi

Contents

Preface

This book provides the basic knowledge necessary to understand how to simulate systems using hardware description languages. Systems here include digital logic circuits, such as adders, multiplexers, flip-flops, latches, counters and sequential-state machines, biological mechanisms that describe the operation of organs (e.g., kidneys), mathematical models (e.g., factorial, greatest of *N* numbers, polynomials), and artificial intelligence (e.g., artificial neural networks).

This book covers Very High-Speed Integrated Circuit Hardware Description Language (VHDL) and Verilog Hardware Description Language (HDL). Mixed-language descriptions are also covered, where both VHDL and Verilog constructs are implemented in one HDL program. The book also covers fundamentals of hardware synthesis. HDL writing styles are classified into six groups: data flow, behavioral, structural or gate level, switch level, mixed type, and mixed-language description.

BOOK ORGANIZATION

The following is a brief description of the subjects that are covered in each chapter.

Chapter 1: The "Introduction" covers the structure of the HDL module and operators, including logical, arithmetic, relational, and shift. Data types are examined, such as scalar, composite and file, and a brief comparison is made between VHDL and Verilog.

Chapter 2: "Data-Flow Descriptions" covers other data types, such as bit vectors, as well as introduces and reviews the concept of designing simple combinational circuits, such as adders, comparators, and multiplexers.

Chapter 3: "Behavioral Descriptions" are covered, including the statements if, case, and loop. VHDL and Verilog are quite similar in behavioral statements. The chapter also covers the concept of designing some sequential circuits, such as counters and flips-flops.

Chapter 4: "Structural Descriptions" introduces gate-level and Register Transfer Level (RTL) descriptions. The chapter also covers digital logic design for counters and sequential-state machines. Again, the languages have many similarities, except that VHDL does not have the built-in components that Verilog has. By including packages, VHDL can use components that are very similar to those of Verilog.

Chapter 5: "Switch-Level Descriptions" introduces switch (transistor) level descriptions. VHDL does not have built-in constructs for switch-level description, but packages can be included that enable writing VHDL switch-level statements similar to those of Verilog.

Chapter 6: "Procedures, Tasks, and Functions" covers VHDL procedures and functions, and Verilog tasks and functions, and discusses their similarities.

Chapter 7: Introduces "Mixed-Type Descriptions." The design of basic computers is also discussed.

Chapter 8: "Advanced HDL Descriptions" covers advanced topics such as files and the type record.

Chapter 9: Mixed languages are introduced in "Mixed-Language Descriptions," where both VHDL and Verilog can be implemented in the same program. The reader now knows both VHDL and Verilog; this chapter shows how to mix their constructs.

Chapter 10: "Synthesis Basics" covers the basics of hardware synthesis.

WHO SHOULD USE THIS BOOK?

This textbook is appropriate for first- or second-year electrical engineering, computer engineering, or computer science college students; some of the advanced topics can be skipped if desired by the instructor. This book is also appropriate for third-year students; all topics of the book can be covered.

Short courses for digital design engineers are also appropriate. Suggested courses that could use this book include HDL programming or synthesis, Application-Specific Integrated Circuit (ASIC) design, or digital design projects.

ABOUT THE EXAMPLES IN THIS BOOK

The examples in this book are comprehensive and numerous. They cover the rules of HDL and also review the digital logic design material that students have learned in their first and/or second years of college. The examples cover a wide span of topics, such as digital design logic, artificial neural networks, and simple biological mechanisms. The examples, in addition to explaining the code, show the locations of the statements within the module and also any Library or package that should be included.

The location of statements is very important in HDL. For example, the VHDL statement case has to be written inside the process statement; if it does not appear inside `process`, even if the syntax is correct, the simulator halts the simulation and declares an error.

There might not be enough time available to cover all the examples. In this case, the instructor can select to cover only those examples that fit the students' background.

HOW TO USE THIS BOOK

The book covers the two major hardware description languages: VHDL and Verilog, and focuses (almost) equally on both languages. If the reader wants to learn one language at a time, he/she can read the sections that deal with that language.

Almost all examples in the book are written into two parts: The first part is written in VHDL, and the second part written in Verilog. Some examples, however, are written in only one language, such as when the example deals with a very specific language construct that belongs only to one language, and which has no counterpart in the other language. An example is the VHDL user-defined statement `which`; this statement does not have a clear Verilog counterpart, so it is written only in VHDL.

If the reader wants to learn both languages at the same time, the book is organized to serve as a simultaneous learning tool. VHDL and Verilog are not very different; they have several similarities. I teach both languages in one course in one semester, starting with VHDL. VHDL is covered in Chapters 1 and 2. The student then will be familiar with the basic rules of HDL language and ready to learn Verilog. Verilog material is introduced in Chapters 1 and 2. After Chapter 2 and until the end of the semester, VHDL and Verilog are covered at the same time and in the same order as presented in this book.

INSTRUCTOR AND STUDENT WEB SUPPORT

This book has a Help and Discussion Web page supervised by the author at *http://www.engr.siu.edu/staff1/botrosn/mywebpage/botros.html.* The Help page has a section for students and a password-driven section for instructors. Visitors can read or leave comments concerning the material in this book. Additional material, such as exams and additional labs, are also posted on the Web site.

1 Introduction

In This Chapter

- Learn the history of HDL Development
- Learn how the HDL module is structured
- Learn the use of operators in HDL modules
- Learn the different types of HDL objects
- Understand the function of a simulator
- Understand the function of a synthesizer
- Understand the major differences between VHDL and Verilog HDL

1.1 WHY HDL?

Hardware Description Language (HDL) is a Computer-Aided Design (CAD) tool for the modern design and synthesis of digital systems. The recent, steady advances in semiconductor technology continue to increase the power and complexity of digital systems. Due to their complexity, such systems cannot be realized using discrete Integrated Circuits (ICs). They are usually realized using high-density, programmable chips, such as Application-Specific Integrated Circuits (ASICs) and Field-Programmable Gate Arrays (FPGAs), and require sophisticated CAD tools. HDL is an integral part of such tools. HDL offers the designer a very efficient tool for implementing and synthesizing designs on chips.

The designer uses HDL to describe the system in a computer language that is similar to several commonly used software languages, such as C. Debugging the design is easy, since HDL packages implement simulators and test benches. The two widely used hardware description languages are VHDL and Verilog. Since each language is equally implemented in both academia and industry, this book covers both individually and also discusses how to use them in the same module.

1.2 A BRIEF HISTORY OF HDL

HDL is a must-have tool for modern digital engineers. There are two major hardware description languages: VHDL and Verilog HDL. Both are popular among industry and academia. In the following, we briefly explore their development history. In Section 1.2.1, we explore VHDL history; and in Section 1.2.2, we explore Verilog HDL. More information about the development of HDL can be found in [Accolade05], [Aldec05], and [Xilinx05].

1.2.1 A Brief History of VHDL

VHDL, which stands for Very High-Speed Integrated Circuit (VHSIC) Hardware Description Language, was developed in the early 1980s under the VHSIC program. In this program, a number of high-tech companies were involved in designing VHSIC chips for the U.S. Department of Defense (DoD). At that time, each company used its own primitive hardware-description language. Moreover, these primitive, company-based languages provided the researchers with only gate-level design tools. They did not support large-scale design and also prevented these companies from unifying their efforts in developing VHSIC chips. So the need for a standardized, extensive hardware-description language was generated.

To meet this need, a research team from three companies—IBM, Texas Instruments, and Intermetrics—was assembled by the DoD and instructed to develop a standard for powerful hardware-description language-based tools. The team produced the first publicly available standard, VHDL Version 7.2, in 1985. A wide variety of companies, especially those who were involved in developing VHSIC chips, extensively implemented this version in their designs. The standardization of the language, however, was not enough to satisfy the design requirements for such a wide variety of companies. In 1986, the Institute of Electrical and Electronics Engineers (IEEE) was tasked with globally standardizing the language. In 1987, the IEEE completed their mission and added several enhancements to the language; the result was the IEEE Standard 1076-1987 version of VHDL, which was also recognized by the American National Standards Institute (ANSI). The official reference manual of this version is available from IEEE *(http://www.ieee.org)*.

In 1993, VHDL was updated and more features were added; the result of this update was IEEE Standard 1076-1993. The language described in this book is based on the 1993 version. One of the major enhancements to the language was the introduction of several packages that added important features. One of these packages, std_logic_1164, added seven additional logic levels to the existing two levels, logic 0 and logic 1. (See Section 1.5.1.5 for details.)

Nowadays, VHDL is a very popular design tool among industry and academia. Additional tools have been added to the language, such as graphics-based simulators that allow the user to interact graphically on the screen with the simulator to compile, simulate, test, and verify the design. Also, an analog extension to the language is underway.

1.2.2 A Brief History of Verilog

The history of Verilog HDL goes back to 1983 when a company called Gateway Design Automation developed a hardware-description language for its newly introduced logic simulator, Verilog-XL. Gateway was bought by Candence in 1989; and in 1990, Cadence made Verilog available as public domain, with the intention that it should become a standard, nonproprietary language.

In December 1995, Verilog HDL became IEEE Standard 1364-1995. The language is presently maintained by the Open Verilog International (OVI) organization. Verilog code structure is based on C software language. Work is currently underway to define analog extensions to Verilog.

1.3 STRUCTURE OF THE HDL MODULE

HDL modules follow the general structure of software languages such as C. The module has a source code that is written in high-level language style. Text editors supplied by the HDL package vendor can be used to write the module, or can be written using external text editors and imported to the HDL package by Copy and Paste. The most recently introduced feature in HDL packages allows automatic generation of HDL code from C-language code. VHDL has a somewhat different structure than HDL Verilog. In this book, Verilog HDL will be simply be referred to as Verilog. In Section 1.3.1 we discuss VHDL structure, and Section 1.3.2 we will cover Verilog structure.

1.3.1 Structure of the VHDL Module

The VHDL module has two major constructs: entity and architecture. Entity declares the input and output signals of the system to be described, and is given a name or identifier by the user. VHDL is case insensitive; the two entity names `Half_ADDER` and `half_adder` are treated as the same name. The name should start with an alphabetical letter and can include the special character underscore (_). Declarations include the name and type of the inputs and outputs of the system. The inputs and outputs here are called "input ports" and "output ports"; they are signals (see Chapter 2, "Data Flow Descriptions"). The name of the port is user-selected, and it has the same requirements as the entity's name. An example of an entity is:

```
entity half_adder is
port(I1 : in bit; I2 : in bit; sum_h : out bit;
    carry_out : out bit);
end half_adder;
```

The word entity is a predefined word. The name of the entity is half_adder. This name is user-selected and does not convey any information about the system; it is just an identifier. The entity could have been given any other name. VHDL does not know that the entity half_adder describes a half adder simply by its name. The entity shown in the previous example has two input ports and two output ports. The term is is a predefined word and must be written after the name of the entity. The word port is predefined. The names of the input ports are I1 and I2, and they must be followed by a colon (:). The predefined word in instantiates the mode of the port as an input (see Section 1.3.1.1 for details on ports modes). The type of these input signals is bit, and determines the allowed values that signals I1 and I2 can take. Type bit allows the signal to take either logic 0 or logic 1. There are several other types, such as std_logic, real, and integer (see Section 1.5.1). The entity also has two output ports, sum_h and carry_out; they are declared as outputs with the predefined word out, and their types are bit. The order that the input and output ports are written inside the parentheses is irrelevant. The output ports could have been listed before the input ports.

The last line of the entity's code uses the predefined word end and ends the entity. The name of the entity can follow the word end, as in end half_adder, or the name of the entity can be omitted and only end is written. The semicolon (;) is an important character in HDL. It is used as a separator similar to the carriage return character used in C language. For example, the port statement can be written as:

```
port(I1 : in bit;
I2 : in bit;
sum_h : out bit;
carry_out : out bit);
```

The carriage return between the statements does not convey any information; it is the semicolon that signals a new statement. Ports can be declared in, out, inout, buffer, or linkage (see Section 1.3.1.1).

The architecture includes details about the relationship between the inputs and outputs of the system, and must be bound to an entity. More than one architecture can be bound to the same entity, but each architecture can be bound to only one entity. Listing 1.1 shows an example of an architecture bound to an entity. The entity illustrate has two input ports of type bit and two output ports of type bit. The architecture is declared by the predefined word architecture, followed by a user-selected name; this name follows the same name-selecting guidelines as the entity. In Listing 1.1, the name of the architecture is dtfl_ex. It is followed by the predefined word of, followed by the name of the entity. The predefined word of binds the architecture dtfl_ex to the entity illustrate.

LISTING 1.1 Example of Entity Architecture

```
entity illustrate is
port (I1, I2 : in bit; O1, O2 : out bit);
end;

architecture dtfl_ex of illustrate is
begin
O1 <= I1 xor I2; -- statement 1
O2 <= I1 and I2; -- statement 2

end dtfl_ex;
```

Binding here means that the information listed in the entity is visible to the architecture. In Listing 1.1, the architecture `dtfl_ex` recognizes the information declared in the entity, such as the name and type of ports `I1`, `I2`, `O1`, and `O2`. After the name of the entity, the predefined word `is` must be written. The architecture's body starts with the predefined word `begin`, followed by statements that detail the relationship between the outputs and inputs.

In Listing 1.1, the body of the architecture includes two statements. The two hyphens (--) signal that a comment follows. Statements 1 and 2 constitute the body of the architecture; they are signal assignment statements (see Chapter 2). The two statements describe the relationship between the output ports `O1` and `O2`, and the input ports `I1` and `I2`. The `xor` and the `and` are called "logical operators" (see Section 1.4); they simulate EXCLUSIVE-OR and AND logic, respectively. The architecture describes a half adder. `O1` is the sum I1⊕I2, and `O2` is the carry out I1⊕I2. The architecture is closed by the predefined word `end`. The name of the architecture can follow `end`, if desired. Leaving blank line(s) is allowed in the module; also, spaces between two words or at the beginning of the line are allowed.

1.3.1.1 VHDL Ports

In VHDL, ports can take one of the following modes:

`in`: The port is only an input. In any assignment statement, the port should appear only on the right-hand side of the statement (i.e., the port is read).

`out`: The port is only an output port. In any assignment statement, the port should appear only on the left-hand side of the statement (i.e., the port is updated).

`buffer`: The port can be used as both an input and output, but can have only one source (i.e., limited fan-out). The port can appear on either the left- or right-hand side of an assignment statement. A buffer port can only be connected to another buffer port or to a signal that also has only one source.

`inout`: The port can be used as both an input and output.

`linkage:` Same as `inout`, but the port can only correspond to a signal.

1.3.2 Structure of the Verilog Module

The Verilog module has a declaration and a body. In the declaration, name, inputs, and outputs of the module are listed. The body shows the relationship between the inputs and the outputs. Listing 1.2 shows an example of a Verilog module:

LISTING 1.2 Example of a Verilog Module

```
module half_adder (I1, I2, O1, O2);
    input I1;
    input I2;
    output O1;
    output O2;
    //Blank lines are allowed
    assign O1 = I1 ^ I2; //statement 1
    assign O2 = I1 & I2; //statement 2
endmodule
```

The name of the module is the user-selected `half_adder`. In contrast to VHDL, Verilog is case sensitive. `Half_adder`, `half_adder`, and `half_addEr` are all different names. The name of the module should start with an alphabetical letter and can include the special character underscore (_). The declaration of the module starts with the predefined word `module`, followed by a user-selected name. The names of the inputs and outputs (i.e., the `input` and `output` ports) follow the same guidelines as the module's name. They are written inside parentheses and are separated by commas. The closing parenthesis is followed by a semicolon. In Listing 1.2, `I1`, `I2`, `O1`, and `O2` are the names of the inputs and outputs. The order in which the input and output ports are written inside the parentheses is irrelevant. We could have written the module statement as:

```
module half_adder (O1, I1, I2, O2);
```

The semicolon (;) performs the same function as in VHDL modules; it is a line separator. A carriage return here does not indicate a new line; the semicolon does. Following the module statement, the mode of the input and output ports are declared. For example, the statement `input I1;` declares signal `I1` as an input port. (Port modes are discussed in Section 1.3.2.1.) In contrast to VHDL, the input and output port signal types are implicitly declared (see Section 1.5.2). The order in which the inputs and outputs, and their declarations, is written is irrelevant; the following could have been written:

```
module half_adder (I1, I2, O1, O2);
    output O1;
    output O2;
    input I1;
    input I2;
```

Also, more than one input or output could have been written on the same line by using a comma (,) to separate each input; for example:

```
module half_adder (I1, I2, O1, O2);
    output O1, O2;
    input I1, I2;
```

Statements 1 and 2 in Listing 1.2 are signal assignment statements (see Chapter 2). In statement 1, the symbol ^ represents an `EXCULSIVE-OR` operation; this symbol is called a *logical operator* (see Section 1.4.2). So, statement 1 describes the relationship between `O1`, `I1`, and `I2` as: `O1` = `I1 XOR I2`.

In statement 2, the symbol `&` represents `AND` logic; it is also a logical operator (see Section 1.4.2). So statement 2 describes the relationship between `O2`, `I1`, and `I2` as: `O2` = `I1 AND I2`. Accordingly, Listing 1.2 simulates a half adder. The double slashes (`//`) signal a comment command. If the comment takes more than one line, new double slashes can be used, or the pair (`/*`...`*/`) can be used to write a comment of any length. The module is terminated by the predefined word `endmodule`. Leaving blank line(s) is allowed in the module; also, spaces between two words or at the beginning of the line are allowed.

1.3.2.1 Verilog Ports

Verilog ports can be one of the following three modes:

`input`: The port is only an input port. In any assignment statement, the port should appear only on the right-hand side of the statement (i.e., the port is read).

`output`: The port is an output port. In contrast to VHDL, the Verilog output port can appear on either side of the assignment statement.

`inout`: The port can be used as both an input and output. The inout port represents a bidirectional bus.

1.4 OPERATORS

HDL has an extensive list of operators. These operators are used extensively in every chapter of the book. Operators perform a wide variety of functions. These functions can be classified as:

Logical (see Section 1.4.1), such as AND, OR, and XOR;

Relational (see Section 1.4.2) to express the relation between objects. These operators include equality, inequality, less than, less than or equal, greater than, and greater than or equal;

Arithmetic (see Section 1.4.3), such as addition, subtraction, multiplication, and division; and

Shift (see Section 1.4.4) to move the bits of an object in a certain direction, such as right or left.

In this section, HDL logical operators are extensively discussed. The reader is advised to briefly study the operators presented here in order to understand their concepts. These operators are implemented in almost every chapter of this book. When implemented, the reader can return to this section to read the details of operators used.

1.4.1 Logical Operators

These operators perform logical operations, such as AND, OR, NAND, NOR, NOT, and EXCLUSIVE-OR. The operation can be on two operands or on a single operand. The operand can be single-bit or multiple bits. In Section 1.4.1.1, VHDL logical operators are discussed, and Verilog logical operators are discussed in Section 1.4.1.2.

1.4.1.1 VHDL Logical Operators

Table 1.1 shows a list of VHDL logical operators. Those operators should appear only on the right-hand side of statements.

All VHDL operators are bitwise; they operate on corresponding bits of two signals. For example, consider the statement `Z:= X XOR Y`. If X is the 4-bit signal 1011 and Y is the 4-bit signal 1010, then Z = 0001.

1.4.1.2 Verilog Logical Operators

Verilog has extensive logical operators. These operators perform logical operations such as AND, OR, and EXCULSIVE-OR. Verilog logical operators can be classified into three groups: bitwise, Boolean logical, and reduction. The bitwise operators are similar to VHDL logical operators; they operate on the corresponding bits of two operands. Consider the statement: `Z= X & Y`, where the AND operator (&) 'ANDs' the corresponding bits of X and Y, and stores the result in Y. For example, if X is the 4-bit signal 1011, and Y is the 4-bit signal 1010, then Z = 1010. Table 1.2 shows bitwise logical operators. For example, if we want to perform an NAND operation on X and Y, we write `Z = ~(X & Y)`.

TABLE 1.1 VHDL Logical Operators

Operator	Equivalent Logic	Operand Type	Result Type
AND	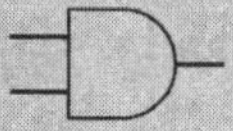	Bit	Bit
OR	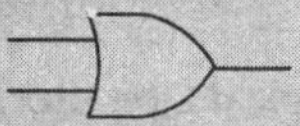	Bit	Bit
NAND	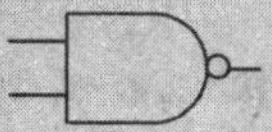	Bit	Bit
NOR	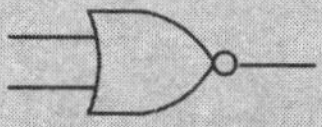	Bit	Bit
XOR		Bit	Bit
XNOR	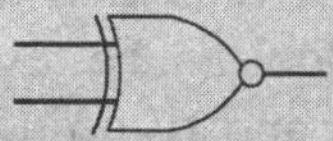	Bit	Bit
NOT	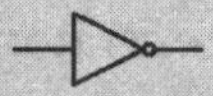	Bit	Bit

TABLE 1.2 Verilog Bitwise Logical Operators

Operator	Equivalent Logic	Operand Type	Result Type
&	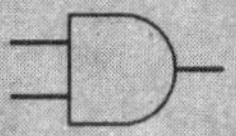	Bit	Bit
|	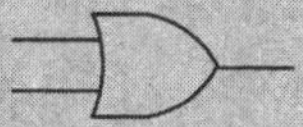	Bit	Bit
~(&)	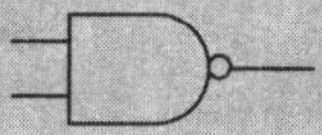	Bit	Bit
~ (|)	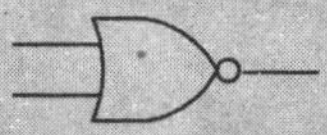	Bit	Bit
^	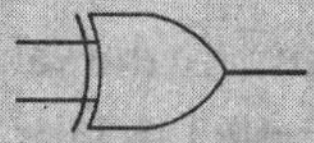	Bit	Bit
~^	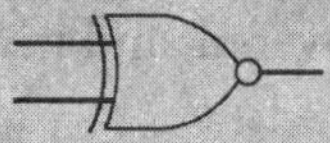	Bit	Bit
~	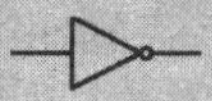	Bit	Bit

Other types of logical operators are the Boolean logical operators. These operators operate on two operands; the result is Boolean, 0 (false) or 1 (true). For example, consider the statement `Z = X && Y`, where `&&` is the Boolean logical AND operator. If X = 1011 and Y = 0001, then Z = 1. If X = 1010 and Y = 0101, then Z = 0. If `Z = !X`, where `!` is the negation operator and X = 1111, then Z = 0. Table 1.3 shows the Boolean logical operators.

TABLE 1.3 Verilog Boolean Logical Operators

Operator	Operation	Number of Operands
&&	AND	two
||	OR	two

The third type of logical operator is the reduction operator. These operators operate on a single operand. The result is Boolean. For example, in the statement `Y = &X`, where `&` is the reduction AND operator and assuming X = 1010, then Y = (1 & 0 & 1 & 0) = 0. Table 1.4 shows the reduction logic operators.

TABLE 1.4 Verilog Reduction Logical Operators

Operator	Operation	Number of Operands
&	Reduction AND	one
|	Reduction OR	one
~&	Reduction NAND	one
~ |	Reduction OR	one
^	Reduction XOR	one
~^	Reduction XNOR	one
!	NEGATION	one

1.4.2 Relational Operators

Relational operators are implemented to compare the values of two objects. The result returned by these operators is Boolean—that is, false (0) or true (1). In Section 1.4.2.1, the VHDL relational operator is covered, and in Section 1.4.2.2 we discuss Verilog relational operators.

1.4.2.1 VHDL Relational Operators

VHDL has extensive relational operators. Their main implementations are in the `if` and `case` statements (see Chapter 3, "Behavioral Descriptions"). Table 1.5 shows VHDL relational operators.

TABLE 1.5 VHDL Relational Operators

Operator	Description	Operand Type	Result Type
=	Equality	Any type	Boolean
/=	Inequality	Any type	Boolean
<	Less than	Scalar	Boolean
<=	Less than or equal	Scalar	Boolean
>	Greater than	Scalar	Boolean
>=	Greater than or equal	Scalar	Boolean

The following statement demonstrates the implementation of some of the above relational operators:

```
If (A = B) then .....
```

`A` is compared to `B`. If `A` is equal to `B`, then the value of the expression `(A = B)` is true (1); otherwise it is false (0).

```
If (A < B) then .....
```

If `A` is less than `B`, the value of the expression `(A < B)` is true (1); otherwise it is false(0).

1.4.2.2 Verilog Relational Operators

Verilog has a set of relational operators similar to VHDL. Table 1.6 shows Verilog relational operators. As in VHDL, the relational operators return Boolean values—false (0) or true (1).

For the equality operator (==) and inequality operator (`!=`), the result can be of type unknown (x) if any of the operands include 'don't care' or 'unknown (x),' or 'high impedance z.' These types are covered in Section 1.5.

The following is an example of a Verilog relational operator:

```
if (A == B).....
```

TABLE 1.6 Verilog Relational Operators

Operator	Description	Result Type
==	Equality	0,1,x
!=	Inequality	0,1,x
===	Equality inclusive	0,1
!==	Inequality inclusive	0,1
<	Less than	0,1,x
<=	Less than or equal	0,1,x
>	Greater than	0,1,x
>=	Greater than or equal	0,1,x

If the value of A or B contains one or more 'don't care' or z bits, the value of the expression is unknown. Otherwise, if A is equal to B, the value of the expression is true (1). If A is not equal to B, the value of the expression is false (0).

```
if (A === B).....
```

This is a bit-by-bit comparison. A or B can include x or z; the result is true (1) if all bits of A match that of B. Otherwise the result is false (0).

1.4.3 Arithmetic Operators

Arithmetic operators can perform a wide variety of operations, such as addition, subtraction, multiplication, and division. In Section 1.4.3.1 we discuss VHDL arithmetic operators, and Section 1.4.3.2 discusses Verilog arithmetic operators.

1.4.3.1 VHDL Arithmetic Operators

VHDL arithmetic operators operate on numeric and physical operand types (see Section 1.5). Physical data types are those that can be measured in units, such as time—for example, `y := 10 ns`, where `ns` is the unit nanoseconds. To illustrate the function of some of these operators, consider the arithmetic operation: `Y := A` (arithmetic operator) `B`. An example of an arithmetic operator is the multiplication operator (*); the statement `Y := (A * B)` calculates the value of `Y` as the product of `A` times `B`. Table 1.7 shows the VHDL arithmetic operators and the types required for A, B, and Y.

TABLE 1.7 VHDL Arithmetic Operators

Operator	Description	A or B Type	Y Type
+	Addition A + B	A numeric B numeric	numeric
-	Subtraction A − B	A numeric B numeric	numeric
*	Multiplication A ? B	A integer or real B integer or real	Same as A
*	Multiplication A ? B	A physical B integer or real	Same as A
*	Multiplication A ? B	A integer or real B physical	Same as B
/	Division A ÷ B	A integer or real B integer or real	Same as A
/	Division A ÷ B	A integer or real B physical	Same as B
/	Division A ÷ B	A physical B integer or real	Same as A
mod	Modulus A mod B	A only integer B only integer	integer
rem	Remainder A rem B	A only integer B only integer	integer
abs	Absolute abs (A)	A numeric	positive numeric
&	Concatenation (A & B)	A numeric or array B numeric or array	Same as A
**	Exponent A ** B	A real or integer B only integer	Same as A

More discussion and examples on how to use these arithmetic operators can be found in subsequent chapters.

1.4.3.2 Verilog Arithmetic Operators

Verilog, in contrast to VHDL, is not an extensive type-oriented language. Accordingly, for most operations, only one type of operation is expected for each operator. To illustrate the function of these operators, consider the arithmetic operation: `Y := A` (arithmetic operator) `B`. An example of an arithmetic operator is the multiplication operator (*); the statement `Y := (A * B)` calculates the value of `Y` as the product of `A` times `B`. Table 1.8 shows the Verilog arithmetic operators.

More discussion and examples on how to use these Verilog arithmetic operators can be found in subsequent chapters.

TABLE 1.8 Verilog Arithmetic Operators

Operator	Description	A or B Type	Y Type
+	Addition A + B	A numeric B numeric	numeric
-	Subtraction A – B	A numeric B numeric	numeric
*	Multiplication A ? B	A numeric B numeric	numeric
/	Division A ÷ B	A numeric B numeric	numeric
%	Modulus A % B	A numeric, not real B numeric, not real	numeric, not real
**	Exponent A ** B	A numeric B numeric	numeric
{,}	Concatenation {A , B}	A numeric or array B numeric or array	Same as A

1.4.4 Shift and Rotate Operators

Shift and rotate operators are implemented in many applications, such as in multiplication and division. A shift left represents multiplication by two, and a shift right represents division by two. VHDL shift operators are discussed in Section 1.4.4.1, and Verilog shift operators are discussed in Section 1.4.4.2.

1.4.4.1 VHDL Shift/Rotate Operators

Shift operators are unary operators; they operate on a single operand. To understand the function of these operators, assume that operand `A` is the 4-bit vector 1110. Table 1.9 shows the VHDL shift operators as they apply to operand `A`.

Notice that rotate `(ror)` keeps all bits of operand `A`. For example, `(A ror 1)` shifts `A` one position to the right and inserts the least significant bit (0) in the vacant, most significant position.

TABLE 1.9 VHDL Shift Operators

Operation	Description	Operand A Before Shift	Operand A After Shift
A sll 1	Shift A one position left logical	1110	110x
A sll 2	Shift A two positions left logical	1110	10xx
A srl 1	Shift A one position right logical	1110	x111
A srl 2	Shift A two positions right logical	1110	xx11
A sla 1	Shift A one position left arithmetic	1110	110x
A sra 1	Shift A one position right arithmetic	1110	1111
A rol 1	Rotate A one position left	1110	1101
A ror 1	Rotate A one position right	1110	0111

1.4.4.2 Verilog Shift Operators

Verilog has the basic shift operators. Shift operators are unary operators; they operate on a single operand. To understand the function of these operators, assume operand A is the 4-bit vector 1110. Table 1.10 shows the Verilog shift operators as they apply to operand A.

TABLE 1.10 Verilog Shift Operators

Operation	Description	Operand A Before Shift	Operand A After Shift
A << 1	Shift A one position left logical	1110	110x
A << 2	Shift A two positions left logical	1110	10xx
A >> 1	Shift A one position right logical	1110	x111
A >> 2	Shift A two positions right logical	1110	xx11

1.5 DATA TYPES

Since HDL is implemented to describe the hardware of a system, the data or operands used in the language must have several types to match the need for describing the hardware. For example, if we are describing a signal, we need to specify its type (i.e., the values that the signal can take), such as type `bit`, which means that the signal can assume only 0 or 1; or type `std_logic`, in which the signal can assume eight values that include 0, 1, and high impedance. Examples of types include `integer`, `real`, `vector`, `bit`, and `array`. HDL, especially VHDL, has an extensive set of types. Many operations will not be executed if we do not satisfy the type requirements for that operation. In Section 1.5.1, data types for VHDL are discussed, and data types for Verilog are discussed in Section 1.5.2.

In this section we extensively discuss HDL data types. The reader is advised to briefly study the data types presented here in order to know their concepts. Data types are implemented in almost every chapter of this book; when implemented, the reader can come back to this section to read the details about a data type.

1.5.1 VHDL Data Types

As previously mentioned, VHDL is a type-oriented language; many operations will not be executed if we do not choose the right type for the operands. The type of any element or object in VHDL determines the allowed values that element can assume. Objects in VHDL can be signal (see Chapter 2), variable (see Chapter 3), or constant (see Chapters 2 and 3). These objects can assume different types; we can classify these types into five groups, depending on the nature of the values the object can assume: scalar, composite, access, file, and other. The following sections discuss each group.

1.5.1.1 Scalar Types

The values that a scalar object type can assume are numeric. Numeric values can be integer, real, physical (such as time), characters when stored as ASCII (American Standard Code for Information Interchange) or compatible code, or Boolean (0 or 1). The following types constitute the scalar types.

Bit Type

The only values allowed here are 0 or 1; `bit` is the most primitive type. It is used to describe a signal that takes only 1 (high) or 0 (low). The signal cannot take other values, such as high impedance (open). An example of implementing this type is when we describe the type of a port signal as:

```
port (I1, I2 : in bit; O1, O2 : out bit);
```

Signals `I1`, `I2`, `O1`, and `O2` can assume only 0 or 1. If any of these signals must assume other levels or values, such as high impedance, `bit` type cannot be used.

Boolean Type

This type has two values: `false` (0) or `true` (1). Both `true` and `false` are predefined words. One of the most frequent applications of the `Boolean` type is in the `if` statement (see Chapter 3). Consider the statements:

```
If (y = B) then
     S := '1';
else
     S := '0';
end if;
```

The output of the first line, `If (y =B)`, is Boolean—that is, it is either true or false. If true, then `S` = 1; if false, `S` = 0. `Boolean` can also be specified as a port type:

```
port (I1, I2 : in bit; O1 : out bit; O2 : Boolean);
```

Integer Type

As the name indicates, this type covers all integer values; the values can be negative or positive. The default range is from –2,147,483,647 to +2,147,483,647. The user can specify a shorter range by using the predefined word `range`. The predefined word `natural` can be used instead of `integer` if the values of the object are always positive, including 0. An example of the `integer` type is in the implementation of the exponent operator (see Section 1.4.3.1). The exponent has to be of type `integer`, such as `X**2` or `X**y`, where `y` is declared as `integer`. The port can also be declared as type `integer`:

```
port (I1 : in natural; I2 : in bit; O1 : out integer; O2 : Boolean);
```

Another predefined type, `positive`, restricts the values an object can take to be positive and higher then 0.

Real Type

This type accepts fractions, such as .4502, 12.5, –5.2E–10, where E–10 = 10^{-10}. The default range is from –1.0E38 to +1.0E38. An example of using `real` type is:

```
port (I1 : in natural; I2 : in real; O1 : out integer; O2 : Boolean);
```

Character Type

This type includes characters that can be used to print a message using the predefined command `report`, such as:

```
report ("Variable x is greater than Y");
```

Notice that each character in the above message is just printed; no value is assigned to them. The `report` statement is very similar to the `print` statement in C language. We can add some format to the characters printed by `report`:

```
report ("Variable x is greater than Y.") & CR &
    ("Variable x is > 2.34.");
```

where `&` is the concatenation operator (see Section 1.4.3.1), and `CR` is a predefined word for carriage return.

If we want to assign a numeric value to each character, `subtype` and `type` can be used as follows:

```
subtype wordChr is character;
type string_chr is array (N downto 0) of wordChr;
```

`subtype`, `type`, and `array` are predefined words (see arrays and user-defined types in this section and in Chapters 6, "Procedures, Tasks, and Functions," 7 "Mixed-Type Descriptions," and 8, "Advanced HDL Descriptions."). The above two statements declare an array of $N + 1$ elements; and each element is a character. The characters are associated with ASCII values. For example, character "A" has the ASCII value of 32. More discussion on characters can be found in Chapter 8.

Physical Type

This type has values that can be measured in units, such as time (e.g., second, millisecond, microsecond, etc.) and voltage (e.g., volt, millivolt, microvolts, etc.). An example of type `time` is as follows:

```
constant Delay_inv : time := 1 ns;
```

The above statement states that the constant `Delay_inv` is of type `time`, and its initial value is one nanosecond `(1 ns)`. The word `time` is predefined; the units of `time` are as follows:

fs	=	smallest unit
ps	=	1,000 fs
ns	=	1,000 ps
us	=	1,000 ns
ms	=	1,000 us
sec	=	1,000 ms
min	=	60 sec
hr	=	60 min

More implementations of the physical type are covered in Chapter 2.

User-Defined Types

The user can define a type by using the predefined word `type` as shown below:

```
type op is (add, mul, divide, none);
variable opcode : op := mul;
```

`op` is a user-defined type. The variable `opcode` is of type `op` and hence can take an initial value of `add, mul, divide,` or `none`. More discussion about user-defined types can be found in Chapter 7, "Mixed-Type Descriptions."

Severity Type

This type is used with the `assert` statement (see Chapter 8). An object with type `severity` can take one of four values: `note, warning, error,` or `failure`. An example of this type is as follows:

```
assert (Flag_full = false);
report "The stack is full";
severity failure;
```

The `assert` condition is `Flag_full = false`. If `Flag_full` is not false, a message is printed to indicate that the stack is full, and simulation is halted.

1.5.1.2 Composite Types

The composite type is a collection of values. There are three composite types: bit vector, arrays (see Chapter 7), and records (see Chapter 8). An array is a collection of values all belonging to a single type; a record is a collection of values with the same or different types.

Bit_vector Types

The `bit_vector` type represents an array of bits; each element of the array is a single bit. The following example illustrates the implementation of type `bit_vector`:

```
Port (I1 : in bit; I2 : in bit_vector (5 downto 0); Sum : out bit);
```

In the above statement, port `I2` is declared as of type `bit_vector`; it has 6 bits. Possible values of `I2` include 110110, 011010, and 000000. More details about `bit_vector` can be found in Chapter 2.

Array Types

This type is declared by using the predefined word `array`. For example, the following statements declare the variable `memory` to be a single-dimensional array of eight elements, and each element is an integer:

```
subtype wordN is integer;
```

```
type intg is array (7 downto 0) of wordN;
...........
variable memory : intg;
```

Arrays can be multidimensional. See Chapter 7, for more details on arrays.

Record Types

An object of `record` type is composed of elements of the same or different types. An example of `record` type is shown below:

```
Type forecast is
record
Tempr : integer range -100 to 100;
Day : real;
Cond : bit;
end record;
............
variable temp : forecast
```

Variable `temp` is of type `forecast`; type `forecast` includes `record`, and `record` has three different types: `integer`, `real`, and `bit`. More details about records can be found in Chapter 8.

1.5.1.3 Access Types

Values belonging to an `access` type are pointers to objects of other types. For example:

```
type ptr_weathr is access forecast;
```

`ptr_weathr` is a pointer to `forecast` shown in last example of Section 1.5.1.2.

1.5.1.4 File Types

Objects of type `file` can be read from and written to using built-in functions and procedures that are provided in the standard library. Some of these procedures and functions are `file_open` to open files, `readline` to read a line from the file, `writeline` to write a line into the file, and `file_close` to close the file. More details about `file` types and operations can be found in Chapter 8.

1.5.1.5 Other Types

There are several other types provided by external Libraries. The external IEEE Library contains a package by the name of std_logic_1164. This package contains an extremely important type: `std_logic`. We have seen that type `bit` has only two values: level 0 and level 1. If we want to simulate a signal that assumes values of more than the two levels, such as high impedance, we can not use `bit` type. Type `std_logic` can be used to declare a signal as high impedance.

Std_Logic Type

This logic has nine values, including 1 and 0. Package std_logic_1164 should be attached to the VHDL module. The nine values of `std_logic` type are shown in Table 1.11:

TABLE 1.11 Values of Std_Logic Type

Value	Definition
U	uninitialized
X	unknown
0	low
1	high
Z	high impedance
W	weak unknown
L	weak low
H	weak high
-	don't care

Std_logic_vector Type

The type `std_logic_vector` represents an array. Each element of the array is a single bit of type `std_logic`. The following example illustrates the implementation of type `std_logic_vector`.

```
Port (I1 : in bit; I2 : in std_logic_vector (5 downto 0);
Sum : out bit);
```

In the above statement, port `I2` is declared as type `std_logic_vector;` it has 6 bits. Possible values of `I2` include 110110, 011010, and 0Z0Z00. More details about `std_logic_vector` can be found in Chapter 2.

Signed

Signed is a numeric type. It is declared in the external package `numeric_std` and represents `signed` integer data in the form of an array. The left-most bit is the sign; objects of type `signed` are represented in 2's complement form. Consider the statement:

```
Variable prod : signed (3 downto 0) := 1010;
```

The above statement declares the variable `prod`. It is of type `signed`, has 4 bits, and its initial value is 1010, or –6. Chapter 3, shows implementations of type `signed`.

Unsigned

The type `unsigned` represents unsigned integer data in the form of an array of std_logic and is a part of the package numeric_std. The following example illustrates type `unsigned`:

```
Variable Qout : unsigned (3 downto 0) := 1010;
```

The above statement declares variable `Qout`. It is of type `unsigned`, it has 4 bits, and its initial value is 1010, or 10.

1.5.2 Verilog Data Types

Verilog, in contrast to VHDL, does not have extensive data types. Verilog supports several data types, including: `nets`, `registers`, `vectors`, `integer`, `real`, `parameters`, and `arrays`. More details on these types can be found in Chapters 2–4.

1.5.2.1 Nets

Nets are declared by the predefined word `wire`. Nets have values that change continuously by the circuits that are driving them. Verilog supports four values for nets, as shown in Table 1.12:

TABLE 1.12 Verilog Net Values

Value	Definition
0	logic 0 (false)
1	logic 1 (true)
x	unknown
z	high impedance

Examples of net types are as follows:

```
wire sum;
wire S1 = 1'b0;
```

The first statement declares a net by the name `sum`. The second statement declares a net by the name of `S1`; its initial value is `1'b0`, which represents 1 bit with value 0. More details on nets can be found in Chapter 2.

1.5.2.2 Registers

Registers, in contrast to nets, store values until they are updated. Registers, as their name suggests, represent data storage elements. Register is declared by the predefined word reg. Verilog supports four values for registers, and shown in Table 1.13:

TABLE 1.13 Verilog Register Values

Value	Definition
0	logic 0 (false)
1	logic 1 (true)
x	unknown
z	high impedance

An example of a register is:

```
reg Sum_total;
```

The above statement declares a register by the name Sum_total. More details on registers can be found in Chapter 3.

1.5.2.3 Vectors

Vectors are multiple bits. A register or a net can be declared as a vector. Vectors are declared by brackets [ ]. Examples of vectors are:

```
wire [3:0] a = 4'b1010;
reg [7:0] total = 8'd12;
```

The first statement declares a net a. It has 4 bits, and its initial value is 1010 (b stands for bit). The second statement declares a register total. Its size is 8 bits, and its value is decimal 12 (d stands for decimal). Vectors are implemented in subsequent chapters.

1.5.2.4 Integers

Integers are declared by the predefined word integer. An example of integer declaration is:

```
integer no_bits;
```

The above statement declares no_bits as an integer.

1.5.2.5 Real

Real (floating-point) numbers are declared with the predefined word `real`. Examples of real values are 2.4, 56.3, and 5e12. The value 5e12 is equal to 5×10^{12}. The following statement declares the register `weight` as `real`.

```
real weight;
```

1.5.2.6 Parameters

Parameters represent global constants. They are declared by the predefined word `parameter`. The following is an example of implementing parameters:

```
module compr_genr (X, Y, xgty, xlty, xeqy);
parameter N = 3;
input [N:0] X, Y;
output xgty, xlty, xeqy;
wire [N:0] sum, Yb;
```

To change the size of the inputs `x` and `y`, and the size of the nets `sum` and `Yb` to 8 bits, we just change the value of `N` as: `parameter N = 7.`

1.5.2.7 Arrays

Verilog, in contrast to VHDL, does not have a predefined word for array. Registers and integers can be written as arrays. Consider the following statements:

```
parameter N = 4;
parameter M = 3;

reg signed [M:0] carry [0:N];
reg [M:0] b [0:N];
integer sum [0:N];
```

The above statements declare an array by the name `sum`. The array has five elements, and each element is an integer type. The array `carry` has five elements, and each element is 4 bits. The 4 bits are in 2's complement form. For example, if the value of a certain element is 1001, then it is equivalent to decimal –7. The array `b` has five elements, and each element is 4 bits. The value of each bit can be 0, 1, x, or z.

Verilog does not support multidimensional arrays. Chapter 7 has more details about arrays.

1.6 STYLES (TYPES) OF DESCRIPTIONS

This section discusses the different styles of writing the description. The styles adopted in this book can be classified as behavioral, structural, switch level, data flow, mixed type/style, or mixed language. The following sections will briefly discuss these styles.

1.6.1 Behavioral Descriptions

A behavioral description models the system as to how the outputs behave with the inputs. The definition of behavioral description is one where the architecture (VHDL) or the module (Verilog) includes the predefined word `process` (VHDL) or `always` (Verilog) or `initial` (Verilog). The description is considered pure behavioral if it does not contain any other features from other styles or descriptions (see Chapter 3). An example of pure behavioral description, according to the definition used in this book, is shown in Listing 1.3. As shown, the architecture (VHDL) or module (Verilog) consists only of a `process` or `always` construct, respectively.

NOTE *Throughout this book, Listings may include both VHDL and Verilog descriptions. For the reader's convenience, the Verilog versions have been given a shaded background.*

LISTING 1.3 Example of Behavioral Description–VHDL and Verilog

VHDL Behavioral Description

```
entity half_add is
    port (I1, I2 : in bit; O1, O2 : out bit);
end half_add;
architecture behave_ex of half_add is
--The architecture consists of a process construct
begin
process (I1, I2)
--The above statement is process statement

    begin
        O1 <= I1 xor I2 after 10 ns;
        O2 <= I1 and I2 after 10 ns;
    end process;
end behave_ex;
```

Verilog Behavioral Description

```
module half_add (I1, I2, O1, O2);
input I1, I2;
output O1, O2;
reg O1, O2;
always @(I1, I2)
//The above abatement is always
//The module consists of always construct
begin
    #10 O1 = I1 ^ I2;
    #10 O2 = I1& I2;
end
endmodule
```

1.6.2 Structural Descriptions

Structural descriptions model the system as components or gates. This description is identified by the presence of the key word component in the architecture (VHDL) or gates construct, such as `and`, `or`, or `not` in the `module` (Verilog). If the VHDL architecture or the Verilog module consists only of components or gates; the style is coined as pure structural. Structural descriptions are covered in Chapter 4, "Structural Descriptions." Listing 1.4 shows an example of pure structural description.

LISTING 1.4 Pure Structural Description–VHDL and Verilog

VHDL Structural Description

```
entity system is

   port (a, b : in bit;
   sum, cout : out bit);
end system;

architecture struct_exple of system is

component xor2
--The above statement is a component statement
   port(I1, I2 : in bit;
   O1 : out bit);
end component;
component and2
   port(I1, I2 : in bit;
   O1 : out bit);
end component;
   begin
      X1 : xor2 port map (a, b, sum);
      A1 : and2 port map (a, b, cout);
   end struct_exple;
```

Verilog Structural Description

```
module system(a, b, sum, cout);
input a, b;
output sum, cout;
   xor X1(sum, a, b);
//The above statement is EXCLUSIVE-OR gate
   and a1(cout, a, b);
//The above statement is AND gate
endmodule
```

1.6.3 Switch-Level Descriptions

The switch-level description is the lowest level of description. The system is described using switches or transistors. The Verilog keywords `nmos`, `pmos`, `cmos`, `tranif0`, `tran`, or `tranif0` describe the system. VHDL does not have built-in switch-level primitives, but we can construct packages to include such primitives and attach them to the VHDL module. More details on switch-level descriptions can be found in Chapter 5, "Switch-Level Descriptions." Listing 1.5 shows an example of switch-level description.

LISTING 1.5 Switch-Level Description—VHDL and Verilog

VHDL Switch-Level Description

```
library IEEE;
use IEEE.STD_LOGIC_1164.ALL;

entity Inverter is
    Port (y : out std_logic; a : in std_logic );
end Inverter;

architecture Invert_switch of Inverter is
component nmos
--nmos is one of the key words for switch-level.
port (O1 : out std_logic; I1, I2 : in std_logic);
end component;

component pmos
--pmos is one of the key words for switch-level.

port (O1 : out std_logic; I1, I2 : in std_logic);
end component;

for all: pmos use entity work. mos (pmos_behavioral);
for all: nmos use entity work. mos (nmos_behavioral);
--The above two statements are referring to a package mos
--See details in Chapter 5
constant vdd : std_logic := '1';
constant gnd : std_logic := '0';
begin
    p1 : pmos port map (y, vdd, a);
    n1 : nmos port map (y, gnd, a);
end Invert_switch;
```

Verilog Switch-Level Description

```
module inver (y, a);
input a;
output y;
supply1 vdd;
supply0 gnd;
pmos p1 (y, vdd, a);
nmos n1 (y, gnd, a);
//The above two statements are using the two primititves pmos and nmos
endmodule
```

1.6.4 Data-Flow Descriptions

Data flow describes how the system's signals flow from the inputs to the outputs. Usually, the description is done by writing the Boolean function of the outputs. The data-flow statements are concurrent; their execution is controlled by events. The VHDL architecture or Verilog module data-flow description, as defined here, does not include any of the key words that identify behavioral, structural, or switch-level descriptions. Data-flow descriptions are covered in Chapter 2. Listing 1.6 shows an example of using data-flow descriptions.

LISTING 1.6 Data-Flow Description–VHDL and Verilog

VHDL Data-Flow Description

```
entity halfadder is
port (
a : in bit;
b : in bit;
s : out bit;
c : out bit);
end halfadder;

architecture HA_DtFl of halfadder is
--The architecture has no process, component, cmos,
--tranif0, tran, or tranif0

begin
    s <= a xor b;
    c <= a and b;
end HA_DtFl;
```

Verilog Data-Flow Description

```
module halfadder (a, b, s, c);
input a;
input b;
output s;
output c;
    assign s = a ^ b;
    assign c = a & b;
/* The module has no always, gates such as and, cmos,
    tranif0, tran, or tranif0*/
endmodule
```

1.6.5 Mixed-Type Descriptions

Mixed-type or mixed-style descriptions use more than one type or style of the previously mentioned descriptions. In fact, most of the descriptions of moderate- to large-size systems are mixed. We may describe some parts of the system using one description type and other parts using another type. Mixed-type descriptions are covered in Chapter 7. Listing 1.7 shows an example of mixed-type descriptions using both data-flow and behavioral descriptions.

LISTING 1.7 Mixed-Type Description—VHDL and Verilog (Not Complete Listing)

VHDL Mixed-Type Description

```
architecture ALU_mixed of ALU_mixed is

    signal c0, c1 : std_logic;
    signal p, g : unsigned (2 downto 0);
    signal temp1 : unsigned (5 downto 0);

begin

    --The following is a data-flow description.
    g(0) <= a(0) and b(0);
    g(1) <= a(1) and b(1);
    g(2) <= a(2) and b(2);
    .......................
    --The following is a behavioral description
    process (a, b, cin, opc, temp1)

    variable temp : unsigned (5 downto 0);
    variable a1, a2, a3 : integer;
    begin
    a1 := TO_INTEGER (a);
    a2 := TO_INTEGER (b);

    case opc is
        when mul =>
    ..............
    end ALU_mixed;
```

Verilog Mixed-Type Description

```
module ALU_mixed (a, b, cin, opc, z);
................
wire [2:0] g, p;
wire c0, c1;

//The following is data-flow description
    assign g[0] = a[0] & b[0];
    assign g[1] = a[1] & b[1];
    assign g[2] = a[2] & b[2];
    assign p[0] = a[0] | b[0];
    assign p[1] = a[1] | b[1];
..........................
//The following is behavioral description

always @ (a, b, cin, opc, temp1)
begin

    case (opc)
    ..........................
endmodule
```

1.6.6 Mixed-Language Descriptions

The mixed-language description is a newly added tool for HDL descriptions. The user now can write a module in one language (VHDL or Verilog) and invoke or import a construct (entity or module) written in the other language. Listing 1.8 illustrates the mixed-language description. In this Listing, inside the Verilog module `Full_Adder1`, we instantiate (import) the VHDL entity `HA`. The information in `HA` is then visible to the Verilog module. Mixed-language descriptions are covered in Chapter 9, "Mixed-Language Descriptions."

LISTING 1.8 Mixed-Language Description (Not Complete Listing)

```
module Full_Adder1 (x, y, cin, sum, carry);
    input x, y, cin;
    output sum, carry;
    wire c0, c1, s0;

HA H1 (y, cin, s0, c0);

// Description of HA is written in VHDL in the entity HA
 ..................

endmodule

library IEEE;
use ieee.std_logic_1164.all;
entity HA is

--For correct binding between this VHDL code and the above Verilog
--code, the entity has to be named HA

    port (a, b : in std_logic; s, c : out std_logic);
end HA;
architecture HA_Dtflw of HA is
begin
    s <= a xor b;
    c <= a and b;
end HA_Dtflw;
```

1.7 SIMULATION AND SYNTHESIS

The ultimate goal for hardware description is to synthesize the system onto an electronic chip. To synthesize an HDL description, it needs to be simulated and tested. Synthesis basics are covered in Chapter 10, "Synthesis Basics." More information about simulators and synthesizers can be found in [Accolade05], [Aldec05], and [Xilinx05]. The steps of simulation and synthesis can be summarized as follows.

Choose the preferred language to describe the system. The language may be VHDL, Verilog, or mixed-language (both VHDL and Verilog). Mixed-language descriptions are covered in Chapter 9.

Choose the style or type of description. Refer to Section 1.6 for selecting a style.

Write the code. If writing a VHDL module, be sure to attach all the necessary packages and Libraries. At this step, some HDL packages require the user to select the type of synthesis technology and electronic chip type before compilation.

Compile the code using the compiler supplied by the HDL package. The compiler checks that the code satisfies the rules of the language and displays any errors. Some compilers suggest how to fix the errors.

After successful compilation, we need to test the code to see that it correctly describes the system. This test is done by selecting the input and output signals that we want to inspect. For example, if a 2x1 multiplexer is being described, the two inputs, the select line, and the output might be selected. The way these signals are selected differs from one simulator to the other; there might be different ways to select signals even within the same simulator. The newer simulators are graphical. All signals in the system are displayed in graphical fashion; the user selects the signals and assigns initial values for them. The user then clicks a button to run the simulation, and a simulation screen appears showing the waveform of the selected signals. Some other simulators require the user to write an HDL code for testing the source code. In this book, we assume that the simulator is graphical, so there is no need to write test code.

After the user's simulation verifies that the signals behave as expected, the compiled code can be synthesized. The simulator CAD package usually has a synthesizer. The synthesizer converts the compiled code into a schematic and generates a net list. The net list can be downloaded onto a chip, usually as field-programmable gate arrays. Chapter 10 illustrates how to convert the HDL code to gate level or RTL, the forms closest to the schematic original that the synthesizer can download onto the chip.

1.8 BRIEF COMPARISON OF VHDL AND VERILOG

As previously mentioned, VHDL and Verilog are languages that are popular in both industry and academia. Each language, however, has some advantages and disadvantages over the other. These advantages and disadvantages may not be very clear to beginners. Verilog is considered better when describing a system at the gate or transistor level due to its use of predefined primitives at this level. VHDL is considered better at the system level; multiple entity/architecture pairs lead to flexibility and ease in writing code for complex systems. Recently, many simulators have acquired the capability to use mixed-language simulations. In mixed-language simulations, a construct of one language can be instantiated into the other. This allows the user to utilize the advantages of both languages (see Chapter 9). In the following, the major differences between VHDL and Verilog are listed.

- **Data Types**

  VHDL: Definitely a type-oriented language, VHDL types are built in, or the user can create and define them. User-defined types give the user a tool to write the code effectively; these types also support flexible coding. VHDL can handle objects with multidimensional array types. Another data type that VHDL supports is the physical type; the physical type supports more synthesizable or targeted design code.

  Verilog: Compared to VHDL, Verilog data types are very simple and easy to use. All types are defined by the language. There are no user-defined types. Some beginners may consider these simple data types as an advantage over VHDL. Verilog, however, cannot handle objects with multidimensional array types.

- **Ease of Learning**

  VHDL: For beginners, VHDL may seem hard to learn because of its rigid type requirements. Advanced users, however, may find these rigid type requirements easier to handle.

  Verilog: Easy to learn, Verilog users just write the module without worrying about what Library or package should be attached. Many of the statements in the language are very similar to those in C language.

- **Libraries and Packages**

  VHDL: Libraries and packages can be attached to the standard VHDL package. Packages can include procedures and functions, and the package can be made available to any module that needs to use it. Packages are used to target a certain design. For example, if the system modeled/designed includes arithmetic functions, a package can be used that includes those functions.

  Verilog: There is no concept of Libraries or packages in Verilog.

- **Operators**

  VHDL: An extensive set of operators is available in VHDL, but it does not have predefined unary operators.

  Verilog: An extensive set of operators is also available in Verilog. It also has predefined unary operators (see Section 1.4).

- **Procedures and Tasks:** Procedures (VHDL) and tasks (Verilog) are implemented to simplify the writing of HDL code for complex systems.

  VHDL: Concurrent procedure calls are allowed. VHDL, in contrast to Verilog, allows a function to be written inside the procedure's body. This feature may contribute to an easier way to describe a complex system.

Verilog: Concurrent task calls are allowed. Functions, however, are not allowed to be written in the task's body.

1.9 SUMMARY

In this chapter several introductory VHDL and Verilog topics have been covered. The structure of the HDL module has been discussed. The VHDL module has two major constructs: an entity and architecture, which are bound to the entity. Verilog has a module construct.

Operators, which perform a wide variety of operations, have been covered. Arithmetic operators (see Table 1.14) perform arithmetic operations, such as multiplication and division. Relational operators (see Table 1.15) perform comparisons, such as greater than and equals. Shift operators (see Table 1.16) perform bit shifts, such as logical shift (a specified number of bit positions) right. Logical operators (see Table 1.17) perform logical operations, such as AND.

TABLE 1.14 Summary of Arithmetic Operators for VHDL and Verilog

Operation	Operator VHDL	Operator Verilog
Addition +	+	
Subtraction	-	-
Multiplication	*	*
Division	/	/
Modulus	mod	%
Exponent	**	**
Concatenation	(&)	{ , }

TABLE 1.15 Summary of Relational Operators for VHDL and Verilog

Operation	Operator VHDL	Operator Verilog
Equality	=	==
Inequality	/=	!=
Less than	<	<
Less than or equal	<=	<=

Operation	Operator VHDL	Operator Verilog
Greater than	>	>
Greater than or equal	>=	>=
Equality inclusive	none	===
Inequality inclusive	none	!==

TABLE 1.16 Summary of Shift Operators for VHDL and Verilog

Operation	Operator VHDL	Operator Verilog
Shift A logical left one position	`A sll 1`	A << 1
Shift A logical right one position	`A slr 1`	A >> 1
Shift A arithmetic left one position	`A sla 1`	none
Shift A arithmetic right one position	`A sra 1`	none
Rotate A left one position	`A rol 1`	none
Rotate A right one position	`A ror 1`	none

TABLE 1.17 Summary of Logical Operators for VHDL and Verilog

Operation	Operator VHDL	Operator Verilog
AND	AND	&
OR	OR	|
NAND	NAND	~(&)
NOR	NOR	~(|)
XOR	XOR	^
XNOR	XNOR	~^
NOT	NOT	~

Data types have also been covered, including `bit`, `std_logic`, `std_logic_vector`, and `array` (VHDL); and [N:0], `real`, `integer`, `reg`, and `wire` (Verilog). The following description styles have been briefly contrasted: behavioral, structural, switch-level, data flow, mixed type, and mixed language. Finally, a brief comparison of VHDL and Verilog has been presented.

1.10 EXERCISES

1.1 Determine whether the following statements are VHDL, Verilog, or can be both. Justify your answer.

a. port (input1 : std_logic; output2 : std_logic; output3 : bit);
b. module vhdl1(I1, I2, O1, O3);
c. input D, E;
d. y = s ^ sel;
e. process Verlog (a, b, c)
f. always @ (a, b,c)
g. begin

1.2 If A and B are two unsigned variables, with A = 1100 and B = 1001, find the value of the following expressions:

a. (A AND B)
b. (A ^ B)
c. (A NOR B)
d. (A & B)
e. (A && B)
f. !(B)
g. ~|(A)
h. A slr 3
i. A >> 1
j. B ror 2

1.3 For the following HDL code, determine the type (style) description.

a.
```
architecture Q1 of Exercise is
    begin
  process (a, b)
    begin
       A <= B;
       Y <= B AND C;
    end process;
  end Q1;
```

b.
```
module NAND2gate(a, b, y);
input a, b;
output y;
supply1 vdd;
supply0 gnd;
```

```
nmos (s1, gnd, b);
nmos (y, s1, a);
pmos (y, vdd, a);
pmos (y, vdd, b);
endmodule
```

1.11 REFERENCES

[Accolade05] *Accolade VHDL Reference*. Available online at *http://www.acceda.com/vhdlref/ index.html.*

[Aldec05] Active-HDL. Available online at *http://www.aldec.com/*.

[Xilinx05] Xilinx Documentation. Available online at *http://www.xilinx.com/*.

2 Data-Flow Descriptions

In This Chapter

- Understand the concept of data-flow description in both VHDL and Verilog.
- Understand events and concurrent statements.
- Identify the basic statements and components of data-flow descriptions, such as logical operators, signal-assignment statements, the statement "assign," time delays, and vectors.
- Review and understand the fundamentals of some digital logic systems, such as half adder, 2x1 multiplexer, 2x2 combinational array multiplier, 2-bit comparator, D-latch, ripple-carry adder, and carry-lookahead adder.

2.1 HIGHLIGHTS OF DATA-FLOW DESCRIPTION

Data flow is one type (style) of hardware description. Other types include behavioral, structural (gate level), switch level, mixed type, and mixed language. Listed below are some facts about data-flow descriptions:

Facts

- Data-flow descriptions simulate the system by showing how the signal flows from system inputs to outputs. For example, the Boolean function of the output or the logical structure of the system shows such a signal flow.
- Signal-assignment statements are concurrent. At any simulation time, all signal-assignment statements that have an event are executed concurrently.

2.2 STRUCTURE OF THE DATA-FLOW DESCRIPTION

Listing 2.1 shows HDL code describing a system using data-flow description. The entity (module) name is `system`. There are two inputs (`I1` and `I2`) and two outputs (`O1` and `O2`). Statements 1 and 2 are used to assign a value to the outputs `O1` and `O2`.

The signal assignment operator <= is used in VHDL, or the predefined word `assign` in Verilog, to assign a value to the left-hand side of a signal-assignment statement (e.g., O1 and O2 in Listing 2.1).

LISTING 2.1 Example of HDL Data-Flow Description—VHDL and Verilog

VHDL Data-Flow Description

```
entity system is
    port (I1, I2 : in bit; O1, O2 : out bit);
end;
architecture dtfl_ex of system is
begin
    O1 <= I1 and I2; -- statement 1.
    O2 <= I1 xor I2; -- statement 2.

--Statements 1 and 2 are signal-assignment statements

end dtfl_ex;
```

Verilog Data-Flow Description

```
module system (I1, I2, O1, O2);
    input I1, I2;
    output O1, O2;

/*by default all the above inputs and outputs are 1-bit signals.*/

    assign O1 = I1&I2; // statement 1
    assign O2 = I1^I2; // statement 2
/*Statements 1 and 2 are continuous signal-assignment statements*/
endmodule
```

2.2.1 Signal Declaration and Assignment Statements

Figure 2.1 shows an AND-OR circuit. Signals a, b, c, and d are the inputs; signal y is the output; and signals s1 and s2 are intermediates.

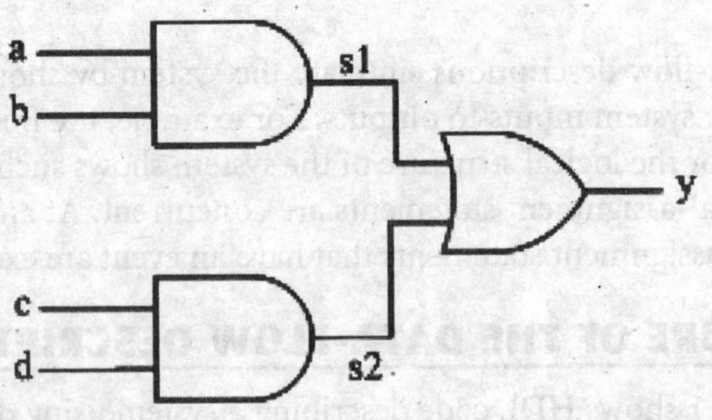

FIGURE 2.1 AND-OR circuit.

Input and output signals are declared in the entity (module) as ports. In HDL, a signal has to be declared before it can be used. Accordingly, signals s1 and s2 have to be declared. In VHDL, s1 and s2 are declared signals by using the predefined word `signal` in the architecture.

```
signal s1, s2 : bit;
```

In Verilog, s1 and s2 are declared as signals by using the predefined word `wire`.

```
wire s1, s2;
```

By default, all ports in Verilog are assumed to be wires. The value of the wire is continuously changing with changes in the device that is deriving it. For example, s1 is the output of the AND gate in Figure 2.1, and s1 may change as a or b changes.

Another type of declaration in Verilog is `reg` (register); the `reg` declaration is used if the object's value needs to be stored (remembered). In Verilog, any object that is assigned a value in an `always` statement must be declared as `reg` (see Chapter 3, "Behavioral Descriptions").

A signal-assignment statement is used to assign a value to a signal. The left-hand side of the statement should be declared as a signal. The right-hand side can be a signal, a variable, or a constant. The operator for signal assignment is `<=` in VHDL or the predefined word `assign` in Verilog.

The execution of the signal-assignment statement is unique to HDL and is different in concept from that of software languages such as C. The execution is done in two phases: calculation and assignment. Consider Listing 2.1, and the execution at time T_0 of the signal-assignment statement `O1 <= I1 and I2 (assign O1 = I1 & I2)`. Assume that an event at T_0 (see Section 2.2.2) occurs on either signal `I1` or `I2`. This event changes the value of `I1` to 1 and also changes the value of `I2` to 1.

1. **Calculation:** The value of `O1` is calculated using the current values of `I1` and `I2` at time T_0. This value is (1 `and` 1) = 1 in VHDL or (1 `&` 1) = 1 in Verilog, where `and` and `(&)` are the logical AND operators in VHDL and Verilog, respectively. This value is not assigned yet to `O1`.
2. **Assignment:** The calculated value is assigned to `O1` after a delay time. The delay time can be implicitly or explicitly specified. For example, to explicitly specify a 10-ns delay time, VHDL is written as: `O1 <= I1 and I2 after 10 ns;` Verilog is written as: `assign #10 O1 = I1 & I2.` In Verilog, we do not specify the units of time; the simulator assumes a delay of 10 screen time units. If the screen units are in seconds, for example, then the delay is 10 seconds. If no delay time is specified, the HDL uses a default, infinitely small delay time of Δ (delta) seconds. At $T_0 + \Delta$, the value of "1" is assigned

to O1. On the simulation screen, Δ cannot be seen, and it looks as if O1 acquired its value at T_0.

2.2.2 Concurrent Signal-Assignment Statements

In HDL data-flow descriptions, concurrent signal-assignment statements constitute the major part of the body of VHDL architectures and Verilog modules. In Listing 2.1, both VHDL and Verilog description statements 1 and 2 are concurrent statements.

Another type of execution is sequential (see Chapter 3, "Behavioral Descriptions"), where the statements are processed sequentially. For the execution of any concurrent statement to start, an event on the right-hand side of the statement has to occur. An event is a change in the value of a signal or a variable, such as a change from 0 to 1 (i.e., from low to high) or from 1 to 0 (i.e., from high to low). The statement remains inactive if no event occurs. If an event occurs on more than one statement, then all of these statements, regardless of their order (locations) in the architecture (module), are executed concurrently—that is, simultaneously.

Referring to Listing 2.1, if at time T_0, I1 changes from 0 to 1 while I2 retains its previous value of 1, then this constitutes an event on I1. Both statements 1 and 2 are executed concurrently, because I1 is on the right-hand side of both statements. This means that the calculation of O1 and O2 values is done at the same time at T_0, using the current values of I1 and I2. At $T_0 + \Delta$, O1 acquires the value of (1 AND 1) = 1, and O2 acquires the value of (1 XOR 1) = 0. Since there is no explicit delay time specified, O1 takes the value of 1 at simulation screen time T_0.

2.2.3 Constant Declaration and Assignment Statements

A constant in HDL is treated as in C language; its value is constant within the segment of the program where it is visible. A constant in VHDL can be declared using the predefined word `constant`. In Verilog, a constant can be declared by its type, such as `time` or `integer`. For example, the following statements declare `period` as a constant of type `time`.

```
constant period : time;       -- VHDL
time period;                  // Verilog
```

To assign a value to a constant, we use the assignment operator := in VHDL or = in Verilog. For example, to assign a value of 100 nanoseconds to the constant period described above:

```
period := 100 ns;       -- VHDL
period = 100;           // Verilog
```

In Verilog there are not explicit units of time; 100 means 100 simulation screen time units. If the simulation screen units are defined as nanoseconds, for example, then 100 will mean 100 nanoseconds. The declaration and assignment can be combined in one statement as:

```
Constant period : time := 100 ns;     -- VHDL
time period = 100;                    // Verilog
```

In the following, several examples of data-flow descriptions are covered.

EXAMPLE 2.1 Data-Flow Description of a Half Adder

A half adder adds 2 input bits and outputs the result as 2 bits—1 bit for the sum and 1 bit for the carryout. Examples of the half addition are: 1 + 0 = 01; 1 + 1 = 10; 0 + 0 = 00. To describe the half adder using data-flow description, we write the Boolean function of the output. The function shows how the data flows from the input to the output of the half adder. Table 2.1 shows the truth table of the half adder. Figure 2.2a shows the logic diagram and Figure 2.2b shows the logic symbol of the half adder.

TABLE 2.1 Truth Table for a Half Adder

Input		Output	
a	b	S	C
0	0	0	0
1	0	1	0
0	1	1	0
1	1	0	1

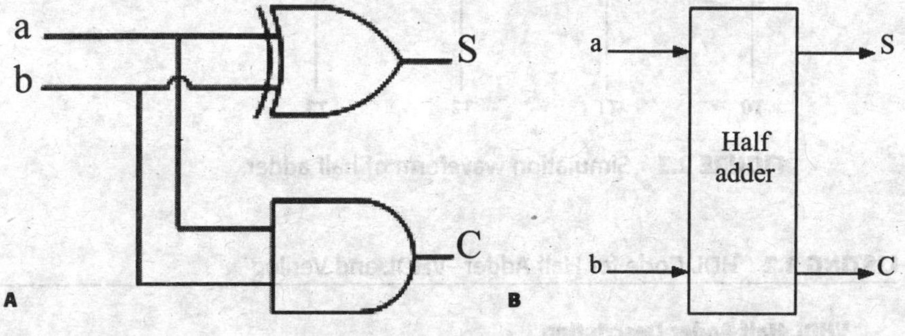

FIGURE 2.2 Half adder. (a) Logic diagram. (b) Logic symbol.

We can obtain the Boolean function from the truth table. The Boolean function of the output is generated using minterms (where the output has value(s) of 1) or maxterms (where the output has value(s) of 0). The Boolean function using minterms in the Sum of Products (SOP) form is:

$$S = \bar{a}\,b + a\,\bar{b} = a \oplus b \tag{2.1}$$

$$C = ab \tag{2.2}$$

or we can use the maxterms in the Product of Sums (POS) forms as:

$$S = (a + b)(\bar{a} + \bar{b}) \tag{2.3}$$

$$C = (a + b)(\bar{a} + b)(a + \bar{b}) \tag{2.4}$$

After minimizing ($a\,\bar{a} = 0$ and $b\,\bar{b} = 0$), the SOP and the POS yield identical Boolean functions. More details about Boolean function minimization can be found in [Ciletti02], [Hayes98], [Mano00], and [Nelson95]. Listing 2.2 shows the HDL program for the half adder. The program is compiled and simulated. Figure 2.3 shows the simulation waveform.

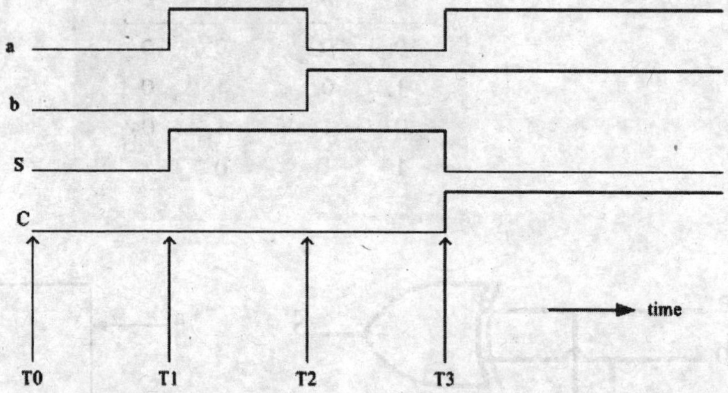

FIGURE 2.3 Simulation waveform of half adder.

LISTING 2.2 HDL Code for Half Adder–VHDL and Verilog

VHDL Half Adder Description

```
entity halfadder is
port (
a : in bit;
```

```
b : in bit;
s : out bit;
c : out bit);
end halfadder;
architecture HA_DtFl of halfadder is
begin
    s <= a xor b; --This is a signal assignment statement.
    c <= a and b; --This is a signal assignment statement.
end HA_DtFl;
```

Verilog Half Adder Description

```
module halfadder (a, b, s, c);
input a;
input b;
output s;
output c;
/*The default type of all inputs and outputs is a single bit. */
    assign s = a ^ b; /* This is a signal assignment statement;
                         ^ is a bitwise xor logical operator. */

    assign c = a & b; /* This is a signal assignment statement
                       & is a bitwise logical "and" operator */
endmodule
```

The waveform in Figure 2.3 correctly describes a half adder. Consider, for example, simulation time T = T1. At this time, signal a changes from 0 to 1, and b stays at 0. This constitutes an event on a. Consider the two signal assignment statements in Listing 2.2. Since a is on the right-hand side of both statements, both statements are executed concurrently (simultaneously). S and C are calculated as `S = (1 XOR 0) = 1`, and `C = (1 AND 0) = 0`. Since there is no delay time specified, both S and C acquire the values 1 and 0, respectively, after the infinitely small delay time, Δ. Since it is very small, Δ cannot be seen on the waveform in Figure 2.3, and both signals S and C look as if they acquire their new values at T = T1. Figure 2.3 shows additional events at T2 and T3.

2.2.4 Assigning a Delay Time to the Signal-Assignment Statement

To assign a delay time to a signal-assignment statement, we use the predefined word `after` in VHDL or `#`(delay time) in Verilog. For example, the following statement assigns a 10-nanosecond delay time to signal `S1`.

```
S1 <= sel and b after 10 ns;    --VHDL
assign #10 S1 = sel & b         // Verilog
```

In Verilog, we cannot specify the units of delay time; the delay is in simulation screen unit time. Let us assume that an event occurs on either `sel` or `b`, or on both at time T_0. `S1` is calculated at T_0 using the current values of `sel` and `b`. `S1` does not acquire this value at T_0, but rather at time = $T_0 + 10$ ns (assuming a screen unit is 1 ns). The following example illustrates the assignment of a delay time.

EXAMPLE 2.2 2x1 Multiplexer with Active Low Enable

A basic 2x1 multiplexer has two 1-bit inputs, a 1-bit select line, and a 1-bit output. Additional control signals may be added, such as enable. The output of the basic multiplexer depends on the level of the select line. If select is high (1), the output is equal to one of the two inputs; if select is low (0), the output is equal to the other input. A truth table for a 2x1 multiplexer with active low enable is shown in Table 2.2.

TABLE 2.2 Truth Table for a 2x1 Multiplexer

Input		Output
SEL	Gbar	Y
X	H	L
L	L	A
H	L	B

If enable (gbar) is high (1), then the output is low (0), regardless of the input. When gbar is low (0), the output is A if SEL is low (0), or the output is B if SEL is high (1). From Table 2.2, we find the Boolean function of the output Y as:

$$Y = (G \text{ and } A \text{ and } \overline{SEL}) \text{ or } (G \text{ and } B \text{ and } SEL);\ G \text{ is the invert of Gbar.}$$

Figure 2.4a shows the gate-level structure of the multiplexer. The logic symbol is shown in Figure 2.4b.

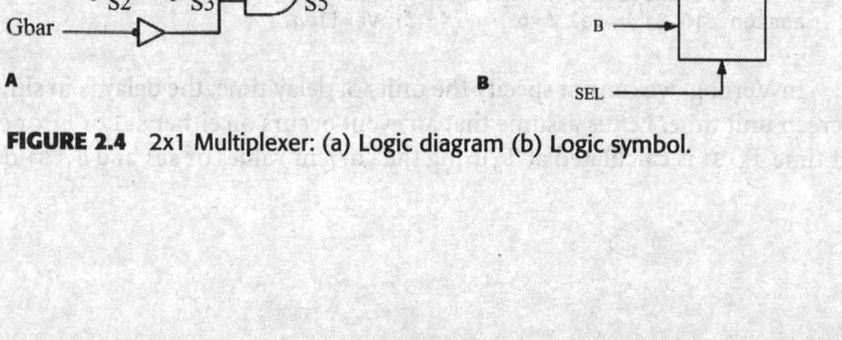

FIGURE 2.4 2x1 Multiplexer: (a) Logic diagram (b) Logic symbol.

Listing 2.3 shows the HDL code. To generate the code we follow Figure 2.4a. We assume propagation delay time for all gates of 7 ns. Since this is a data-flow description, the order that the statements are written is irrelevant. For example, the statement `st6` could have been written at the very beginning instead of statement `st1`. The logical operators in VHDL (and Verilog) implemented in this listing are: `OR (|)`, `AND (&)`, and `NOT (~)`. Figure 2.5 shows the simulation waveform.

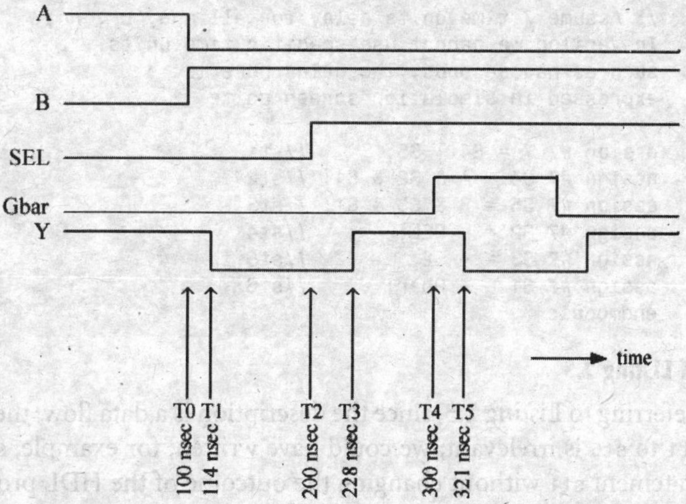

FIGURE 2.5 Simulation waveform for a 2x1 Multiplexer.

LISTING 2.3 HDL Code of a 2x1 Multiplexer—VHDL and Verilog

VHDL 2x1 Multiplexer Description

```
library IEEE;
use IEEE.STD_LOGIC_1164.ALL;
entity mux2x1 is
port (A, B, SEL, Gbar : in std_logic;
    Y : out std_logic);
end mux2x1;

architecture MUX_DF of mux2x1 is
signal S1, S2, S3, S4, S5 : std_logic;
    Begin

--Assume 7 nanoseconds propagation delay
--for all and, or, and not.

st1: Y <= S4 or S5 after 7 ns;
st2: S4 <= A and S2 and S1 after 7 ns;
st3: S5 <= B and S3 and S1 after 7 ns;
st4: S2 <= not SEL after 7 ns;
st5: S3 <= not S2 after 7 ns;
```

```
st6: S1 <= not Gbar after 7 ns;
end MUX_DF;
```

Verilog 2x1 Multiplexer Description

```
module mux2x1 (A, B, SEL, Gbar, Y);
input A, B, SEL, Gbar;
output Y;
wire S1, S2, S3, S4, S5;

/* Assume 7 time units delay for all and, or, not.
In Verilog we cannot use specific time units,
such as nanoseconds. The delay here is
expressed in simulation screen units. */

assign #7 Y = S4 | S5;        //st1
assign #7 S4 = A & S2 & S1; //st2
assign #7 S5 = B & S3 & S1; //st3
assign #7 S2 = ~ SEL;        //st4
assign #7 S3 = ~ S2;         //st5
assign #7 S1 = ~ Gbar;       //st6
endmodule
```

Analysis of Listing 2.3

Referring to Listing 2.3, since the description is a data flow, the order of statements `st1` to `st6` is irrelevant; we could have written, for example, statement `st5` before statement `st1` without changing the outcome of the HDL program. In Figure 2.5, signal A changes from 1 to 0 and signal B changes from 0 to 1 at T0; these changes constitute an event in signal-assignment statements `st2` and `st3`. Accordingly, statements `st2` and `st3` are executed simultaneously. As previously mentioned, execution is done in two phases: calculation and assignment. For statement `st2`, at T0, `A` = 0, `S2` = 1 (the inversion of SEL), and `S1` = 1 (the inversion of Gbar); hence, the calculated new value of `S4` at T0 is (`A` AND `S1` AND `S2`) = 0. This is a change in value for `S4` from 1 to 0, which is assigned to `S4` after 7 ns from time T0 (at 107 ns). For statement `st3`, at T0, `B` = 1, `S3` = 0, and `S1` = 1. The calculated value of `S5` is 0, as it was before T0. At T = 107 ns, an event occurs on `S4`, and this causes execution of statement `st1`. `Y` is calculated as (0 or 1) = 1, and then this value is assigned to `Y` after 7 ns—that is, at T1 = 107 + 7 = 114 ns.

Alternatively, statements `st1` to `st5` can be replaced by one statement:

```
--VHDL:
Y <= not (Gbar) and ((sel and b) or (not sel and A)) after 21 ns;

// Verilog:
assign # 21 Y = ~ (Gbar) & ((SEL & B ) | (~ SEL & A));
```

The delay time of 21 ns is an average delay time. If either of the above two statements is used, individual delay times cannot be assigned, as was done in Listing 2.3 statements `st1` through `st5`.

2.3 DATA TYPE—VECTORS

Vector data types were briefly covered in Chapter 1, "Introduction." A vector is a data type that declares an array of similar elements, such as to declare an object that has a width of more than 1 bit. In the previous examples, all signals have been 1 bit in width. If we want to declare a signal a with a 4-bit width, we can declare each individual bit separately as:

```
signal a0, a1, a2, a3 : bit;      --VHDL
wire a0, a1, a2, a3;              // Verilog
```

Or, the vector declaration can be written as:

```
signal a : bit_vector (3 downto 0);   --VHDL
wire [3:0] a;                         // Verilog
```

In VHDL, `downto` (`[ ]` in Verilog) is a predefined operator that describes the width of the vector. If the value of a is 14_d, or $(1110)_2$, then the elements of vector a are:

$$a[3] = 1, a[2] = 1, a[1] = 1, a[0] = 0.$$

The following declaration can be used:

```
signal a : bit_vector (0 to 3);   --VHDL
wire [0:3];                       // Verilog
```

where `to` is a predefined word. In the above declaration, the elements of the vector are:

$$a[0] = 1, a[1] = 1, a[2] = 1, a[3] = 0.$$

This means the value of A[a] is considered to be 7_d rather than 14_d.

Example 2.3 2x2 Unsigned Combinational Array Multiplier

Consider the multiplication of a × b, where a and b are 2-bit numbers. The multiplication is done as follows:

		a(1)	a(0)
		b(1)	b(0)
		b(0) × a(1)	b(0) × a(0)
	b(1) × a(1)	b(1) × a(0)	
P(3)	P(2)	P(1)	P(0)

P(0) = b(0)a(0)
P(1) = b(0)a(1) *plus* b(1)a(0)
P(2) = b(1)a(1) *plus* carry out of P(1)
P(3) = carry out of P(2)

P(1) and P(2) are realized by half adders. The 1 × 1 bit multiplication (e.g., b(0) × a(0)) is realized by AND logical operator (b(0) AND a(0)). The logic diagram of the multiplier is shown in Figure 2.6. The HDL code is shown in Listing 2.4, and the simulation output of the multiplier is shown in Figure 2.7.

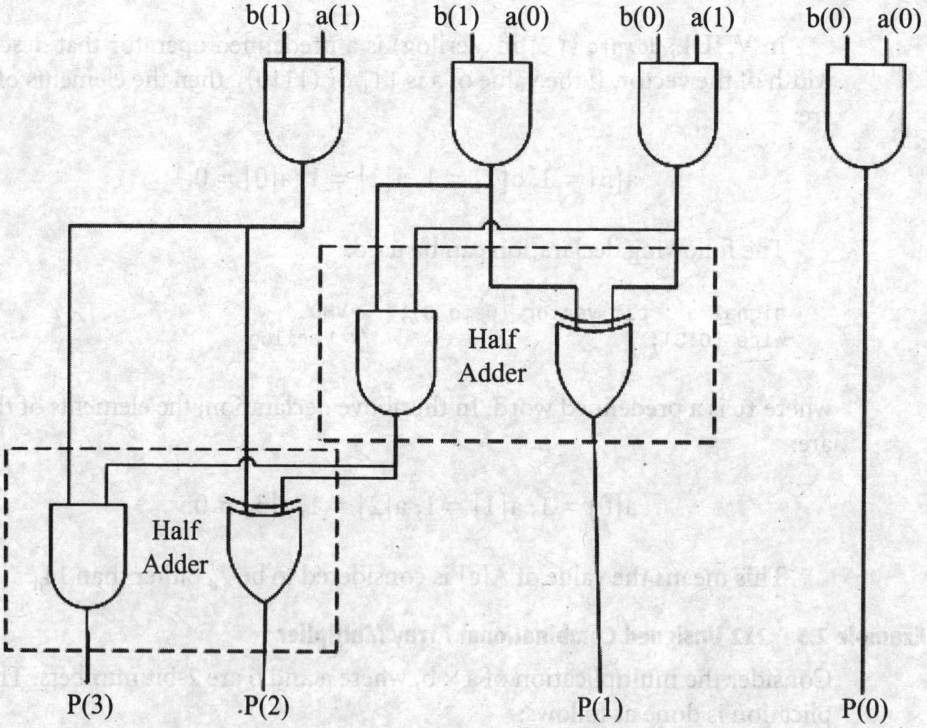

FIGURE 2.6 Gate-level diagram of a 2x2-bit combinational array multiplier.

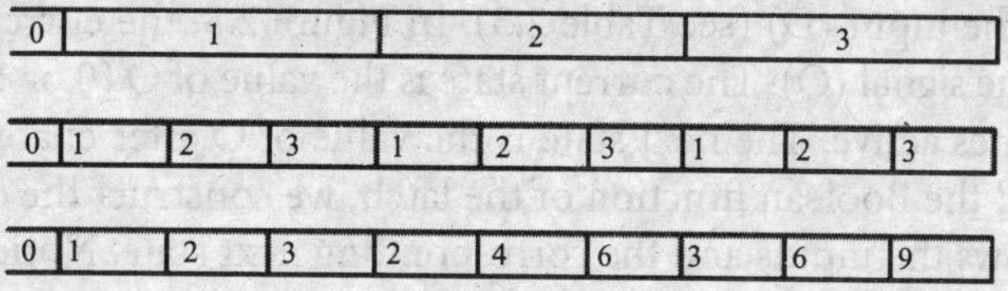

FIGURE 2.7 Simulation output for a 2x2 multiplier. All values are in unsigned format.

LISTING 2.4 HDL Code for a 2x2 Unsigned Combinational Array Multiplier–VHDL and Verilog

VHDL 2x2 Unsigned Combinational Array Multiplier

```
library IEEE;
use IEEE.STD_LOGIC_1164.ALL;
entity mult_arry is
    port (a, b : in std_logic_vector(1 downto 0);
    P : out std_logic_vector (3 downto 0));
end mult_arry;

architecture MULT_DF of mult_arry is
begin
--For simplicity propagation delay times are not considered
--in this example.
P(0) <= a(0) and b(0);
P(1) <= (a(0) and b(1)) xor (a(1) and b(0));
P(2) <= (a(1) and b(1)) xor ((a(0) and b(1)) and (a(1) and b(0)));
P(3) <= (a(1) and b(1)) and ((a(0) and b(1)) and (a(1) and b(0)));
end MULT_DF;
```

Verilog 2x2 Unsigned Combinational Array Multiplier

```
module mult_arry (a, b, P);
input [1:0] a, b;
output [3:0] P;
/*For simplicity, propagation delay times are not considered in this
example.*/

assign P[0] = a[0] & b[0];
assign P[1] = (a[0] & b[1]) ^ (a[1] & b[0]);
assign P[2] = (a[1] & b[1]) ^ ((a[0] & b[1]) & (a[1] & b[0]));
assign P[3] = (a[1] & b[1]) & ((a[0] & b[1])& (a[1] & b[0]));
endmodule
```

Example 2.4 D-Latch

Latches are sequential circuits. Figure 2.8 shows the logic symbol of a D-latch. At any time when the enable (E) is inactive, the present value of Q is called the current state. When enable becomes active, the new value of Q is called the next state Q^+. The value of the next state depends on the value of the present state and the value of the input (D) (see Table 2.3). In Figure 2.8, the current and next states are the same signal (Q). The current state is the value of Q (0 or 1) before the level of E becomes active. The next state is the value of Q after enable (E) becomes active. To find the Boolean function of the latch, we construct the excitation table. Table 2.3 shows the inputs and the corresponding next state. Notice that the current state is considered an input in addition to the input D. Assume an active high enable (E).

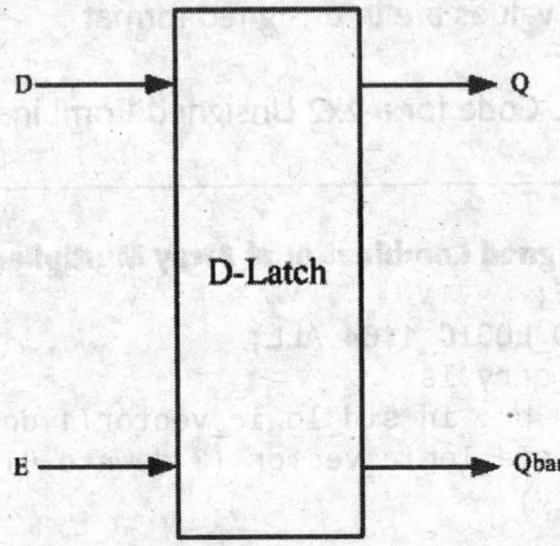

FIGURE 2.8 Logic symbol of D-latch.

TABLE 2.3 Excitation table of D-latch with active high enable. Qbar (Qbar+) is always the inverse of Q (Q+).

Inputs			Next State
E	D	Q	Q+
0	x	0	0
0	x	1	1
1	0	x	0
1	1	x	1

To find the Boolean function, we use K-maps to minimize the minterms. The K-map is shown in Figure 2.9.

From Figure 2.9, we find:

$$Q = \overline{E}\,Q + ED\,; \;\; Qbar = \overline{Q}$$

Figure 2.10 shows the logic diagram of D-latch. Listing 2.5 shows the HDL description of D-latch. A delay time of 9 ns is assumed between the input and Qbar, and 1 ns between Q and Qbar.

E \ DQ	00	01	11	10
0	0	1	1	0
1	0	0	1	1

Q

FIGURE 2.9 K-map for Q.

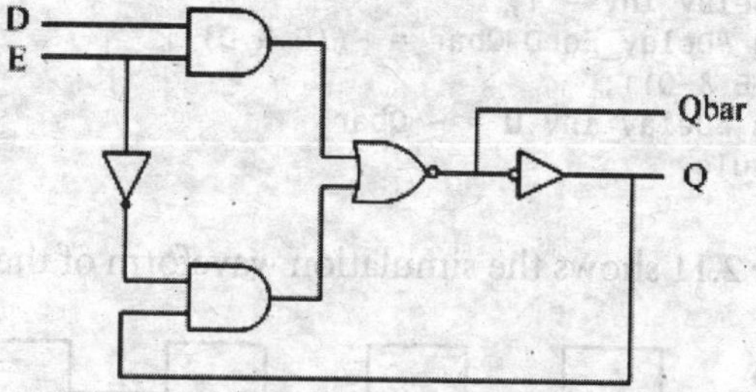

FIGURE 2.10 Gate-level diagram of one D-latch unit.

LISTING 2.5 HDL Code for a D-Latch—VHDL and Verilog

VHDL D-Latch Description

```
library IEEE;
use IEEE.STD_LOGIC_1164.ALL;

entity D_Latch is
port (D, E : in std_logic;
    Q, Qbar : buffer std_logic);
--Q and Qbar are declared as buffer because they act as
--both input and output, they appear on the right- and left-
--hand side of signal assignment statements. inout or
--linkage could have been used instead of buffer.
end D_Latch;

architecture DL_DtFl of D_Latch is
constant Delay_EorD : Time := 9 ns;
constant Delay_inv : Time := 1 ns;
begin
--Assume 9-ns propagation delay time between
--E or D and Qbar; and 1 ns between Qbar and Q.

Qbar <= (D and E) nor (not E and Q) after Delay_EorD;
```

```
Q <= not Qbar after Delay_inv;
end DL_DtFl;
```

Verilog D-Latch Description

```
module D_latch (D, E, Q, Qbar);
input D, E;
output Q, Qbar;

/* Verilog treats the ports as internal ports,
so Q and Qbar are not considered here as
both input and output. If the port is
connected externally as bidirectional,
then we should use inout. */

time Delay_EorD = 9;
time Delay_inv = 1;
assign #Delay_EorD Qbar = ~((E & D) |
    (~E & Q));
assign #Delay_inv Q = ~ Qbar;
endmodule
```

Figure 2.11 shows the simulation waveform of the latch.

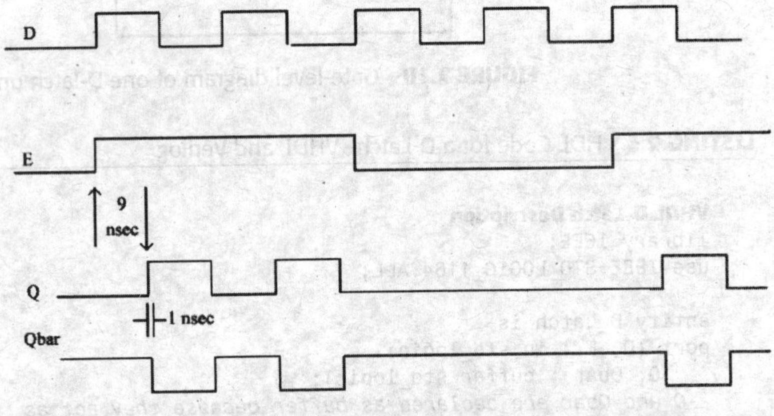

FIGURE 2.11 Simulation waveform of a D-latch with active high enable.

Example 2.5 2-Bit Magnitude Comparator

A 2-bit comparator is a combinational circuit that compares two words (numbers), and each word has 2 bits. Figure 2.12 shows the logic symbol of the comparator. In Figure 2.12, the two words are X and Y. The output of the comparator indicates the result of the comparison: X > Y, X = Y, or X < Y. Since the number of input bits is small (a total of 4 bits), a truth table of the comparator (see Table 2.4) can be used to find the Boolean function.

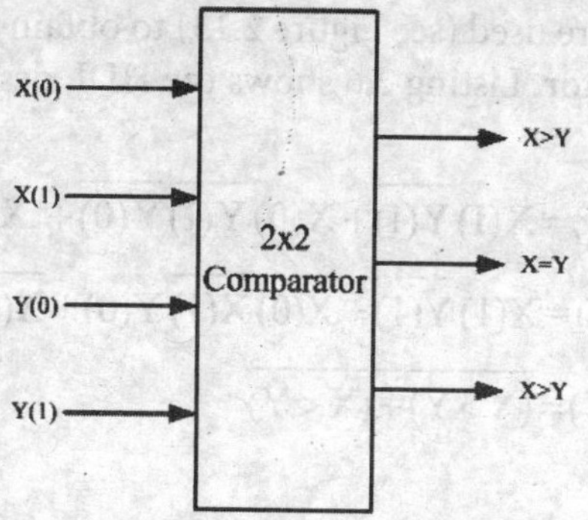

FIGURE 2.12 Logic symbol of a 2x2 magnitude comparator.

TABLE 2.4 Truth Table for a 2x2 Comparator

Input				Output		
X(1)	**X(0)**	**Y(1)**	**Y(0)**	**X > Y**	**X < Y**	**X = Y**
0	0	0	0	0	0	1
0	0	0	1	0	1	0
0	0	1	0	0	1	0
0	0	1	1	0	1	0
0	1	0	0	1	0	0
0	1	0	1	0	0	1
0	1	1	0	0	1	0
0	1	1	1	0	1	0
1	0	0	0	1	0	0
1	0	0	1	1	0	0
1	0	1	0	0	0	1
1	0	1	1	0	1	0
1	1	0	0	1	0	0
1	1	0	1	1	0	0
1	1	1	0	1	0	0
1	1	1	1	0	0	1

If the number of bits increases, the table becomes huge, and other approaches should be used, such as implementation of n-full adders to construct $n \times n$ comparators (see Chapter 4, "Structural Descriptions"). After constructing the truth table, K-maps are used (see Figure 2.13) to obtain the minimized Boolean function of the comparator. Listing 2.6 shows the HDL description.

$$(X>Y)=X(1)\,\overline{Y(1)}+X(0)\,\overline{Y(1)}\,\overline{Y(0)}+X(0)X(1)\,\overline{Y(0)}$$

$$(X<Y)=X(1)\,\overline{Y(1)}+\overline{X(0)}\,\overline{X(1)}\,Y(0)+\overline{X(0)}\,Y(0)Y(1)$$

$$(X=Y)=\overline{(X>Y)+(X<Y)}$$

Y(1)Y(0) \ X(1)X(0)	00	01	11	10
00	0	1	1	1
01	0	0	1	1
11	0	0	0	0
10	0	0	1	0

X>Y

Y(1)Y(0) \ X(1)X(0)	00	01	11	10
00	0	0	0	0
01	1	0	0	0
11	1	1	0	1
10	1	1	0	0

X>Y

FIGURE 2.13 K-maps for Table 2.4.

LISTING 2.6 HDL Code of a 2x2 Magnitude Comparator–VHDL and Verilog

VHDL 2x2 Magnitude Comparator Description

```
library IEEE;
use IEEE.STD_LOGIC_1164.ALL;

entity COMPR_2 is
port (x, y : in std_logic_vector(1 downto 0); xgty,
    xlty : buffer std_logic; xeqy : out std_logic);
end COMPR_2;

architecture COMPR_DFL of COMPR_2 is
begin
xgty <= (x(1) and not y(1)) or (x(0) and not y(1) and
    not y(0)) or
x(0) and x(1) and not y(0));
xlty <= (y(1) and not x(1)) or ( not x(0) and y(0)
    and y(1)) or
(not x(0) and not x(1) and y(0));
xeqy <= xgty nor xlty;
end COMPR_DFL;
```

Verilog 2x2 Magnitude Comparator Description

```
module compr_2 (x, y, xgty, xlty, xeqy);
input [1:0] x, y;
output xgty, xlty, xeqy;
assign xgty = (x[1] & ~ y[1]) | (x[0] & ~ y[1]
    & ~ y[0]) | (x[0] &
x[1] & ~ y[0]);
assign xlty = (y[1] & ~ x[1] ) | (~ x[0] & y[0] & y[1]) |
    (~ x[0] & ~ x[1] & y[0]);
assign xeqy = ~ (xgty | xlty);
endmodule
```

Figure 2.14 shows the simulation waveform of the 2x2 comparator.

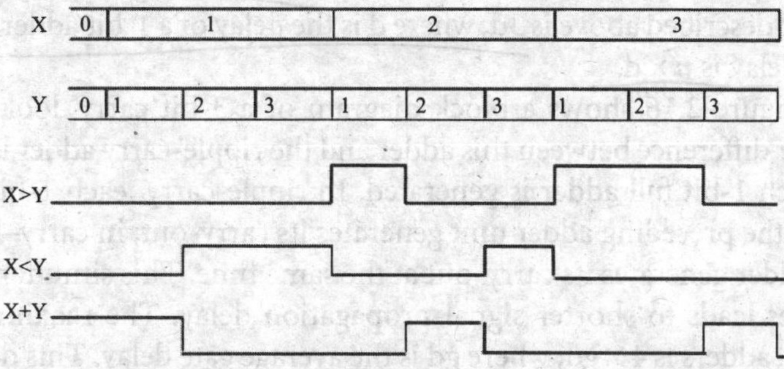

FIGURE 2.14 Simulation waveform of a 2x2 comparator.

Case Study 2.1

In this case study, a 3-bit adder will be described. The adder is designed using two approaches, ripple-carry and carry–look ahead. We simulate the description and compare timing characteristics of the two adders. Figure 2.15 shows a block diagram of a 3-bit ripple-carry.

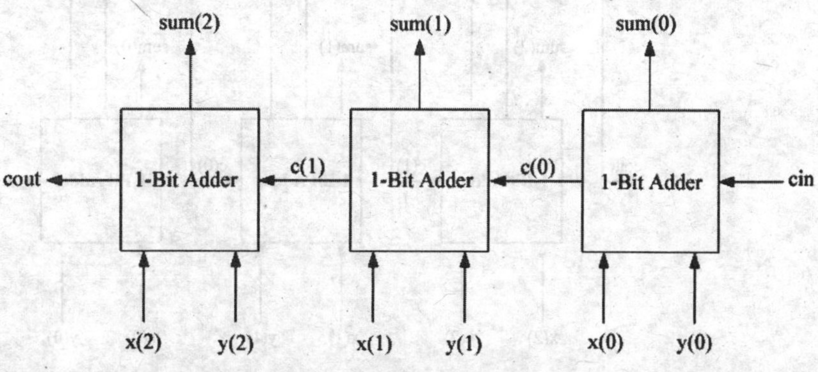

FIGURE 2.15 Block diagram of a 3-bit ripple-carry adder.

The Boolean functions of a 3-bit ripple-carry adder can be written as:

$$\text{sum}(i) = \text{x}(i) \text{ XOR y}(i) \text{ XOR c}(i-1), 0 \leq i \leq 2 \quad (2.5)$$

$$\text{c}(i) = \text{x}(i)\text{y}(i) + \text{x}(i)\text{c}(i-1) + \text{y}(i)\text{c}(i-1), 0 \leq i \leq 2 \quad (2.6)$$

$$\text{cout} = \text{c}(2), \text{c}(-1) = \text{cin} \quad (2.7)$$

Each 1-bit adder in Figure 2.15 is described by Equations 2.5 and 2.6. To produce the sum, each 1-bit adder has to wait until the preceding 1-bit adder generates its carry-out (c(0), c(1), or cout). The maximum signal propagation delay of the adder described above is 3d, where d is the delay of a 1-bit adder; for an n-bit adder, this delay is $n \times$ d.

Figure 2.16 shows a block diagram of a 3-bit carry–look ahead adder. The major difference between this adder and the ripple-carry adder is how the carry-out of each 1-bit full adder is generated. In ripple-carry, each 1-bit adder has to wait until the preceding adder unit generates its carry-out; in carry–look ahead, each 1-bit adder generates its carry-out at the same time. This simultaneous generation of carries leads to shorter signal-propagation delay. The maximum delay in look-ahead adders is 4 × gd, where gd is the average gate delay. This delay is independent of the number of 1-bit adders. More details on these adders can be found in [Ciletti02], [Hayes98], [Mano00], and [Nelson95].

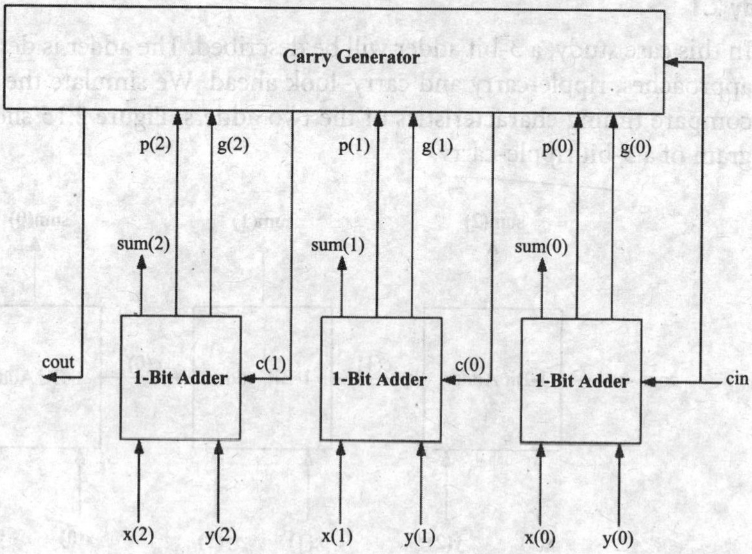

FIGURE 2.16 Block diagram of a 3-bit carry–look ahead adder.

The Boolean functions of a carry–look ahead adder are:

$$\mathrm{sum}(i) = x(i)\ \mathrm{XOR}\ y(i)\ \mathrm{XOR}\ c(i-1),\ 0 \le i \le 2 \quad (2.8)$$

$$g(i) = x(i)\,y(i) \quad (2.9)$$

$$p(i) = x(i) + y(i) \quad (2.10)$$

$$c(0) = g(0) + p(0)\mathrm{cin},\ c(1) = g(1) + p(1)g(0) + p(1)p(0)\mathrm{cin} \quad (2.11)$$

$$\mathrm{cout} = c(2) = g(2) + p(2)g(1) + p(2)p(1)g(0) + P(2)p(1)p(0)\mathrm{cin} \quad (2.12)$$

Listings 2.7 and 2.8 show the HDL code for the ripple-carry adder and the carry–look ahead adders, respectively. A 4.0-nanosecond delay is assumed for all gate types. A constant of type time `delay_gt` is declared, and 4 ns is assigned to it:

```
constant delay_gt : time := 4 ns;       -- VHDL
time delay_gt = 4;                      // Verilog
```

Figure 2.17 shows the waveform for both ripple-carry and carry–look ahead adders, without taking gate delay into consideration. Since there is no delay, the two adders have identical waveforms. From the waveform, it can be concluded that both adders function correctly. Figures 2.18a and b show the waveforms for ripple-carry and carry–look ahead after taking the gate delay into consideration, respectively.

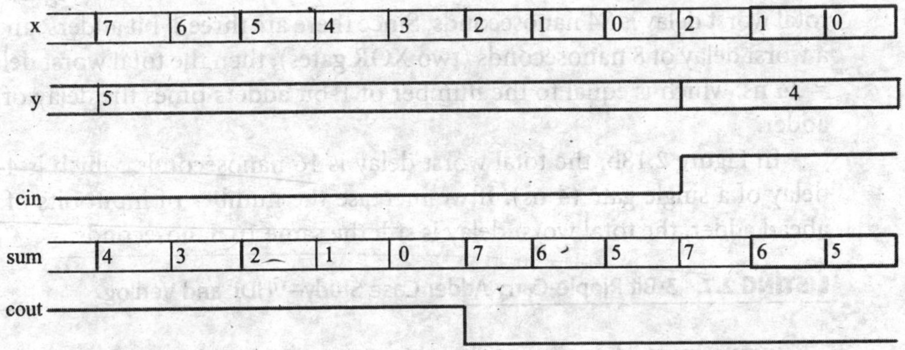

FIGURE 2.17 Simulation waveform for a 3-bit adder with no gate delay.

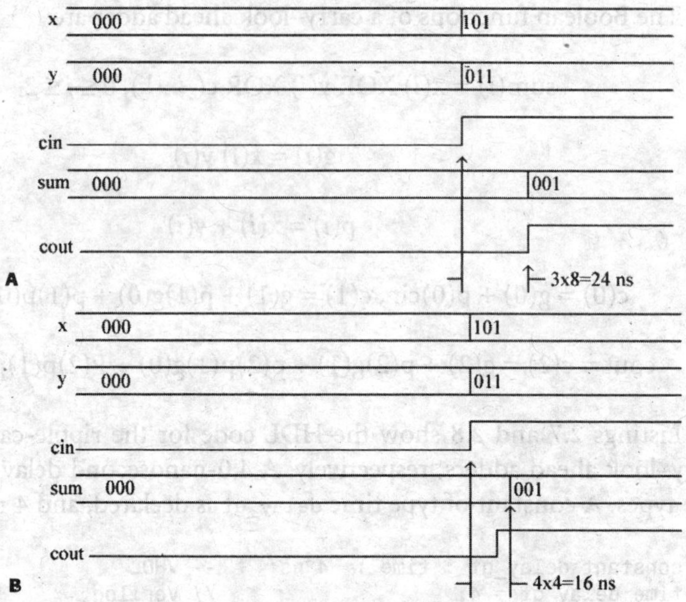

FIGURE 2.18 Simulation waveforms for a 3-bit adder with a 4-ns gate delay: a) Ripple-carry b) Carry–look ahead.

To calculate the worst delay, values are selected for the inputs x, y, and cin to obtain the maximum possible delay; this is done by selecting those values that cause a change in all the carry-out signals. We select x = y = cin = 0 to generate a zero signal on all the outputs, and then select x = 5, y = 3, and cin = 1. In Figure 2.18a, the total worst delay is 24 nanoseconds. Since there are three 1-bit adders, and each has a worst delay of 8 nanoseconds (two XOR gates), then the total worst delay is 8 × 3 = 24 ns, which is equal to the number of 1-bit adders times the delay of one 1-bit adder.

In Figure 2.18b, the total worst delay is 16 nanoseconds, which is 4 times the delay of a single gate (4 ns). If we increase the number of input bits of the look-ahead adder, the total worst delay is still the same 16 nanoseconds.

LISTING 2.7 3-Bit Ripple-Carry Adder Case Study–VHDL and Verilog

VHDL 3-Bit Ripple-Carry Adder Case Study

```
library IEEE;
use IEEE.STD_LOGIC_1164.ALL;
entity adders_RL is
    port (x, y : in std_logic_vector (2 downto 0);
    cin : in std_logic;
    sum : out std_logic_vector (2 downto 0);
    cout : out std_logic);
```

```
end adders_RL;

--I. RIPPLE-CARRY ADDER

architecture RCarry_DtFl of adders_RL is
--Assume 4.0-ns propagation delay for all gates.
signal c0, c1 : std_logic;
constant delay_gt : time := 4 ns;

begin
sum(0) <= (x(0) xor y(0)) xor cin after 2*delay_gt;

--Treat the above statement as two 2-input XOR.

sum(1) <= (x(1) xor y(1)) xor c0 after 2*delay_gt;

--Treat the above statement as two 2-input XOR.
sum(2) <= (x(2) xor y(2)) xor c1 after 2*delay_gt;
--Treat the above statement as two 2-input XOR.
c0 <= (x(0) and y(0)) or (x(0) and cin) or (y(0) and cin)
    after 2*delay_gt;
c1 <= (x(1) and y(1)) or (x(1) and c0) or (y(1) and c0)
    after 2*delay_gt;
cout <= (x(2) and y(2)) or (x(2) and c1) or (y(2) and c1)
    after 2*delay_gt;
end RCarry_DtFl;
```

Verilog 3-Bit Ripple-Carry Adder Case Study

```
module adr_rcla (x, y, cin, sum, cout);
input [2:0] x, y;
input cin;
output [2:0] sum;
output cout;
// I. RIPPLE CARRY ADDER
wire c0, c1;
time delay_gt = 4;
//Assume 4.0-ns propagation delay for all gates.
assign #(2*delay_gt) sum[0] = (x[0] ^ y[0]) ^ cin;
//Treat the above statement as two 2-input XOR.

assign #(2*delay_gt) sum[1] = (x[1] ^ y[1]) ^ c0;
//Treat the above statement as two 2-input XOR.

assign #(2*delay_gt) sum[2] = (x[2] ^ y[2]) ^ c1;
//Treat the above statement as two 2-input XOR.

assign #(2*delay_gt) c0 = (x[0] & y[0]) | (x[0] & cin) | (y[0] & cin);

assign #(2*delay_gt) c1 = (x[1] & y[1]) | (x[1] & c0) | (y[1] & c0);

assign #(2*delay_gt) cout = (x[2] & y[2]) | (x[2] & c1) | (y[2] & c1);
endmodule
```

LISTING 2.8 3-Bit Carry–Look ahead Adder Case Study–VHDL and Verilog

VHDL 3-Bit Carry–Look Ahead Adder Case Study

```
--II. CARRY-LOOKAHEAD ADDER
architecture lkh_DtFl of adders_RL is
--Assume 4.0-ns propagation delay for all gates
--including a 3-input xor.
signal c0, c1 : std_logic;
signal p, g : std_logic_vector (2 downto 0);
constant delay_gt : time := 4 ns;
begin

g(0) <= x(0) and y(0) after delay_gt;
g(1) <= x(1) and y(1) after delay_gt;
g(2) <= x(2) and y(2) after delay_gt;
p(0) <= x(0) or y(0) after delay_gt;
p(1) <= x(1) or y(1) after delay_gt;
p(2) <= x(2) or y(2) after delay_gt;
c0 <= g(0) or (p(0) and cin) after 2*delay_gt;

c1 <= g(1) or (p(1) and g(0)) or (p(1) and p(0)
    and cin) after 2*delay_gt;
cout <= g(2) or (p(2) and g(1)) or (p(2) and p(1)
    and g(0)) or
    (p(2) and p(1) and p(0) and cin) after 2*delay_gt;

sum(0) <= (p(0) xor g(0)) xor cin after delay_gt;
sum(1) <= (p(1) xor g(1)) xor c0 after delay_gt;
sum(2) <= (p(2) xor g(2)) xor c1 after delay_gt;
end lkh_DtFl;
```

Verilog 3-Bit Carry–Look Ahead Adder Case Study

```
// II. CARRY-LOOKAHEAD ADDER
module lkahd_adder (x, y, cin, sum, cout);
input [2:0] x, y;
input cin;
output [2:0] sum;
output cout;
/*Assume 4.0-ns propagation delay for all gates
    including a 3-input xor.*/

wire c0, c1;
wire [2:0] p, g;
time delay_gt = 4;
assign #delay_gt g[0] = x[0] & y[0];
assign #delay_gt g[1] = x[1] & y[1];
assign #delay_gt g[2] = x[2] & y[2];
assign #delay_gt p[0] = x[0] | y[0];
assign #delay_gt p[1] = x[1] | y[1];
assign #delay_gt p[2] = x[2] | y[2];
assign #(2*delay_gt) c0 = g[0] | (p[0] & cin);

assign #(2*delay_gt) c1 = g[1] | (p[1] & g[0]) |
```

```
        (p[1] & p[0] & cin);

    assign #(2*delay_gt) cout = g[2] | (p[2] & g[1]) | (p[2] &
        p[1] & g[0]) | (p[2] & p[1] & p[0] & cin);

    assign #delay_gt sum[0] = (p[0] ^ g[0]) ^ cin;
    assign #delay_gt sum[1] = (p[1] ^ g[1]) ^ c0;
        assign #delay_gt sum[2] = (p[2] ^ g[2]) ^ c1;
    endmodule
```

2.4 COMMON PROGRAMMING ERRORS

This section discusses common programming errors. These errors are classified as either syntax or semantic errors. Syntax errors are those that result from not following the rules of the language. For example, consider the sentence: "Jim am a policeman."; the sentence has a syntax error. According to the rules of English language, "is" should replace "am." The sentence, after correcting the syntax error, may still have a semantic error if Jim is not a policeman. A semantic error is an error in the meaning of the statement, rather than an error in the mechanics of the statement.

The above example applies to HDL; there can be syntax and semantic errors. Syntax errors terminate compilation of the program. Semantic errors may not terminate the program, but the outcome of the program may not be as expected.

2.4.1 Common VHDL Programming Errors

This section briefly discusses some common syntax and semantic errors when writing VHDL programs. Listing 2.4 (VHDL) is considered, and some possible errors are discussed in modified code. Table 2.5 shows errors in Listing 2.4 (VHDL) modified code.

TABLE 2.5 Possible Errors in Modified Listing 2.4 (VHDL)

Modified Code	Error
`entity mult_arry`	"is" is missing.
`port (a; b : in std_logic_vector (1 downto 0);`	instead of comma (a, b). Semicolon is inserted
`P : std_logic_vector (3 downto 0)`	The direction of the port `P` is missing (`out`).
`architecture MULT_DF of mult_ary is`	The name of the entity is misspelled; it should be (`mult_arry`).
`P(0) = a(0) and b(0);`	The signal assignment statement operator is wrong ("<=" should replace "=").
`P(1) <= (a(0) and b(1)) xor (a(1) and b(0);`	Closing parenthesis ")" is missing at the end of the statement. →

Modified Code	Error
`P(0) <= a(0) and b(2);`	The index of "b" is out of range; it should be 0 or 1.
`end MUL_DF;`	The name of the architecture is misspelled; it should be `MULT_DF`.
`P(0) <= a(0) and b(2);` `P(0) <= a(0) or b(2);`	The syntax may be correct, but the logic (semantics) is wrong; `P(0)` cannot have two different logics (`and` & `or`).
No Library listed on first line of code. `entity mult_arry is`	The Library declaration is missing; `std_logic` is not recognized without attaching the IEEE library.

2.4.2 Common Verilog Programming Errors

Here, we briefly discuss some common syntax and semantic errors in writing Verilog programs. One of the most common errors for beginners is in not adhering to Verilog's case-sensitive nature. Consider the modified Listing 2.4 (Verilog). Some possible errors in this modified Listing are discussed (see Table 2.6).

TABLE 2.6 Possible Errors in Modified Listing 2.4 (Verilog)

Modified Code	Error
`module mult_arry (a, b, P)`	Semicolon (;) is missing at the end of the statement.
`input [1:0] A, b;`	"A" is not defined; it should be lowercase.
`output (3:0) P;`	Brackets `[3:0]` should be used instead of parentheses.
`P[0] = a[0] & b[0];`	"`assign`" is missing.
`assign P[0] = a[0] and b[0];`	"and" cannot be used here; in Verilog, the logical operator "&" should be used.
`endmodule;`	No semicolon at the end of "`endmodule`."

2.5 SUMMARY

This chapter discussed data-flow descriptions based mainly on writing the Boolean function(s) of the system. The Boolean function is coded as signal-assignment statements. In VHDL, the signal assignment operator <= is implemented to assign a value to a signal; in Verilog, the signal-assignment operator is `assign`. Logical operators such as and (&), or (|), and xor (^) have been implemented to describe the Boolean function in VHDL (Verilog) code. The following table summarizes the commands that we have used in this Chapter. Table 2.7 lists data-flow commands/components in VHDL and their counterparts (if any) in Verilog.

TABLE 2.7 VHDL Versus Verilog Data-Flow Components

VHDL Command/Components	Verilog Counterpart
`entity`	`module`
`<=`	`assign`
`and, or, xor, not`	`&, |, ^, ~`
`signal`	`wire`
`after`	`#`
`in, out, inout`	`input, output, inout`

2.6 EXERCISES

2.1 Write a data-flow description (in both VHDL and Verilog) of a full adder with enable. If the enable is low (0), the sum and carry are zero; otherwise, the sum and carry are the usual output of the adder. Use a 5-ns delay for any gate including XOR. Draw the truth table of this adder, and derive the Boolean function after minimization. Simulate and verify the circuit.

2.2 Write a data-flow description (in both VHDL and Verilog) of a system that has three 1-bit inputs, a(1), a(2), and a(3); and one 1-bit output b. The least significant bit is a(1); and b is 1 only when (a(1)a(2)a(3)) = 1, 3, 6, or 7 (all in decimal), otherwise b is 0. Derive a minimized Boolean function of the system and write the data-flow description. Simulate the system and verify that it works as designed. What is the function of this system?

2.3 Given the following Verilog description code, fill the values of s1 and s2 into the table; T = time in nanoseconds. Do not use a computer to solve this problem.

```
module problem (a, b, s1, s2);
input a, b;
output s1, s2;
assign #10 s1 = a ^ b;
assign #10 s2 = a | s1;
endmodule
```

	T=100	T=150	T=165	T=200	T=250	T=300
a	1	0	0	1	0	1
b	1	1	1	0	0	1
s1	0					
s2	0					

Explain how you obtained the values for s1 and s2 at time T = 165 ns. Translate the Verilog code to VHDL.

2.4 Referring to Case Study 2.1, increase the number of bits from 3 to 4. Drive the Boolean functions of both the ripple-carry and the carry–look ahead adders. Simulate the adders, and calculate the worst delay between the input and output using Verilog description. Contrast your results with Figure 2.16 and explain.

2.5 The following VHDL code describes an SR-latch. Translate the code to Verilog.

```
entity SR is
    port (S, R : in bit; Q : buffer bit; Qb : out bit);
end SR;
architecture SR_DtFL of SR is
begin
Q <= S or (not R and Q);
Qb <= not Q;
end SR_DtFL;
```

2.7 REFERENCES

[Ciletti02] Ciletti, M. D., *Advanced Digital Design with The VERILOG HDL.* Prentice Hall, 2002.

[Hayes98] Hayes, J., *Computer Architecture and Organization*, 3d ed. McGraw Hill Companies, 1998.

[Mano00] Mano, M. M. and C. R. Kime, *Logic and Computer Design Fundamentals.* Prentice Hall, 2000.

[Nelson95] Nelson, V. P., H. T. Nagle, B. D. Carroll, and J. D. Irwin, *Digital Logic Circuit Analysis & Design.* Prentice Hall, 1995.

3 Behavioral Descriptions

In This Chapter

- Understand the concept of sequential statements and how they differ from concurrent statements.
- Identify the basic statements and components of behavioral descriptions, such as process, variable assignment statements, `if`, `case`, `casex`, `casez`, `when`, `report`, `loop`, `exit`, `next`, `always`, `repeat`, `forever`, and `initial`.
- Review and understand the basics of digital logic systems such as D flip-flop, JK flip-flop, binary counters, and shift register.
- Understand the concept of some basic genetic and renal systems.
- Both VHDL and Verilog descriptions are discussed.

3.1 BEHAVIORAL DESCRIPTION HIGHLIGHTS

In Chapter 2, "Data-Flow Descriptions," data-flow simulations were implemented to describe digital systems for known digital structures, such as adders, multiplexers, and latches. The behavioral description is a powerful tool to describe systems for which the digital logic structures are not known or are hard to generate. Examples of such systems are complex arithmetic units, computer control units, and biological mechanisms that describe the physiological action of certain organs, such as the kidney or heart.

Facts

- The behavioral description describes the system by showing how the outputs behave according to changes in the inputs.
- In this description, we do not need to know the logic diagram of the system; what must be known is how the output behaves in response to change in the input.
- In VHDL, the major behavioral description statement is `process`. In Verilog, the major behavioral description statements are `always` and `initial`.

■ For VHDL, the statements inside the process are sequential. In Verilog, all statements are concurrent (see "Analysis of VHDL Code" in Section 3.4.2).

3.2 STRUCTURE OF THE HDL BEHAVIORAL DESCRIPTION

Listing 3.1 shows a simple example of HDL code describing a system (`half_add`) using behavioral description. The code mainly consists of signal-assignment statements. Referring to the VHDL code, the entity `half_add` has two input ports, `I1` and `I2`, and two output ports, `O1` and `O2`. The ports are of type `bit`; this type is recognized by the VHDL package without the need to attach a Library. If the type is, for example, `std_logic`, the IEEE Library must be attached.

The name of the architecture is `behave_ex`; it is bound to the entity `half_add` by the predefined word `of`. `Process` is the VHDL behavioral description keyword. Every VHDL behavioral description has to include a process. The statement `process (I1, I2)` is a concurrent statement; so its execution is determined by the occurrence of an event.

`I1` and `I2` constitute a sensitivity list. The process is executed (activated) only if an event occurs on any element of the sensitivity list; otherwise the process remains inactive. If the process has no sensitivity list, the process is executed continuously. The process in Listing 3.1 includes two signal-assignment statements, statement 1 and statement 2. (See Section 2.2.2 for details on signal-assignment statements.)

LISTING 3.1 Example of an HDL Behavioral Description–VHDL and Verilog

VHDL Behavioral Description

```
entity half_add is
    port (I1, I2 : in bit; O1, O2 : out bit);
        --Since we are using type bit,
        --no need for attaching a Library.
        --If we use std_logic, we should
        --attach the IEEE Library.

end half_add;
architecture behave_ex of half_add is
begin
process (I1, I2)
    begin
        O1 <= I1 xor I2 after 10 ns; – statement 1
        O2 <= I1 and I2 after 10 ns; – statement 2

--The above two statements are signal-assignment statements
--with 10-nanosecond delays.
--Other behavioral (sequential) statements can be added here
    end process;
end behave_ex;
```

Verilog Behavioral Description

```
module half_add (I1, I2, O1, O2);
input I1, I2;
output O1, O2;
reg O1, O2;
/* Since O1 and O2 are outputs and they are
written inside "always," they should be
declared as reg */
always @(I1, I2)

     begin

          #10 O1 = I1 ^ I2; // statement 1.
          #10 O2 = I1 & I2; // statement 2.

/*The above two statements are procedural (inside always)
 signal-assignment statements with 10 simulation screen
units delay*/

/*Other behavioral (sequential) statements can be added here*/

     end
endmodule
```

All statements inside the body of the process are executed *sequentially*. Recall from Section 2.2.1 that the execution of a signal-assignment statement has two phases: calculation and assignment. The sequential execution here means *sequential calculation*. That means the calculation of a statement will not wait until the preceding statement is assigned, only until the calculation is done.

To illustrate this sequential execution, assume that in Listing 3.1, at $T = T_0$, `I1` changes from 0 to 1, while `I2` stays at 1. This change constitutes an event on `I1`, which in turn activates the process. Statement 1 is calculated as O1 = (I1 XOR I2) = (1 XOR 0) = 1. This value of 1 is not assigned to `O1` at T_0, but rather at $T_0 + 10$ ns. Still at T_0, statement 2 is calculated by using the values of `I1` and `I2` at T_0; so O2 = (1 AND 0) = 0. The value of 0 is assigned to `O2` at $T_0 + 10$ ns.

For the above example, both data-flow and behavioral descriptions yield the same output for the two signal-assignment statements. This is not the case when a signal appears on both the right-hand side of the statement and the left-hand side of another statement, which will be seen later.

Referring to the Verilog code in Listing 3.1, `always` is the Verilog behavioral statement. In contrast to VHDL, all Verilog statements inside `always` are treated as concurrent, the same as in the data-flow description (see Section 2.2.2). Any signal that is declared as an output should also be declared as a register (`reg`) if it appears inside `always`. In Listing 3.1, `O1` and `O2` are declared outputs, so they should also be declared as `reg`.

3.3 THE VHDL VARIABLE-ASSIGNMENT STATEMENT

The use of variables inside processes is common practice in VHDL behavioral descriptions. Consider the following two signal-assignment statements inside a process where S1, S2, and t1 are signals.

```
Signl : process(t1)
begin
st1 : S1 <= t1;
st2 : S2 <= not S1;
end process;
```

In VHDL, we can label any statement. The label should be followed by a colon. In the above code, Signl, st1, and st2 are labels. VHDL code in this example does not use these labels for compilation or simulation; they are optional. They are used here to refer to a certain statement by its label. For example, to explain the statement S1 <= t1, it can be referred to by statement st1.

In the above code, signal S1 appears on both the left-hand side of statement st1 and on the right-hand side of statement st2. Assume that at simulation time T_0, t1 = 0 and S1 = 0, and at simulation time T_1, t1 changes from 0 to 1. This change constitutes an event, and the process labeled Signl is activated. For statement st1, S1 is calculated as 1. S1 does not acquire this new value of 1 at T_1, but rather at $T_1 + \Delta$. For the statement st2, S2 at T_1 is calculated using the old value of S1 (0). Now, if we use variable assignment statements as follows:

```
Varb : process(t1)
variable temp1, temp2 : bit; --This is a variable
                              --declaration statement
begin
st3 : temp1 := t1; -- This is a variable assignment statement
st4 : temp2 := not temp1; --This is a variable
                            --assignment statement
st5 : S1 <= temp1;
st6 : S2 <= temp2;
end process;
```

Variable assignment statements, as in C language, are calculated and assigned immediately with no delay time between calculation and assignment. The assignment operator is :=. If t1 acquires a new value of 1 at T_1, then momentarily temp1 = 1 and temp2 = 0. For statements st5 and st6, S1 acquires the value of temp1 (1) at $T_1 + \Delta$, and S2 acquires value of temp2 (0) at $T_1 + \Delta$. Because Δ is infinitesimally short, S1 and S2 appear on the simulation screen as if they acquire their new values at T_1.

3.4 SEQUENTIAL STATEMENTS

There are several statements associated with behavioral descriptions. These statements have to appear inside `process` in VHDL, or inside `always` or `initial` in Verilog. The following sections discuss some of these statements.

3.4.1 IF Statement

`IF` is a sequential statement that appears inside `process` in VHDL, or inside `always` or `initial` in Verilog. It has several formats, some of which are as follows:

VHDL IF Formats

```
if (Boolean Expression) then
statement 1;
statement 2;
statement 3;
.......
    else
statement a;
statement b;
statement c;
.......
end if;
```

Verilog IF Formats

```
if (Boolean Expression)
begin
    statement 1; /* if only one statement, begin and end
                    can be omitted */
    statement 2;
        statement 3;
        .......
        end
    else
begin
    statement a; /* if only one statement, begin and end
                    can be omitted */
        statement b;
        statement c;
        .......
end
```

The execution of `if` is controlled by the Boolean expression. If the Boolean expression is true, then statements 1, 2, 3, ... are executed. If the expression is false, statements a, b, c, ... are executed.

EXAMPLE 3.1 Boolean Expression and Execution of `IF`

VHDL

```
if (clk = '1') then
temp := s1;
```

```
else
temp := s2;
end if;
```

```
Verilog
if (clk == 1)
temp = s1;
else
temp = s2;
```

In Example 3.1, if `clk` is high (1), then the value of `s1` is assigned to variable `temp`. Otherwise, `s2` is assigned to variable `temp`.

The `else` statement can be eliminated, and in this case the `if` statement simulates a latch, as shown in Example 3.2.

EXAMPLE 3.2 Execution of `IF` as a Latch

```
VHDL
if clk = '1' then
    temp := s1;
end if;
```

```
Verilog
if (clk == 1)
begin
    temp = s1;
end
```

If `clk` is high, then the value of s1 is assigned to temp. If `clk` is not high, temp retains its current value, thus simulating a latch.

Another format for the `if` statement is `else-if`.

EXAMPLE 3.3 Execution of `IF` as `ELSE-IF`

```
VHDL
if (Boolean Expression1) then
statement1; statement2;...
elsif (Boolean expression2) then
statement i; statement ii;...
else
statement a; statement b;...
end if;
```

```
Verilog
if (Boolean Expression1)
begin
    statement1; statement 2;....
end
else if (Boolean expression2)
begin
```

→

```
    statementi; statementii;
end
else
begin
    statementa; statementb;
end
```

EXAMPLE 3.4 Implementing ELSE-IF

VHDL

```
if signal1 ='1' then
temp := s1;
elsif signal2 = '1' then
temp := s2;
else
temp := s3;
end if;
```

Verilog

```
if (signal1 == 1)
temp = s1;
else if (signal2 == 1)
temp = s2;
else
temp = s3;
```

After execution of the above `if` statement, `temp` acquires the values shown in Table 3.1.

TABLE 3.1 Output Signals (`temp`) for `else-if` Statement in Example 3.4

signal1	signal2	temp =
0	0	s3
1	0	s1
0	1	s2
1	1	s1

The Boolean expression may specify other relational operations, such as inequality, or greater than or less than (see Chapter 1, "Introduction," for details on relational operators). In Example 3.5, the `if` statement and variable assignment statements are used to describe a 2x1 multiplexer.

EXAMPLE 3.5 Behavioral Description of a 2x1 Multiplexer with Tristate Output

To describe the behavior of the output of a multiplexer with a change in input, we develop a flowchart for the multiplexer. The flowchart shows how the output behaves with the input. The output is high impedance if the enable is high. When the enable is low, the output is equal to input B if select is high, otherwise the output is equal to A. We do not need to know the logic diagram of the multiplexer to write the HDL behavioral description. Figure 3.1a shows the flowchart, and Figure 3.1b shows the logic symbol of the multiplexer. In this example, for simplicity, the propagation delays between the input and the output are not considered.

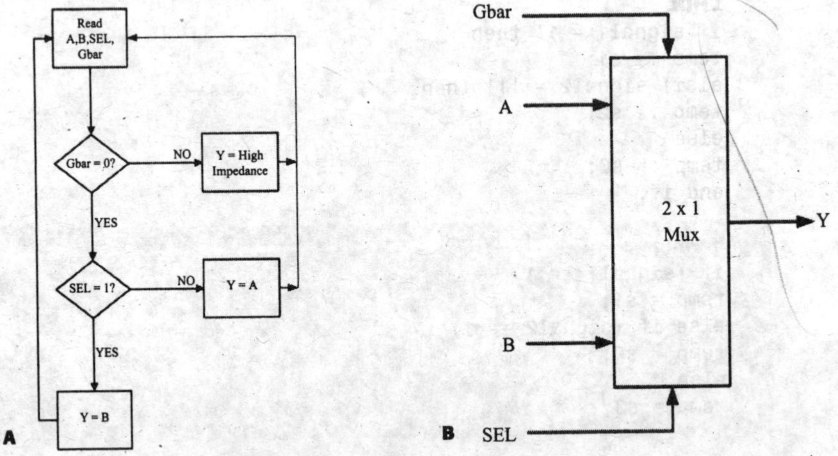

FIGURE 3.1 2x1 Multiplexer. (a) Flow chart. (b) Logic symbol.

Listing 3.2 shows the HDL description of the multiplexer using the `if-else` statement, and Listing 3.3 shows the HDL description with the `else-if` statement. The VHDL code uses variable assignment statements to describe the function of the multiplexer. VHDL executes variable assignment statements as does C language; no delay time is involved in the execution. The signal-assignment statements `Y <= 'Z';` in VHDL, and `Y = 1'bz;` in Verilog assign high impedance to the single-bit `Y`. If `Y` is a 3-bit signal, then the two statements are: `Y <= "ZZZ";` and `Y = 3'bzzz;`, respectively.

LISTING 3.2 HDL Description of a 2x1 Multiplexer Using IF-ELSE—VHDL and Verilog

VHDL 2x1 Multiplexer Using IF-ELSE

```
library IEEE;
use IEEE.STD_LOGIC_1164.ALL;
entity MUX_if is
port (A, B, SEL, Gbar : in std_logic; Y : out std_logic);
end MUX_if;
architecture MUX_bh of MUX_if is
begin
process (SEL, A, B, Gbar)
```

```
--SEL, A, B, and Gbar are the sensitivity list of the process.
variable temp : std_logic;

--It is common practice in behavioral description to use
--variable(s) rather than signal(s). This is done to avoid
--any timing errors that may arise due to the sequential
--execution of signal statements by the behavioral
--description. Execution of variable assignment statements
--is the same as in C language. After calculating the value
--of the variable, it is assigned to the output signal.
--In this example, temp is calculated as the output of the
--multiplexer. After calculation, temp is assigned to
   —the output signal Y.

begin
    if Gbar = '0' then
        if SEL = '1' then
            temp := B;
            else
            temp := A;
        end if;
    Y <= temp;
    else
    Y <= 'Z';
    end if;
end process;

end MUX_bh;
```

Verilog 2x1 Multiplexer Using IF-ELSE

```
module mux2x1 (A, B, SEL, Gbar, Y);
input A, B, SEL, Gbar;
output Y;
reg Y;
always @ (SEL, A, B, Gbar)
begin
    if (Gbar == 1)
    Y = 1'bz;
    else
    begin
        if (SEL)
        Y = B;
/* This is a procedural assignment. Procedural assignments are used to
assign values to variables declared as regs (as Y here in this module).
Procedural statements have to appear inside always, blocks, initial,
tasks, or functions*/

        else
        Y = A;
    end
end

endmodule
```

LISTING 3.3 HDL Description of a 2x1 Multiplexer Using ELSE-IF—VHDL and Verilog

VHDL 2x1 Multiplexer Using ELSE-IF

```
library IEEE;
use IEEE.STD_LOGIC_1164.ALL;
entity MUXBH is
    port (A, B, SEL, Gbar : in std_logic;
Y : out std_logic);
end MUXBH;
architecture MUX_bh of MUXBH is
begin
process (SEL, A, B, Gbar)
variable temp : std_logic;
    begin
        if (Gbar = '0') and (SEL = '1') then
        temp := B;
        elsif (Gbar = '0') and (SEL = '0')then
        temp := A;
        else
        temp := 'Z'; – Z is high impedance.
    end if;
Y <= temp;
end process;
end MUX_bh;
```

Verilog 2x1 Multiplexer Using ELSE-IF

```
module MUXBH (A, B, SEL, Gbar, Y);
input A, B, SEL, Gbar;
output Y;
reg Y; /* since Y is an output and appears inside always,
          Y has to be declared as reg (register) */

always @ (SEL, A, B, Gbar)
begin
    if (Gbar == 0 & SEL == 1)
    begin
        Y = B;
    end
    else if (Gbar == 0 & SEL == 0)
    Y = A;
    else
    Y = 1'bz; //Y is assigned to high impedance
end

endmodule
```

Figure 3.2 shows the simulation waveform of the multiplexer.

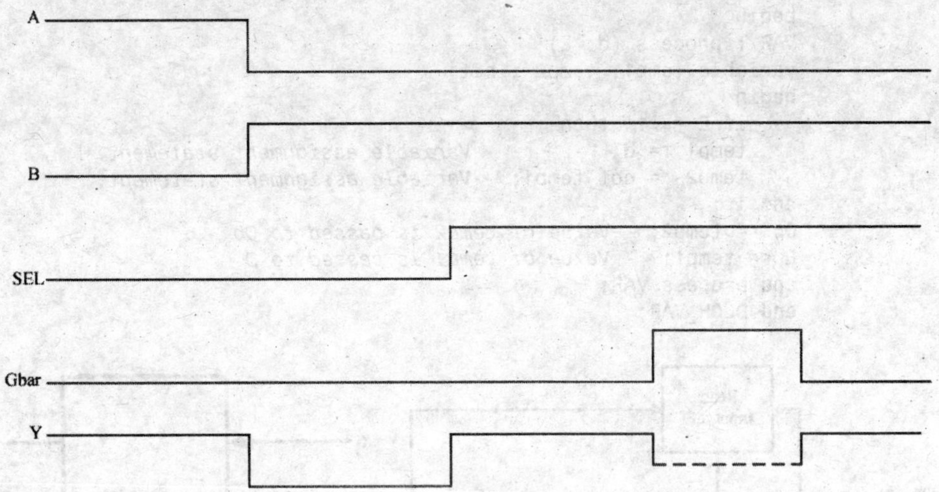

FIGURE 3.2 Simulation waveform of a 2x1 multiplexer.

3.4.2 Signal and Variable Assignment

To illustrate the difference between signal- and variable-assignment statements in VHDL code, the behavioral description of a D-latch is written. A process is written based on signal-assignment statements, and then another process is written based on variable-assignment statements. A comparison of the simulation waveforms of the two processes will highlight the differences between the two assignment statements.

EXAMPLE 3.6 Behavioral Description of a Latch Using Variable and Signal Assignments

The functionality of a D-latch can be explained as follows: if the enable (E) is active, the output of the latch (Q) follows the input (d); otherwise, the outputs remain unchanged. Also, Qb, the invert output, is always the invert of Q. A flowchart that illustrates this functionality is shown in Figure 3.3a. Figure 3.3b shows the logic symbol of a D-latch.

We first write the VHDL code using variable assignment statements. Listing 3.4 shows that code.

LISTING 3.4 VHDL Code for Behavioral Description of D-Latch Using Variable-Assignment Statements

```
entity DLTCH_var is
    port (d, E : in bit; Q, Qb : out bit);
--Since we are using type bit, no need for attaching a Library.
--If we use std_logic, we should attach the IEEE Library.
end DLTCH_var;
architecture DLCH_VAR of DLTCH_var is
```

```
begin
VAR : process (d, E)
variable temp1, temp2 : bit;
begin
    if E = '1' then
    temp1 := d;          --Variable assignment statement.
    temp2 := not temp1; --Variable assignment statement.
end if;
Qb <= temp2; --Value of temp2 is passed to Qb
Q <= temp1;  --Value of temp1 is passed to Q
end process VAR;
end DLCH_VAR;
```

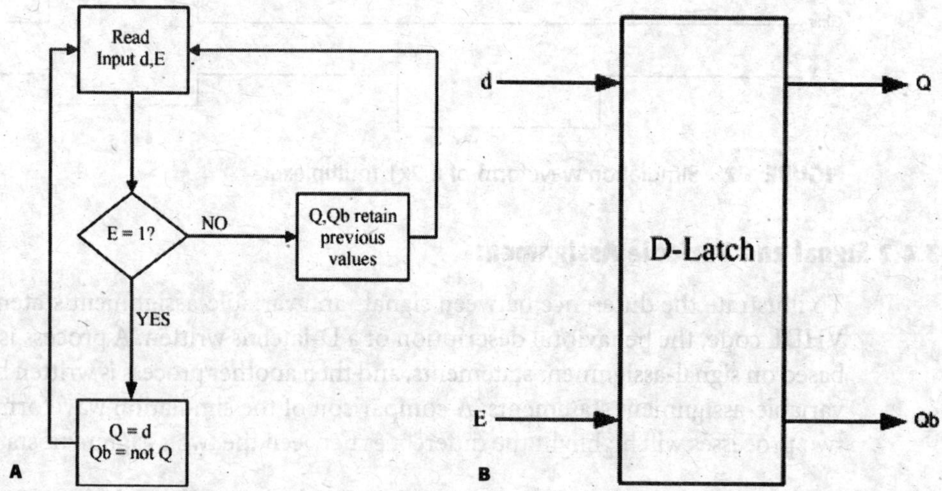

FIGURE 3.3 D-Latch. (a) Flowchart. (b) Logic symbol.

Figure 3.4 shows the waveform for Listing 3.4. Clearly from the waveform, the code correctly represents a D-latch where `Q` follows `d` when `E` is high; otherwise, `d` retains its previous value. Also, `Qb` is the invert of `Q` at all times.

Next, the same VHDL code from Listing 3.4 is written using signal-assignment statements. Listing 3.5 shows the VHDL behavioral code for D-Latch using signal-assignment statements.

LISTING 3.5 VHDL Code for Behavioral Description of D-Latch Using Signal-Assignment Statements

```
entity Dltch_sig is
port (d, E : in bit; Q : buffer bit; Qb : out bit);
--Q is declared as a buffer because it is an input/output
--signal; it appears on both the left- and right-hand
--sides of the assignment statements.
```

```
end Dltch_sig;
architecture DL_sig of Dltch_sig is
begin
process (d, E)
begin
    if E = '1' then
        Q <= d;        -- signal assignment
        Qb <= not Q; -- signal assignment
    end if;
end process;

end DL_sig;
```

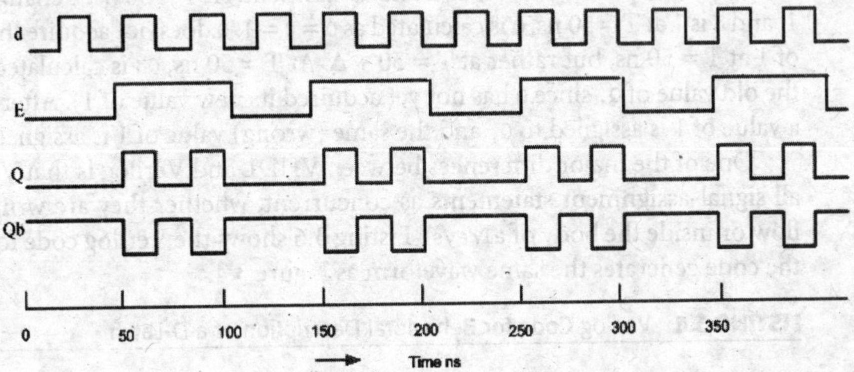

FIGURE 3.4 Simulation waveform of D-Latch using variable-assignment statement. The waveform correctly describes a D-latch.

Figure 3.5 shows the simulation waveform of Listing 3.5. The figure shows Q following Qb, which is an error because Qb should be the invert of Q. This error is due to the sequential execution of the signal-assignment statements in the behavioral description (see details in the following Analysis).

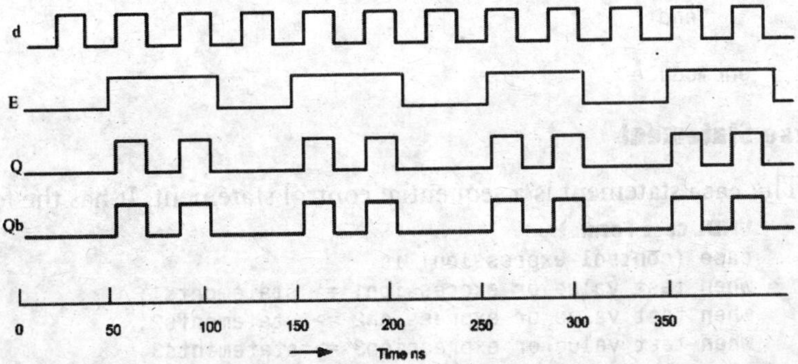

FIGURE 3.5 Simulation waveform of D-Latch using signal-assignment statement. Qb is following Q instead of being the invert of Q.

Analysis of VHDL Code in Listings 3.4 and 3.5

The variable-assignment statements in Listing 3.4 are: `temp1 := d` and `temp2 := not temp1`. Referring to Figure 3.4, at simulation time T = 0 ns, initial values are: E = 0, d = 0, Q = 0, and Qb = 0. At T = 50 ns, signal E changes from 0 to 1. Because temp1 and temp2 are variables, they instantaneously acquire their new values 1 and 0, respectively. These correct values are passed to Q and Qb.

Listing 3.5 shows two signal assignment statements inside the body of the process, `Q <= d` and `Qb <= not q`. Initial values at T ≤ 50 ns are : `E` = 0, `d` = 0, `Q` = 0, and `Qb` = 0. Recall that execution of a signal-assignment statement inside a process is done in two phases: calculation and assignment. At T = 50 ns, `E` changes from 0 to 1, and `d` is 1 at T = 50 ns. `Q` is calculated as `Q` = `d` = 1. `Q` does not acquire this new value of 1 at T = 50 ns, but rather at T = 50 + Δ. At T = 50 ns, `Qb` is calculated as 1 (using the old value of `Q`, since `Q` has not yet acquired its new value of 1). After calculation, a value of 1 is assigned to `Q`, and the same (wrong) value of 1 is assigned to `Qb`.

One of the major differences between VHDL and Verilog is that Verilog treats all signal-assignment statements as concurrent, whether they are written as data-flow or inside the body of `always`. Listing 3.6 shows the Verilog code for a D-latch; the code generates the same waveform as Figure 3.4.

LISTING 3.6 Verilog Code for Behavioral Description of a D-Latch

```
module D_latch (d, E, Q, Qb);
input      d, E;
output Q, Qb;
reg Q, Qb;
always @ (d, E)
begin
    if (E == 1)
        begin
        Q = d;
        Qb = ~ Q;
        end
    end

endmodule
```

3.4.3 Case Statement

The `case` statement is a sequential control statement. It has the following format:

VHDL Case Format

```
case (control-expression) is
when test value or expression1 => statements1;
when test value or expression2 => statements2;
when test value or expression3 => statements3;
when others => statements4;
end case;
```

```
Verilog Case Format
case (control-expression)
test value1 : begin statements1; end
test value2 : begin statements2; end
test value3 : begin statements3; end
default : begin default statements end
endcase
```

If, for example, `test value1` is true (i.e., the value of the control expression), then `statements1` is executed. The `case` statement must include all possible conditions (values) of the `control-expression`. The statement `when others` (VHDL) or `default` (Verilog) can be used to guarantee that all conditions are covered. The `case` resembles `if`, except that the correct condition in `case` is determined directly, not serially as in `if` statements. The `begin` and `end` are not needed in Verilog if only a single statement is included for any test value.

EXAMPLE 3.7

```
VHDL
case sel is
when "00" => temp := I1;
when "01" => temp := I2;
when "10" => temp := I3;
when others => temp := I4;
end case;
```

```
Verilog
case sel
2'b00 : temp = I1;
2'b01 : temp = I2;
2'b10 : temp = I3;
default : temp = I4;
endcase
```

In Example 3.7, the control is `sel`. If `sel` = 00, then `temp` = `I1`; if `sel` = 01, then `temp` = `I2`; if `sel` = 10, then `temp` = `I3`; if `sel` = 11 (others or default), then `temp` = `I4`. All four values have the same priority; it means that if `sel` = 10, for example, then the third (VHDL) statement (`temp := I3`) is executed directly without checking the first and second expressions (00 and 01).

EXAMPLE 3.8 Behavioral Description of a Positive Edge-Triggered JK Flip-Flop Using the CASE Statement

Edge-triggered flip-flops are sequential circuits. They are triggered by the edge of the clock, in contrast to latches where flip-flops are triggered by the level of the clock (enable). Positive (negative) edge flip-flops sample the input only at the positive (negative) edges of the clock; any change in the input that does not occur at the edges is not sampled by the output. Figures 3.6a and 3.6b show the logic symbol and the state diagrams of a positive edge-triggered JK flip-flop. respectively.

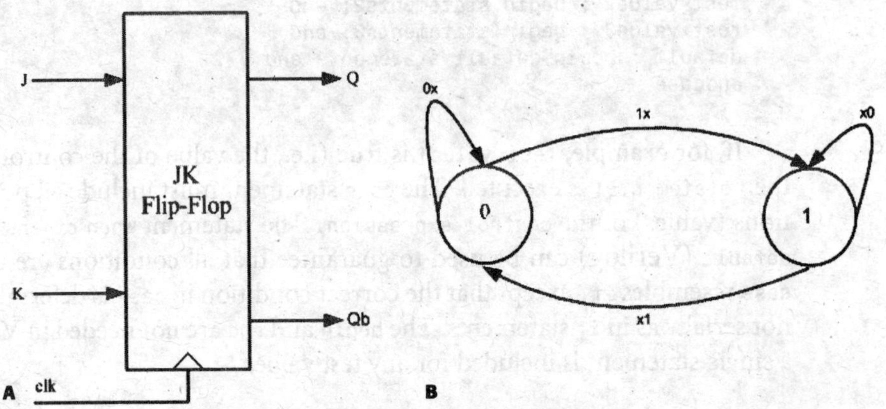

FIGURE 3.6 JK flip-flop. (a) Logic symbol. (b) State diagram.

Table 3.2 shows the excitation table of the JK flip-flop. It conveys the same information as the state diagram. The state diagram (Figure 3.6b) shows the possible states (two in this case: q can take 0 or 1), state 0 and state 1. Transition between these states has to occur only at the positive edges of the clock. If the current state is 0 (q = 0), then the next state is 0(1) if JK = 0x(1x), where x is "don't care." If the current state is 1 (q = 1), then the next state is 1(0) if JK = x0(x1). Table 3.2 shows the same results as the state diagram. For example, a transition from 0 to 1, according to the excitation table, can occur if JK = 10 or JK = 11, which is JK = 1x.

TABLE 3.2 Excitation Table of a Positive Edge-Triggered JK Flip-Flop

J	K	clk	q (next state)
0	0	↑	No change (hold), next = current
1	0	↑	1
0	1	↑	0
1	1	↑	Toggle (next state) = invert of (current state)
x	x	no +ve edge	No change (hold), next = current

Listing 3.7 shows the HDL code for a positive edge-triggered JK flip-flop using the `case` statement. In the Listing, `rising_edge` (VHDL) and `posedge` (Verilog) are

predefined words called "attributes." They represent the positive edge of the clock (`clk`). Other attributes are discussed in Chapters 6, "Procedres, Tasks, and Functions," 7, "Mixed-Type Media," and 10, "Synthesis Basics." Any of the four case statements can be replaced with `others` (VHDL) or `default` (Verilog). For example:

```
when "00" => temp1 := temp1; --VHDL
2'd3 : q =~ q;                 // Verilog
```

can be replaced by:

```
when others => temp1 := not temp1; --VHDL
default : q =~ q;                    // Verilog
```

Since `others` here refers to `"00"`, this replacement does not change the output of the simulation as long as J and K values are either 0 or 1.

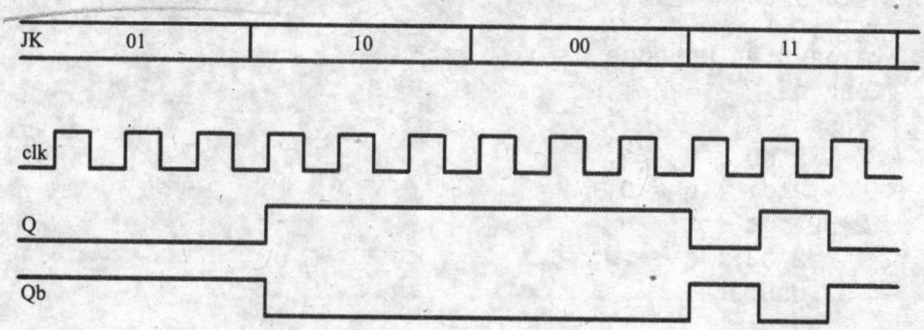

FIGURE 3.7 Simulation waveform of a positive edge-triggered JK flip-flop.

The waveform of the flip-flop is shown in Figure 3.7.

LISTING 3.7 HDL Code for a Positive Edge-Triggered JK Flip-Flop Using the `Case` Statement–VHDL and Verilog

VHDL Positive Edge-Triggered JK Flip-Flop Using Case

```
library ieee;
use ieee.std_logic_1164.all;
entity JK_FF is
port(JK : in bit_vector (1 downto 0);
clk : in std_logic; q, qb : out bit);
end JK_FF;

architecture JK_BEH of JK_FF is
begin
P1 : process (clk)
variable temp1, temp2 : bit;
   begin
      if rising_edge (clk) then
case JK is
```

```
when "01" => temp1 := '0';
when "10" => temp1 := '1';
when "00" => temp1 := temp1;
when "11" => temp1 := not temp1;
end case;
        q <= temp1;
        temp2 := not temp1;
        qb <= temp2;
        end if;
end process P1;

end JK_BEH;
```

Verilog Positive Edge-Triggered JK Flip-Flop Using Case

```
module JK_FF (JK, clk, q, qb);
input [1:0] JK;
input clk;
output q, qb;
reg q, qb;

always @ (posedge clk)
begin
case (JK)
    2'd0 : q = q;
    2'd1 : q = 0;
2'd2 : q = 1;
    2'd3 : q =~ q;
    endcase
qb =~ q;
end

endmodule
```

EXAMPLE 3.9 Behavioral Description of a 3-bit Binary Counter with Active High Synchronous Clear

Counters are sequential circuits. For up counters, the next state is the increment of the present state. For example, if the present state is 101, then the next state is 110. For down counters, the next state is the decrement of the present state. For example, if the present state is 101, then the next state is 100. A 3-bit binary up counter counts from 0 to 7 (Mod 8). Decade counters count from 0 to 9 (Mod10). Synchronous clear means that `clear` resets the counter when the clock is active; in contrast, asynchronous clear resets the counter instantaneously. More details about counters can be found in [Nelson95]. The excitation table for the 3-bit binary counter is as shown in Table 3.3. The logic symbol is shown in Figure 3.8.

The most efficient approach to describe the above counter is to use the fact that the next state is the increment of the present. The goal here, however, is to use `case` statement. We treat Table 3.3 as a lookup table. Listing 3.8 shows the HDL code for the counter. To assign initial values, such as 101, to the count at the start of simulation, in Verilog, the procedural `initial` is used as follows:

```
initial
begin
    q = 3'b101;
end
```

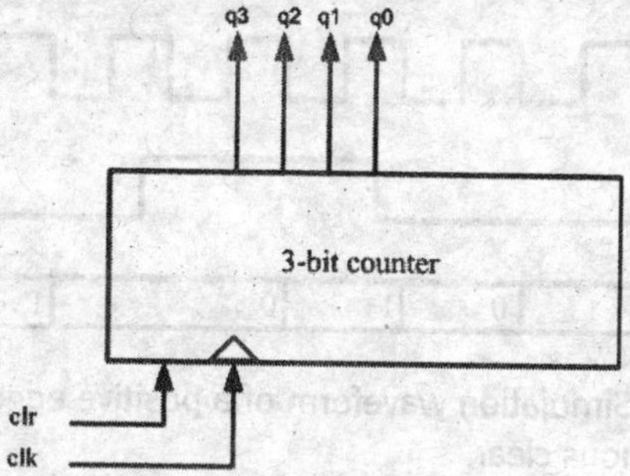

FIGURE 3.8 Logic symbol of a 3-bit counter with clear.

TABLE 3.3 Excitation Table of a 3-Bit Binary Counter with Synchronous Active High Clear

		Input	Output
Clock	**Clear**	**Current State**	**Next State**
↑	H	xxx	000
↑	L	000	001
↑	L	001	010
↑	L	010	011
↑	L	011	100
↑	L	100	101
↑	L	101	110
↑	L	110	111
↑	L	111	000
L	x		hold

The `begin` and `end` can be omitted if there is a single `initial` statement. In VHDL, we assign the initial value to the variable `temp` after the statement `process`, as shown below:

```
ctr : process (clk)
variable temp : std_logic_vector (2 downto 0) := "101";
begin
```

Any value assigned to a variable between process and its begin is acquired only once at the beginning of the simulation; subsequent execution of the process will not reassign that value to the variable unless a new simulation is executed. Figure 3.9 shows the simulation waveform of the counter.

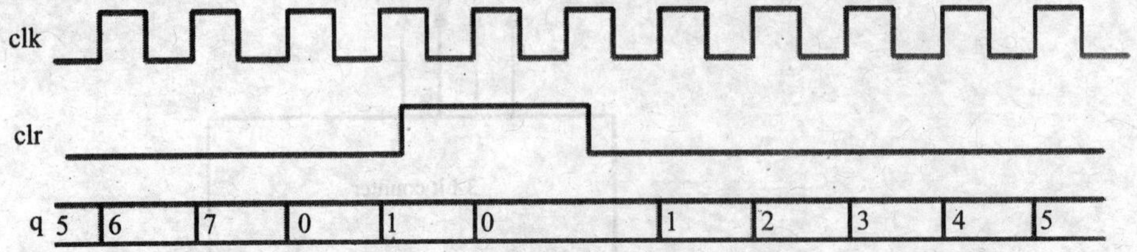

FIGURE 3.9 Simulation waveform of a positive edge-triggered counter with active .high synchronous clear.

LISTING 3.8 HDL Code for a 3-Bit Binary Counter Using the Case Statement

VHDL 3-Bit Binary Counter Case Statement Description

```
library IEEE;
use IEEE.STD_LOGIC_1164.ALL;
entity CT_CASE is
    port (clk, clr : in std_logic;
    q : buffer std_logic_vector (2 downto 0));
end CT_CASE;
architecture ctr_case of CT_CASE is
begin
ctr : process(clk)
variable temp : std_logic_vector (2 downto 0) := "101";
--101 is the initial value, so the counter starts from 110
    begin
    if rising_edge (clk) then
        if clr = '0' then
            case temp is
                when "000" => temp := "001";
                when "001" => temp := "010";
                when "010" => temp := "011";
                when "011" => temp := "100";
                when "100" => temp := "101";
                when "101" => temp := "110";
                when "110" => temp := "111";
                when "111" => temp := "000";
                when others => temp := "000";
            end case;
        else
```

```
                temp := "000";
                end if;
            end if;
            q <= temp;
            end process ctr;
        end ctr_case;
```

Verilog 3-Bit Binary Counter Case Statement Description

```
module CT_CASE (clk, clr, q);
input clk, clr;

output [2:0] q;
reg [2:0] q;
initial /* The initial procedure is to force the counter
           to start from initial count q=110 */

q = 3'b101;
always @ (posedge clk)
begin
if (clr == 0)
begin
    case (q)
        3'd0 : q = 3'd1;
        3'd1 : q = 3'd2;
        3'd2 : q = 3'd3;
        3'd3 : q = 3'd4;
        3'd4 : q = 3'd5;
        3'd5 : q = 3'd6;
        3'd6 : q = 3'd7;
        3'd7 : q = 3'd0;
    endcase
end
else
q = 3'b000;
end
endmodule
```

EXAMPLE 3.10 Modeling the Genotype and Phenotype of Human Blood

In this example some basics of genetics are discussed. The different types of human blood are introduced, and it is shown how these types are determined by the parents' blood types. More details on genetics can be found in [Lewin97]. First, consider some definitions related to genotype and phenotype.

Cells: The simplest basic structural units that make up all living things.

Chromosomes: Rod-like structures that appear in the nucleus of the cell, they contain the genes responsible for heredity. Humans have a total 46 different chromosomes in most cells: 23 paternal (from the father) and 23 maternal (from the mother). Sex cells (sperm and ova) contain half the number of chromosomes (i.e., 23).

DNA: Deoxyribonucleic acid (DNA) is a polymer of deoxyribonucleotides in the form of a double helix. It is the genetic molecule of life and codes the sequence of amino acids in proteins. Only identical twins have identical DNA, otherwise it differs from one person to the other.

Gene: A heritable unit in a chromosome, a gene is a series of nucleotide bases on the DNA molecule that codes for polypeptides (chains of amino acids). Humans have about 30,000 genes.

Allele: An alternate form of a gene.

Dominant allele: An allele that, if combined with other recessive alleles, suppresses their expressions. In blood types, alleles A and B are dominant.

Recessive allele: An allele that, if combined with other dominant alleles, is suppressed. For example, the brown-eye allele is dominant to the blue-eye allele. If a male with blue eyes mates with a female with brown eyes, their children (assuming complete dominance of the brown-eye allele) will have brown eyes. For blood types, the O allele is recessive to A and B.

Codominant alleles: Both alleles are expressed equally. The alleles for blood types A and B are codominant. If combined from a male and a female, the children will be blood type AB.

Gametes: Sex cells that contain half of the number of chromosomes. In humans these cells comprise the genetic makeup of eggs and sperm. Each gamete cell contains 23 chromosomes. When a male mates with a female, the two sex cells (egg and sperm) combined to form a single cell called a "zygote." Gametes for blood types have a single allele—A, B, or O.

Homozygous genes: These cells contain the same alleles of the gene. A person who is homozygous for the brown-eye gene has inherited two alleles for brown eyes—one from their mother and one from their father. A person who is homozygous for blood type A has two A alleles—one parental and one maternal.

Heterozygous in a Gene: Two different alleles are inherited. For blood types, heterozygous alleles can be AB, AO, or BO.

Genotype: The type of alleles in the cell; for example, AO is a genotype for blood.

Phenotype: The expression that results from allele combinations. For example, the phenotype of the genotype AO is blood type A, since A is dominant and O is recessive. The phenotype of genotype AB is blood type AB, since A and B are codominant.

To find all possible genotypes and phenotypes of human blood, we construct a table that shows all possible blood alleles (A, B, O) from male and female gametes. Then we determine the offspring's genotype. From the genotype, the phenotype is determined according to the type of allele (recessive, dominant, or codominant). Table 3.4A shows all possible genotypes, and Table 3.4B shows all possible phenotypes for the offspring.

TABLE 3.4 Genotypes and Phenotypes of Human Blood–A. Genotypes and B. Phenotypes

A. Genotypes

♂ ♀	A	B	O
A	AA	AB	AO
B	AB	BB	BO
O	AO	BO	OO

B. Phenotypes

♂ ♀	A	B	O
A	A	AB	A
B	AB	B	B
O	A	B	O

We treat Tables 3.4A and 3.4B as lookup tables and use the `case` statement to code the table. Listing 3.9 shows the code for describing the genotypes and phenotypes using `case`. The two statements

```
geno := allelm & allelf; -- VHDL
geno = {allelm , allelf}; // Verilog
```

concatenate `allelm` and `allelf` into one vector, `geno`, using the concatenation operator `&` (VHDL) or { , } (Verilog). For example, if `allelm` = 10 and `allelf` = 11, after concatenation, `geno` = 1011.

Figure 3.10 shows the simulation output for genotypes and phenotypes of human blood.

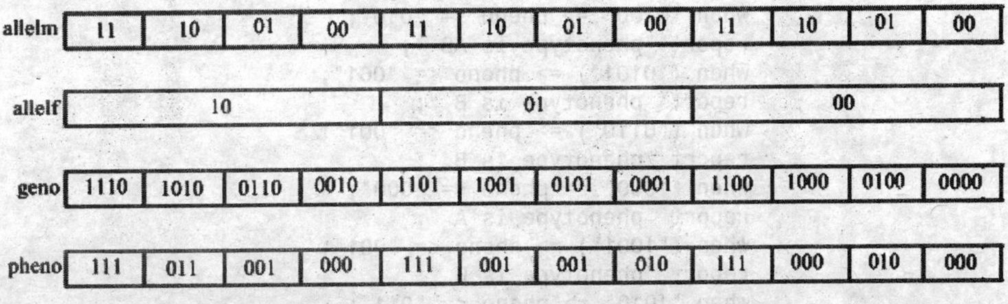

FIGURE 3.10 Simulation output for genotypes and phenotypes of human blood. The phenotype is also printed (not shown here) on the main screen of the simulator.

LISTING 3.9 HDL Code for Genotypes and Phenotypes Using the Case Statement—VHDL and Verilog

This program takes the blood genotypes (alleles) of a male and a female, and generates the possible blood phenotypes of their offspring. The statement `report` *(VHDL) or* `display` *(Verilog) is used to print the phenotype on the screen of the simulator. The male allele is* `allelm`*, and* `allelf` *is the female allele. Both* `allelm` *and* `allelf` *are 00 for genotype A, 01 for B, or 10 for O. Phenotype A is decoded as 000, B as 001, AB as 010, O as 011, and an illegal allele entry as 111.*

VHDL Genotypes and Phenotypes Using `Case`

```
library ieee;
use ieee.std_logic_1164.all;
entity Bld_type is
    port (allelm, allelf : in bit_vector (1 downto 0);
        pheno : out bit_vector (2 downto 0));
end Bld_type;
architecture GEN_BLOOD of Bld_type is
begin
Bld : process (allelm, allelf)
variable geno : bit_vector(3 downto 0);
begin
    geno := allelm & allelf;

    --The operator (&) concatenates the two 2-bit vectors allelf
    --and allelm into one 4-bit vector geno.

    case geno is
        when "0000" => pheno <= "000";
        report "phenotype is A ";

    --report statement is close to printf in C language.
    --The statement prints on the screen whatever
    --is written between the quote marks.

        when "0001" => pheno <= "010";
        report "phenotype is AB ";
        when "0010" => pheno <= "000";
        report "phenotype is A ";
        when "0100" => pheno <= "010";
        report "phenotype is AB ";
        when ("0101") => pheno <= "001";
        report "phenotype is B ";
        when ("0110") => pheno <= "001";
        report "phenotype is B ";
        when "1000" => pheno <= "000";
        report "phenotype is A ";
        when ("1001") => pheno <= "001";
        report "phenotype is B ";
        when "1010" => pheno <= "011";
        report "phenotype is O ";
```

```
        when others =>pheno <= "111";
        report "illegal allele entry ";
    end case;
end process;
end GEN_BLOOD;
```

Verilog Genotypes and Phenotypes Using Case

```
module bld_type (allelm, allelf, pheno);
input [1:0] allelm, allelf;
output [2:0] pheno;
reg [2:0] pheno;
reg [3:0] geno;
always @ (allelm, allelf)
begin
geno = {allelm , allelf};

/* { , } concatenates the two 2-bit vectors allelm and allelf
   into one 4-bit vector geno */

case (geno)
4'd0 : begin pheno = 3'd0;
$display ("phenotype is A "); end
4'd1 : begin pheno = 3'd2;
$display ("phenotype is AB "); end
4'd2 : begin pheno = 3'd0;
$display ("phenotype is A "); end
4'd4 : begin pheno = 3'd2;
$display ("phenotype is AB "); end
4'd5 : begin pheno = 3'd1;
$display ("phenotype is B "); end
4'd6 : begin pheno = 3'd1;
$display ("phenotype is B "); end
4'd8 : begin pheno = 3'd0;
$display ("phenotype is A "); end
4'd9 : begin pheno = 3'd1;
$display ("phenotype is B "); end
4'd10 : begin pheno = 3'd3;
$display ("phenotype is O "); end
default: begin pheno = 3'd7;
$display ("illegal allele entry "); end
    endcase
end

endmodule
```

3.4.3.1 Verilog Casex and Casez

Section 3.4 covered the case statement for both VHDL and Verilog. Verilog has another two variations of `case`: `casex` and `casez`; `casex` ignores the "don't care" values of the control expression, and `casez` ignores the high impedance in control expression values. For example, in the code:

```
casex (a)
    4'bxxx1: b = 4'd1;
    4'bxx10: b = 4'd2;
    ................
    endcase;
```

all occurrences of x are ignored. b = 1 if, and only if, the least significant bit of a (bit order 0) is 1, regardless of the value of the higher order bits of a. b = 2 if the bits of order 0 and 1 are 10, regardless of the value of all other bits. For the Verilog variation casez, all high-impedance values (z) in control expressions are ignored. For example:

```
casez (a)
        4'bzzz1 : b = 4'd1;
        4'bzz10 : b = 4'd2;
        ................
    endcase;
```

b = 1 if, and only if, the least significant bit (bit of order 0) of a = 1. b = 2 if bit 0 of a = 0 and bit 1 of a = 1.

EXAMPLE 3.11 Verilog Description of a Priority Encoder Using Casex

A priority encoder encodes the inputs according to a priority set by the user—for example, when the inputs represent interrupt requests. If two or more interrupt requests are issued at the same time by devices needing service, and the Central Processing Unit (CPU) can only serve one device at a time, then one of these requests should be given priority over the others and be served first. A priority encoder can handle this task. The input to the encoder is the interrupt requests and the output of the encoder can be memory addresses where the service routine is located or can be an address leading to the actual address of the routines. Table 3.5 shows the truth table of a 4-bit encoder; bit 0 of input a has the highest priority.

TABLE 3.5 Truth Table for a 4-bit Encoder

Input	Output
a	b
xxx1	1
xx10	2
x100	4
1000	8
Others	0

Listing 3.10 shows the Verilog description for a 4-bit priority encoder.

LISTING 3.10 Verilog Description for a 4-Bit Priority Encoder

```
module Encoder_4 (Int_req, Rout_addrs);
input [3:0] Int_req;
output [3:0] Rout_addrs;
    reg [3:0] Rout_addrs;

always @ (Int_req)
            begin
                casex (Int_req)
                    4'bxxx1 : Rout_addrs=4'd1;
                    4'bxx10 : Rout_addrs=4'd2;
                    4'bx100 : Rout_addrs=4'd4;
                    4'b1000 : Rout_addrs= 4'd8;
                    default : Rout_addrs=4'd0;

                endcase
            end
endmodule
```

Figure 3.11 shows the simulation output of Listing 3.10.

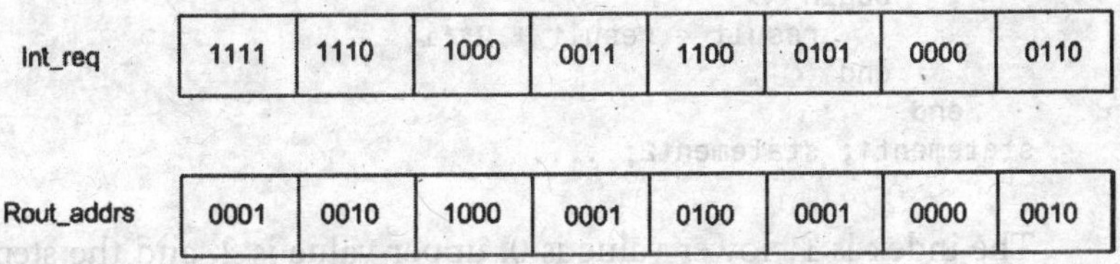

FIGURE 3.11 Simulation output of a 4-bit priority encoder.

3.4.4 Loop Statement

`Loop` is a sequential statement that has to appear inside `process` in VHDL or inside `always` or `initial` in Verilog. `Loop` is used to repeat the execution of statements written inside its body. The number of repetitions is controlled by the range of an `index` parameter. The loop allows the code to be shortened. Instead of writing a block of code as individual statements, it can be written as one general statement that, if repeated, reproduces all statements in the block. In Sections 3.4.4.1–3.4.4.5, several formats for the `loop` statement are discussed.

3.4.4.1 For-Loop

The general format for a `for-loop` is:

```
for <lower index value> <upper index value> <step>
statements1; statement2; statement3; ….
end loop
```

If the value of `index` is between `lower` and `upper`, all statements written inside the body of the loop are executed. For each cycle, the index is modified at the `end loop` according to the `step`. If the value of `index` is not between the lower and upper values, the loop is terminated.

EXAMPLE 3.12 For-Loop–VHDL and Verilog

VHDL For-Loop

```
for i in 0 to 2 loop
if temp(i) = '1' then
result := result + 2**i;
end if;
end loop;
statement1; statement2; ....
```

Verilog For-Loop

```
for (i = 0; i <= 2; i = i + 1)
begin
    if (temp[i] == 1)
        begin
            result = result + 2**i;
        end
    end
statement1; statement2; ....
```

The index is `i`, lower value is 0, upper value is 2, and the step is 1. All statements between the `for` statement and `end loop` (VHDL) or `end` (Verilog) are executed until the index `i` goes out of range. At the very beginning of the loop, `i` takes the value of 0, and the statements `if` and `result` are executed as:

```
if temp(0) = '1' then
result := result + 2**0;
```

When the program encounters the end of the loop it increments `i` to 1. If `i` is less than or equal to 2, the loop is repeated; otherwise, the program exits the loop and executes statement1, statement2, and so on. In VHDL, we do not have to declare index `i`; in Verilog, it has to be declared.

3.4.4.2 While-Loop

The general format of the `while-loop` is:

```
while (condition)
Statement1;
```

```
Statement2;
..........
end
```

As long as the condition is true, all statements written before the end of the loop are executed, otherwise the program exits the loop.

EXAMPLE 3.13 While-Loop—VHDL and Verilog

VHDL While-Loop

```
while (i < x)loop
    i := i + 1;
    z := i * z;
end loop;
```

Verilog While-Loop

```
while (i < x)
    begin
        i = i + 1;
        z = i * z;
    end
```

In the above example the condition is `(i < x)`. As long as `i` is less than `x`, `i` is incremented, and the product `i * z` (`i` multiplied by `z`) is calculated and assigned to `z`.

3.4.4.3 Verilog Repeat

In Verilog, the sequential statement `repeat` causes the execution of statements between its `begin` and `end` to be repeated a fixed number of times; no condition is allowed in `repeat`.

EXAMPLE 3.14 Verilog Repeat

```
repeat (32)
begin
        #100 i = i + 1;
    end
```

In the above example, `i` is incremented 32 times with a delay of 100 screen time units. This describes a 5-bit binary counter with a clock period of 100 screen time units.

3.4.4.4 Verilog Forever

The statement `forever` in Verilog repeats the loop endlessly. One common use for `forever` is to generate clocks in code-oriented test benches. The following code describes a clock with a period of 20 screen time units.

```
initial
begin
```

```
        Clk = 1'b0;
        forever #20 clk = ~clk;
    end
```

3.4.4.5 VHDL Next and Exit

In VHDL, `next` and `exit` are two sequential statements associated with `loop`. `exit` causes the program to exit the loop; `next` causes the program to jump to the end of the loop, skipping all statements written between `next` and `end loop`. The index is incremented, and if its value is still within the loop's range, the loop is repeated, otherwise the program exits the loop.

EXAMPLE 3.15 VHDL Next-Exit

```
for i in 0 to 2 loop
......

.....
next When z = '1';
statements1;
end loop;
statements2;
```

In the above example, at the very beginning of the loop's execution, `i` takes the value 0; at the statement `next When z = '1'`, the program checks the value of `z`. If $z = 1$, then `statements1` is skipped and `i` is incremented to 1. The loop is then repeated with `i` = 1. If `z` is not equal to 1, then `statements1` is executed and `i` is incremented to 1, and the loop is repeated.

EXAMPLE 3.16 Behavioral Description of a 4-bit Positive Edge-Triggered Counter

In this example, the `loop` statement is used to convert values between binary and integer, and use this conversion to describe a binary counter. The HDL package is assumed to not contain predefined functions that will increment a binary input or convert values between binary and integer. Describing a counter using the above loop-conversion approach is not the most efficient way; the main goal here is to demonstrate the implementation of the `loop` statement.

The next state of a binary counter is generated by incrementing the current state. Since in this example a binary cannot be incremented directly, it is first converted to an integer. HDL packages can easily increment integers. We increment the integer and convert it back to binary. To convert an integer to binary, the predefined `MOD` function is used. X MOD 2 equals 1 if X is odd, or equals 0 if X is even (divisible by 2); by successively dividing the integer by 2 and recording the remainder from the outcome of the MOD2, we convert the integer to binary. To convert a binary to integer, we multiply each bit by its weight and accumulate the products; so: $1010 = (0 \times 1) + (1 \times 2) + (0 \times 4) + (1 \times 8) = 10$.

Listing 3.11 shows the HDL code of the counter. The simulation waveform is the same as that shown in Figure 3.9, except the count here is from 0 to 15 rather than from 0 to 7 as in the figure.

A more efficient approach to describe a binary counter is to directly increment the current state. As mentioned before, the approach implemented in Listing 3.11 is not the most efficient way to describe a counter. To write an efficient code for a 4-bit counter, direct increment of the current state is used. The following Verilog code describes a 4-bit binary counter using direct increment of the current state.

```
module countr_direct (clk, Z);
input clk;
output [3:0] Z;
reg [3:0] Z;
initial
Z = 4'b0000;

/*This initialization is needed if we want to start counting
        from 0000 */

always @ (posedge clk)
Z = Z + 1;
endmodule
```

LISTING 3.11 HDL Code for a 4-Bit Counter with Synchronous Clear–VHDL and Verilog

VHDL 4-Bit Counter with Synchronous Clear Description

```
library ieee;
use ieee.std_logic_1164.all;
entity CNTR_LOP is
port (clk, clr : in std_logic; q :
    buffer std_logic_vector (3 downto 0));
end CNTR_LOP;
architecture CTR_LOP of CNTR_LOP is
begin
ct : process(clk)
variable temp : std_logic_vector (3 downto 0) := "0000";
variable result : integer := 0;
begin
if rising_edge (clk) then
    if (clr = '0') then
        result := 0;
--change binary to integer
        lop1 : for i in 0 to 3 loop
            if temp(i) = '1' then
            result := result + 2**i;
            end if;
        end loop;
--increment result to describe a counter
        result := result + 1;
--change integer to binary
```

```
        for j in 0 to 3 loop
        if (result MOD 2 = 1) then
            temp (j) := '1';
            else temp (j) := '0';
        end if;
--integer division by 2
        result := result/2;
        end loop;
    else temp := "0000";
    end if;
q <= temp;
end if;
end process ct;
end CTR_LOP;
```

Verilog 4-Bit Counter with Synchronous Clear Description

```
module CNTR_LOP (clk, clr, q);
input clk, clr;
output [3:0] q;
reg [3:0] q;
integer i, j, result;
initial
begin
q = 4'b0000; //initialize the count to 0
end
always @ (posedge clk)
begin
    if (clr == 0)
    begin
result = 0;
        //change binary to integer
        for (i = 0; i < 4; i = i + 1)
                begin
            if (q[i] == 1)
            result = result + 2**i;
        end
        result = result + 1;
        for (j = 0; j < 4; j = j + 1)
        begin
            if (result %2 == 1)
            q[j] = 1;
            else
            q[j] = 0;
            result = result/2;
        end
    end
    else q = 4'b0000;
end
endmodule
```

EXAMPLE 3.17 Behavioral Description of a 4-Bit Counter with Synchronous Hold

To write the code for the counter, we use binary-integer conversion. As mentioned, this approach is not the most efficient way to describe a counter, but will be used to demonstrate the use of `loop`. The hold signal in a counter, when active, retains the value of the output and keeps it unchanged until the hold is inactivated. In VHDL, an `exit` statement is used to exit the loop when the hold is active. Verilog, however, does not have an exit statement, but the loop can be exited by assigning the index a value higher than its upper value. Listing 3.12 shows the HDL code for the counter.

LISTING 3.12 HDL Code for a 4-Bit Counter with Synchronous Hold–VHDL and Verilog

VHDL 4-Bit Counter with Synchronous Hold Description

```
library ieee;
use ieee.std_logic_1164.all;
entity CNTR_Hold is
port (clk, hold : in std_logic;
    q : buffer std_logic_vector (3 downto 0));
end CNTR_Hold;
architecture CNTR_Hld of CNTR_Hold is
begin
ct : process (clk)
variable temp : std_logic_vector
    (3 downto 0) := "0000";
    --temp is initialized to 0 so count starts at 0
    variable result : integer := 0;
    begin
    if rising_edge (clk) then
        result := 0;
    --change binary to integer
        lop1 : for i in 0 to 3 loop
        if temp(i) = '1' then
            result := result + 2**i;
            end if;

        end loop;
    --increment result to describe a counter
        result := result + 1;
        --change integer to binary
        lop2 : for i in 0 to 3 loop
    --exit the loop if hold = 1
        exit when hold = '1';
    --"when" is a predefined word
        if (result MOD 2 = 1) then
            temp (i) := '1';
        else
            temp (i) := '0';
        end if;
    --Successive division by 2
        result := result/2;
```

```
            end loop;
            q <= temp;
        end if;
        end process ct;
        end CNTR_Hld;
```

Verilog 4-Bit Counter with Synchronous Hold Description

```
module CT_HOLD (clk, hold, q);
input clk, hold;
output [3:0] q;
reg [3:0] q;
integer i, result;
initial
begin
q = 4'b0000; //initialize the count to 0
end
always @ (posedge clk)
begin
result = 0;

//change binary to integer

for (i = 0; i <= 3; i = i + 1)
begin
if (q[i] == 1)
result = result + 2**i;
end
result = result + 1;
for (i = 0; i <= 3; i = i + 1)
begin
if (hold == 1)
i = 4; //4 is out of range, exit.
else
    begin
        if (result %2 == 1)
        q[i] = 1;
        else
        q[i] = 0;
        result = result/2;
        end
end
end
endmodule
```

Figure 3.12 shows the simulation waveform of the counter.

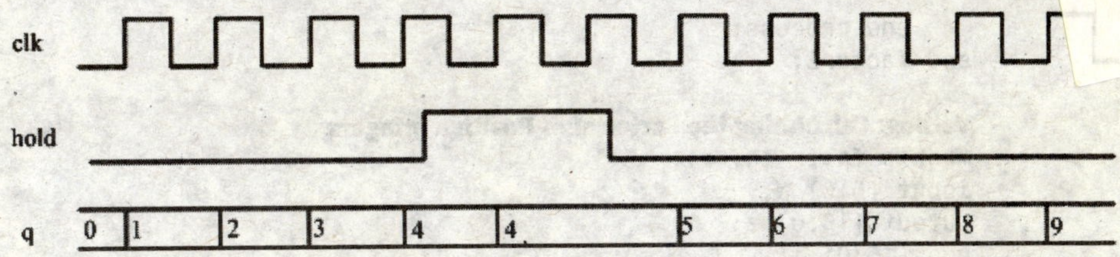

FIGURE 3.12 Simulation waveform of a 4-bit binary counter with synchronous hold.

EXAMPLE 3.18 Calculating the Factorial Using Behavioral Description with `While-Loop`

In this example, an HDL behavioral description is written to find the factorial of a positive number N. The factorial of $N, N! = N(N-1)(N-2)(N-3)...1$. For example, $4! = 4 \times 3 \times 2 \times 1 = 24$. In VHDL, `N` and the output `z` are declared as natural; this restricts the values that `N` and `z` can assume to positive integers. If `N` and `z` are declared as `std_logic`, the multiplication operator (*) cannot be used directly; they must be converted to integers before multiplication.

In VHDL, be sure to include all the necessary libraries. If the appropriate libraries are not included in the code, the simulator will not accept the declaration and will report it as undefined. In Verilog, the default declaration of inputs and outputs allows for direct use of arithmetic operators, such as multiplication. Listing 3.13 shows the HDL code for calculating the factorial.

LISTING 3.13 HDL Code for Calculating the Factorial of Positive Integers—VHDL and Verilog

VHDL: Calculating the Factorial of Positive Integers

```
library IEEE;
use IEEE.STD_LOGIC_1164.ALL;
--The above library statements can be omitted; however,
--it is not an error if they are not omitted.
--The basic VHDL has type "natural."
entity factr is
port(N : in natural; z : out natural);
end factr;
architecture factorl of factr is
begin
    process (N)
    variable y, i : natural;
    begin
        y := 1;
        i := 0;
        while (i < N) loop
        i := i + 1;
        y := y * i;
        end loop;
        z <= y;
```

```
    end process;
end factorl;
```

Verilog: Calculating the Factorial of Positive Integers

```
module factr (N, z);
input [5:0] N;
output [15:0] z;
reg [15:0] z;
/* Since z is an output, and it will appear inside "always," then
Z has to be declared "reg" */
integer i;
always @ (N)
begin
    z = 1;
//z can be written as 16'b0000000000000001 or 16'd1.
    i = 0;
    while (i < N)
        begin
            i = i + 1;
            z = i * z;
    end
end
endmodule
```

Case Study 3.1 Booth Algorithm

The Booth algorithm is used to multiply two signed numbers. The signed numbers are in twos-complement format. The function of the algorithm is to determine the beginning and end of a string of ones in the multiplier and perform multiplicand addition-accumulation at the end of the string, or perform subtraction-accumulation at the beginning of the string. A string consists of one or more consecutive ones: 01110 has one string, and 1011 has two strings. Any signed number can be written in terms of its bit order of the beginning and end of the string. For example, the number 0111011 has the following bit order:

Bit order	6	5	4	3	2	1	0
	0	1	1	1	0	1	1

The above number has two strings. One string has two 1s, begins at bit 0, and ends at bit 1. The other string has three 1s, begins at bit 3, and ends at bit 5. The value of any binary number is equal to $(2^{end1+1} - 2^{begin1}) + (2^{end2+1} - 2^{begin2}) + \ldots$, where begin1 and begin2 are the bit orders of the beginnings of string1 and string2, respectively; and end1 and end2 are the bit orders of the ends of string1 and string2, respectively. So, . For the multiplication Z = multiplier (X) × multiplicand (Y), we can write:

$$X = \{(2^{end1+1} - 2^{begin1}) + (2^{end2+1} - 2^{begin2}) + \ldots\}$$

$$Z=\{(2^{end1+1}Y-2^{begin1}Y)+(2^{end2+1}Y-2^{begin2}Y)+...\} \tag{3.1}$$

Multiplication of Y by positive power(s) of 2 is a shift left of Y. For example, Y $\times 2^3$ is a three-left-shift of Y. From Equation 3.1, it can be seen that the calculation of the product Z consists of addition at the end of the string, subtraction at the beginning of the string, and a shift after addition or subtraction. To guarantee no overflow, Z is selected to be double the width of X or Y. For example, if X is 4-bit, then Z is 8-bit. The beginning of a string is the transition from 0 to 1, while the end is the transition from 1 to 0. To detect the transition, the 1-bit register (E) is used to hold 0 initially. By comparing E with the bits of X, the beginning and end of the string can be detected. More details about this algorithm can be found in [Hayes98]. The flowchart of the algorithm is shown in Figure 3.12.

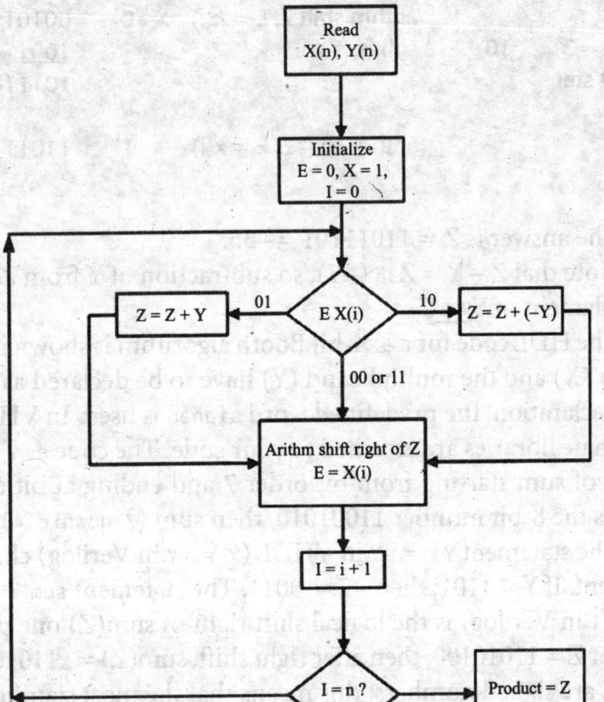

FIGURE 3.13 Flowchart of Booth multiplication algorithm.

To illustrate the algorithm, consider multiplication of two 4-bit numbers –5 (1011) multiplied by 7 (0111). To avoid any possibility of overflow in the product, we assign 8 bits to the product. The steps of the Booth algorithm are shown in Table 3.6.

TABLE 3.6 Example of Booth Algorithm

X = 1011, Y = 0111, –Y = 1001

Step	X(i)E	Action	E	Z
Initial			0	00000000
1, i = 0	10	subtract Y		1001
				10010000
		arithm shift Z, E = x(i)	1	11001000
2, i = 1	11	arithm shift Z, E = x(i)	1	11100100
3, i = 2	01	add Y		0111
				01010100
		arithm shift Z, E = x(i)	0	00101010
4, i = 3	10	subtract Y		1001
last step				10111010
		arithm shift Z, E = x(i)	1	11011101

The answer is Z = 11011101 = –35.

Note that Z – Y = Z + (–Y), so subtraction of Y from Z is addition of the twos-complement of Y to Z.

The HDL code for a 4x4-bit Booth algorithm is shown in Listing 3.14. The multiplier (X) and the multiplicand (Y) have to be declared as signed numbers. To do this declaration, the predefined word `signed` is used. In VHDL, be sure that the appropriate libraries are attached to your code. The code `sum (7 downto 4)` represents 4 bits of sum starting from bit order 7 and ending at bit order 4. For example, if sum is the 8-bit number 11001010, then sum (`7 downto 4`) is 1100.

The statement `Y := -Y` in VHDL (`Y = -Y` in Verilog) changes Y to its twos complement. If Y = 1101, then –Y = 0011. The statement `sum := sum srl` in VHDL (`Z = Z >> 1` in Verilog) is the logical shift right of sum(Z) one position. For example, if sum or Z = 11010100, then after right shift, sum(Z) = x1101010. In Listing 3.14, sum and Z are signed numbers; this means that the most significant bit is the sign bit. If this bit is 0, the number is positive; if it is 1, the number is negative. Notice that after the logical shift, the sign may change, as in our example where sum(Z) changes from 11010100 (negative number) to 01101010 (positive number) after a one-position right shift. Another type of shift is arithmetic, where the sign is preserved. An arithmetic right shift of 11010100 yields 11101010. The shift in the Booth algorithm is arithmetic; the following two statements perform arithmetic shift:

VHDL
sum := sum srl 1;
sum (7):= sum(6);

Verilog
Z = Z >> 1;
Z[7] = Z[6];

The first statement performs logic shift, and the second performs sign preservation. VHDL code has a predefined arithmetic shift operator, `sra`; for example, `sum := sum sra 2` executes a right shift of two positions and preserves the sign. To use this shift, be sure that the appropriate libraries are attached to the VHDL code.

LISTING 3.14 4x4-Bit Booth Algorithm—VHDL and Verilog

VHDL 4x4-Bit Booth Algorithm

```
library ieee;
use ieee.std_logic_1164.all;
use ieee.numeric_std.all;
entity booth is
port (X, Y : in signed (3 downto 0);
Z : buffer signed (7 downto 0));
end booth;
architecture booth_4 of booth is
begin
process (X, Y)
variable temp : signed (1 downto 0);
variable sum : signed (7 downto 0);
variable E1 : unsigned (0 downto 0);
variable Y1 : signed (3 downto 0);
begin
sum := "00000000"; E1 := "0";
for i in 0 to 3 loop
temp := X(i) & E1(0);
Y1 := - Y;
case temp is
    when "10" => sum (7 downto 4) :=
    sum (7 downto 4) + Y1;
    when "01" => sum (7 downto 4) :=
    sum (7 downto 4) + Y;
    when others => null;
end case;
sum := sum srl 1; --This is a logical
                  --shift of one position to the right
sum (7) := sum(6);

--The above two statements perform arithmetic shift where
--the sign of the number is preserved after the shift.

E1(0) := x(i);
end loop;
    if (y = "1000") then

--If Y = 1000; then according to our code,
```

```
--Y1 = 1000 (-8 not 8 because Y1 is 4 bits only).
--The statement sum = -sum adjusts the answer.

        sum := - sum;
    end if;

z <= sum;
end process;
end booth_4;
```

Verilog 4x4-Bit Booth Algorithm

```
module booth (X, Y, Z);
input signed [3:0] X, Y;
output signed [7:0] Z;
reg signed [7:0] Z;
reg [1:0] temp;
integer i;
reg E1;
reg [3:0] Y1;
always @ (X, Y)
begin
Z = 8'd0;
E1 = 1'd0;for (i = 0; i < 4; i = i + 1)
begin
temp = {X[i], E1};
    //The above statement is catenation
Y1 = - Y;
    //Y1 is the 2' complement of Y
case (temp)
2'd2 : Z [7 : 4] = Z [7 : 4] + Y1;
2'd1 : Z [7 : 4] = Z [7 : 4] + Y;
default : begin end
endcase
Z = Z >> 1;
/*The above statement is a logical shift of one position to the right*/

Z[7] = Z[6];
/*The above two statements perform arithmetic shift where the sign of
the number is preserved after the shift. */

E1 = X[i];
    end
if (Y == 4'd8)

/*If Y = 1000; then according to our code,
 Y1 = 1000 (-8 not 8, because Y1 is 4 bits only).
 The statement sum = - sum adjusts the answer.*/
    begin
        Z = - Z;
    end
end
endmodule
```

The simulation output of the Booth algorithm is shown in Figure 3.14.

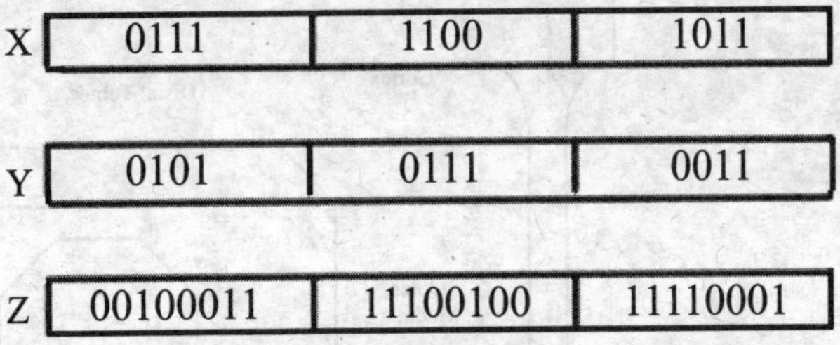

FIGURE 3.14 Simulation output of a Booth Multiplication Algorithm.

Case Study 3.2 Behavioral Description of a Simplified Renal Antidiuretic Hormone Mechanism

In this case study, the action of Antidiuretic Hormone (ADH) on water excreted by the kidney is discussed. One function of the kidney is to regulate the amount of water excreted by the body as urine. Human blood is 70% water by volume. Regulation of the water volume is directly related to blood pressure regulation. An excessive amount of water in the body raises blood pressure; and if the body excretes more water than it needs to maintain proper functions, then the blood pressure will drop. Kidney failure has a direct effect on blood pressure. The main functional unit in the kidney is the nephron. Figure 3.15 illustrates a schematic of nephron functions.

Nephrons are tiny tubules through which blood flows. In nephrons, some components in the blood, such as sodium and potassium, are reabsorbed by the body; and other components, such as urea, are excreted because they are toxic to the body. Any extra water that the body does not need is also excreted as urine. Several hormones control the amount of water excreted. One of those hormones is ADH. The function of ADH is summarized as follows:

The biological action of ADH is to conserve body water and regulate tonicity of body fluids.

DH is released by the hypothalamic cells in the brain.

Water deprivation (and subsequent low blood pressure) stimulates ADH release. Conversely, excess water (and subsequent high blood pressure) decreases ADH release.

The major target of ADH is the renal cells—specifically, the collecting ducts of the nephrons.

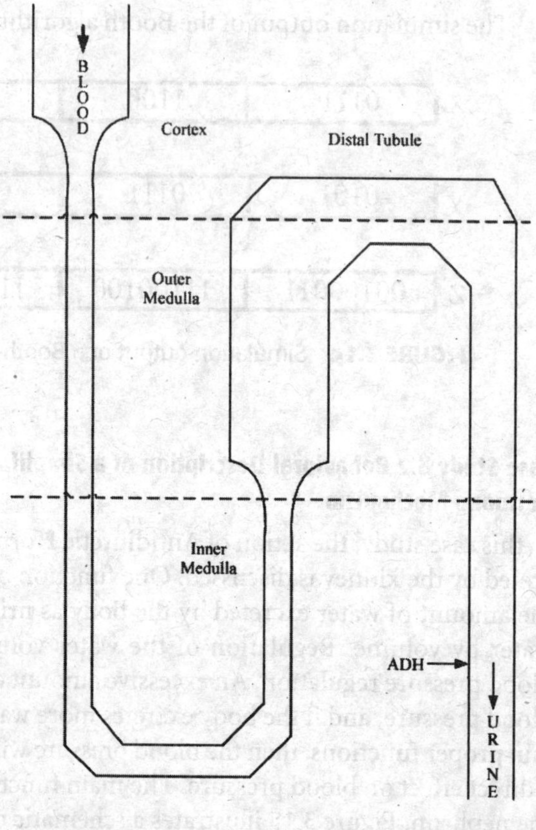

FIGURE 3.15 Nephron function in the human body.

ADH causes the kidney to reabsorb (conserve) water. Absence of ADH causes the kidney to excrete water as urine.

ΣAlcohol and caffeine inhibit ADH release, and promote more urine.

More details about the physiology of the kidney can be found in [Campbell01] and [Vander94]. Figure 3.16 describes the relationship between the concentration of ADH and Blood Pressure (BP). We assume that the relationship is linear and BP takes only positive integer values.

The HDL code is shown in Listing 3.15. It is assumed that the body samples its blood pressure at intervals—each interval represented in the code by the period of the clock. The major sequential statement in the code is `ELSE-IF`. For simplification of the code, we assume that the pressure and the ADH take only integer-positive values. In VHDL, this means that BP and ADH are declared as natural, allowing the application of the equation ADH = BP * (-4) + 180.0. If BP and ADH are declared as `std_logic_vectors`, VHDL cannot directly multiply or add. In contrast, Verilog allows for direct add and multiply if BP and ADH are declared as bit vectors.

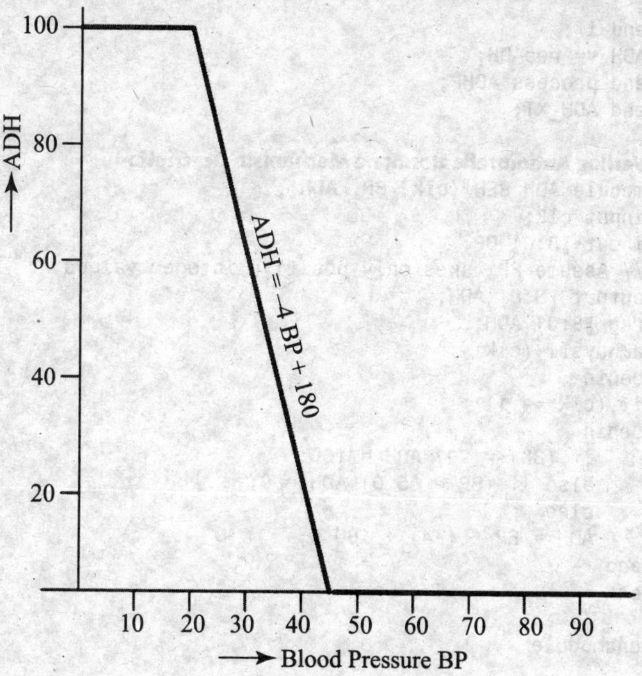

FIGURE 3.16 Concentration of ADH Versus Blood Pressure. Units in the figure are arbitrary.

LISTING 3.15 Antidiuretic Hormone Mechanism—VHDL and Verilog

VHDL Antidiuretic Hormone Mechanism Description

```
library IEEE;
use IEEE.STD_LOGIC_1164.ALL;
use IEEE.STD_LOGIC_ARITH.ALL;
use IEEE.STD_LOGIC_UNSIGNED.ALL;
entity ADH_BEH is
    port (clk : in std_logic; BP : in natural;
ADH : out natural);
-- Assume BP takes only positive integer values
end;
architecture ADH_XT of ADH_BEH is
begin
ADHP : process (clk)
variable resADH : natural := 0;
begin
if (clk = '1') then
    if Bp <= 20 then resADH := 100;
    elsif Bp > 45 then resADH := 0;
    else
        resADH := Bp * (-4) + 180;
    end if;
```

```
end if;
ADH <= resADH;
end process ADHP;
end ADH_XT;
```

Verilog Antidiuretic Hormone Mechanism Description

```
module ADH_BEH (clk, BP, ADH);
input clk;
input [8:0] BP;
// Assume BP takes only positive integer values
output [8:0] ADH;
reg [8:0] ADH;
always @ (clk)
begin
if (clk == 1)
begin
    if (BP <= 20) ADH = 100;
    else if (BP > 45.0) ADH = 0;
    else
    ADH = BP * (-4) + 180.0;
end
end

endmodule
```

Figure 3.17 shows the simulation waveform of an ADH-BP relationship.

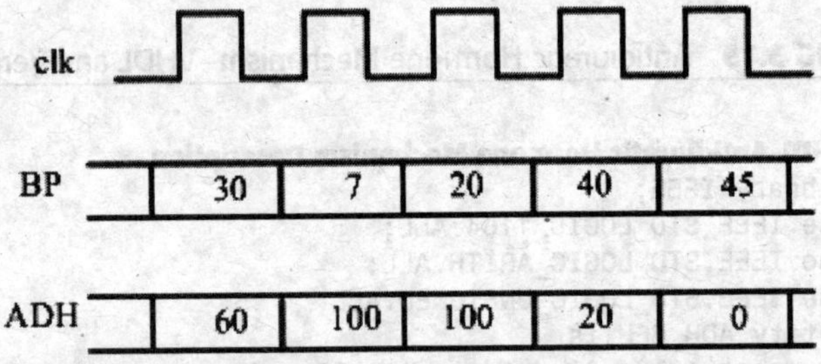

FIGURE 3.17 Simulation waveform of ADH Versus Blood Pressure.

3.5 COMMON PROGRAMMING ERRORS

This section discusses some common programming errors. Additional common errors are discussed in Chapter 2.

3.5.1 Common VHDL Programming Errors

Following is a brief discussion of some common syntax and semantic errors in writing VHDL programs. Table 3.7 considers Listing 3.13 (VHDL) and some possible errors if the code is modified.

TABLE 3.7 Possible Errors in Modified VHDL Listing 3.13

Modified Code	Error
`process (Z)`	Sensitivity list cannot include output ports.

`process (N)`
`begin`
`  variable y, i : natural;`
	Variable declaration should be before `begin`.

`port (N : in integer;` `z : out natural);`	The syntax is correct, but if `N` is forced to a negative value, the loop will not terminate, causing the program to hang up.
`y <= y * i;`	`y` has been declared as variable. The variable assignment operator := should be used instead of the signal-assignment operator <=.
`Z := y * i;`	`Z` has been declared as signal; the variable assignment operator := cannot be used.

`while (i < N) loop`
`  i := i + 1;`
`  y := y * i;`
`   end;`
	`end;` should be written as `end loop;`

3.5.2 Common Verilog Programming Errors

Here, some common Verilog syntax and semantic errors are briefly discussed. One of the most common errors for beginners is in not adhering to Verilog's case-sensitive nature. Table 3.8 considers Listing 3.13 (Verilog) and discusses some possible errors if the code is modified.

TABLE 3.8 Possible Errors in Modified Verilog Listing 3.13

Modified Code	Error

`module factr (N, z);`
`input [15:0] N;`
`output [15:0] z;`
`integer i;`
`    always @(N)`
	Since `z` is an output, it has to be declared as `reg`.

`always @ (N)`
`begin`
`    z = 1;`
`.........`
`end always`
	To end `always`, write only end.

`while (i <= N)`	There is no syntax error, but the result of the program is not correct. Try `N = 2` and find `z`.

3.6 SUMMARY

In this chapter, the basics of behavioral descriptions have been covered, including the statements `process` (VHDL) and `always` (Verilog). Some sequential statements have also been discussed, such as `if`, `case`, and `loop`. These sequential statements have to appear inside process in VHDL, or inside always or initial in Verilog. In VHDL, all signal-assignment statements inside process are executed sequentially. Sequentially here means calculating the values of the left-hand side of the statements in the order they are written. After calculation, the values are assigned, taking into consideration delay times. In Verilog, all statements inside `always` are executed concurrently, based on events. Execution of variable-assignment statements inside `process` in VHDL, in contrast to signal-assignment statements, do not involve any timing delays; execution here is the same as in C language. Table 3.9 shows a list of the VHDL statements covered in this chapter, along with their Verilog counterparts (if any).

TABLE 3.9 Summary of VHDL Behavioral Statements and Their Verilog Counterparts

VHDL	Verilog
`process`	`always`
`variable`	`------`
`-------`	`reg`
`if; else; endif`	`if; else; begin end`
`if; elsif; else; endif`	`if; else if; else; begin end`
`case; endcase`	`case begin end`
`for loop`	`for`
`while loop`	`while`
`next, exit`	`-----`
`-------`	`repeat, forever`
`MOD`	`%`
`Signed`	`signed`
`Srl 1`	`>> 1`
`integer`	`integer`

3.7 EXERCISES

3.1 Change the code in Example 3.8 to describe an asynchronous clear. Simulate your code and verify the simulation.

3.2 Use the `case` statement to describe a 3-bit logical shift register. The register should have a right/left control signal to control the direction of shift.

3.3 In Listing 3.7, a JK flip-flop was described by using a `case` statement on `JK`. Change the code to describe the flip-flop by using `case` on `Q`. Simulate and verify your description.

3.4 Use binary-to-integer conversion to describe a 4-bit even counter with active low clear. Use Verilog, simulate, and verify.

3.5 Using the Booth algorithm (see Case Study 3.1), modify the code to satisfy all the following requirements:

- The multiplier and the multiplicand are 5-bit each.
- If the multiplier or the multiplicand is 0; then the product should be 0 without going through the multiplication steps.

- If the multiplier or the multiplicand is 1 (decimal), then the product should be equal to the multiplicand or the multiplier, respectively, without going through the multiplication steps.

3.6 In the ADH Case Study 3.2, it was assumed that the relationship between ADH and BP is linear: `Bp * (-4) + 180` (VHDL). Change this relationship to be exponential: `ADH = a exp (-b * BP)`. The value of ADH is 100 for BP 20 and stays at 10 for BP 45. Write the VHDL code using the `case` statement to describe this relationship. You can approximate the values of ADH to be integers, but be as accurate as possible.

3.8 REFERENCES

[Campbell01] Campbell, N. A. and J. B. Reece, *Biology*, 6th ed. Benjamin Cummings, 2001.

[Hayes98] Hayes, J. P., *Computer Architecture and Organization*, 3d ed. McGraw Hill, 1998.

[Lewin97] Lewin B., *GENES*. Oxford University Press, 1997.

[Nelson95] Nelson V. P., H. T. Nagle, B. D. Carroll, and J. D. Irwin, *Digital Logic Circuit Analysis & Design*. Prentice Hall, 1995.

[Vander94] Vander A. J., J. H. Sherman, and D. S. Luciano, *Human Physiology*. McGraw Hill Companies, 1994.

4 Structural Descriptions

In This Chapter

- Understand the concept of structural description, including the binding of modules.
- Identify the basic statements of structural description, such as `component`, `use`, `and`, `or`, `not`, `xor`, `nor`, `generate`, `generic`, and `parameter`.
- Review and understand the fundamentals of digital logic design for digital systems, such as adders, multiplexers, decoders, comparators, encoders, latches, flip-flops, counters, and memory cells.
- Understand the concept of sequential finite-state machines.

4.1 HIGHLIGHTS OF STRUCTURAL DESCRIPTIONS

Structural description is best implemented when the digital logic of the system's hardware components is known. An example of such a system is a 2x1 multiplexer. The components of the system are known: AND, OR, and invert gates. Structural description can easily describe these components. On the other hand, it is hard (if not impossible) to describe the digital logic of, say, hormone secretion in the blood; therefore, another description, such as behavioral or mixed, may be implemented. Structural description is very close to schematic simulation.

In this chapter, structural description is covered. Both gate-level and register-level descriptions are discussed for VHDL and Verilog.

Facts

- Structural description simulates the system by describing its logical components. The components can be gate level, such as AND gates, OR gates, or NOT gates; or components can be in a higher logical level, such as Register Transfer Level (RTL) or processor level.

- It is more convenient to use structural description rather than behavioral description for systems that required a specific design. Consider, for example, a system is performing the operation A + B = C. In behavioral description, we usually write C = A + B and we have no choice in the type of adders used to perform this addition. In structural description, we can specify the type of adders, for example, look-ahead adders.
- All statements in structural description are concurrent. At any simulation time, all statements that have an event are executed concurrently.
- A major difference between VHDL and Verilog structural description is the availability of components (especially primitive gates) to the user. Verilog recognizes all the primitive gates, such as AND, OR, XOR, NOT, and XNOR gates. Basic VHDL packages do not recognize any gates unless the package is linked to one or more libraries, packages, or modules that have the gate description. Usually, the user develops these links, as will be done in this chapter.
- Although we use structural description in this chapter to simulate digital systems, this does not mean that only one type of description can be used in a module. In fact, in most descriptions of complex systems, mixed types of descriptions (e.g., data flow, behavioral, structural, or switch-level) are used in the same module (see Chapter 7, "Mixed-Type Descriptions").

4.2 ORGANIZATION OF THE STRUCTURAL DESCRIPTION

Listing 4.1 shows a simple example of HDL code that describes a system, using structural description. The entity (VHDL) or module (Verilog) name is `system`; there are two inputs, `a` and `b`, and two outputs, `sum` and `cout`.

In the VHDL description, the structural code has two parts: declaration and instantiation. In declaration, all of the different types of components are declared. For example, the statements:

```
component xor2
port (I1, I2 : in std_logic; O1 : out std_logic);
end component;
```

declare a generic component by the name of `xor2`; the component has two inputs (`I1, I2`) and one output (`O1`). The name (identifier) `xor2` is not a reserved or predefined word in VHDL; it is a user-selected name. To specify the type of the component (e.g., AND, OR, XOR, etc.) additional information should be given to the simulator (see Listing 4.2). If the system has two or more identical components, only one declaration is needed. The instantiation part of the code maps the generic inputs/outputs to the actual inputs/outputs of the system. For example, the statement:

```
X1 : xor2 port map (a, b, sum);
```

maps input a to input I1 of xor2, input b to input I2 of xor2, and output sum to output O1 of xor2. This mapping means that the logic relationship between a, b, and sum is the same as between I1, I2, and O1. If xor2 is specified through additional statements to be an XOR gate, for example, then sum = a ⊕ b. A particular order of mapping can be specified as:

```
X1 : xor2 port map (O1 => S, I1 => b , I2 => a);
```

S is mapped to O1, b is mapped to I1, and a is mapped to I2. Note that we wrote the mapping of S before writing the mapping of the inputs; we could have used any other order of mapping.

As previously mentioned, structural description statements are concurrent and are driven by events. This means that their execution depends on events, not on the order that the statements are placed in the module. So, placing statement A1 before statement X1 in Listing 4.1 does not change the outcome of the VHDL program.

LISTING 4.1 HDL Structural Description—VHDL and Verilog

VHDL Structural Description

```
library IEEE;
use IEEE.STD_LOGIC_1164.ALL;
    entity system is
    port (a, b : in std_logic;
sum, cout : out std_logic);
    end system;
    architecture struct_exple of system is
    --start declaring all different types of components
    component xor2
        port (I1, I2 : in std_logic;
        O1 : out std_logic);
    end component;
    component and2
        port (I1, I2 : in std_logic;
        O1 : out std_logic);
    end component;
        begin
    --Start of instantiation statements
    X1 : xor2 port map (a, b, sum);
    A1 : and2 port map (a, b, cout);
    end struct_exple;
```

Verilog Structural Description
```
module system (a, b, sum, cout);
input a, b;
output sum, cout;
xor X1 (sum, a, b);
/* X1 is an optional identifier; it can be omitted.*/
and a1 (cout, a, b);
/* a1 is optional identifier; it can be omitted.*/
endmodule*
```

Verilog has a large number of built-in gates; for example, the statement:

```
Xor X1 (sum, a, b);
```

describes a two-input XOR gate. The inputs are `a` and `b`, and the output is `sum`. `X1` is an optional identifier for the gate; we can omit the identifier and write the same XOR gate as:

```
Xor (sum, a, b);
```

Verilog has a complete list of built-in primitive gates. The output of the gate `sum` has to be listed before the inputs `a` and `b`. Figure 4.1 shows a list of gates and their code in Verilog. As in structural VHDL, Verilog statements are concurrent; the order of appearance of statements in the module is irrelevant.

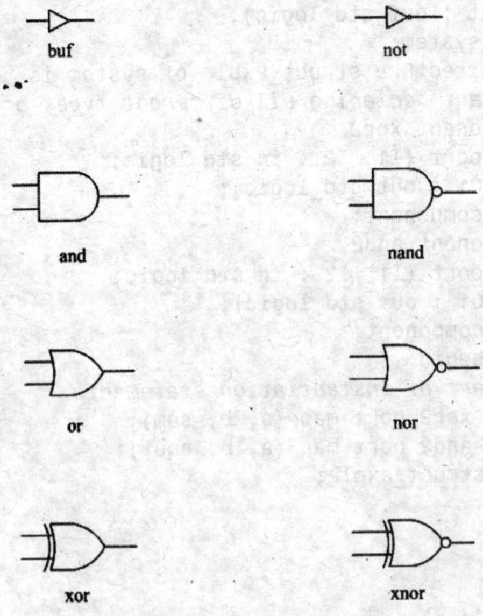

FIGURE 4.1 Verilog built-in gates.

In Example 4.1, the complete structural code for half adder will be written.

EXAMPLE 4.1 Structural Description of a Half Adder

The logic and symbol diagrams of the half adder have been shown before (see Figure 2.2). Listing 4.2 shows the HDL code for the half adder. As mentioned above, VHDL does not have built-in gates. To specify `xor2` as an EXCLUSIVE-OR gate, we bind (link) the component `xor2` with an entity bearing the same name, `xor2`. By having the same name, all information in the entity is visible to the component. The entity specifies the relationship between `I1`, `I2`, and `O1` as EXCLUSIVE-OR; accordingly, the inputs and output of `xor2` behave as EXCLUSIVE-OR. The same is done for component `and2`; it is bound to the entity `and2`.

LISTING 4.2 HDL Code of Half Adder—VHDL and Verilog

VHDL Half Adder Description

```
library IEEE;
use IEEE.STD_LOGIC_1164.ALL;
entity xor2 is
port(I1, I2 : in std_logic; O1 : out std_logic);
end xor2;
architecture Xor2_0 of xor2 is
    begin
    O1 <= I1 xor I2;
end Xor2_0;
library IEEE;
use IEEE.STD_LOGIC_1164.ALL;
entity and2 is
    port (I1, I2 : in std_logic; O1 : out std_logic);
end and2;
architecture and2_0 of and2 is
    begin
    O1 <= I1 and I2;
end and2_0;
library IEEE;
use IEEE.STD_LOGIC_1164.ALL;

entity half_add is
    port (a, b : in std_logic; S, C : out std_logic);
end half_add;

architecture HA_str of half_add is
    component xor2
    port (I1, I2 : in std_logic; O1 : out std_logic);
end component;
component and2
    port (I1, I2 : in std_logic; O1 : out std_logic);
end component;
begin
X1 : xor2 port map (a, b, S);
```

```
A1 : and2 port map (a, b, C);
end HA_str;
```

Verilog Half Adder Description

```
module half_add (a, b, S, C);
input a, b;
output S, C;
xor (S, a, b);
and (C, a, b);
endmodule
```

The VHDL code looks much longer than the Verilog code. This is due to the assumption that the basic VHDL packages do not have built-in libraries or packages for logical gates. The above binding method becomes impractical when the number of gates becomes large. Every time a new description is written, the entities of all gates used also must be written. In the following sections, more efficient ways of binding are discussed.

4.3 BINDING

Binding in HDL is common practice. Binding (linking) segment1 in HDL code to segment2 makes all information in segment2 visible to segment1. Consider the VHDL code in Listing 4.3.

LISTING 4.3 Binding Between Entity and Architecture in VHDL

```
entity one is
port (I1, I2 : in std_logic; O1 : out std_logic);
end one;
architecture A of one is
signal s : std_logic;
..........
end A;

architecture B of one is
signal x : std_logic;
.......
end B;
```

Architecture `A` is bound to entity `one` through the predefined word `of`. Also, architecture `B` is bound to entity `one` through the predefined word `of`. Accordingly, `I1`, `I2`, and `O1` can be used in both architecture `A` and architecture `B`. Architecture `A` is not bound to architecture `B`, and hence signal `s` is not recognized in architecture `B`. Likewise, signal `x` is not recognized in architecture `A`.

Now consider Listing 4.4 where an entity is bound to a component.

LISTING 4.4 Binding Between Entity and Component in VHDL

```
entity orgate is
port (I1, I2 : in std_logic; O1 : out std_logic);
end orgate;

architecture Or_dataflow of orgate is
begin
O1 <= I1 or I2;
end Or_dataflow;

entity system is
port (x, y, z : in std_logic; out r : std_logic_vector (3 downto 0);
end system;

architecture system_str of system is
component orgate
port (I1, I2 : in std_logic; O1 : std_logic);
end component;
begin
orgate port map (x, y, r(0));
.......
end system_str;
```

The component `orgate` is bound to the entity `orgate` because it has the same name. Architecture `Or_dataflow` is bound to entity `orgate` by the `of`. All information in the entity is now visible to the component. Accordingly, the relationship between `I1`, `I2`, and `O1` defined in the architecture `or_dataflow` is visible to the component `orgate`; hence the component `orgate` is an OR gate.

Now consider another way of VHDL binding, where a library or a package is bound to a module. Listing 4.5 shows how a Library can be bound to a module.

LISTING 4.5 Binding Between Library and Module in VHDL

```
library IEEE;
use IEEE.STD_LOGIC_1164.ALL;
entity system is
port (I1, I2 : in std_logic;
    O1 : out std_logic_vector (3 downto 0));
end system;
architecture lib_bound of system is
signal s : std_logic;
.............
end lib_bound;
```

`Library (library)` is a predefined word, `IEEE` is the name of the library, `use` is a predefined word, and `IEEE.STD_LOGIC_1164.ALL` refers to the part of the Library to be linked. Library IEEE provides the definition for the `standard_logic` type. By entering the name of the Library and the statement use, all information in the Library is visible to the whole module. If we do not write the first two statements in Listing 4.5, the standard_logic type cannot be used. Libraries can also be generated by the user. The HDL simulator generates a Library named work every time it compiles HDL code. This Library can be bound to another module by using the statement use, as follows:

```
use entity work.gates (or_gates);
```

The entity to be bound to the module is gates; gates has an architecture by the name of or_gates; and all information in this architecture is visible to the module wherever the use statement is written. Listing 4.6 shows an example of binding architecture in one module to a component written in another module.

LISTING 4.6 Binding Between a Library and Component in VHDL

```
--First, write the code that will be bound to another module
library IEEE;
use IEEE.STD_LOGIC_1164.ALL;
entity bind2 is
port (I1, I2 : in std_logic; O1 : out std_logic);
end bind2;

architecture xor2_0 of bind2 is
begin
    O1 <= I1 xor I2;
end xor2_0;

architecture and2_0 of bind2 is
begin
    O1 <= I1 and I2;
end and2_0;

architecture and2_4 of bind2 is
begin
    O1 <= I1 and I2 after 4 ns;
end and2_4;

--After writing the above code; compile it and store it in a known
--location. Now, open another module
--where the above information is to be used.
library IEEE;
use IEEE.STD_LOGIC_1164.ALL;
    entity half_add is
    port (a, b : in std_logic; S, C : out std_logic);
    end half_add;

    architecture HA_str of half_add is
    component xor2
```

```
port (I1, I2 : in std_logic; O1 : out std_logic);
end component;
component and2
port (I1, I2 : in std_logic; O1 : out std_logic);
end component;
for all : xor2 use entity work.bind2 (xor2_0);
for all : and2 use entity work.bind2 (and2_4);
begin
X1 : xor2 port map (a, b, S);
A1 : and2 port map (a, b, C);
end HA_str;
```

The statement: `for all : xor2 use entity work.bind2 (xor2_0)` binds the architecture `xor2_0` of the entity `bind2` to the component `xor2`. By this binding, component `xor2` behaves as a two-input XOR gate with zero propagation delay. The statement `for all : and2 use entity work.bind2 (and2_4)` binds the architecture `and2_4` of the entity `bind2` to the component `and2`. By this binding, component `and2` behaves as a two-input AND gate with a 4-ns propagation delay time. In Listing 4.6, it is assumed that both entities `bind2` and `half_add` have the same path (stored in the same directory), otherwise the path of the Library work has to be entered.

Throughout this chapter the binding shown in Listing 4.6 is adopted. The codes for all the gates expected are written, and the module is compiled and stored. Whenever we want to use any component from the stored module, we bind it to the current module. Listing 4.28 includes VHDL binding code used in all of the Examples in this chapter.

As previously mentioned, Verilog has all primitive gates built in and ready to use. We can bind modules by just writing the name of the module to be bound. Listing 4.7 shows such binding.

LISTING 4.7 Binding Between Two Modules in Verilog

```
module one (O1, O2, a, b);
    input [1:0] a;
    input [1:0] b;
    output [1:0] O1, O2;

two M0 (O1[0], O2[0], a[0], b[0]);
two M1 (O1[1], O2[1], a[1], b[1]);
endmodule

module two (s1, s2, a1, b1);
    input a1;
    input b1;
    output s1, s2;
xor (s1, a1, b1);
and (s2, a1, b1);
endmodule
```

The statement: `two M0 (O1[0], O2[0], a[0], b[0]);` written in module `one` binds module `two` to module `one`. Accordingly, the relationship between `O1`, `O2`, `a`, and `b` is as follows:

`O1[0]` is the output of a two-input XOR gate with `a[0]` and `b[0]` as the inputs.
`O2[1]` is the output of a two-input AND gate with `a[1]` and `b[1]` as the inputs.

Other methods of binding are discussed in Chapter 6, "Procedures, Tasks, and Functions," and in Chapter 8, "Advanced HDL Descriptions." The following Examples will enable practice in using binding and structural descriptions.

EXAMPLE 4.2 Structural Description of a 2x1 Multiplexer with Active Low Enable

The truth table and logic diagram of this multiplexer have been covered in Chapter 2, "Data-Flow Descriptions." The logic diagram is redrawn here for convenience (see Figure 4.2).

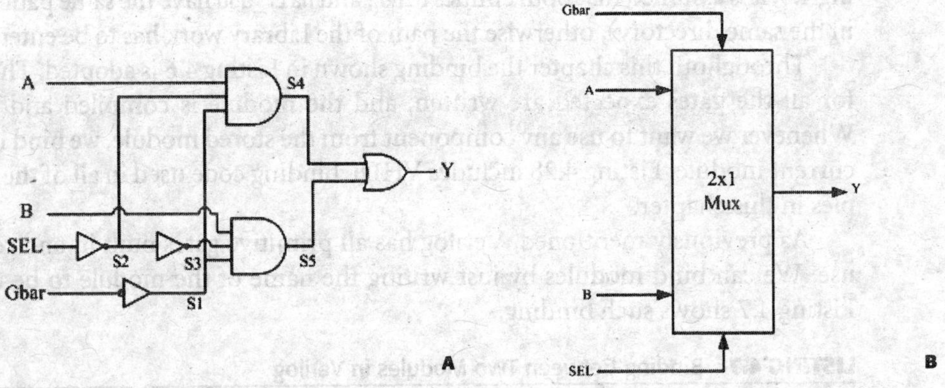

FIGURE 4.2 Multiplexer. (a) Logic diagram. (b) Logic symbol.

From Figure 4.2, we see that the components of the multiplexer are: two three-input AND gates, three inverters, and one two-input OR gate. Each gate, including the inverter, is assumed to have a 7-ns propagation delay time. For VHDL, we adopt the binding method shown in Listing 4.6. First, we write a code to describe these gates; it is compiled and then stored. Some other gates are included here that might be used for other Examples. Listing 4.8 shows the code for several gates.

LISTING 4.8 VHDL Code for Several Gates

```
library IEEE;
use IEEE.STD_LOGIC_1164.ALL;
```

```
entity bind1 is
port (I1 : in std_logic; O1 : out std_logic);
end bind1;
architecture inv_0 of bind1 is
begin
O1 <= not I1; --This is an inverter with zero delay
end inv_0;

architecture inv_7 of bind1 is
begin
O1 <= not I1 after 7 ns; --This is an inverter with a 7-ns delay
end inv_7;

library IEEE;
use IEEE.STD_LOGIC_1164.ALL;

entity bind2 is
port (I1, I2 : in std_logic; O1 : out std_logic);
end bind2;

architecture xor2_0 of bind2 is
begin
O1 <= I1 xor I2; --This is exclusive-or with zero delay.
end xor2_0;

architecture and2_0 of bind2 is
begin
O1 <= I1 and I2; --This is a two input and gate with zero delay.
end and2_0;

architecture and2_7 of bind2 is
begin
O1 <= I1 and I2 after 7 ns; --This is a two input and gate
                            --with 7-ns delay.
end and2_7;

architecture or2_0 of bind2 is
begin
O1 <= I1 or I2; --This is a two input or gate with zero delay.
end or2_0;

architecture or2_7 of bind2 is
begin
O1 <= I1 or I2 after 7 ns; --This is a two input or gate
                           --with 7-ns delay.
end or2_7;

library IEEE;
use IEEE.STD_LOGIC_1164.ALL;

entity bind3 is
```

```
port (I1, I2, I3 : in std_logic; O1 : out std_logic);
end bind3;

architecture and3_0 of bind3 is
begin
O1 <= I1 and I2 and I3; --This is a three input and gate
                        --with zero delay.
end and3_0;

architecture and3_7 of bind3 is
begin
O1 <= I1 and I2 and I3 after 7 ns; --This is a three input
                                   --and gate with 7-ns
                                   --delay.
end and3_7;

architecture or3_0 of bind3 is
begin
O1 <= I1 or I2 or I3; --This is a three input or gate
                      --with zero delay.
end or3_0;

architecture or3_7 of bind3 is
begin
O1 <= I1 or I2 or I3 after 7 ns; --This is a three input or gate
                                 --with 7-ns delay.
end or3_7;
```

After we compile the above code, we store it in a known directory (path). A new module is started to write the code for the multiplexer. Listing 4.9 shows the HDL code for a 2x1 multiplexer with active low enable.

LISTING 4.9 HDL Description of a 2x1 Multiplexer with Active Low Enable—VHDL and Verilog

VHDL 2x1 Multiplexer with Active Low Enable

```
library IEEE;
use IEEE.STD_LOGIC_1164.ALL;
entity mux2x1 is
    port (A, B, SEL, Gbar : in std_logic;
        Y : out std_logic);
    end mux2x1;

architecture mux_str of mux2x1 is

    --Start Components Declaration
    component and3
    port (I1, I2, I3 : in std_logic; O1 : out std_logic);
end component;

--Only different types of components need be declared.
```

```
--Since the multiplexer has two identical AND gates,
--only one is declared.

component or2
port (I1, I2 : in std_logic; O1 : out std_logic);
end component;
component Inv
port (I1 : in std_logic; O1 : out std_logic);
end component;

signal S1, S2, S3, S4, S5 : std_logic;
for all : and3 use entity work.bind3 (and3_7);
for all : Inv use entity work.bind1 (inv_7);
for Or1 : or2 use entity work.bind2 (or2_7);
begin
    --Start instantiation
A1 : and3 port map (A,S2, S1, S4);
A2 : and3 port map (B,S3, S1, S5);
IV1 : Inv port map (SEL, S2);
IV2 : Inv port map (Gbar, S1);
IV3 : Inv port map (S2, S3);
or1 : or2 port map (S4, S5, Y);
end mux_str;
```

Verilog 2x1 Multiplexer with Active Low Enable

```
module mux2x1 (A, B, SEL, Gbar, Y);
input A, B, SEL, Gbar;
output Y;
and #7 (S4, A, S2, S1);
or #7 (Y, S4, S5);
and #7 (S5, B, S3, S1);
not #7 (S2, SEL);
not #7 (S3, S2);
not #7 (S1, Gbar);
endmodule
```

Referring to Listing 4.9, since the multiplexer has two identical AND gates (both three-input and gates), we declare only one of them in the VHDL description by the statements:

```
component and3
port (I1, I2, I3 : in std_logic; O1 : out std_logic);
end component;
```

Similarly, only one inverter is declared. If the two AND gates do not have the same delay time—say, `A1` has 0 ns and `A2` has 7 ns—then instead of `all` in the `use` statement, we write:

```
for A1 : and3 use entity work.bind3 (and3_0);
for A2 : and3 use entity work.bind3 (and3_7);
```

For the Verilog description, the statement:

```
and #7 (S4, A, S2, S1);
```

declares a three-input (A, s2, s1) AND gate with propagation delay of seven simulation screen units. Note that s2 or s1 do not need to be declared as wire; Verilog assumes that they are of the same type as A. If a four input and gate are needed, we write

```
and (o1, in1, in2, in3, in4)
```

where O1 is the output, and in1, in2, in3, and in4 are the inputs. We can give a name to the gates in Verilog, as:

```
or #7 orgate1 (O1, in1, in2)
```

The above statement describes an OR gate by the name orgate1; it has two inputs (in1, in2) and an output (O1). The name is optional and can be omitted.

The simulation waveform of the multiplexer is identical to that of Figure 2.5.

EXAMPLE 4.3 Structural Description of a 2x4 Decoder with Three-State Output

A decoder is a combinational circuit. A 2x4 decoder has two inputs and four outputs. For any input, only one output is active; all others are inactive. For an active-high output decoder, only one output is high. The output can be deactivated or put in high impedance if the decoder has enable. For a tristate output, if the enable is inactive, then all the outputs are in high impedance. The output of an n-bit input decoder is 2^n bits. Table 4.1 shows the truth table of the decoder.

TABLE 4.1 Truth Table for a 2x4 Decoder with Tristate Output

	Inuts		Outputs			
Enable	**I1**	**I2**	**D3**	**D2**	**D1**	**D0**
0	x	x	Z	Z	Z	Z
1	0	0	0	0	0	1
1	0	1	0	0	1	0
1	1	0	0	1	0	0
1	1	1	1	0	0	0

Tristate buffers are used at the output. If the enable is low, then all outputs are in high impedance (Z). From Table 4.1, we can write the Boolean function of the outputs.

$$D0 = \overline{I0}\ \overline{I1}$$

$$D1 = I0\ \overline{I1}$$

$$D2 = \overline{I0}\ I1$$

$$D3 = I0\ I1$$

Figure 4.3 shows the logic diagram of the decoder.

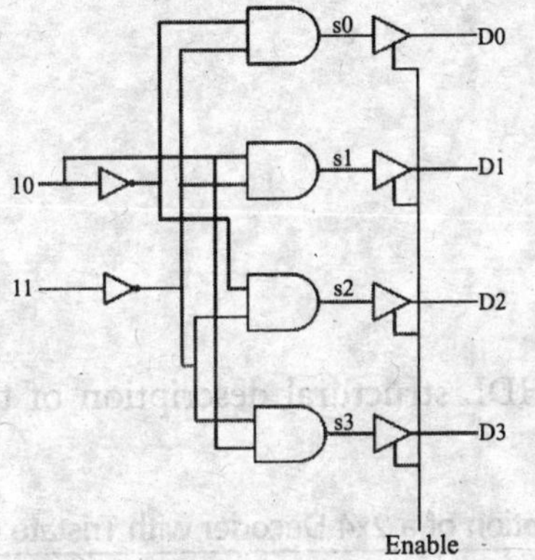

FIGURE 4.3 Logic diagram of a 2x4 Decoder with tristate output.

To write the VHDL code, we need first to write a description of the tri-state buffer gate. The easiest description type that can be written for the tristate buffer is behavioral, using the `if` statement. This description is attached to the entity `bind2` (see Listing 4.8). Listing 4.10 shows a behavioral description of a tristate buffer. The Verilog has built-in buffers (see Figure 4.4).

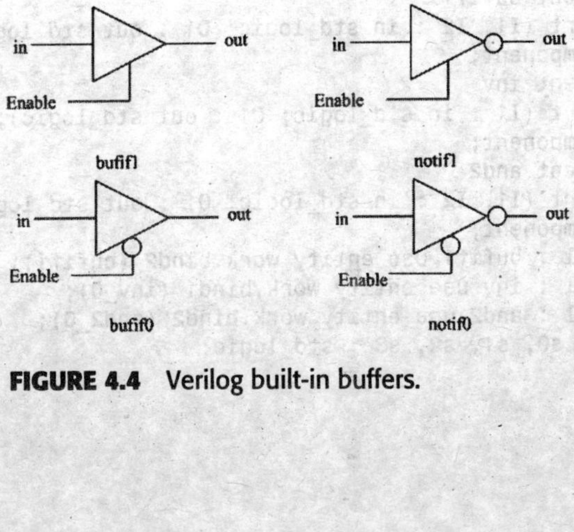

FIGURE 4.4 Verilog built-in buffers.

LISTING 4.10 VHDL Behavioral Description of a Tristate Buffer

```
entity bind2 is
port (I1, I2 : in std_logic; O1 : out std_logic);
end bind2;
...........
--Add the following architecture to
--the entity bind2 of Listing 4.8
architecture bufif1 of bind2 is
begin
buf : process (I1, I2)
variable tem : std_logic;
begin
if (I2 ='1') then
tem := I1;
else
tem := 'Z';
end if;
O1 <= tem;
end process buf;
end bufif1;
```

Now we write the HDL structural description of the decoder as shown in Listing 4.11.

LISTING 4.11 HDL Description of a 2x4 Decoder with Tristate Output—VHDL and Verilog

VHDL 2x4 Decoder with Tristate Output

```
library IEEE;
use IEEE.STD_LOGIC_1164.ALL;

entity decoder2x4 is
    port (I : in std_logic_vector(1 downto 0);
        Enable : in std_logic;
        D : out std_logic_vector (3 downto 0));
end decoder2x4;

architecture decoder of decoder2x4 is
component bufif1
    port (I1, I2 : in std_logic; O1 : out std_logic);
end component;
component inv
    port (I1 : in std_logic; O1 : out std_logic);
end component;
component and2
    port (I1, I2 : in std_logic; O1 : out std_logic);
end component;
for all : bufif1 use entity work.bind2 (bufif1);
for all : inv use entity work.bind1 (inv_0);
for all : and2 use entity work.bind2 (and2_0);
signal s0, s1, s2, s3 : std_logic;
```

```
signal Ibar : std_logic_vector (1 downto 0);
--The above signals have to be declared before they can be used
begin
    B0 : bufif1 port map (s0, Enable, D(0));
    B1 : bufif1 port map (s1, Enable, D(1));
    B2 : bufif1 port map (s2, Enable, D(2));
    B3 : bufif1 port map (s3, Enable, D(3));
    iv0 : inv port map (I(0), Ibar(0));
    iv1 : inv port map (I(1), Ibar(1));
    a0 : and2 port map (Ibar(0), Ibar(1), s0);
    a1 : and2 port map (I(0), Ibar(1), s1);
    a2 : and2 port map (Ibar(0), I(1), s2);
    a3 : and2 port map (I(0), I(1), s3);
end decoder;
```

Verilog 2x4 Decoder with Tristate Output

```
module decoder2x4 (I, Enable, D);
input [1:0] I;
input Enable;
output [3:0] D;
wire [1:0] Ibar;
    bufif1 (D[0], s0, Enable);
    bufif1 (D[1], s1, Enable);
    bufif1 (D[2], s2, Enable);
    bufif1 (D[3], s3, Enable);
    not (Ibar[0], I[0]);
    not (Ibar[1], I[1]);
    and (s0, Ibar[0], Ibar[1]);
    and (s1, I[0], Ibar[1]);
    and (s2, Ibar[0], I[1]);
    and (s3, I[0], I[1]);
endmodule
```

Figure 4.5 shows the simulation waveform of the decoder.

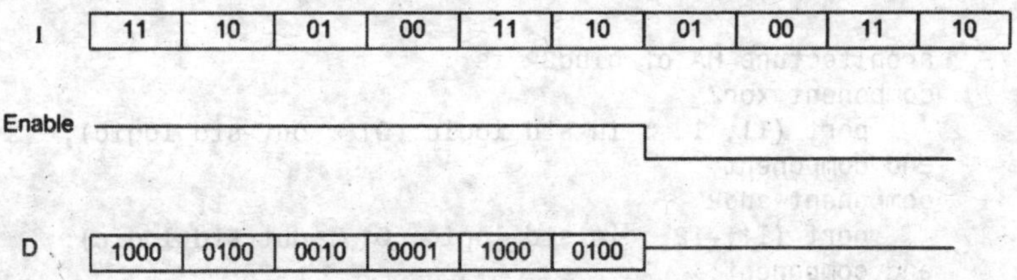

FIGURE 4.5 Simulation waveform of a 2x1 decoder with tristate output.

EXAMPLE 4.4 Structural Description of a Full Adder

In this example, a full adder (Listing 4.13) is built from two half adders (Listing 4.12). The full adder adds `(a + b + cin)` to give `sum` and `carry`. Half adder is used to add (a+b), to give sum1 and carry1. Another half adder is used to add (sum1 + cin), to give sum and carry2. The carry of the summation (a + b + cin) is the logical OR of carry1 and carry2. Figures 4.6a and 4.6b show the logical symbol and diagram of this full adder, respectively.

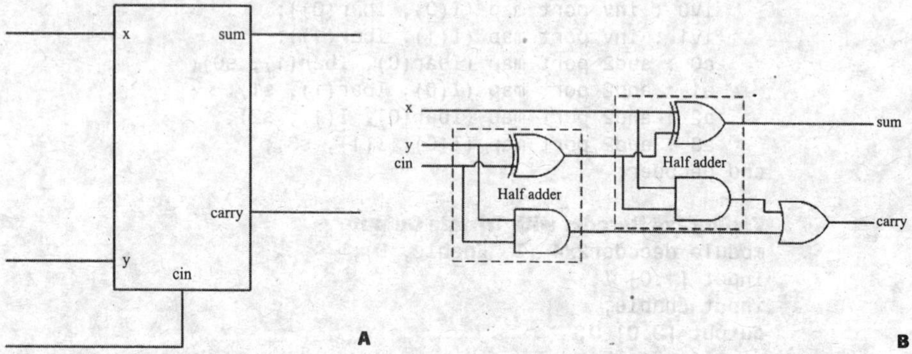

FIGURE 4.6 Full adder as two half adders. (a) Logic symbol. (b) Logic diagram.

For the VHDL code, we first write the code for half adder. We include this code in Listing 4.8. Listing 4.12 shows the code of the half adder as part of Listing 4.8.

LISTING 4.12 VHDL Code for the Half Adder

```
--This code is to be appended to Listing 4.8
library IEEE;
use IEEE.STD_LOGIC_1164.ALL;
entity bind22 is
    Port (I1, I2 : in std_logic; O1, O2 : out std_logic);
end bind22;

architecture HA of bind22 is
component xor2
    port (I1, I2 : in std_logic; O1 : out std_logic);
end component;
component and2
    port (I1, I2 : in std_logic; O1 : out std_logic);
end component;

for A1 : and2 use entity work.bind2 (and2_0);
for X1 : xor2 use entity work.bind2 (xor2_0);
begin
    X1 : xor2 port map (I1, I2, O1);
    A1 : and2 port map (I1, I2, O2);
end HA;
```

Now we write the structural description of the full adder as two half adders. Listing 4.13 shows the HDL code for a full adder.

LISTING 4.13 HDL Description of a Full Adder (Figures 4.6a and 4.6b)—VHDL and Verilog

VHDL Full Adder Description

```
library IEEE;
use IEEE.STD_LOGIC_1164.ALL;
entity FULL_ADDER is
    Port (x, y, cin : in std_logic; sum, carry : out std_logic);
end FULL_ADDER;
architecture full_add of FULL_ADDER is
component HA
    Port (I1, I2 : in std_logic; O1, O2 : out std_logic);
end component;
component or2
    Port (I1, I2 : in std_logic; O1 : out std_logic);
end component;

for all : HA use entity work.bind22 (HA);
for all : or2 use entity work.bind2 (or2_0);
signal s0, c0, c1 : std_logic;

begin
    HA1 : HA port map (y, cin, s0, c0);
    HA2 : HA port map (x, s0, sum, c1);
    r1 : or2 port map (c0, c1, carry);
end full_add;
```

Verilog Full Adder Description

```
module FULL_ADDER (x, y, cin, sum, carry);
input x, y, cin;
output sum, carry;
HA H1 (y, cin, s0, c0);
HA H2 (x, s0, sum, c1);
//The above two statements bind module HA
//to the present module FULL_ADDER
or (carry, c0, c1);
endmodule

module HA (a, b, s, c);
input a, b;
output s, c;
xor (s, a, b);
and (c, a, b);
endmodule
```

To use the above VHDL code in future examples, it is appended to entity `bind32` in Listing 4.28.

EXAMPLE 4.5 Structural Description of an SR-Latch

An SR (Set-Reset) latch is a sequential circuit. It memorizes one of its state when S = R = 0. Memorization is achieved through feedback between the outputs Q and its complement $\overline{Q}$, and the inputs. The inputs receive the values of the current outputs through the feedback lines. The state where S = R = 1 is prohibited, since it may lead to unstable output (both Q and $\overline{Q}$ acquire the same logic level). The latch is implemented in digital systems as a switch or as a memory cell for Static Random-Access Memory (SRAM). The excitation table of the latch is shown in Table 4.2.

TABLE 4.2 Excitation Table of an SR-Latch

S	R	Current State	Next State
1	0	x	1
0	1	x	0
0	0	q	q
1	1	x	prohibited

Figures 4.7a and 4.7b show the logic symbol and diagram, respectively, of an SR-latch using NOR gates. Notice the connection (feedback) between the output Q and the input of NOR gate in Figure 4.7b.

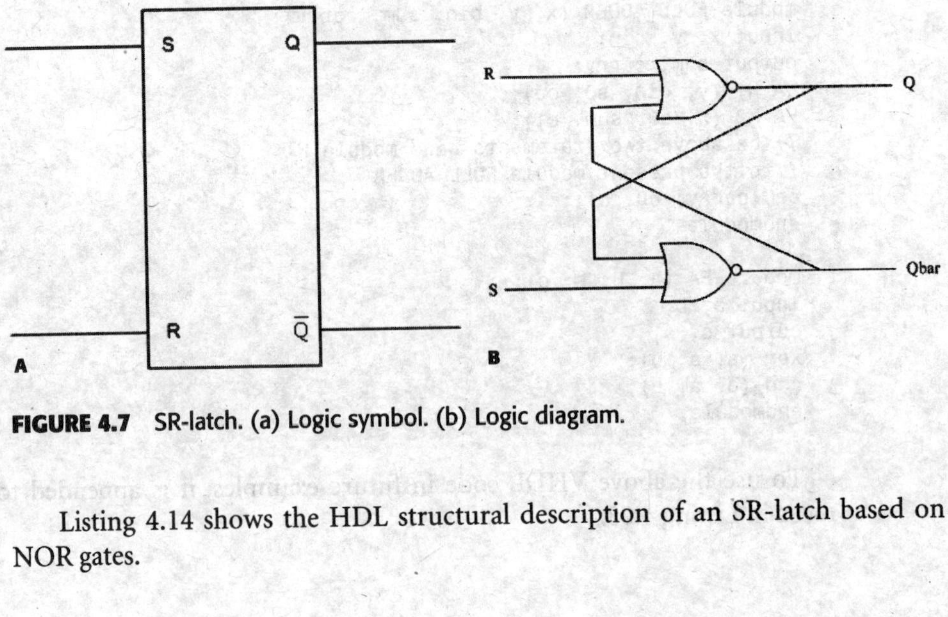

FIGURE 4.7 SR-latch. (a) Logic symbol. (b) Logic diagram.

Listing 4.14 shows the HDL structural description of an SR-latch based on NOR gates.

LISTING 4.14 HDL Description of an SR-Latch with NOR Gates

VHDL SR-Latch with NOR Gates

```
library IEEE;
use IEEE.STD_LOGIC_1164.ALL;
entity SR_latch is
port (R, S : in std_logic;
     Q, Qbar : buffer std_logic);

--Q, Qbar are declared buffer because
--they behave as input and output.

end SR_latch;

architecture SR_strc of SR_latch is
--Some simulators would not allow mapping between
--buffer and out. In this
--case, change all out to buffer.
component nor2
port (I1, I2 : in std_logic; O1 : out std_logic);
end component;
for all : nor2 use entity work.bind2 (nor2_0);
begin
    n1 : nor2 port map (S, Q, Qbar);
    n2 : nor2 port map (R, Qbar, Q);
end SR_strc;
```

Verilog SR-Latch with NOR Gates

```
module SR_Latch (R, S, Q, Qbar);
input R, S;
output Q, Qbar;
nor (Qbar, S,Q);
nor (Q, R, Qbar);
endmodule
```

To use the above code in future Examples, it is appended to Listing 4.28. Figure 4.8 shows the simulation waveform of the SR-latch.

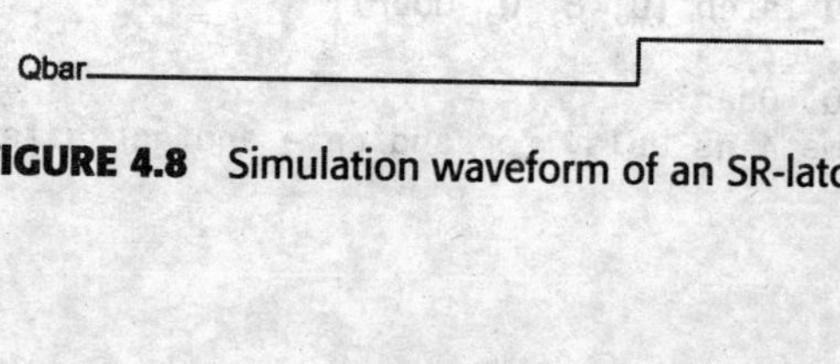

FIGURE 4.8 Simulation waveform of an SR-latch.

EXAMPLE 4.6 Structural Description of a D-Latch

A D-latch (Delay latch) is a sequential circuit. The output of the latch (Q) follows the input (D) as long as the enable (E) is high. $\overline{Q}$ is the complement of Q. The latch has been discussed in Chapter 2. The logic symbol and diagram are as shown in Figures 2.8 and 2.10, respectively. Listing 4.15 shows the HDL structural description of a D-latch.

LISTING 4.15 HDL Description of a D-Latch—VHDL and Verilog

VHDL D-Latch Description

```
library IEEE;
use IEEE.STD_LOGIC_1164.ALL;

entity D_Latch is
   port (D, E : in std_logic; Q, Qbar : buffer std_logic);
end D_Latch;

architecture D_latch_str of D_Latch is
--Some simulators will not allow mapping between
--buffer and out. In this
--case, change all out to buffer.

component and2
   port (I1, I2 : in std_logic; O1 : out std_logic);
end component;
component nor2
   port (I1, I2 : in std_logic; O1 : out std_logic);
end component;
component inv
   port (I1 : in std_logic; O1 : out std_logic);
end component;
for all : and2 use entity work.bind2 (and2_4);
for all : nor2 use entity work.bind2 (nor2_4);
for all : inv use entity work.bind1 (inv_1);
signal Eb, s1, s2 : std_logic;
begin
   a1 : and2 port map (D, E, s1);
   a2 : and2 port map (Eb, Q, s2);
   in1 : inv port map (E, Eb);
   in2 : inv port map (Qbar, Q);
   n2 : nor2 port map (s1, s2, Qbar);
   end D_latch_str;
```

To use the above code in future Examples, it is appended to Listing 4.28.

Verilog D-Latch Description

```
module D_latch (D, E, Q, Qbar);
input D, E;
output Q, Qbar;
/* assume 4 ns delay for and gate and nor gate,
```

→

```
    and 1 ns for inverter */

and #4 gate1 (s1, D, E);

/* the name "gate1" is optional; we could have
    written and #4 (s1, D, E) */
    and #4 gate2 (s2, Eb, Q);
    not #1 (Eb, E);
    nor #4 (Qbar, s1, s2);
    not #1 (Q, Qbar);
endmodule
```

The simulation waveform is the same as in Figure 2.11.

EXAMPLE 4.7 Structural Description of a Pulse-Triggered, Master-Slave D Flip-Flop

The D-latch discussed in Listing 4.15 has a characteristic that may not be desirable in digital circuits such as counters. The D-latch output follows its input as long as the enable is high. In counters, for example, we may like to have the output change only once during the active phase of the clock. To achieve this, we need flip-flops.

A master-slave D flip-flop is a sequential circuit where the output follows the input only once at the transition of the clock from inactive to active. Figure 4.9 shows the logic symbol of the master-slave D flip-flop. Table 4.3 shows the excitation table of the flip-flop.

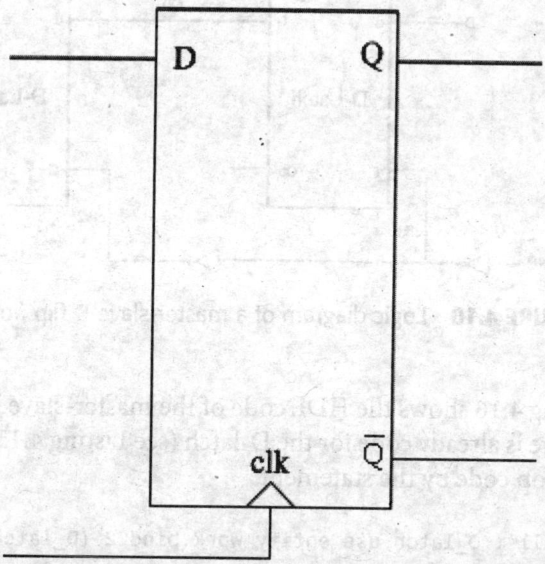

FIGURE 4.9 Logic symbol of the master-slave D flip-flop.

TABLE 4.3 Excitation Table for the Master-Slave D Flip-Flop

Input	Current State	Clock	Next State
D	Q	clk	Q+
0	0	⎍	0
0	1	⎍	0
1	0	⎍	1
1	1	⎍	1

The logic diagram of the master-slave flip-flop is shown in Figure 4.10. The flip-flop consists of two active-high enable D-latches; the first latch is called the "master," and the second is called the "slave." The master latch drives the slave. The clock of the master is the invert of the clock of the slave. Since the clock of one of the latches is the invert of the other, at any time, one latch is active while the other is inactive. At the high level of the clock, the slave is active; its output Q follows its input QM (QM is the output of the master). Since the master is inactive at the high level of the clock, any change in D (the input of the slave) is not transmitted to QM; so QM and Q stay the same during the high level of the clock, unaffected by any change in D. Thus, the flip-flop is sensitive to the clock pulse rather than the level, as in a D-latch.

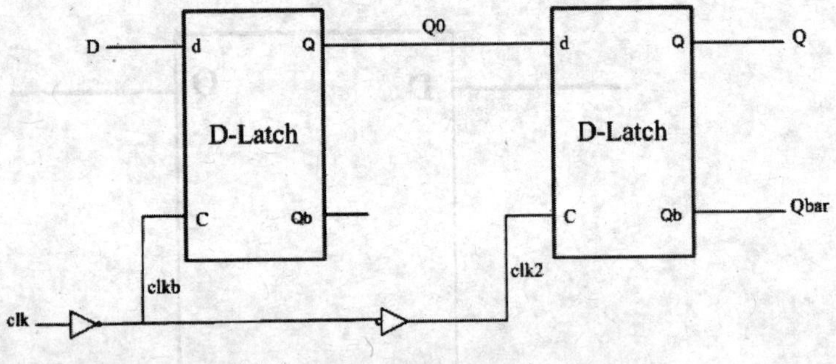

FIGURE 4.10 Logic diagram of a master-slave D flip-flop.

Listing 4.16 shows the HDL code of the master-slave D flip-flop. In the VHDL code, there is already code for the D-latch (see Listing 4.15); this code is attached to the flip-flop code by the statement:

```
for all : D_latch use entity work.bind22 (D_latch);
```

which links the architecture `D_latch` to the current module. In Verilog, we link the module `D_latch` to the module `D_FFMaster` by the statement:

```
D_latch D0 (D, clkb, Q0, Qb0);
```

Note that the order of the linked parameters `(D, clkb, Q0, Qb0)` has to match `D, E, Q,` and `Qbar` of the `D_latch` module, respectively.

LISTING 4.16 HDL Description of a Master-Slave D Flip-Flop—VHDL and Verilog

VHDL Master-Slave D Flip-Flop

```
library IEEE;
use IEEE.STD_LOGIC_1164.ALL;

entity D_FFMaster is
    Port (D, clk : in std_logic; Q, Qbar : buffer std_logic);
end D_FFMaster;

architecture D_FF of D_FFMaster is
--Some simulators would not allow mapping between
--buffer and out. In this
--case, change all out to buffer.

component inv
    port (I1 : in std_logic; O1 : out std_logic);
end component;
component D_latch
    port (I1, I2 : in std_logic; O1, O2 : buffer std_logic);
end component;
for all : D_latch use entity work.bind22 (D_latch);
for all : inv use entity work.bind1 (inv_1);
signal clkb, clk2, Q0, Qb0 : std_logic;
begin
    D0 : D_latch port map (D, clkb, Q0, Qb0);
    D1 : D_latch port map (Q0, clk2, Q, Qbar);
    in1 : inv port map (clk, clkb);
    in2 : inv port map (clkb, clk2);
end D_FF;
```

Verilog Master-Slave D Flip-Flop

```
module D_FFMaster (D, clk, Q, Qbar);
input D, clk;
output Q, Qbar;
    not #1 (clkb, clk);
    not #1 (clk2, clkb);
    D_latch D0 (D, clkb, Q0, Qb0);
    D_latch D1 (Q0, clk2, Q, Qbar);
endmodule

module D_latch (D, E, Q, Qbar);
input D, E;
output Q, Qbar;
    and #4 gate1 (s1, D, E);
```

```
        and #4 gate2 (s2, Eb, Q);
        not #1 (Eb, E);
        nor #4 (Qbar, s1, s2);
        not #1 (Q, Qbar);
    endmodule
```

To use the above VHDL code in future Examples, it is appended to entity `bind22` in Listing 4.28. Listing 4.28 shows the code that has been used in all Examples in this chapter.

Figure 4.11 shows the simulation waveform of the master-slave D flip-flop. It is clear from the figure that signal D is sampled only at the transition of the clock from low to high. If D changes during the high level (or the low level) of the clock, the output Q remains the same; it does not respond to this change. Compare Figure 4.11 with Figure 2.11, and notice the difference between a latch and a flip-flop. During the high level of the clock (called enable in the latch), Q follows D for the latch. In the flip-flop, Q follows D only at the clock transition from low to high.

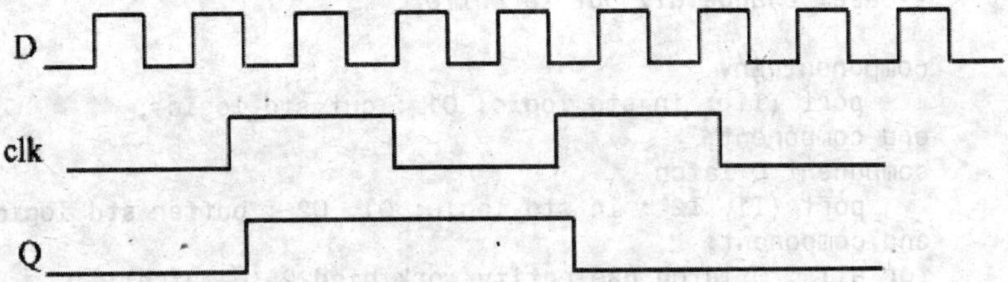

FIGURE 4.11 Simulation waveform of a master-slave D flip-flop.

EXAMPLE 4.8 Structural Description of a Pulse-Triggered Master-Slave JK Flip-Flop

A JK flip-flop can be viewed as an extension of the SR-latch. The flip-flop has all the allowed states of the SR. The prohibited state in the SR-latch is replaced by a toggle state, where the output of the flip-flop is complemented every time J = K = 1. Table 4.4 shows the excitation table of a pulse-triggered JK flip-flop.

TABLE 4.4 Excitation Table for a Pulse-Triggered JK Flip-Flop

J	K	Q	clk	Q+
0	0	Q0	⎍	Q0
0	1	x	⎍	0
1	0	x	⎍	1
1	1	Q0	⎍	$\overline{Q0}$

The Boolean function of a JK flip-flop can be derived from that of D flip-flop. Table 4.5 shows the J and K values, and the corresponding D values.

TABLE 4.5 Relationship between JK Flip-Flop and D Flip-Flop.

J	K	Q	clk	Q+	D
0	0	0	⎍	0	0
0	0	1	⎍	1	1
0	1	0	⎍	0	0
0	1	1	⎍	0	0
1	0	0	⎍	1	1
1	0	1	⎍	1	1
1	1	0	⎍	1	1
1	1	1	⎍	0	0

To find the Boolean function of D, we form K-maps as shown in Figure 4.12.

J \ KQ	00	01	11	10
00	0	1	0	0
01	1	1	0	1

D

FIGURE 4.12 K-maps of Table 4.5.

From Figure 4.12, the Boolean functions are:

$$D = \overline{K}Q + J\overline{Q} \tag{4.1}$$

Equation 4.1 is used to generate a master-slave JK flip-flop from a master- slave D flip-flop. Figure 4.13 shows a JK master-slave flip-flop generated from a master-slave D flip-flop (see Figure 4.10).

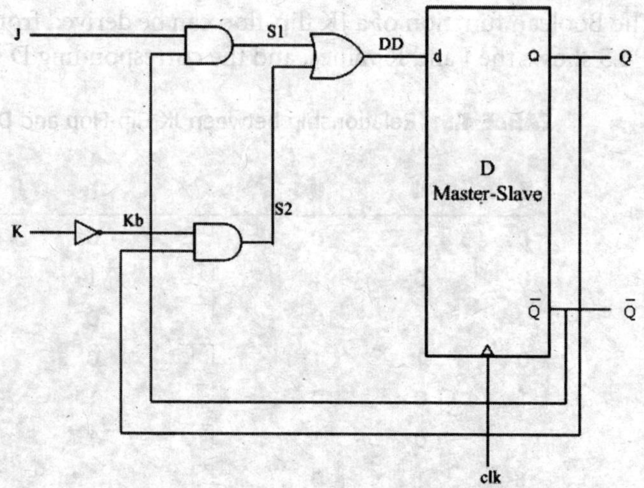

FIGURE 4.13 Pulse-triggered master-slave JK flip-flop.

Listing 4.17 shows the HDL code for the master-slave JK flip-flop illustrated in Figure 4.13.

LISTING 4.17 HDL Description of a Master-Slave JK Flip-Flop—VHDL and Verilog

VHDL Master-Slave JK Flip-Flop

```
library IEEE;
use IEEE.STD_LOGIC_1164.ALL;

entity JK_FF is
port (J, K, clk : in std_logic; Q, Qbar : buffer std_logic);

--Q and Qbar are declared buffer so they can be input or output

end JK_FF;

architecture JK_Master of JK_FF is
--Some simulators will not allow mapping between
--buffer and out. In this
--case, change all out to buffer.

component and2
    port (I1, I2 : in std_logic; O1 : out std_logic);
end component;
component or2
    port (I1, I2 : in std_logic; O1 : out std_logic);
```

```
end component;
component inv
    port (I1 : in std_logic; O1 : out std_logic);
end component;
component D_flip
    port (I1, I2 : in std_logic; O1, O2 : buffer std_logic);
end component;
for all : and2 use entity work.bind2 (and2_4);
for all : or2 use entity work.bind2 (or2_4);
for all : inv use entity work.bind1 (inv_1);
for all : D_flip use entity work.bind22 (D_FFMaster);
signal s1, s2, Kb, DD : std_logic;
begin
    a1 : and2 port map (J, Qbar, s1);
    a2 : and2 port map (Kb, Q, s2);
    in1 : inv port map (K, Kb);
    or1 : or2 port map (s1, s2, DD);
    DFF : D_flip port map (DD, clk, Q, Qbar);
end JK_Master;
```

Verilog Master-Slave JK Flip-Flop

```
module JK_FF (J, K, clk, Q, Qbar);
input J, K, clk;
output Q, Qbar;
wire s1, s2;
    and #4 (s1, J, Qbar);
    and #4 (s2, Kb, Q);
    not #1 (Kb, K);
    or #4 (DD, s1, s2);
    D_FFMaster D0 (DD, clk, Q, Qbar);
endmodule

module D_FFMaster (D, clk, Q, Qbar);

/* We do not have to rewrite the module if the simulator
   used can attach it to the above module (JK_FF). */

input D, clk;
output Q, Qbar;
wire clkb, clk2, Q0, Qb0;
not #1 (clkb, clk);
not #1 (clk2, clkb);
D_latch D0 (D, clkb, Q0, Qb0);
D_latch D1 (Q0, clk2, Q, Qbar);
endmodule

module D_latch (D, E, Q, Qbar);
input D, E;
output Q, Qbar;
wire Eb, s1, s2;
```

→

```
//assume 4-ns delay for and gate and nor gate,
//and 1 ns for inverter
and #4 gate1 (s1, D, E);
//The name gate1 is optional and could have been omitted.

    and (s1, D, E);
    and #4 gate2 (s2, Eb, Q);
    not #1 (Eb, E);
    nor #4 (Qbar, s1, s2);
    not #1 (Q, Qbar);
endmodule
```

Notice here that the VHDL code in Listing 4.17 is getting shorter compared to the Verilog code. This is due to the fact that VHDL user-built components are being linked, such as `and2`, `or2`, and `inv`. Their codes do not need to be rewritten because they are linked to the current module.

EXAMPLE 4.9 Structural Description of a 3-bit Ripple-Carry Adder

In this Example, a 3-bit ripple-carry adder is described. Then in Example 4.10, we implement this adder to build a magnitude comparator. The logic diagram of the adder is as shown in Figure 2.13 of Chapter 2. Listing 4.18 shows the structural description of the 3-bit ripple-carry adder.

LISTING 4.18 HDL Description of a 3-Bit Ripple-Carry Adder—VHDL and Verilog

VHDL 3-Bit Ripple-Carry Adder

```
library IEEE;
use IEEE.STD_LOGIC_1164.ALL;

entity three_bit_adder is
port(x, y : in std_logic_vector (2 downto 0);
    cin : in std_logic; sum : out std_logic_vector (2 downto 0);
    cout : out std_logic);
end three_bit_adder;

architecture three_bitadd of three_bit_adder is
component full_adder
port (I1, I2, I3 : in std_logic; O1, O2 : out std_logic);
end component;
for all : full_adder use entity work.bind32 (full_add);
signal carry : std_logic_vector (1 downto 0);
begin
    M0 : full_adder port map (x(0), y(0), cin, sum(0), carry(0));
    M1 : full_adder port map (x(1), y(1), carry(0), sum(1), carry(1));
    M2 : full_adder port map (x(2), y(2), carry(1), sum(2), cout);
end three_bitadd;
```

Verilog 3-Bit Ripple-Carry Adder

```
module three_bit_adder (x, y, cin, sum, cout);
input [2:0] x, y;
input cin;
output [2:0] sum;
output cout;
wire [1:0] carry;
    FULL_ADDER M0 (x[0], y[0], cin, sum[0], carry[0]);
    FULL_ADDER M1 (x[1], y[1], carry[0], sum[1], carry[1]);
    FULL_ADDER M2 (x[2], y[2], carry[1], sum[2], cout);

/* It is assumed that the module FULL_ADDER
    (Listing 4.13) is attached by the simulator to
    the module three_bit_adder so, no need to
    rewrite the module FULL_ADDER.*/

endmodule
```

Inspect the code in Listing 4.18 and notice that there may be lag time between the steady state of each of the adders and the carryout (`cout`). This lag time produces transient states before the values of the sum and carryout settle. For example, if the inputs to the adder are 101 and 001, and the previous output of the adder is 1001, some transient states can be 0100 and 1010 before the output settles at 0110. The appearance of these transient states is called "hazards." These transient states, however, have short duration and may not be noticed.

EXAMPLE 4.10 Structural Description of a 3-Bit Magnitude Comparator Using a 3-Bit Adder

Chapter 2 covered a 2x2-bit comparison using truth tables. If the number of bits to be compared is more than two bits, the truth tables become so huge that it is too difficult to handle. In this Example, a different approach is taken. Given two numbers X and Y, each of *n* bits; if we assume X is greater than Y, then we have:

$$X - Y > 0 \tag{4.2}$$

–Y is the twos complement of $Y = \overline{Y} + 1$; substituting in Equation 4.2, the condition of $X > Y$ is rewritten as:

$$X + \overline{Y} + 1 > 0 \tag{4.3}$$

Or, Equation 4.3 can be rewritten as:

$$X + \overline{Y} > -1 \tag{4.4}$$

For n bits, –1 is $1n\ldots1111$, so Equation 4.4 can be rewritten as:

$$X+\overline{Y}>1n\ldots1111 \quad (4.5)$$

Equation 4.5 states that if X is greater than Y, then the sum of X and $\overline{Y}$ should be greater than $1n\ldots1111$. If n adders are used to add X plus $\overline{Y}$, then for X to be greater than Y, the n-bit sum should be greater than n ones; this can only happen if the n-bit adders have a final carryout of 1. So, if X is added to $\overline{Y}$ using n-bit adders, and the final carryout is 1, then it can be concluded that X > Y. If there is no final carryout, then X ≤ Y. To check for equality, it is noticed that if X = Y then:

$$X+\overline{Y}=1n\ldots1111 \quad (4.6)$$

In this Example, $n = 3$ is being considered. Figure 4.14 shows the logic diagram of the comparator.

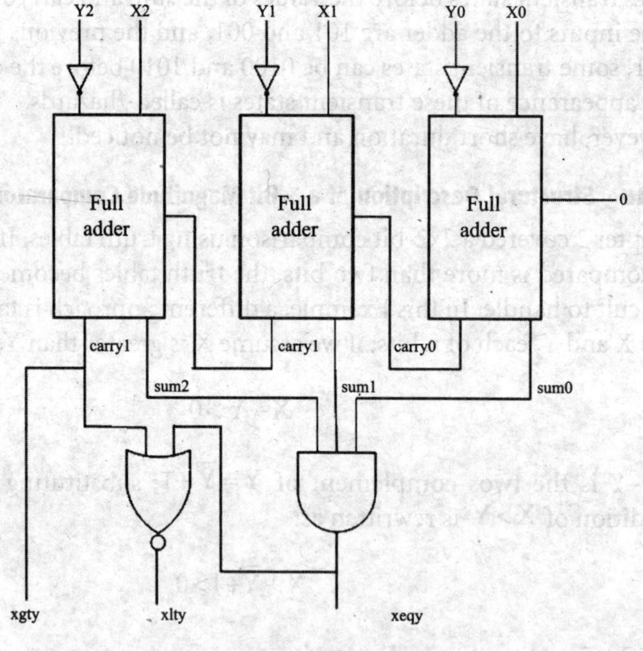

FIGURE 4.14 A full adder-based comparator.

Listing 4.19 shows the HDL code for the comparator. The HDL code for a full adder has already been written (see Listing 4.13). The full adder components (macros) are used in Listing 4.19. Since they are identical, we declare only one generic full adder as:

```
component full_adder
port(I1, I2, I3 : in std_logic; O1, O2 : out std_logic);
end component;
```

To use these components, we link their `work` Library from Listing 4.13 as:

```
for all : full_adder use entity work.bind32 (full_add); –VHDL
```

or, in Verilog, we link the module built in Listing 4.13 as:

```
FULL_ADDER M0 (X[0], Yb[0], 1'b0, sum[0], carry[0]); //Verilog
```

LISTING 4.19 HDL Description of a 3-Bit Comparator Using Adders–VHDL and Verilog

VHDL 3-Bit Comparator Using Adders

```
library IEEE;
use IEEE.STD_LOGIC_1164.ALL;

entity three_bit_cmpare is
port (X, Y : in std_logic_vector (2 downto 0);
    xgty, xlty, xeqy : buffer std_logic);
end three_bit_cmpare;

architecture cmpare of three_bit_cmpare is

--Some simulators will not allow mapping between
--buffer and out. In this
--case, change all out to buffer.

component full_adder
    port (I1, I2, I3 : in std_logic; O1, O2 : out std_logic);
end component;
component Inv
    port (I1 : in std_logic; O1 : out std_logic);
end component;
component nor2
    port (I1, I2 : in std_logic; O1 : out std_logic);
end component;
component and3
    port (I1, I2, I3 : in std_logic; O1 : out std_logic);
end component;
for all : full_adder use entity work.bind32 (full_add);
for all : Inv use entity work.bind1 (inv_0);
for all : nor2 use entity work.bind2 (nor2_0);
for all : and3 use entity work.bind3 (and3_7);
```

```
    --To reduce hazards, an AND gate is
      --implemented with a 7-ns delay.
signal sum, Yb : std_logic_vector (2 downto 0);
signal carry : std_logic_vector (1 downto 0);
begin
    in1 : inv port map (Y(0), Yb(0));
    in2 : inv port map (Y(1), Yb(1));
    in3 : inv port map (Y(2), Yb(2));
    F0 : full_adder port map (X(0), Yb(0), '0', sum(0), carry(0));
    F1 : full_adder port map (X(1), Yb(1), carry(0),
        sum(1), carry(1));
    F2 : full_adder port map (X(2), Yb(2), carry(1),
        sum(2), xgty);

--The current module could have been linked to the 3-bit adders
--designed in Listing 4.18 instead of linking to
--F0, F1, and F2, as was done here.

    a1 : and3 port map (sum(0), sum(1), sum(2), xeqy);
    n1 : nor2 port map (xeqy, xgty, xlty);
end cmpare;
```

Verilog 3-Bit Comparator Using Adders

```
module three_bit_cmpare (X, Y, xgty, xlty, xeqy);
input [2:0] X, Y;
output xgty, xlty, xeqy;
wire [1:0] carry;
wire [2:0] sum, Yb;
    not (Yb[0], Y[0]);
    not (Yb[1], Y[1]);
    not (Yb[2], Y[2]);
    FULL_ADDER M0 (X[0], Yb[0], 1'b0, sum[0], carry[0]);
    FULL_ADDER M1 (X[1], Yb[1], carry[0], sum[1], carry[1]);
    FULL_ADDER M2 (X[2], Yb[2], carry[1], sum[2], xgty);

/* The current module could have been linked to the
   3-bit adders designed in Listing 4.18 instead of
   linking to F0, F1, and F2, as was done here.*/

    and #7 (xeqy, sum[0], sum[1], sum[2]);

/* To reduce hazard use an AND gate with a delay of 7 units*/

    nor (xlty, xeqy, xgty);
endmodule
```

EXAMPLE 4.11 Structural Description of an SRAM Cell

A simple memory cell has been designed using an SR-latch, but we could have used any other latches, such as a D-latch. The cell has tri-state output. If select line (Sel) is low, the output of the cell is in high impedance. A Read/Write (R/W) input signal controls the cell's cycle mode. If R/W is high, the cell is in read cycle; if low, the cell is in write cycle. Table 4.6 shows the excitation table of the cell, with inputs (Select, R/W, Data-In, Current State) and the corresponding outputs (Next State, Output). From the current state and next state, we determine S and R of the latch according to Table 4.2. For example, if the current state is 0 and next state 0, then two combinations of SR can generate this transition: S = 0, R = 0, and S = 0, R = 1; so SR = 0x where x is "don't care."

TABLE 4.6 Excitation Table of an SRAM Memory Cell

Select	R/W	Data-in	Current State	Next State	Output	Latch	
Sel	RW	Din	Q	Q+	O1	S	R
0	x	x	Q	Q	Z	0	0
1	0	0	0	0	0	0	x
1	0	0	1	0	0	0	1
1	0	1	0	1	1	1	0
1	0	1	1	1	1	x	0
1	1	0	0	0	0	0	x
1	1	0	1	1	1	x	0
1	1	1	0	0	0	0	x
1	1	1	1	1	1	x	0

From Table 4.6, K-maps are constructed (see Figure 4.15). From the K-maps, find that:

$$S = \mathrm{Sel}\,\overline{\mathrm{RW}}\,\mathrm{Din}$$

$$R = \mathrm{Sel}\,\overline{\mathrm{RW}}\,\overline{\mathrm{Din}}$$

$$\mathrm{O1} = \mathrm{Sel}\,\overline{\mathrm{RW}}\,\mathrm{Din} + \mathrm{Sel}\,\mathrm{RW}\,\mathrm{O} = R + \mathrm{Sel}\,\mathrm{RW}\,\mathrm{O} \quad (\text{for Sel} = 1)$$

$$\mathrm{O1} = Z \quad (\text{for Sel} = 0)$$

Din Q / sel R/W	00	01	11	10
00	0	0	0	0
01	0	0	0	0
11	0	x	x	0
10	0	0	x	1

S

DinQ / sel R/W	00	01	11	10
00	0	0	0	0
01	0	0	0	0
11	x	0	0	x
10	x	1	0	0

R

Din Q / Sel R/W	00	01	11	10
00	Z	Z	Z	Z
01	Z	Z	Z	Z
11	0	1	1	0
10	0	0	1	1

O1

FIGURE 4.15 K-maps for Table 4.6.

The logic symbol and logic diagram of the cell are shown in Figures 4.16a and 4.16b, respectively.

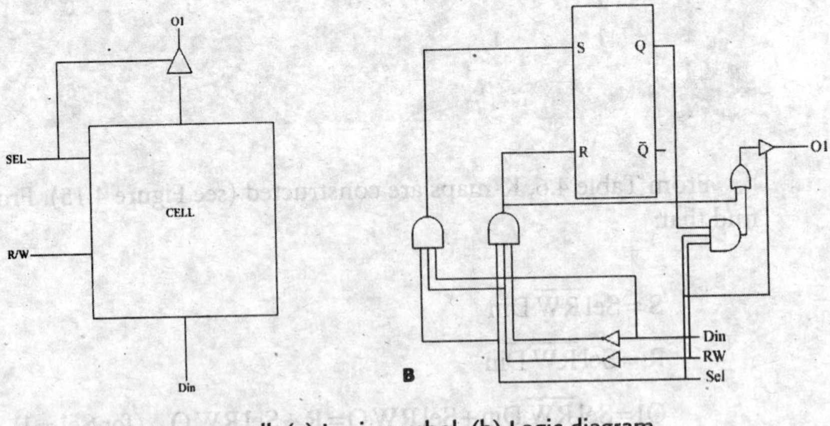

FIGURE 4.16 SRAM memory cell. (a) Logic symbol. (b) Logic diagram.

The code for the memory cell is shown in Listing 4.20. The VHDL code uses the SR-latch that we designed in Listing 4.14 as a component (macro), using the statement:

```
component SR_Latch
port (I1, I2 : in std_logic; O1, O2 : buffer std_logic);
end component;
```

which declares a generic SR-latch. This latch is linked to the memory cell code by the statement:

```
for all : SR_Latch use entity work.bind22 (SR_Latch);
```

The VHDL statement:

```
SR1 : SR_Latch port map (R, S, Q, open);
```

assigns R and S as the inputs of the SR-latch `SR1`. The noninverted output of the latch is assigned to `Q`, and the inverted output is left open; `open` is a VHDL predefined word. For Verilog, we link the module of the SR-latch that we designed in Listing 4.14 to the memory cell code by the statement:

```
SR_Latch RS1 (R, S, Q, Qbar);
```

which links the module `SR_Latch` to the current module `memory`.

LISTING 4.20 HDL Description of an SRAM Memory Cell—VHDL and Verilog

VHDL SRAM Memory Cell Description

```
library IEEE;
use IEEE.STD_LOGIC_1164.ALL;

entity memory is
    port (Sel, RW, Din : in std_logic; O1: buffer std_logic);
end memory;

architecture memory_str of memory is
--Some simulators will not allow mapping between
--buffer and out. In this
--case, change all out to buffer.

component and3
    port (I1, I2, I3 : in std_logic; O1 : out std_logic);
end component;

component inv
    port (I1 : in std_logic; O1 : out std_logic);
```

```
end component;

component or2
    port (I1, I2 : in std_logic; O1 : out std_logic);
end component;

component bufif1
    port (I1, I2 : in std_logic; O1 : out std_logic);
end component;

component SR_Latch
    port (I1, I2 : in std_logic; O1, O2 : buffer std_logic);
end component;
for all : and3 use entity work.bind3 (and3_0);
for all : inv use entity work.bind1 (inv_0);
for all : or2 use entity work.bind2 (or2_0);
for all : bufif1 use entity work.bind2 (bufif1);
for all : SR_Latch use entity work.bind22 (SR_Latch);
signal RWb, Dinb, S, S1, R, O11, Q : std_logic;
begin
    in1 : inv port map (RW, RWb);
    in2 : inv port map (Din, Dinb);
    a1 : and3 port map (Sel, RWb, Din, S);
    a2 : and3 port map (Sel, RWb, Dinb, R);
    SR1 : SR_Latch port map (S, R, Q, open);
--open is a predefined word;
--it indicates that the port is left open.
    a3 : and3 port map (Sel, RW, Q, S1);
    or1 : or2 port map (S1, S, O11);
    buf1 : bufif1 port map (O11, Sel, O1);
end memory_str;
```

Verilog SRAM Memory Cell Description

```
module memory (Sel, RW, Din, O1);
input Sel, RW, Din;
output O1;
    not (RWb, RW);
    not (Dinb, Din);
    and (S, Sel, RWb, Din);
    and (R, Sel, RWb, Dinb);
    SR_Latch RS1 (R, S, Q, Qbar);
    and (S1, Sel, RW, Q);
    or (O11, S1, S);
    bufif1 (O1, O11, Sel);
endmodule
```

4.4 STATE MACHINES

Synchronous sequential circuits are called "state machines." The main components of the state machine are latches and flip-flops; additional combinational components may also be present. Synchronous clock pulses are fed to all flip-flops and latches of the machine. There are two types of synchronous sequential circuits: Mealy and Moore circuits. The output or next state of Mealy circuits depends on the inputs and the present state of the flip-flops/latches. The output or next state of the Moore circuit depends only on the present states. Present state and next state for a particular flip-flop are the same pin (output Q). The current state is the value of Q just before the present clock pulse or edge; the next state is the value of Q after the clock pulse or the edge. To analyze a state machine, we perform the following steps:

1. Determine the number of states. If the system is *n*-bit, then the number of flip-flops is *n*. The number of flip-flops here is calculated according to the "classical method," where the number of flip-flops is the minimum possible. Another method in which each state is represented by one flip-flop is frequently used because analysis of the system is easier than when using the classical method. For example, if the system is 3-bit, then the classical method requires three flip-flops, while the one flip-flop per state requires eight flip-flops. In this chapter, the classical method is implemented.
2. Construct a state diagram that shows the transition between states. At each state, consider it current state; after the clock is active (edge or pulse), the system moves from current state to next state. Determine the next state according to the input if the system is Mealy, or according to the current state only if the system is Moore. Also, determine the output (if any) of the system at this current state.
3. From the state diagram, construct the excitation table that tabulates the inputs and the outputs. The inputs include the current states, and the outputs include the next states. The table also includes the inputs of the flip-flops or latches that constitute the state machine. For example, if the flip-flops implemented in a certain machine are JK flip-flops, then the inputs J and K of the flip-flop are determined according to the transition from current to next state. If, for example, the current state is 0 and the next is 0, then J = 0 and K = x (don't care). If the flip-flops are D flip-flops, then the D's of the flip-flops are equal to the corresponding next states.
4. Find J and K in terms of the inputs and minimize using K-maps or any other appropriate method.
5. If using structural description to simulate the system, draw a logic diagram of the system using appropriate available macros, such as latches, adders, and flip-flops.

More details about state machines can be found in [Hayes98] and [Nelson95]. Following are some examples of state machines. More examples of state machines and counters will be discussed in Chapter 6, "Procedures, Tasks, and Functions"; and Chapter 7, "Mixed-Type Descriptions."

Example 4.12 Structural Description of a 3-Bit Synchronous Counter with Active Low Clear

The logic symbol of the counter is shown in Figure 4.17. The counter is constructed from JK flip-flops.

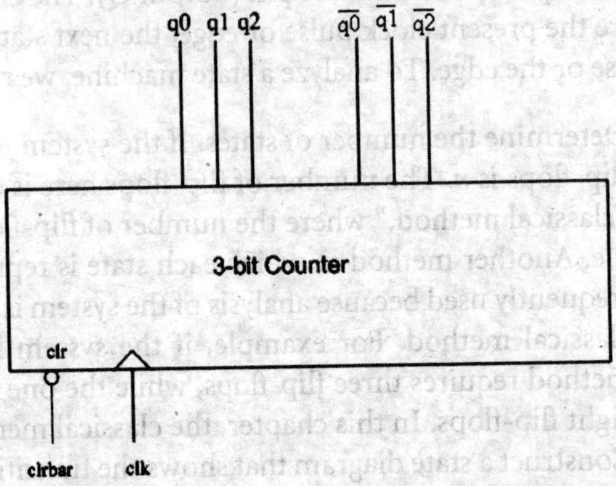

FIGURE 4.17 Logic symbol of a 3-bit counter with active low clear.

The state diagram of the counter is shown in Figure 4.18. Since the counter counts from 0 to 7, we need three flip-flops to cover that count. The transition depends on current state and the input (clear). The next step is to construct the excitation table.

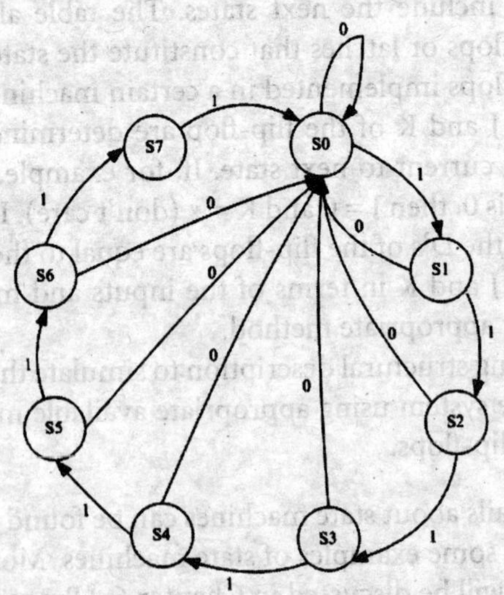

FIGURE 4.18 State diagram of a 3-bit counter with active low clear.

Table 4.7a shows the excitation table of a JK flip-flop, and Table 4.7b shows the excitation table of the counter.

TABLE 4.7A Excitation Table for a JK Flip-Flop

Inputs Current State	Outputs Next State	J	K
0	1	1	x
0	0	0	x
1	0	x	1
1	1	x	0

TABLE 4.7B Excitation Table for 3-Bit Synchronous Counter with Active High Clear

Inputs				Outputs					
Input	Current State			Next State			Flip-Flops		
clrbar	q2	q1	q0	q2+	q1+	q0+	J2K2	J1K1	J0K0
0	x	x	x	0	0	0	01	01	01
1	0	0	0	0	0	1	0x	0x	1x
1	0	0	1	0	1	0	0x	1x	x1
1	0	1	0	0	1	1	0x	x0	1x
1	0	1	1	1	0	0	1x	x1	x1
1	1	0	0	1	0	1	x0	0x	1x
1	1	0	1	1	1	0	x0	1x	x1
1	1	1	0	1	1	1	x0	x0	1x
1	1	1	1	0	0	0	x1	x1	x1

Now we construct the K-maps of the previous table. Figure 4.19 shows the K-maps of Table 4.7b.

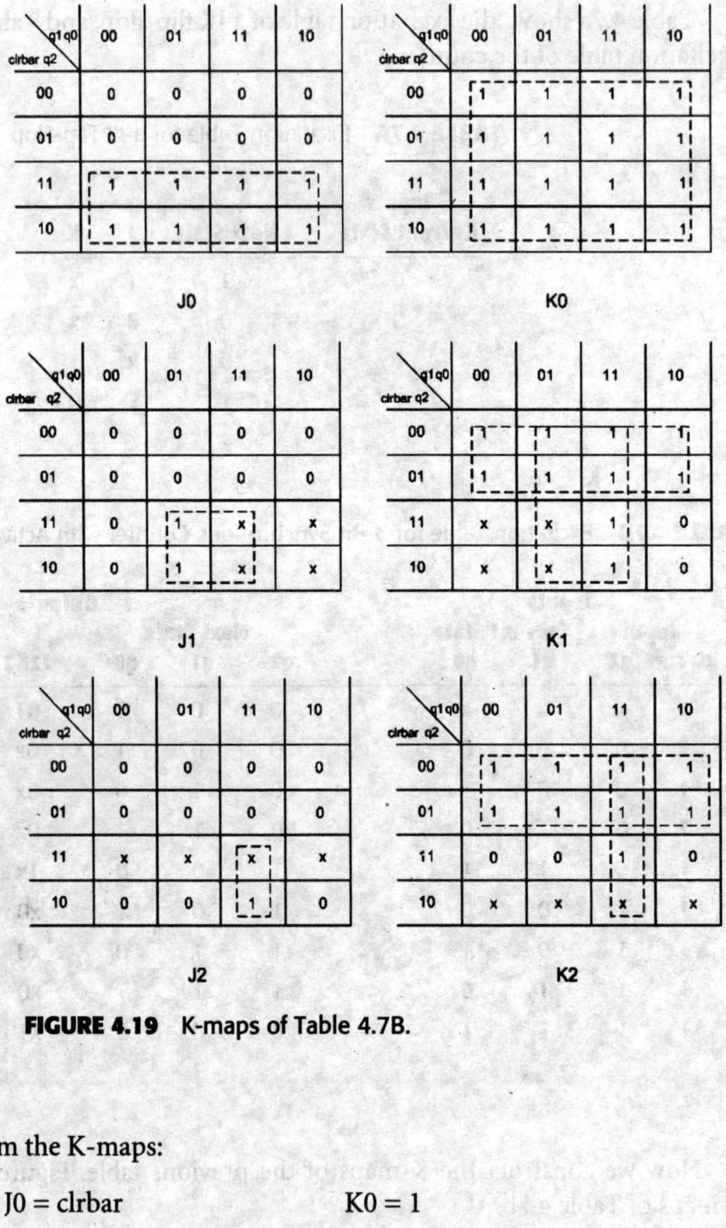

FIGURE 4.19 K-maps of Table 4.7B.

From the K-maps:

J0 = clrbar K0 = 1

J1 = clrbar q0 K1 = q0 + $\overline{clrbar}$

J2 = clrbar q0 q1 K2 = q0 q1 + $\overline{clrbar}$

Next, draw the logic diagram of the counter (see Figure 4.20).

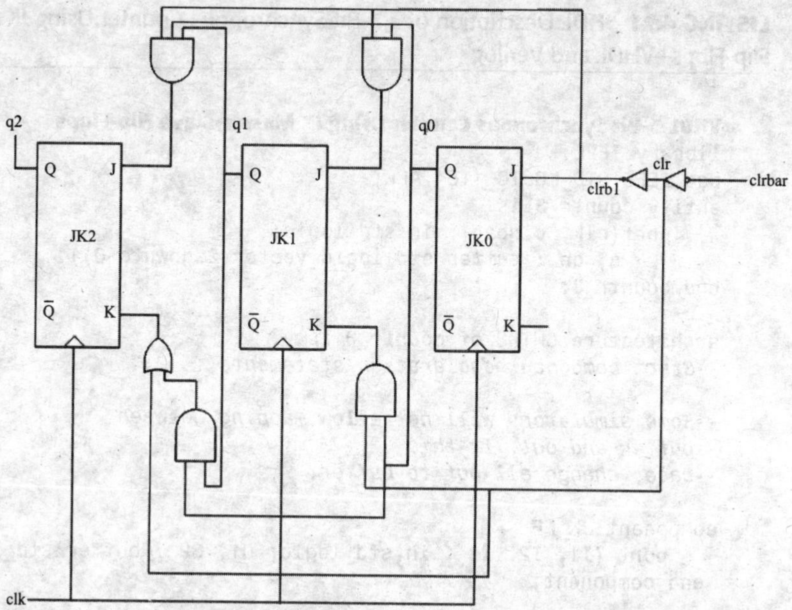

FIGURE 4.20 Logic diagram of a 3-bit synchronous counter with active low clear using JK master-slave flip-flops.

Now we write the structural description of the counter. The previously built macros and modules are used, as well as the JK flip-flop designed in Listing 4.17. In VHDL, we declare it as `component`:

```
component JK_FF
    port (I1, I2, I3 : in std_logic; O1, O2 : buffer std_logic);
end component;

for all : JK_FF use entity work.bind32 (JK_Master);
```

The entity where the code of the JK flip-flop was written is `bind32`; `JK_Master` is the name of the architecture.

In Verilog, we link the current module to the `JK_FF` module designed in Listing 4.17B as:

```
JK_FF FF0 (clrb1, 1'b1, clk, q[0], qb[0]);
```

Listing 4.21 shows the HDL code of the counter. The basic VHDL package does not include definitions of the components `JK_FF`, `inv`, `and2`, or `or2`. Several CAD vendors can provide packages that contain these definitions; if these packages are included in Listing 4.21, then there is no need for component declaration statements.

LISTING 4.21 HDL Description of a 3-Bit Synchronous Counter Using JK Master-Slave Flip-Flops—VHDL and Verilog

VHDL 3-Bit Synchronous Counter Using JK Master-Slave Flip-Flops

```
library IEEE;
use IEEE.STD_LOGIC_1164.ALL;
entity countr_3 is
    port(clk, clrbar : in std_logic;
        q, qb : buffer std_logic_vector(2 downto 0));
end countr_3;

architecture CNTR3 of countr_3 is
--Start component declaration statements

--Some simulators will not allow mapping between
--buffer and out. In this
--case, change all out to buffer.

component JK_FF
    port (I1, I2, I3 : in std_logic; O1, O2 : buffer std_logic);
 end component;

component inv
    port (I1 : in std_logic; O1 : out std_logic);
end component;

component and2
    port (I1, I2 : in std_logic; O1 : out std_logic);
end component;

component or2
    port (I1, I2 : in std_logic; O1 : out std_logic);
end component;
for all : JK_FF use entity work.bind32 (JK_Master);
for all : inv use entity work.bind1 (inv_0);
for all : and2 use entity work.bind2 (and2_0);
for all : or2 use entity work.bind2 (or2_0);
signal J1, K1, J2, K2, clr, clrb1, s1 : std_logic;
begin
    FF0 : JK_FF port map (clrb1, '1', clk, q(0), qb(0));
    -- clrb1 has the same logic as clrbar

    A1 : and2 port map (clrb1, q(0), J1);
    inv1 : inv port map (clr, clrb1);
    inv2 : inv port map (clrbar, clr);

    r1 : or2 port map (q(0), clr, K1);
    FF1 : JK_FF port map (J1, K1, clk, q(1), qb(1));
    A2 : and2 port map (q(0), q(1), s1);
    A3 : and2 port map (clrb1, s1, J2);
    r2 : or2 port map (s1, clr, K2);
```

```
    FF2 : JK_FF port map (J2, K2, clk, q(2), qb(2));
end CNTR3;
```

Verilog 3-Bit Synchronous Counter Using JK Master-Slave Flip-Flops

```
module countr_3 (clk, clrbar, q, qb);
input clk, clrbar;
output [2:0] q, qb;

    JK_FF FF0(clrb1, 1'b1, clk, q[0], qb[0]);
// clrb1 has the same logic as clrbar
    and A1 (J1, q[0], clrb1);

/*The name of the and gate "A1" and all other
 gates in this code are optional; it can be omitted.*/

    not inv1 (clrb1, clr);
    not inv2 (clr, clrbar);

    or r1 (K1, q[0], clr);
    JK_FF FF1 (J1, K1, clk, q[1], qb[1]);
    and A2 (s1, q[0], q[1]);
    and A3 (J2, clrb1, s1);
    or or2 (K2, s1, clr);
    JK_FF FF2(J2, K2, clk, q[2], qb[2]);
endmodule
```

The simulation waveform of the counter is shown in Figure 4.21. The waveform shows the clear signal (clrbar) to be synchronous; it has to wait for the clock to be active.

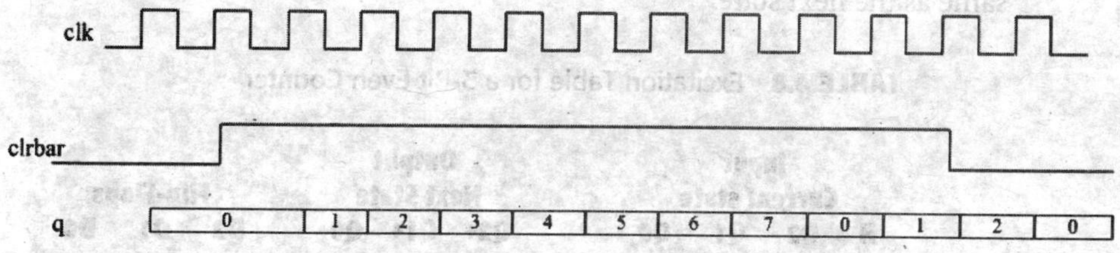

FIGURE 4.21 Simulation waveform of a 3-bit synchronous counter with active low clear.

EXAMPLE 4.13 Structural Description of a 3-Bit Synchronous Even Counter with Active High Hold

The counter here is counting up. The number of flip-flops is three. First, draw the state diagram of the counter, as shown in Figure 4.22. For all even current states, the next state is the next even. For example, if the current state is 010 (2), then the next state is 100 (4). For any odd state that is invalid, the next state can be any state that ensures the continuity of the count. For example, if the current state is the invalid state 001, the next state can be 000. In the case of invalid states, we choose the next state that yields the minimum number of minterms. This will be explained when the excitation table is formed.

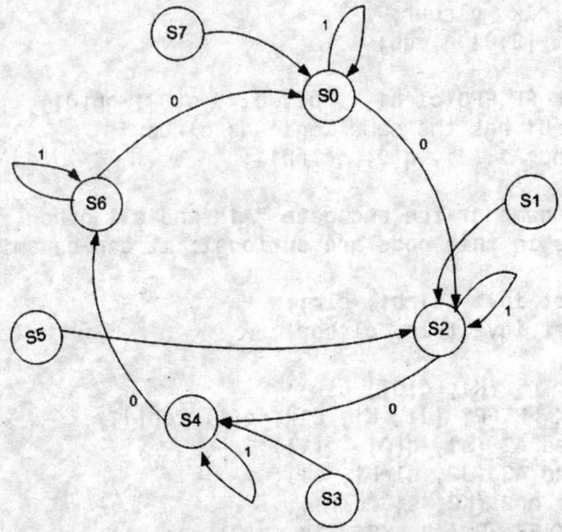

FIGURE 4.22 State diagram of an even 3-bit counter. The Hold is shown in the diagram as input.

From the state diagram, we generate the excitation table. Table 4.8 shows the excitation table of the counter using D flip-flops. The Ds of the flip-flop are the same as the next state.

TABLE 4.8 Excitation Table for a 3-Bit Even Counter

Input				Output					
Current state				Next State			Flip-Flops		
H	**Q2**	**Q1**	**Q0**	**Q2+**	**Q1+**	**Q0+**	**D2**	**D1**	**D0**
0	0	0	0	0	1	0	0	1	0
0	0	0	1	0	1	0	0	0	0
0	0	1	0	1	0	0	1	0	0
0	0	1	1	1	0	0	0	0	0
0	1	0	0	1	1	0	1	1	0
0	1	0	1	0	1	0	0	0	0
0	1	1	0	0	0	0	0	0	0
0	1	1	1	0	0	0	0	0	0

Input				Output			Flip-Flops		
Current state				Next State					
H	Q2	Q1	Q0	Q2+	Q1+	Q0+	D2	D1	D0
1	0	0	0	0	0	0	0	0	0
1	0	0	1	0	0	0	0	0	0
1	0	1	0	0	1	0	0	1	0
1	0	1	1	0	0	0	0	0	0
1	1	0	0	1	0	0	1	0	0
1	1	0	1	0	0	0	0	0	0
1	1	1	0	1	1	0	1	1	0
1	1	1	1	0	0	0	0	0	0

From the excitation table, we generate the K-maps. Figure 4.23 shows the K-maps of the counter. Referring to the K-maps, for odd states, any next state can be assigned, since odd states are not valid. The only restriction is that the next state should yield a valid state. We select the next state that yields elimination of more terms. For example, if the current state is 101, we select the next state 100; this yields less minterms.

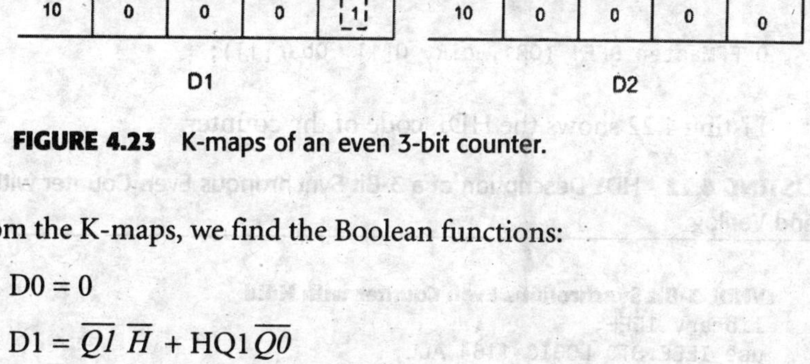

FIGURE 4.23 K-maps of an even 3-bit counter.

From the K-maps, we find the Boolean functions:

$$D0 = 0$$

$$D1 = \overline{Q1}\,\overline{H} + HQ1\overline{Q0}$$

$$D2 = Q2\overline{Q1}\,\overline{Q0} + \overline{Q0}HQ2 + \overline{H}\,\overline{Q2}Q1$$

Using the above the Boolean functions, we draw the logic diagram of the counter. Figure 4.24 shows the logic symbol and logic diagram of the counter.

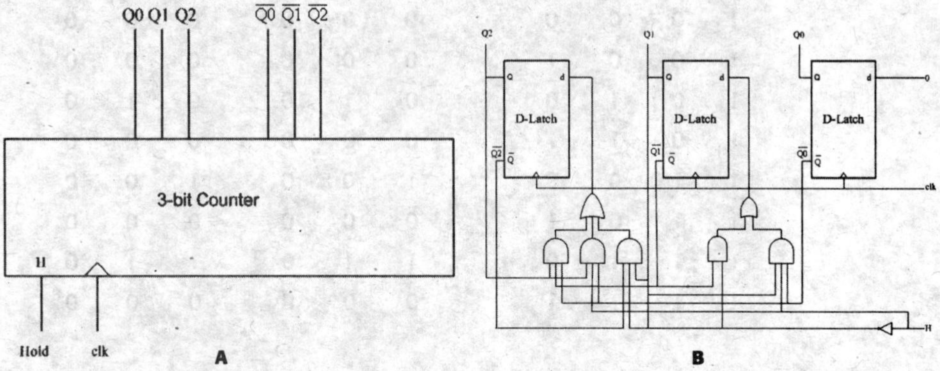

FIGURE 4.24 Three-bit even counter. (a) Logic symbol. (b) Logic diagram.

Next, we write the HDL code for the counter. The macros for the D master-slave flip-flops developed in Listing 4.16 are used. In VHDL code, we write:

```
component D_FF
port (I1, I2 : in std_logic; O1, O2 : buffer std_logic);
end component;

for all : D_FF use entity work.bind22 (D_FFMaster);
```

In Verilog, we write the code that links the `D_FFMaster` designed in Listing 4.16 to the new module:

```
D_FFMaster DFF1 (OR1, clk, Q[1], Qbar[1]);
```

Listing 4.22 shows the HDL code of the counter.

LISTING 4.22 HDL Description of a 3-Bit Synchronous Even Counter with Hold—VHDL and Verilog

VHDL 3-Bit Synchronous Even Counter with Hold

```
library IEEE;
use IEEE.STD_LOGIC_1164.ALL;

entity CTR_EVEN is
    port (H, clk : in std_logic;
        Q, Qbar : buffer std_logic_vector (2 downto 0));
```

```
end CTR_EVEN;

architecture Counter_even of CTR_EVEN is
--Some simulators will not allow mapping between
--buffer and out. In this
--case, change all out to buffer.

component inv
    port (I1 : in std_logic; O1 : out std_logic);
end component;

component and2
    port (I1, I2 : in std_logic; O1 : out std_logic);
end component;

component or2
    port (I1, I2 : in std_logic; O1 : out std_logic);
end component;

component and3
    port (I1, I2, I3 : in std_logic; O1 : out std_logic);
end component;

component or3
    port (I1, I2, I3 : in std_logic; O1 : out std_logic);
end component;

component D_FF
    port (I1, I2 : in std_logic; O1, O2 : buffer std_logic);
end component;

for all : D_FF use entity work.bind22 (D_FFMaster);
for all : inv use entity work.bind1 (inv_0);
for all : and2 use entity work.bind2 (and2_0);
for all : and3 use entity work.bind3 (and3_0);
for all : or2 use entity work.bind2 (or2_0);
for all : or3 use entity work.bind3 (or3_0);
signal Hbar, a1, a2, a3, a4, a5, OR11, OR22 : std_logic;
begin
    DFF0 : D_FF port map ('0', clk, Q(0), Qbar(0));
    inv1 : inv port map (H, Hbar);
    an1 : and2 port map (Hbar, Qbar(1), a1);
    an2 : and3 port map (H, Q(1), Qbar(0), a2);
    r1 : or2 port map (a2, a1, OR11);

    DFF1 : D_FF port map (OR11, clk, Q(1), Qbar(1));
    an3 : and3 port map   (Q(2), Qbar(1), Qbar(0), a3);
    an4 : and3 port map (Qbar(0), H, Q(2), a4);
    an5 : and3 port map (Hbar, Qbar(2), Q(1), a5);
    r2 : or3 port map (a3, a4, a5, OR22);

    DFF2 : D_FF port map (OR22, clk, Q(2), Qbar(2));
```

```
end Counter_even;
```

Verilog 3-Bit Synchronous Even Counter with Hold

```
module CTR_EVEN (H, clk, Q, Qbar);

input H, clk;
output [2:0] Q, Qbar;
    D_FFMaster DFF0 (1'b0, clk, Q[0], Qbar[0]);
    not (Hbar, H);
    and (a1, Qbar[1], Hbar);
    and (a2, H, Q[1], Qbar[0]);
    or (OR1, a1, a2);

    D_FFMaster DFF1 (OR1, clk, Q[1], Qbar[1]);

    and (a3, Q[2], Qbar[1], Qbar[0]);
    and (a4, Qbar[0], H, Q[2]);
    and (a5, Hbar, Qbar[2], Q[1]);
    or (OR2, a3, a4, a5);

    D_FFMaster DFF2 (OR2, clk, Q[2], Qbar[2]);

endmodule
```

The simulation waveform of the counter is shown in Figure 4.25. As shown in the figure, the Hold is active high. If it is high and the clock pulse is present, the counter holds its output Q to the present value. Some transient states may appear in the simulation due to hazards.

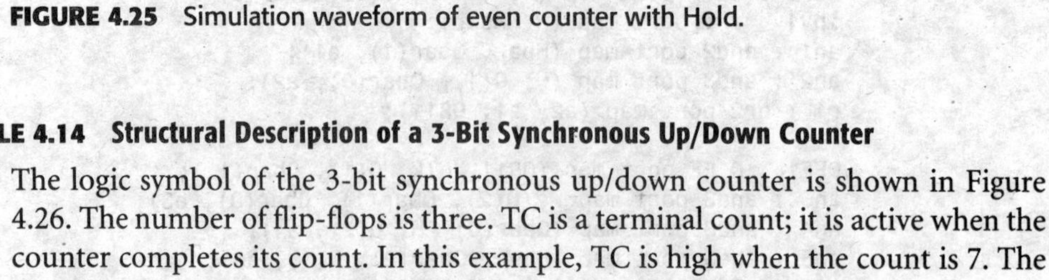

FIGURE 4.25 Simulation waveform of even counter with Hold.

EXAMPLE 4.14 Structural Description of a 3-Bit Synchronous Up/Down Counter

The logic symbol of the 3-bit synchronous up/down counter is shown in Figure 4.26. The number of flip-flops is three. TC is a terminal count; it is active when the counter completes its count. In this example, TC is high when the count is 7. The clear here is active high; if it is high, the output of the counter is reset to zero.

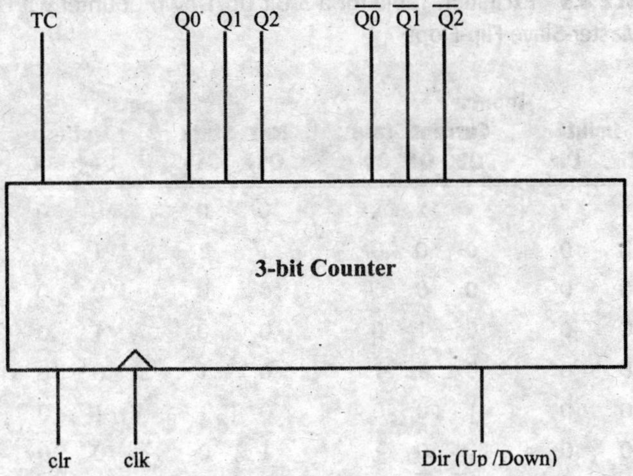

FIGURE 4.26 Symbol logic diagram of an up/down 3-bit counter.

The state diagram of the counter is shown in Figure 4.27. The input signal Dir determines whether the counter counts up or down. If Dir = 0, the counter counts down; if Dir = 1, the counter counts up. TC is an output; it is only high when the count is 7. From the state diagram we form the excitation table of the counter (see Table 4.9).

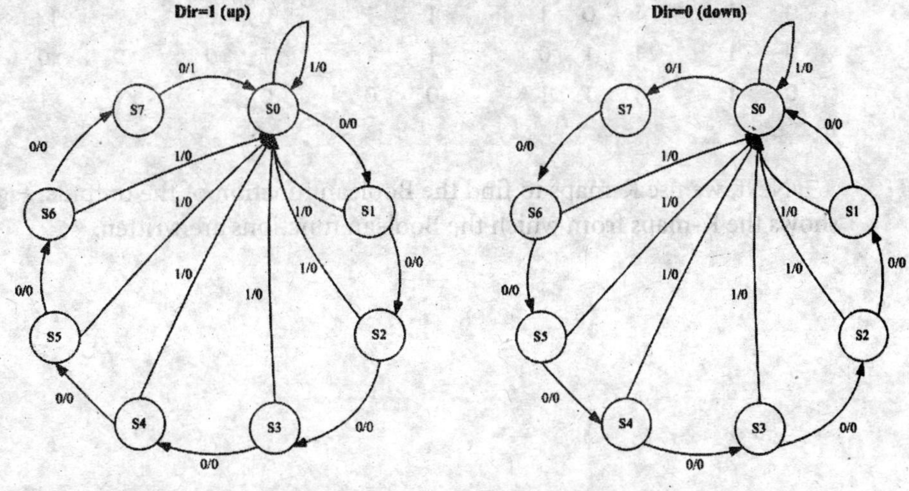

FIGURE 4.27 State diagram of a 3-bit synchronous up/down counter.

TABLE 4.9 Excitation Table for a 3-Bit Up/Down Counter with a Terminal Count, Using JK Master-Slave Flip-Flops

Inputs					Outputs						
Input		Current State			Next State		Output		Flip-Flop		
Clr	Dir	Q2	Q1	Q0	Q2+	Q1+	Q0+	TC	J2K2	J1K1	J0K0
1	x	x	x	x	0	0	0	0	01	01	01
0	0	0	0	0	1	1	1	1	1x	1x	1x
0	0	0	0	1	0	0	0	0	0x	0x	x1
0	0	0	1	0	0	0	1	0	0x	x1	1x
0	0	0	1	1	0	1	0	0	0x	1x	x1
0	0	1	0	0	0	1	1	0	x1	1x	1x
0	0	1	0	1	1	0	0	0	x0	0x	x1
0	0	1	1	0	1	0	1	0	x0	x1	1x
0	0	1	1	1	1	1	0	0	x0	x0	x1
0	1	0	0	0	0	0	1	0	0x	0x	1x
0	1	0	0	1	0	1	0	0	0x	1x	x1
0	1	0	1	0	0	1	1	0	0x	x0	1x
0	1	0	1	1	1	0	0	0	1x	x1	x1
0	1	1	0	0	1	0	1	0	x0	0x	1x
0	1	1	0	1	1	1	0	0	x0	1x	x1
0	1	1	1	0	1	1	1	0	x0	x0	1x
0	1	1	1	1	0	0	0	1	x1	x1	x1

Next, we use K-maps to find the Boolean function of the outputs. Figure 4.28 shows the K-maps from which the Boolean functions are written.

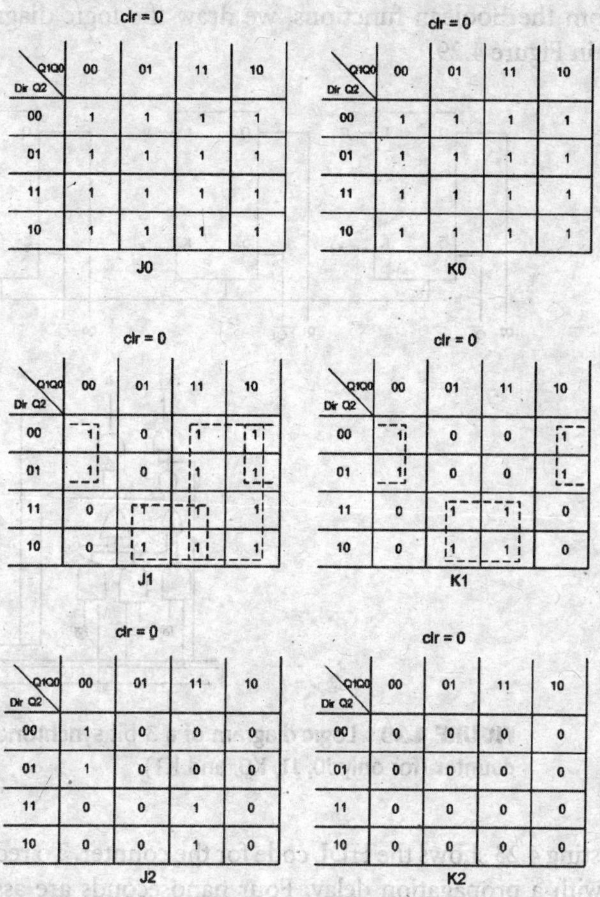

FIGURE 4.28 K-maps of a 3-bit synchronous up/down counter.

$$J0=\overline{clr}=0=\overline{clr} \quad K0=\overline{clr}+1. \quad clr=1$$

$$J1=\overline{clr}(\overline{Dir}\,\overline{Q0}+Q1+Dir\,Q0), \quad K1=\overline{clr}(\overline{Dir}\,\overline{Q0}+Dir\,Q0)=clr$$

$$J1=\overline{clr}(\overline{Dir}\,\overline{Q0}+Q1+Dir\,Q0), \quad K1=\overline{clr}(\overline{Dir}\,\overline{Q0}+Dir\,Q0)=clr$$

$$TC=\overline{clr}(\overline{Q0}\,\overline{Q1}\,\overline{Q2}\,\overline{Dir}+Q0\,Q1\,Q2\,Dir)$$

From the Boolean functions, we draw the logic diagram of the counter, as shown in Figure 4.29.

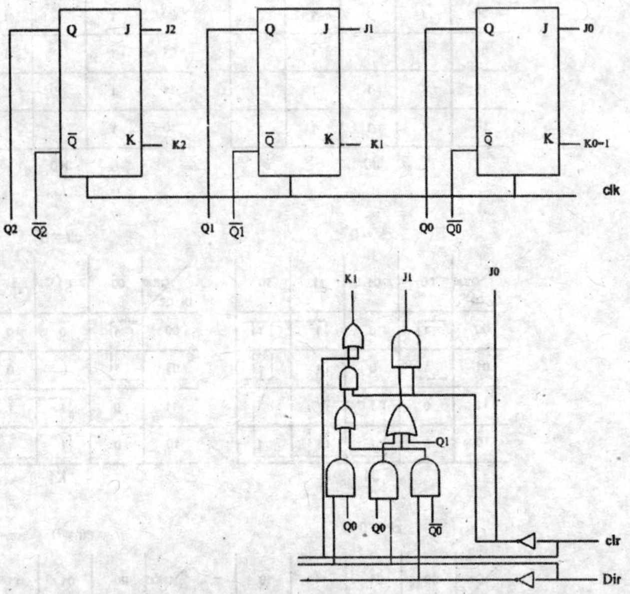

FIGURE 4.29 Logic diagram of a 3-bit synchronous up/down counter (for only J0, J1, K0, and K1).

Listing 4.23 shows the HDL code for the counter. To reduce the hazards, we use gates with a propagation delay. Four nanoseconds are assigned for all primitive gates, except an inverter that is assigned 1 ns.

LISTING 4.23 HDL Description of a 3-Bit Synchronous Up/Down Counter with Clear and Terminal Count–VHDL and Verilog

VHDL 3-Bit Synchronous Up/Down Counter with Clear and Terminal Count

```
library IEEE;
use IEEE.STD_LOGIC_1164.ALL;

entity up_down is
    port (clr, Dir, clk : in std_logic; TC : out std_logic;
        Q, Qbar : buffer std_logic_vector (2 downto 0));
end up_down;

architecture Ctr_updown of up_down is
--Some simulators will not allow mapping between
--buffer and out. In this
--case, change all out to buffer.
```

```
component inv
    port (I1 : in std_logic; O1 : out std_logic);
end component;

component and2
    port (I1, I2 : in std_logic; O1 : out std_logic);
end component;

component or2
    port (I1, I2 : in std_logic; O1 : out std_logic);
end component;

component and3
    port (I1, I2, I3 : in std_logic; O1 : out std_logic);
end component;

component JK_FF
port (I1, I2, I3 : in std_logic; O1, O2 : buffer std_logic);
end component;

for all : JK_FF use entity work.bind32 (JK_Master);
for all : inv use entity work.bind1 (inv_1);
for all : and2 use entity work.bind2 (and2_4);
for all : and3 use entity work.bind3 (and3_4);
for all : or2 use entity work.bind2 (or2_4);

signal clrbar, Dirbar, J1, K1, J2, K2 : std_logic;
signal s : std_logic_vector (11 downto 0);
begin
    in1 : inv port map (clr, clrbar);
    in2 : inv port map (Dir, Dirbar);
    an1 : and2 port map (Dirbar, Qbar(0), s(0));
    an2 : and2 port map (Dir, Q(0), s(1));
    r1 : or2 port map (s(0), s(1), s(2));
    an3 : and2 port map (s(2), clrbar, s(3));
    r2 : or2 port map (s(3), clr, K1);
    r3 : or2 port map (s(2), Q(1), s(4));
    an4 : and2 port map (clrbar, s(4), J1);
    an5 : and3 port map (Dirbar, Qbar(1), Qbar(0), s(5));
    an6 : and3 port map (Dir, Q(1), Q(0), s(6));
    r4 : or2 port map (s(6), s(5), s(7));
    an7 : and2 port map (s(7), clrbar, J2);
    r5 : or2 port map (J2, clr, K2);

    JKFF0 : JK_FF port map (clrbar, '1', clk, Q(0), Qbar(0));
    JKFF1 : JK_FF port map (J1, K1, clk, Q(1), Qbar(1));
    JKFF2 : JK_FF port map (J2, K2, clk, Q(2), Qbar(2));

    an8 : and3 port map (clrbar, Qbar(1), Qbar(0), S(8));
    an9 : and3 port map (Dirbar, Qbar(2), s(8), S(9));
```

```
--For an8 and an9,  we could have used 5-input and gate;
--but two and gates with a reasonable number of
--fan-in (three-input) is preferred. Same
--argument for an10 and an11*/

    an10 : and3 port map (clrbar, Q(0), Q(1), S(10));
    an11 : and3 port map (Dir, Q(2), s(10), S(11));
    r6 : or2 port map (s(9), s(11), TC);
end Ctr_updown;
```

Verilog 3-Bit Synchronous Up/Down Counter with Clear and Terminal Count

```
module up_down (clr, Dir, clk, Q, Qbar, TC);
input clr, Dir, clk;
output [2:0] Q, Qbar;
output TC;
    not #1 (clrbar, clr);
    not #1 (Dirbar, Dir);
    and #4 (s0, Dirbar, Qbar[0]);
    and #4 (s1, Dir, Q[0]);        or #4 (s2, s0, s1);
    and #4 (s3, s2, clrbar);
    or #4 (K1, s3, clr);
    or #4 (s4, s2, Q[1]);
    and #4 (J1, clrbar, s4);
    and #4 (s5, Dirbar, Qbar[1], Qbar[0]);
    and #4 (s6, Dir, Q[1], Q[0]);
    or #4 (s7, s6, s5);
    and #4 (J2, s7, clrbar);
    or #4 (K2, J2, clr);

    JK_FF JKFF0 (clrbar, 1'b1, clk, Q[0], Qbar[0]);
    JK_FF JKFF1 (J1, K1, clk, Q[1], Qbar[1]);
    JK_FF JKFF2 (J2, K2, clk, Q[2], Qbar[2]);

    and #4 an8 (s8, clrbar, Qbar[1], Qbar[0]);
    and #4 an9 (s9, Dirbar, Qbar[2], s8);

/* For an8 and an9, a five-input and gate could have been used;
    but two and gates with a reasonable number of fan-in
    (three-input) is preferred. Same argument for an10 and an11*/

    and #4 an10 (s10, clrbar, Q[0], Q[1]);
    and #4 an11 (s11, Dir, Q[2], s10);
    or #4 (TC, s9, s11);
endmodule
```

The simulation waveform of the counter is shown in Figure 4.30.

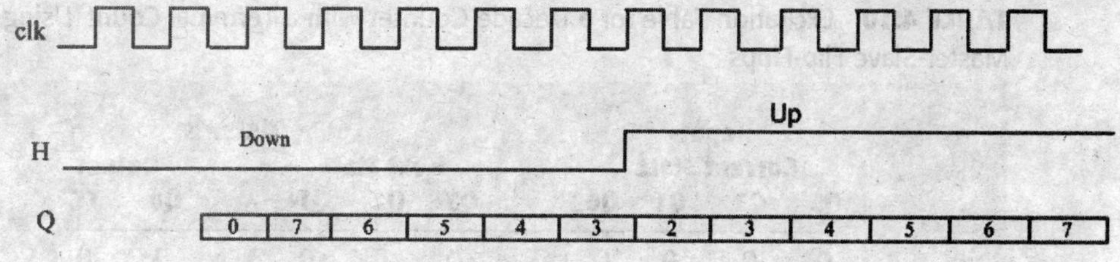

FIGURE 4.30 Simulation waveform of an up/down counter. When the count is 3, the Dir (up/down) changes from down to up count. Due to the synchronous nature of the Dir signal, the counter continues counting down to 2, and then starts counting up to 3, 4, 5, and so forth.

EXAMPLE 4.15 Structural Description of a 3-Bit Synchronous Decade Counter

Decade up counters count from 0 to 9, and the number of flip-flops to cover all counts is four. The state diagram of the counter is shown in Figure 4.31a. There are invalid states from 10 to 14. If any one of these invalid states is a current state, then the next state can be any state that restores continuity of the count. As before, the next states selected yield more minimization. This is determined when we generate the K-maps.

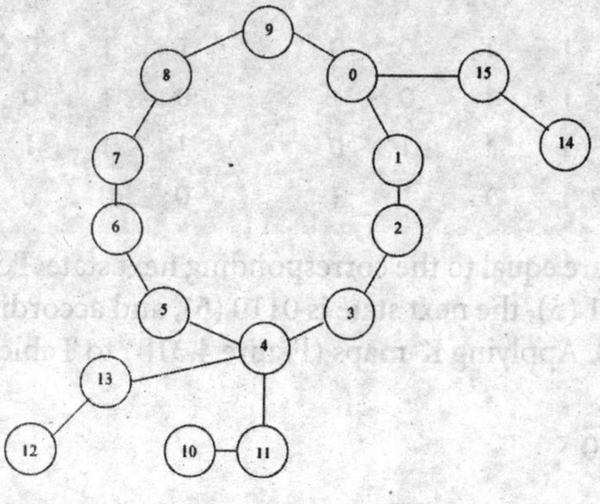

FIGURE 4.31A State diagram of a decade counter.

Next we construct the excitation table. Table 4.10 shows the excitation table of the decade counter.

TABLE 4.10 Excitation Table for a Decade Counter with a Terminal Count, Using D Master-Slave Flip-Flops

Inputs				Outputs				
Current State				Next State			Output	
Q3	Q2	Q1	Q0	Q3+	Q2+	Q1+	Q0+	TC
0	0	0	0	0	0	0	1	0
0	0	0	1	0	0	1	0	0
0	0	1	0	0	0	1	1	0
0	0	1	1	0	1	0	0	0
0	1	0	0	0	1	0	1	0
0	1	0	1	0	1	1	0	0
0	1	1	0	0	1	1	1	0
0	1	1	1	1	0	0	0	0
1	0	0	0	1	0	0	1	0
1	0	0	1	0	0	0	0	1
1	0	1	0	1	0	1	1	0
1	0	1	1	0	1	0	0	0
1	1	0	0	1	1	0	1	0
1	1	0	1	0	1	0	0	0
1	1	1	0	1	1	1	1	0
1	1	1	1	0	0	0	0	0

All Ds are equal to the corresponding next state. For example, when the current state is 0101 (5), the next state is 0110 (6), and accordingly D0 = 0, D1 = 1, D2 = 1, and D3 = 0. Applying K-maps (Figure 4.31b) to Table 4.9 we find:

$$D0=\overline{Q0}$$

$$D1=\overline{Q3}\,\overline{Q1}Q0+Q1\overline{Q0}$$

$$D2=Q2\overline{Q1}+Q2\overline{Q0}+Q1Q0\overline{Q2}$$

$$D3=Q3\overline{Q0}+Q0Q1Q2\overline{Q3}$$

$$TC=Q0\overline{Q1}\,\overline{Q2}Q3$$

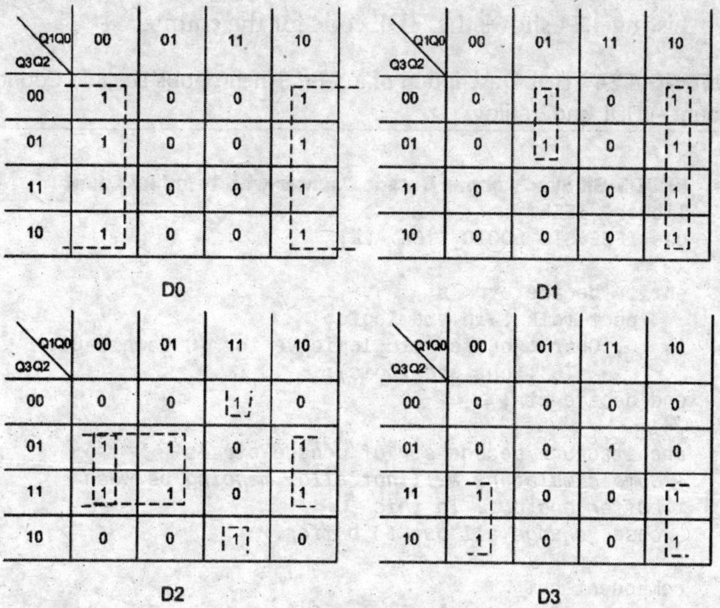

FIGURE 4.31B K-maps for a decade counter.

From the Boolean functions, we draw the logic diagram of the counter. Figure 4.32 shows the logic diagram of the counter.

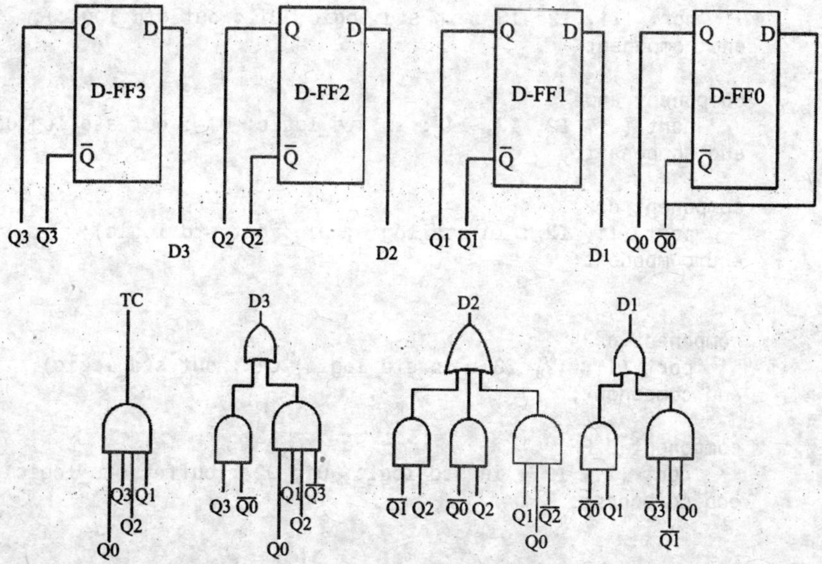

FIGURE 4.32 Logic diagram of a decade counter.

Listing 4.24 shows the HDL code for the counter.

LISTING 4.24 HDL Description of a 3-Bit Synchronous Decade Counter with Terminal Count–VHDL and Verilog

VHDL 3-Bit Synchronous Decade Counter with Terminal Count

```
library IEEE;
use IEEE.STD_LOGIC_1164.ALL;

entity decade_ctr is
    port (clk : in std_logic;
    Q, Qbar : buffer std_logic_vector (3 downto 0);
         TC : out std_logic);
end decade_ctr;

architecture decade_str of decade_ctr is
--Some simulators will not allow mapping between
--buffer and out. In this
--case, change all out to buffer.

component buf
    port (I1 : in std_logic; O1 : out std_logic);
end component;

component and2
    port (I1, I2 : in std_logic; O1 : out std_logic);
end component;

component and3
    port (I1, I2, I3 : in std_logic; O1 : out std_logic);
end component;

component and4
    port (I1, I2, I3, I4 : in std_logic; O1 : out std_logic);
end component;

component or2
    port (I1, I2 : in std_logic; O1 : out std_logic);
end component;


component or3
    port (I1, I2, I3 : in std_logic; O1 : out std_logic);
end component;

component D_FF
    port (I1, I2 : in std_logic; O1, O2 : buffer std_logic);
end component;


for all : D_FF use entity work.bind22 (D_FFMaster);
```

```
for all : buf use entity work.bind1 (buf_1);
for all : and2 use entity work.bind2 (and2_4);
for all : and3 use entity work.bind3 (and3_4);
for all : and4 use entity work.bind4 (and4_4);
for all : or2 use entity work.bind2 (or2_4);
for all : or3 use entity work.bind3 (or3_4);
signal s : std_logic_vector (6 downto 0);
signal D : std_logic_vector (3 downto 0);
begin

    b1 : buf port map (Qbar(0), D(0));
    DFF0 : D_FF port map (D(0), clk, Q(0), Qbar(0));

--Assume and gates and or gates have 4 ns propagation
--delay and invert has 1 ns.
    a1 : and3 port map (Qbar(3), Qbar(1), Q(0), s(0));
    a2 : and2 port map (Q(1), Qbar(0), s(1));
    r1 : or2 port map (s(0), s(1), D(1));
    DFF1 : D_FF port map (D(1), clk, Q(1), Qbar(1));

    a3 : and2 port map (Q(2), Qbar(1), s(2));
    a4 : and2 port map (Q(2), Qbar(0), s(3));
    a5 : and3 port map (Q(1), Q(0), Qbar(2), s(4));
    r2 : or3 port map (s(2), s(3), s(4), D(2));
    DFF2 : D_FF port map (D(2), clk, Q(2), Qbar(2));

    a6 : and2 port map (Q(3), Qbar(0), s(5));
    a7 : and4 port map (Q(0), Q(1), Q(2), Qbar(3), s(6));
    r3 : or2 port map (s(5), s(6), D(3));
    DFF3 : D_FF port map (D(3), clk, Q(3), Qbar(3));
    a8 : and4 port map (Q(0), Qbar(1), Qbar(2), Q(3), TC);

end decade_str;
```

Verilog 3-Bit Synchronous Decade Counter with Terminal Count

```
module decade_ctr (clk, Q, Qbar, TC);
input clk;
output [3:0] Q, Qbar;
output TC;
wire [3:0] D;
wire [6:0] s;
buf #1 (D[0], Qbar[0]);
D_FFMaster FF0(D[0], clk, Q[0], Qbar[0]);

/*Assume and gates and or gates have 4 ns propagation
    and #4 (s[0], Qbar[3], Qbar[1], Q[0]);

    and #4 (s[0], Qbar[3], Qbar[1], Q[0]);
    and #4 (s[1], Q[1], Qbar[0]);
    or #4 (D[1], s[0], s[1]);
    D_FFMaster FF1 (D[1], clk, Q[1], Qbar[1]);
```

```
    and #4 (s[2],Q[2], Qbar[1]);
    and #4 (s[3],Q[2], Qbar[0]);
    and #4 (s[4],Q[1], Q[0], Qbar[2]);

    or #4 (D[2], s[2], s[3], s[4]);
    D_FFMaster FF2 (D[2], clk, Q[2], Qbar[2]);

    and #4 (s[5], Q[3], Qbar[0]);
    and #4 (s[6], Q[0], Q[1], Q[2], Qbar[3]);
    or #4 (D[3], s[5], s[6]);
    D_FFMaster FF3 (D[3], clk, Q[3], Qbar[3]);
    and #4 (TC, Q[0], Qbar[1], Qbar[2], Q[3]);

endmodule
```

4.5 GENERATE (HDL), GENERIC (VHDL), AND PARAMETER (VERILOG)

The predefined word `generate` is mainly used for repetition of concurrent statements. Its counterpart in behavioral description is the `for-loop`, and it can be used to replicate structural or gate-level description statements. `Generate` has several formats, one of which is covered here. See Chapter 7 for more formats.

In VHDL, the format for the `generate` statement is:

```
L1 : for i in 0 to N generate

v1 : inv port map (Y(i), Yb(i));
--other concurrent statements
end generate;
```

The above statement describes $N + 1$ inverters (assuming `inv` was declared as an inverter with input Y and output `Yb`); the input to inverter i is `Y(i)`, and the output is `Yb(i)`. `L1` is a required label for the generate statement.

An equivalent `generate` statement in Verilog is:

```
generate

genvar i;
for (i = 0; i <= N; i = i + 1)
    begin : uF
    not (Yb[i], Y[i]);

end
endgenerate
```

The statement `genvar i` declares the index `i` of the `generate` statement; genvar is a predefined word. `uF` is a label for the predefined word `begin`; and `begin` must have a label.

In VHDL, generic, and parameter in Verilog, are used to define global constants. The generic statement can be placed within entity, component, or instantiation statements. The following generic VHDL statement inside the entity declares N as a global constant of value 3.

```
entity compr_genr is
generic (N : integer := 3);
port (X, Y : in std_logic_vector (N downto 0);
    xgty, xlty, xeqy : buffer std_logic);
```

The following Verilog statement declares N as a global constant with a value of 3.

```
parameter N = 3;
input [N:0] X, Y;
```

The following Examples cover generate, generic, and parameter.

EXAMPLE 4.16 Structural Description of (N+1)-Bit Magnitude Comparator Using Generate Statement

In Listing 4.19, a 3-bit comparator is described. Here we design an $(N+1)$-bit comparator using the generate statement to replicate the full adder designed in Example 4.12. Listing 4.25 shows the HDL code for the $(N+1)$-bit comparator. Referring to Listing 4.25, the following statements replicate the N+1 inverters, $N+1$ full adders, and N+1 two-inputs and gates:

```
G1 : for i in 0 to N generate
v1 : inv port map (Y(i), Yb(i));
FA : full_adder port map (X(i), Yb(i), carry(i), sum(i), carry(i+1));
a1 : and2 port map (eq(i), sum(i), eq(i+1));

end generate G1;
```

The following Verilog statements also replicate $N+1$ inverters, $N+1$ full adders, and $N+1$ two-inputs and gates.

```
generate

genvar i;
for (i = 0; i <= N; i = i + 1)
    begin : uF
    not (Yb[i], Y[i]);
    FULL_ADDER FA (X[i], Yb[i], carry [i], sum [i], carry[i+1]);
    and (eq[i+1], sum[i], eq[i]);
end
```

LISTING 4.25 HDL Description of *N*-Bit Magnitude Comparator Using Generate Statement—VHDL and Verilog

VHDL N-Bit Magnitude Comparator Using Generate Statement

```
library IEEE;
use IEEE.STD_LOGIC_1164.ALL;

entity compr_genr is
generic (N : integer := 3);

   port (X, Y : in std_logic_vector (N downto 0);
      xgty, xlty, xeqy : buffer std_logic);
end compr_genr;

architecture cmpare_str of compr_genr is
--Some simulators will not allow mapping between
--buffer and out. In this
--case, change all out to buffer.

component full_adder
   port (I1, I2, I3 : in std_logic; O1, O2 : out std_logic);
end component;
component inv
   port (I1 : in std_logic; O1 : out std_logic);
end component;
component nor2
   port (I1, I2 : in std_logic; O1 : out std_logic);
end component;
component and2
   port (I1, I2 : in std_logic; O1 : out std_logic);
end component;
signal sum, Yb : std_logic_vector (N downto 0);
signal carry, eq : std_logic_vector (N + 1 downto 0);

for all : full_adder use entity work.bind32 (full_add);
for all : inv use entity work.bind1 (inv_0);
for all : nor2 use entity work.bind2 (nor2_7);
for all : and2 use entity work.bind2 (and2_7);
begin
   carry(0) <= '0';
   eq(0) <= '1';
G1 : for i in 0 to N generate
   v1 : inv port map (Y(i), Yb(i));
   FA : full_adder port map (X(i), Yb(i), carry(i),
      sum(i), carry(i+1));
   a1 : and2 port map (eq(i), sum(i), eq(i+1));

   end generate G1;
   xgty <= carry(N+1);
   xeqy <= eq(N+1);
   n1 : nor2 port map (xeqy, xgty, xlty);
```

```
end cmpare_str;
```

Verilog N-Bit Magnitude Comparator Using Generate Statement

```
module compr_genr (X, Y, xgty, xlty, xeqy);
parameter N = 3;
input [N:0] X, Y;
output xgty, xlty, xeqy;
wire [N:0] sum, Yb;
wire [N+1 : 0] carry, eq;
    assign carry[0] = 1'b0;
    assign eq[0] = 1'b1;

    generate

genvar i;
    for (i = 0; i <= N; i = i + 1)
        begin : uC
        not (Yb[i], Y[i]);

/* The above statement is equivalent to assign Yb = ~Y if
   outside the generate loop */

        FULL_ADDER FA(X[i], Yb[i], carry [i], sum [i], carry[i+1]);
        and (eq[i+1], sum[i], eq[i]);
    end
    endgenerate
assign xgty = carry[N+1];
assign xeqy = eq[N+1];
nor (xlty, xeqy, xgty);

endmodule
```

EXAMPLE 4.17 Structural Description of an *N*-Bit Asynchronous Down Counter Using Generate

Asynchronous counters differ from synchronous counters in the way the clock is connected to each flip-flop. In synchronous counters, all flip-flops are driven by the same clock. In asynchronous counters, each flip-flop may be driven by a different clock. Figure 4.33 shows an n-bit asynchronous counter using JK flip-flops. The clock of the first flip-flop is the main clock. The clock of the second flip-flop is the output of the first JK flip-flop. We repeat this pattern where the clock of the ith flip-flop is driven by the output of (*i*–1)th flip-flop.

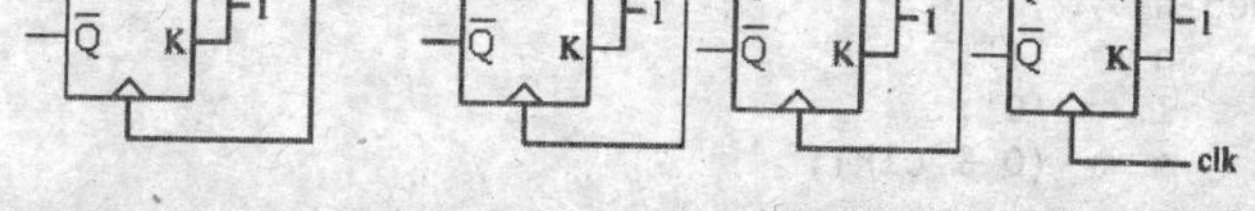

FIGURE 4.33 Logic diagram of an n-bit asynchronous down counter when n = 3.

Asynchronous counters suffer from hazards more than synchronous counters do. This is due to the way the clock of each flip-flop is connected. Each flip-flop has to wait until the output of the preceding flip-flop settles. During the period before the flip-flop settles, there will be transient states. Listing 4.26 shows the HDL code for an n-bit asynchronous counter. To use `generate` effectively we should be able to describe the *n* flip-flops by a general statement that will be replicated. All flip-flops, except the first, have a repeated pattern; the clock of the ith flip-flop is the output of the (*i*–1)th. To bring the first flip-flop into this pattern, we concatenate the clock and the Qs of all flip-flops in one vector.

```
s <= (Q & clk);          --VHDL
assign s = {Q, clk};     //Verilog
```

LISTING 4.26 HDL Description of an N-Bit Asynchronous Down Counter Using `Generate`—VHDL and Verilog

VHDL N-Bit Asynchronous Down Counter Using `Generate`

```
library IEEE;
use IEEE.STD_LOGIC_1164.ALL;

entity asynch_ctr is
Generic (N : integer := 3);

--This is a 3-bit counter. If a different number of bits
--is needed, simply change the value of N here only.

    port (clk : in std_logic;
        Q, Qbar : buffer std_logic_vector (N-1 downto 0));
end asynch_ctr;

architecture CT_strgnt of asynch_ctr is
--Some simulators will not allow mapping between
--buffer and out. In this
--case, change all out to buffer.

component JK_FF is
    port(I1, I2, I3 : in std_logic; O1, O2 : buffer std_logic);
end component ;
for all : JK_FF use entity work.bind32 (JK_Master);

--For bind32, see Listing 4.17a

signal h, l : std_logic;
signal s : std_logic_vector (N downto 0);
begin
    h <= '1';
    l <= '0';
    s <= (Q & clk);

--s is the concatenation of Q and clk. We need
```

```
--this concatenation to
--describe the clock of each JK flip-flop.

   Gnlop : for i in (N-1) downto 0 generate

   G1 : JK_FF port map (h, h, s(i), Q(i), Qbar(i));
   end generate GnLop;

end CT_strgnt;
```

Verilog N-Bit Asynchronous Down Counter Using Generate

```
module asynch_ctr (clk, Q, Qbar);
parameter N = 3;
/* This is a 3-bit counter. If a different number of bits
   is needed, simply change the value of N here only.*/
input clk;
output [N-1:0] Q, Qbar;
wire [N:0] s;
    assign s = {Q, clk};
/* s is the concatenation of Q and clk.
 This concatenation is needed to describe the clock
 of each JK flip-flop. */

    generate
    genvar i;
for (i = 0; i < N; i = i + 1)

    begin : uC

    JK_FF JKFF0 (1'b1, 1'b1, s[i], Q[i], Qbar[i]);
// JK_FF is as shown in Listing 4.17b
    end

endgenerate

endmodule
```

Figure 4.34 shows the simulation waveform of the counter with $N = 3$. The waveform may contain several transient states.

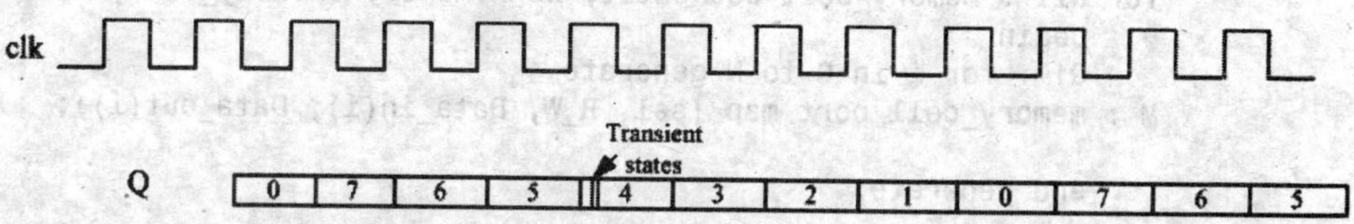

FIGURE 4.34 Simulation waveform of an N-bit asynchronous down counter (N = 3).

EXAMPLE 4.18 Structural Description of an N-Bit Memory Word Using `Generate`

In Listing 4.20, a single memory cell is described. This cell is expanded to *N* bits using the `generate` statement. Listing 4.27 shows the HDL code for the N-bit memory word. Referring to Listing 4.27, the VHDL statements

```
G1 : for i in 0 to N generate
M : memory_cell port map (sel, R_W, Data_in(i), Data_out(i));

end generate;
```

and the Verilog statements

```
generate
genvar i;
for (i = 0; i <= N; i = i + 1)
    begin : uM
    memory M1 (sel, R_W, Data_in [i], Data_out[i]);
    end
endgenerate
```

replicate the memory cell designed in Listing 4.29 N times.

LISTING 4.27 HDL Description of an N-Bit Memory Word Using `Generate`—VHDL and Verilog

VHDL N-Bit Memory Word Using `Generate`

```
library IEEE;
use IEEE.STD_LOGIC_1164.ALL;
entity Memory_word is
    Generic (N : integer := 7);
port (Data_in : in std_logic_vector (N downto 0); sel, R_W : in
    std_logic; Data_out : out std_logic_vector (N downto 0));
end Memory_word;

architecture Word_generate of Memory_word is
component memory_cell
    Port (Sel, RW, Din : in std_logic; O1 : buffer std_logic );
end component;

for all : memory_cell use entity work.memory (memory_str);
    begin
    G1 : for i in 0 to N generate
M : memory_cell port map (sel, R_W, Data_in(i), Data_out(i));

    end generate;

end Word_generate;
```

Verilog N-Bit Memory Word Using Generate

```
module Memory_Word (Data_in, sel, R_W, Data_out);

parameter N = 7;
input [N:0] Data_in;
input sel, R_W;
output [N:0] Data_out;

    generate
    genvar i;
    for (i = 0; i <= N; i = i + 1)

    begin : u
    memory M1M (sel, R_W, Data_in [i], Data_out[i]);

    end

    endgenerate

endmodule
```

LISTING 4.28 VHDL Code for All Components Used for Binding in Chapter 4

```
library IEEE;
use IEEE.STD_LOGIC_1164.ALL;
entity bind1 is
    port (O1 : out std_logic; I1 : in std_logic);
end bind1;
architecture inv_0 of bind1 is
begin
    O1 <= not I1;
end inv_0;

architecture inv_1 of bind1 is
begin
    O1 <= not I1 after 1 ns;

end inv_1;


architecture inv_7 of bind1 is
begin
    O1 <= not I1 after 7 ns;
end inv_7;

library IEEE;
use IEEE.STD_LOGIC_1164.ALL;

entity bind2 is
    port (O1 : out std_logic; I1, I2 : in std_logic);
end bind2;
```

```
architecture xor2_0 of bind2 is
begin
    O1 <= I1 xor I2;
end xor2_0;

architecture and2_0 of bind2 is
begin
    O1 <= I1 and I2;
end and2_0;

architecture and2_4 of bind2 is
begin
    O1 <= I1 and I2 after 4 ns;
end and2_4;

architecture and2_7 of bind2 is
begin
    O1 <= I1 and I2 after 7 ns;
end and2_7;

architecture or2_0 of bind2 is
begin
    O1 <= I1 or I2;
end or2_0;

architecture or2_7 of bind2 is
begin
    O1 <= I1 or I2 after 7 ns;
end or2_7;

architecture nor2_0 of bind2 is
begin
    O1 <= I1 nor I2;
end nor2_0;

architecture nor2_7 of bind2 is
begin
    O1 <= I1 nor I2 after 7 ns;
end nor2_7;

architecture nor2_4 of bind2 is
begin
    O1 <= I1 nor I2 after 4 ns;
end nor2_4;

architecture bufif1 of bind2 is
begin
    buf : process (I1, I2)
    variable tem : std_logic;
    begin
if (I2 ='1')then
    tem := I1;
else
```

```
        tem := 'Z';
    end if;
        O1 <= tem;
        end process buf;
    end bufif1;

    library IEEE;
    use IEEE.STD_LOGIC_1164.ALL;


    entity bind3 is
        port (O1 : out std_logic; I1, I2, I3 : in std_logic);
    end bind3;

    architecture and3_0 of bind3 is
    begin
        O1 <= I1 and I2 and I3;
    end and3_0;

    architecture and3_7 of bind3 is
    begin
        O1 <= I1 and I2 and I3 after 7 ns;
    end and3_7;

    architecture or3_0 of bind3 is
    begin
        O1 <= I1 or I2 or I3;
    end or3_0;

    architecture or3_7 of bind3 is
    begin
        O1 <= I1 or I2 or I3 after 7 ns;
    end or3_7;

    library IEEE;
    use IEEE.STD_LOGIC_1164.ALL;
    entity bind22 is
        Port (O1, O2 : buffer std_logic; I1, I2 : in std_logic);
    end bind22;

    architecture HA of bind22 is
    --Some simulators will not allow mapping between
    --buffer and out. In this
    --case, change all out to buffer.
    component xor2
        port (I1, I2 : in std_logic; O1 : out std_logic);
    end component;
        component and2
        port (I1, I2 : in std_logic; O1 : out std_logic);
        end component;
        for A1 : and2 use entity work.bind2 (and2_0);
        for X1 : xor2 use entity work.bind2 (xor2_0);
            begin
```

```
        X1 : xor2 port map (I1, I2, O1);
        A1 : and2 port map (I1, I2, O2);
    end HA;

architecture SR_Latch of bind22 is
component nor2
    port (I1, I2 : in std_logic; O1 : out std_logic);
end component;
for all : nor2 use entity work.bind2 (nor2_0);
begin
    n1 : nor2 port map (I1, O1, O2);
    n2 : nor2 port map (I2, O2, O1);
end SR_Latch;

architecture D_latch of bind22 is
component and2
    port (I1, I2 : in std_logic; O1 : out std_logic);
end component;
component nor2
    port (I1, I2 : in std_logic; O1 : out std_logic);
end component;
component inv
    port (I1 : in std_logic; O1 : out std_logic);
end component;
for all : and2 use entity work.bind2 (and2_4);
for all : nor2 use entity work.bind2 (nor2_4);
for all : inv use entity work.bind1 (inv_1);
signal I2b, s1, s2 : std_logic;
begin
    a1 : and2 port map (I1, I2, s1);
    a2 : and2 port map (I2b, O1, s2);
    in1 : inv port map (I2, I2b);
    in2 : inv port map (O2, O1);
    n2 : nor2 port map (s1, s2, O2);
end D_latch;

library IEEE;
use IEEE.STD_LOGIC_1164.ALL;

    entity bind32 is
        port (O1, O2 : out std_logic; I1, I2, I3 : in std_logic);
    end bind32;

architecture full_add of bind32 is
component HA
    port (I1, I2 : in std_logic; O1, O2 : buffer std_logic);
end component;
component or2
    port (I1, I2 : in std_logic; O1 : out std_logic);
end component;
for all : HA use entity work.bind22 (HA);
for all : or2 use entity work.bind2 (or2_0);
signal s0, c0, c1 : std_logic;
```

```
begin
    HA1 : HA port map (I2, I3, s0, c0);
    HA2 : HA port map (I1, s0, O1, c1);
    r1 : or2 port map (c0, c1, O2);
end full_add;

architecture JK_FF of bind32 is
begin
P1 : process (I1, I2, I3)
variable temp1, temp2 : std_logic;
variable jk : std_logic_vector (1 downto 0);
begin
    if rising_edge (I3) then
    jk := (I1 & I2);
        case jk is
            when "01" => temp1 := '0';
            when "10" => temp1 := '1';
            when "11" => temp1 := not temp1;
            when "00" => temp1 := temp1;
            when others => temp1 :='0';
        end case;
O1 <= temp1;
temp2 := not temp1;
O2 <= temp2;
end if;
end process P1;
end JK_FF;
```

4.6 SUMMARY

In this chapter, the fundamentals of structural description have been covered. Gate-level description has been discussed and used to build more-complex structures (macros). Verilog has built-in gates, such as `and`, `or`, `nand`, `nor`, and `buf`. Basic VHDL does not have built-in gates but we can build these gates by using the predefined word component. Both VHDL and Verilog have the predefined command `generate` for replicating structural macros. Table 4.11 shows a list of the VHDL statements covered in this chapter along with their Verilog counterparts (if any).

TABLE 4.11 Summary of VHDL Statements and Their Verilog Counterparts

VHDL	Verilog
generate	generate
port map	Built-in already.
and2, or2, xor2, nor2,xnor2, inv	and, or, xor, nor, xnor, not (The above gates are user-built.)
use library	Built-in already.

4.7 EXERCISES

4.1 Design a 4-bit parity generator. The output is 0 for even parity and 1 for odd parity. Write both the VHDL and Verilog codes.

4.2 Design a 3-bit priority encoder. The input I is 3-bit, and the output P is 3-bit. I(0), when high, has the highest priority, followed by I(1) and (I2). The output P for highest priority to lowest is 0, 1, and 2d, respectively. Construct a truth table, minimize, and write both the VHDL and Verilog codes.

4.3 In Listing 4.19, three 1-bit full adders were used for a 3-bit magnitude comparison. Modify the Listing by using one 3-bit adder macro.

4.4 Design a counter that counts 0, 2, 3, 5, 7, 0, 2, … using the state machine approach. Show all details of your answer. Write both the VHDL and Verilog codes.

4.5 Referring to Listing 4.26 (Verilog), change the count from down to up and rewrite the code.

4.6 Translate the VHDL code shown in Listing 4.29 to Verilog. What is the logic function of the system?

LISTING 4.29 Code for Exercise 4.6

```
library IEEE;
use IEEE.STD_LOGIC_1164.ALL;


entity system is
    Port (a, b, c : in std_logic; d, e : out std_logic );
end system;

architecture prob_6 of system is
component xor2
port (I1, I2 : in std_logic; O1 : out std_logic);
end component;

component and2
port (I1, I2 : in std_logic; O1 : out std_logic);
end component;

component or3
port (I1, I2, I3 : in std_logic; O1 : out std_logic);
end component;

component inv
port (I1 : in std_logic; O1 : out std_logic);
```

```
end component;
for all : xor2 use entity work.bind2 (xor2_0);
for all : and2 use entity work.bind2 (and2_0);
for all : inv use entity work.bind1 (inv_0);
for all : or3 use entity work.bind3 (or3_0);
signal s1, s2, s3, s4, abar, bbar, cbar : std_logic;
begin
x1 : xor2 port map (a, b, s1);
x2 : xor2 port map (s1, c, d);
c1 : inv port map (a, abar);
c2 : inv port map (b, bbar);
c3 : inv port map (a, cbar);
a1 : and2 port map (abar, b, s2);
a2 : and2 port map (abar, c, s3);
a3 : and2 port map (b, c, s4);
r1 : or3 port map (s2, s3, s4, e);

end prob_6;
```

4.7 Add active high clear to the asynchronous counter shown in Figure 4.33 by adding a clear signal to the macro JK_FF. Use the modified JK flip-flops to rebuild the counter. Write both the VHDL and Verilog codes.

4.8 Construct a two-digit decade counter that counts from 0 to 99. Use the module of the decade counter in Listing 4.24. Write both the VHDL and Verilog codes. (Hint: use the terminal count TC to cascade the decade counters.)

4.8 REFERENCES

[Hayes98] Hayes, J. P., *Computer Architecture and Organization*, 3d ed. McGraw Hill, 1998.

[Nelson95] Nelson V. P., H. T. Nagle, B. D. Carroll, and J. D. Irwin, *Digital Logic Circuit Analysis & Design*. Prentice Hall, 1995.

5 Switch-Level Descriptions

In This Chapter

- Understand the concept of describing and simulating digital systems using transistors.
- Identify the basic statements of switch-level description in Verilog, such as `nmos`, `pmos`, `cmos`, `supply1`, `supply0`, `tranif0`, `tran`, and `tranif0`.
- Develop a counterpart VHDL switch-level package that matches the switch-level functions of the Verilog description.
- Review and understand the fundamentals of transistors, and how they can be implemented as switches.
- Review Boolean functions for combinational circuits.

5.1 HIGHLIGHTS OF THE SWITCH-LEVEL DESCRIPTION

Facts

- Switch-level description implements switches (transistors) to describe relatively small-scale digital systems.
- Switch-level description is usually implemented in Very Large-Scale Integrated (VLSI) circuit layouts.
- Switch-level description is the lowest HDL logic level that can be used to simulate digital systems.
- Only small-scale systems can be simulated using pure switch-level description. If the system is not small, a huge number of switches are needed that may render the simulation impractical.
- Switch-level description is routinely used along with other types of modeling to describe digital systems.

- The switches used in this chapter are assumed to be perfect; they are either open (high impedance) or closed (zero impedance).
- In contrast to Verilog, basic VHDL does not have built-in statements such as `nmos`, `pmos`, and `cmos`. To use these statements in VHDL, user-built packages must be developed.

5.2 USEFUL DEFINITIONS

Valence electrons: Electrons in the outer shell of the atom that can interact with the valence electrons of another atom.

N-type semiconductor: The free carriers are negatively charged electrons.

P-type semiconductor: The free carriers are positively charged holes.

MOS: Metal Oxide Semiconductor.

5.3 SINGLE NMOS AND PMOS SWITCHES

Figure 5.1a shows a single NMOS switch, and Figure 5.1b shows a single PMOS switch. The switch has three signals: drain, gate, and source. If the gate is at logic 1, then the NMOS is closed (ON) and the PMOS is open (OFF). If the gate is at logic 0, then the NMOS is open (OFF) and the PMOS is closed (ON).

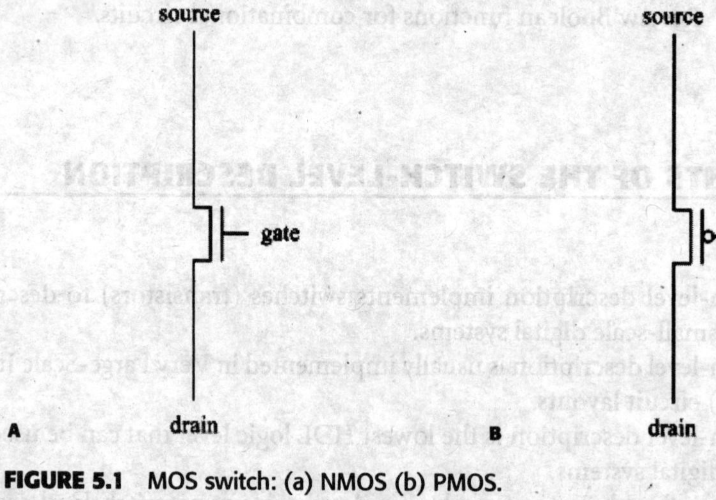

FIGURE 5.1 MOS switch: (a) NMOS (b) PMOS.

5.3.1 Verilog Description of NMOS and PMOS Switches

Verilog has built-in code for NMOS and PMOS switches. In Verilog, there are four logical levels: 1, 0, X (don't care), and Z (high impedance). Table 5.1A shows the relationship between the drain, source, and gate of a NMOS switch, and Table 5.1B shows the same for a PMOS switch.

TABLE 5.1A Relationship Between Source, Drain, and Gate in NMOS Switches

Drain \ Gate	0	1	X	Z
0	Z	0	L	L
1	Z	1	H	H
X	Z	X	X	X
Z	Z	Z	Z	Z

TABLE 5.1B Relationship Between Source, Drain, and Gate in PMOS Switches

Drain \ Gate	0	1	X	Z
0	0	Z	L	L
1	1	Z	H	H
X	X	Z	X	X
Z	Z	Z	Z	Z

For an NMOS switch, the Verilog code is:

```
nmos n1 (drain, source, gate) //The switch name "n1" is optional.
```

The code can be written as:

```
nmos n1 (O1, I1, I2);
```

For the PMOS switch, the Verilog code is:

```
pmos p1 (drain, source, gate) //The switch name "p1" is optional.
```

The code can be written as:

```
pmos p1 (O1, I1, I2);
```

5.3.2 VHDL Description of NMOS and PMOS Switches

Basic VHDL does not have built-in descriptions for NMOS or NMOS switches. Switches are built using behavioral description. Listing 5.1 shows the code, which does not include any consideration of delay times.

LISTING 5.1 VHDL Behavioral Code for NMOS and PMOS Switches

```
library IEEE;
use IEEE.STD_LOGIC_1164.ALL;

entity mos is
    Port (O1 : out std_logic; I1, I2 : in std_logic);
end mos;

architecture nmos_behavioral of mos is

--All switches presented here do not include any
--time parameters, such as rise time and fall time.
--They only mimic the logical functions of their
--Verilog counterparts.

begin
switch : process (I1, I2)
variable temp : std_logic;
begin
case I2 is
when '0'=> temp := 'Z';
when '1' => temp := I1;
when others => case I1 is
    when '0' => temp := 'L';
    when '1' => temp := 'H';
    when others => temp := I1;
    end case;
end case;
O1 <= temp;
end process switch;
end nmos_behavioral;

architecture pmos_behavioral of mos is

begin
switch : process (I1, I2)
variable temp : std_logic;
begin

case I2 is
when '1'=> temp := 'Z';
when '0' => temp := I1;
when others => case I1 is
    when '0' => temp := 'L';
    when '1' => temp := 'H';
```

```
        when others => temp := I1;
        end case;
    end case;
    O1 <= temp;
    end process switch;
    end pmos_behavioral;
```

To write the NMOS and PMOS codes as components, we bind the entity of Listing of 5.1 to a component statement. Listing 5.2 shows such binding.

LISTING 5.2 VHDL Code for NMOS and PMOS Switches as Components

```
architecture nmos of mos is
component nmos
port (O1 : out std_logic; I1, I2 : in std_logic);
end component;

component pmos
port (O1 : out std_logic; I1, I2 : in std_logic);
end component;

for all : pmos use entity work.mos (pmos_behavioral);
for all : nmos use entity work.mos (nmos_behavioral);
```

5.3.3 Serial and Parallel Combinations of Switches

Consider two NMOS switches connected in serial as shown in Figure 5.2a. Assume the gates g1 and g2 can only take logic 0 or logic 1. If g1 or g2 is at 0, then the path between y and d is open (OFF). If g1 and g2 are at 1, then the path between y and d is closed (ON), and y = d.

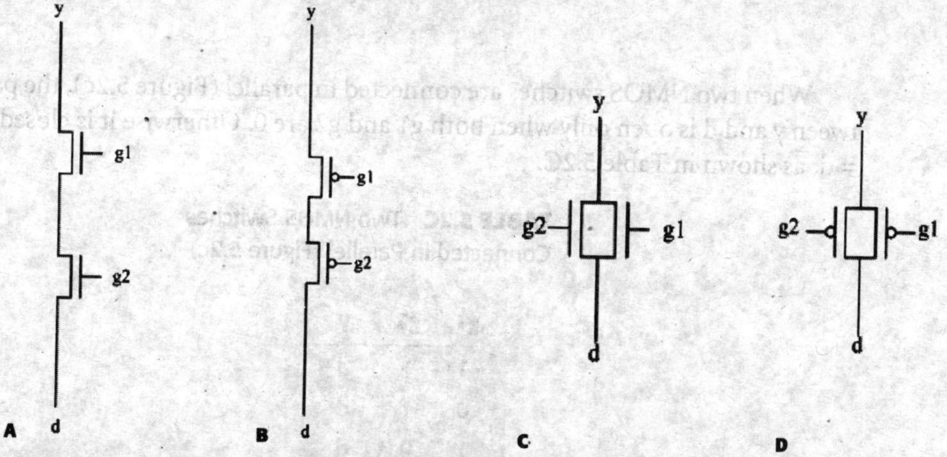

FIGURE 5.2 Combination of switches. (a) Two NMOS switches in serial. (b) Two PMOS switches in serial. (c) Two NMOS switches in parallel. (d) Two PMOS switches in parallel.

Table 5.2A summarizes the relationship between y, d, g1, and g2.

TABLE 5.2A Two NMOS Switches Connected in Serial (Figure 5.2a)

g1	g2	y
1	1	d
0	1	Z
1	0	Z
0	0	Z

Now, consider two PMOS switches connected in serial (Figure 5.2b). The path between y and d is closed (ON) only when both g1 and g2 are at 0; at this instant, y = d. The path is open (OFF) if g1 or g2 is at 1. Table 5.2B summarizes the relation between y and d.

TABLE 5.2B Two PMOS Switches Connected in Serial (Figure 5.2b)

g1	g2	y
1	1	Z
0	1	Z
1	0	Z
0	0	d

When two NMOS switches are connected in parallel (Figure 5.2c), the path between y and d is open only when both g1 and g2 are 0. Otherwise it is closed, and y = d, as shown in Table 5.2C.

TABLE 5.2C Two NMOS Switches Connected in Parallel (Figure 5.2c)

g1	g2	y
1	1	d
0	1	d
1	0	d
0	0	Z

For two PMOS switches connected in parallel (Figure 5.2d), the path between y and d is open only when both g1 and g2 are at 1. Otherwise it is closed, and y = d, as shown in Table 5.2D.

TABLE 5.2D Two PMOS Switches Connected in Parallel (Figure 5.2d)

g1	g2	y
1	1	Z
0	1	d
1	0	d
0	0	d

5.4 SWITCH-LEVEL DESCRIPTION OF PRIMITIVE GATES

This section describes primitive gates. The easy approach is taken to design the gates—one which may yield a greater number of transistors. If the reader is interested in finding the minimum possible number of transistors or the minimum power consumption, he/she is advised to investigate [Weste03] and [Wang95]. Tables 5.2A–D are used to build the gate from a combination of switches. After constructing the switches, we write the code using Listings 5.1 and 5.2.

EXAMPLE 5.1 Switch-Level Description of an Inverter

The truth table of the inverter is shown in Table 5.3.

TABLE 5.3 Truth Table for an Inverter

Input	Output
a	y
0	1
1	0

For any switch circuit, level 1 is represented by the power supply voltage (vdd), and level 0 is represented by ground (gnd). To design the inverter, two complementary switches are needed—one to pull y down to 0 (ground) and the other to pull y up to 1 (vdd). Figure 5.3 shows this connection.

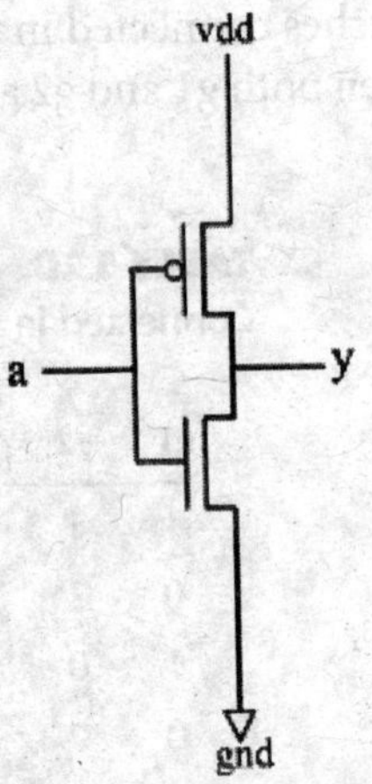

FIGURE 5.3 An inverter.

The HDL code is shown in Listing 5.3, and the statement:

```
pmos port map (y, vdd, a);
```

represents a PMOS switch with source y, drain vdd, and gate a. In the Verilog statements:

```
supply1 vdd;
supply0 gnd;
```

`supply1` and `supply0` are predefined words that represent high voltage and ground, respectively. In VHDL, these two voltage levels are created by using `constant` declaration statements:

```
constant vdd : std_logic := '1';
constant gnd : std_logic := '0';
```

LISTING 5.3 HDL Code for an Inverter—VHDL and Verilog

VHDL Inverter Description

```
library IEEE;
use IEEE.STD_LOGIC_1164.ALL;

entity Inverter is
    Port (y : out std_logic; a : in std_logic);
end Inverter;

architecture Invert_switch of Inverter is
component nmos
```

```
port (O1 : out std_logic; I1, I2 : in std_logic);
end component;

component pmos
port (O1 : out std_logic; I1, I2 : in std_logic);
end component;

for all : pmos use entity work.mos (pmos_behavioral);
for all : nmos use entity work.mos (nmos_behavioral);
constant vdd : std_logic := '1';
constant gnd : std_logic := '0';
begin
p1 : pmos port map (y, vdd, a);
n1 : nmos port map (y, gnd, a);
end Invert_switch;
```

Verilog Inverter Description

```
module invert (y, a);
input a;
output y;
supply1 vdd; //supply1 is a predefined word for the high voltage.
supply0 gnd; //supply0 is a predefined word for the ground.
pmos p1 (y, vdd, a); //the name "p1" is optional; it can be omitted.
nmos n1 (y, gnd, a); //the name "n1" is optional; it can be omitted.
endmodule
```

EXAMPLE 5.2 Switch-Level Description of a Two-Input AND Gate

In this Example, a two-input AND gate is described. The truth table of the two-input AND gate is shown in Table 5.4.

From Table 5.4 we see that we need two switch combinations: one to pull y up to vdd only when both gates of the combination are at level 1 (Table 5.2A satisfies this requirement), and another combination to pull y to ground whenever one of the gates is at level 0 (Table 5.2B satisfies this requirement). So, the final design is composed of two serial NMOS switches and two parallel PMOS switches. Figure 5.4 shows the switch-level diagram of the AND gate.

TABLE 5.4 Truth Table for a Two-Input AND Gate

Input		Output
a	b	y
0	0	0
1	0	0
0	1	0
1	1	1

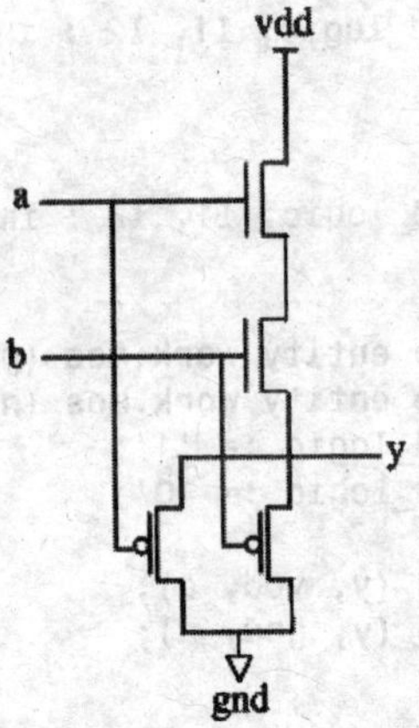

FIGURE 5.4 Switch-level logic diagram of an AND gate.

From Figure 5.4 we write the HDL code. Listing 5.4 shows the HDL code of two-input AND gate.

LISTING 5.4 HDL Code for a Two-Input AND Gate—VHDL and Verilog

VHDL Two-Input AND Gate

```
library IEEE;
use IEEE.STD_LOGIC_1164.ALL;

entity and2gate is
    Port (y : out std_logic; a, b : in std_logic);
end and2gate;

architecture and_switch of and2gate is
component nmos
port (O1 : out std_logic; I1, I2 : in std_logic);
end component;

component pmos
port (O1 : out std_logic; I1, I2 : in std_logic);
end component;

for all : pmos use entity work.mos (pmos_behavioral);
for all : nmos use entity work.mos (nmos_behavioral);
constant vdd : std_logic := '1';
constant gnd : std_logic := '0';
signal s1 : std_logic;
begin

n1 : nmos port map (s1, vdd, a);
n2 : nmos port map (y, s1, b);
```

```
p1 : pmos port map (y, gnd, a);
p2 : pmos port map (y, gnd, b);
end and_switch;
```

Verilog Two-Input AND Gate

```
module and2gate (y, a, b);
input a, b;
output y;

supply1 vdd;
supply0 gnd;

nmos (s1, vdd, a);
nmos (y, s1, b);
pmos (y, gnd, a);
pmos (y, gnd, b);
endmodule
```

As shown in Figure 5.4, the PMOS switches pull y down to ground level, and the NMOS switches pull y up to vdd level. This arrangement results in degraded output and should be avoided; more details can be found in [Dillinger88], [Kang99], [Nelson95], and [Weste03]. When cascaded, degraded outputs can deteriorate the final outputs and render them unrecognizable. To generate strong outputs, the NMOS switches should pull the output down to ground, and the PMOS switches should pull the output up to vdd. So, to design a switch-level AND gate with strong output, a different approach should be followed (see Section 5.5).

EXAMPLE 5.3 Switch-Level Description of a Two-Input OR Gate

In this Example, a two-input OR gate is designed. The truth table of a two-input OR gate is shown in Table 5.5.

TABLE 5.5 Truth Table for a Two-Input OR Gate

Input		Output
a	b	y
0	0	0
1	0	1
0	1	1
1	1	1

From the Table, notice that to design switch-level circuits for the OR gate, two complementary combinations are needed (see Table 5.2). The first combination pulls y down to ground level only when both gates are at level 0; Table 5.2B satisfies this requirement. The second combination pulls y up to vdd when either g1 or g2 is at level 1; Table 5.2C satisfies this requirement. So, the switch-level OR gate consists of two complementary combinations: two serial PMOS switches and two parallel NMOS switches. Figure 5.5 shows the switch-level diagram of a two-input OR gate.

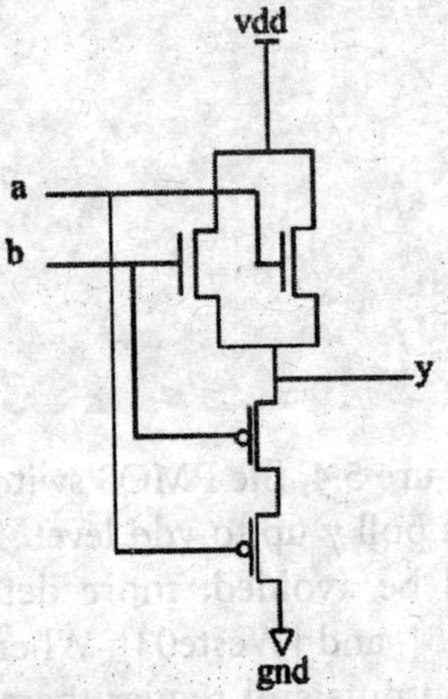

FIGURE 5.5 Switch-level logic diagram of an OR gate.

From Figure 5.5, the HDL code is written using the macros `pmos` and `nmos`. Listing 5.5 shows the HDL code of the switch-level two-input OR gate.

LISTING 5.5 HDL Code of a Two-Input OR Gate—VHDL and Verilog

VHDL Two-Input OR Gate Description

```
library IEEE;
use IEEE.STD_LOGIC_1164.ALL;

entity or2gate is
    Port (y : out std_logic; a, b : in std_logic);
end or2gate;

architecture or_switch of or2gate is
component nmos
port (O1 : out std_logic; I1, I2 : in std_logic);
end component;

component pmos
```

```
port (O1 : out std_logic; I1, I2 : in std_logic);
end component;

for all : pmos use entity work.mos (pmos_behavioral);
for all : nmos use entity work.mos (nmos_behavioral);
constant vdd : std_logic := '1';
constant gnd : std_logic := '0';
signal s1 : std_logic;
begin

n1 : nmos port map (y, vdd, a);
n2 : nmos port map (y, vdd, b);
p1 : pmos port map (y, s1, a);
p2 : pmos port map (s1, gnd, b);
end or_switch;
```

Verilog Two-Input OR Gate Description

```
module OR2gate (a, b, y);

input a, b;
output y;

supply1 vdd;
supply0 gnd;

nmos (y, vdd, a);
nmos (y, vdd, b);
pmos (y, s1, a);
pmos (s1, gnd, b);
endmodule
```

As shown in Figure 5.5, the PMOS switches pull y down to ground level, and the NMOS switches pull y up to vdd level. This arrangement results in degraded outputs and should be avoided; more details can be found in [Dillinger88], [Kang99], [Nelson95], and [Weste03]. Degraded outputs, when cascaded, can deteriorate the final outputs and render them unrecognizable. To generate strong outputs, the NMOS switches should pull the output down to ground, and the PMOS switches should pull the output up to vdd. So, if we want to design a switch-level OR gate with strong output, we should follow a different approach (see Section 5.5).

EXAMPLE 5.4 Switch-Level Description of a Two-Input NAND Gate

In this Example, a switch-level NAND two-input gate is designed. The truth table of the two-input NAND gate is shown in Table 5.6.

Referring to Table 5.6; we can design the gate using two complementary switch combinations (see Table 5.2). The first combination pulls y up to vdd when either of the two switch gates is at level 0; Table 5.2D satisfies this requirement. The second combination pulls y to ground level only when both gates are at level 1; Table

5.2A satisfies this requirement. So, the final design consists of two complementary combinations: two parallel PMOS switches and two serial NMOS switches. Figure 5.6 shows the switch-level logic diagram of an NAND gate.

TABLE 5.6 Truth Table for a Two-Input NAND Gate

Input		Output
a	b	y
0	0	1
1	0	1
0	1	1
1	1	0

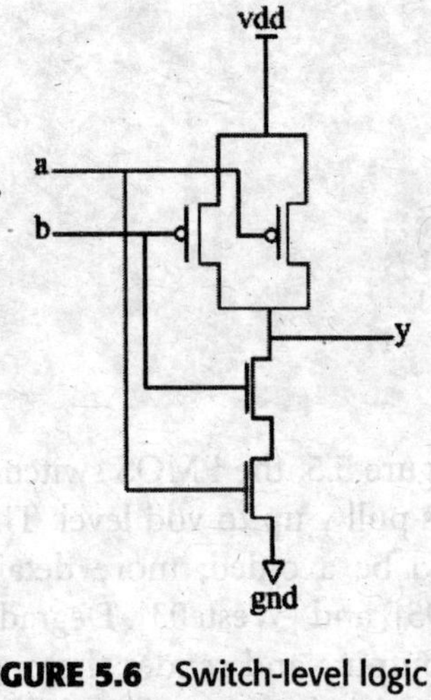

FIGURE 5.6 Switch-level logic diagram of an NAND gate.

From Figure 5.6, we write the HDL code. Listing 5.6 shows the HDL code of the NAND gate, using the two macros pmos and nmos.

LISTING 5.6 HDL Code for a Two-Input NAND Gate—VHDL and Verilog

VHDL Two-Input NAND Gate

```
library IEEE;
use IEEE.STD_LOGIC_1164.ALL;

entity nand2gate is
```

```
    Port (y : out std_logic; a, b : in std_logic);
end nand2gate;

architecture nand_switch of nand2gate is
component nmos
port (O1 : out std_logic; I1, I2 : in std_logic);
end component;

component pmos
port (O1 : out std_logic; I1, I2 : in std_logic);
end component;

for all : pmos use entity work.mos (pmos_behavioral);
for all : nmos use entity work.mos (nmos_behavioral);
constant vdd : std_logic := '1';
constant gnd : std_logic := '0';
signal s1 : std_logic;
begin
n1 : nmos port map (s1, gnd, b);
n2 : nmos port map (y, s1, a);
p1 : pmos port map (y, vdd, a);
p2 : pmos port map (y, vdd, b);
end nand_switch;
```

Verilog Two-Input NAND Gate

```
module NAND2gate (a, b, y);
input a, b;
output y;
supply1 vdd;
supply0 gnd;
nmos (s1, gnd, b);
nmos (y, s1, a);
pmos (y, vdd, a);
pmos (y, vdd, b);
endmodule
```

EXAMPLE 5.5 Switch-Level Description of a Two-Input NOR Gate

Here, a switch-level two-input NOR gate is designed. The truth table of the two-input NOR gate is shown in Table 5.7.

Referring to Table 5.7, we can design the gate using two complementary switch combinations (see Table 5.2). The first combination pulls y up to vdd when the gate levels of both switches are at 0; Table 5.2B satisfies this requirement. The second combination pulls y to ground level when either switch gate is at level 1; Table 5.2C satisfies this requirement. So, the final design consists of two complementary combinations: two serial PMOS switches and two parallel NMOS switches. Figure 5.7 shows the switch-level logic diagram of the NOR gate.

TABLE 5.7 Truth Table for a Two-Input NOR Gate

Input		Output
a	b	y
0	0	1
1	0	0
0	1	0
1	1	0

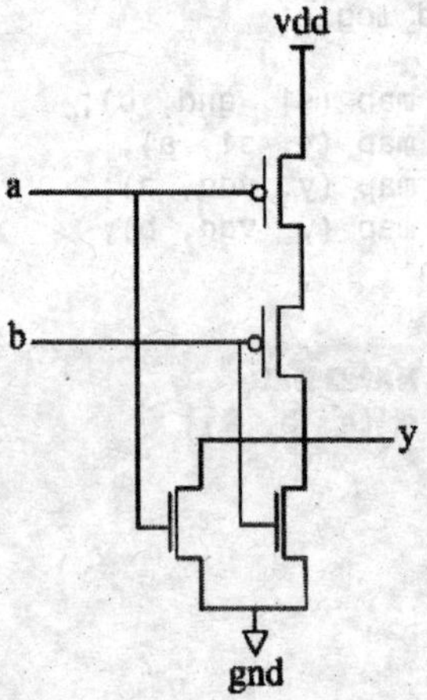

FIGURE 5.7 Switch-level logic diagram of an NOR gate.

From Figure 5.7 we write the HDL code. Listing 5.7 shows the HDL code of the NOR gate, using the two macros `pmos` and `nmos`.

LISTING 5.7 HDL Code for a Two-Input NOR Gate—VHDL and Verilog

VHDL Two-Input NOR Gate

```
library IEEE;
use IEEE.STD_LOGIC_1164.ALL;

entity nor2gate is
    Port (y : out std_logic; a, b : in std_logic );
end nor2gate;
```

```
architecture nor_switch of nor2gate is
component nmos
port (O1 : out std_logic; I1, I2 : in std_logic);
end component;

component pmos
port (O1 : out std_logic; I1, I2 : in std_logic);
end component;

for all : pmos use entity work.mos (pmos_behavioral);
for all : nmos use entity work.mos (nmos_behavioral);
constant vdd : std_logic := '1';
constant gnd : std_logic := '0';
signal s1 : std_logic;
begin
n1 : nmos port map (y, gnd, a);
n2 : nmos port map (y, gnd, b);
p1 : pmos port map (s1, vdd, a);
p2 : pmos port map (y, s1, b);
end nor_switch;
```

Verilog Two-Input NOR Gate

```
module nor2gate (a, b, y);
input a, b;
output y;
supply1 vdd;
supply0 gnd;
nmos (y, gnd, a);
nmos (y, gnd, b);
pmos (s1, vdd, a);
pmos (y, s1, b);
endmodule
```

5.5 SWITCH-LEVEL DESCRIPTION OF SIMPLE COMBINATIONAL LOGICS

In this section, simple combinational circuits will be designed using single PMOS and NMOS switches. The same logic is implemented as in Section 5.4, where Table 5.2 was used to come up with switch-level logics. Unless otherwise mentioned, all switch-level circuits here are designed to produce *strong outputs* (i.e., the output is either the ground or the vdd).

EXAMPLE 5.6 Switch-Level Description of a Two-Input AND Gate with Strong Output

As mentioned in Section 5.4, to produce strong output, the NMOS switches should pull the output down to ground, and the PMOS should pull the output up to vdd. The design of NAND, Invert, and NOR systems discussed in Section 5.4 satisfy this requirement. One approach is to convert the AND gate to an NAND and inverter. Figure 5.8 shows a switch-level logic diagram of an AND gate constructed from an NAND gate and an inverter.

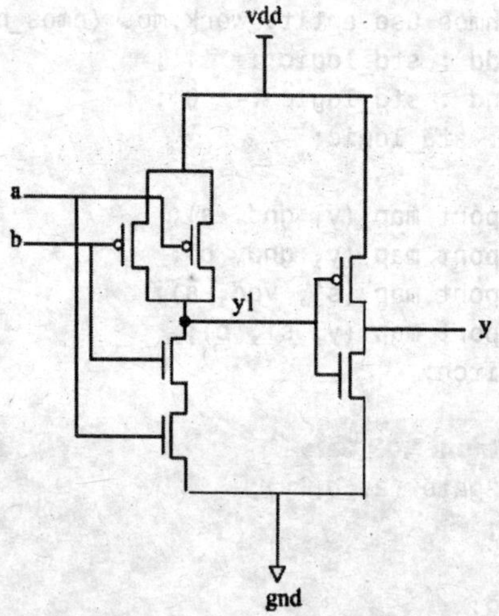

FIGURE 5.8 Switch-level logic diagram of an AND gate constructed from an NAND gate and an inverter.

Listing 5.8 shows the HDL code for the AND gate. The code is longer than that of Listing 5.4, but it should produce strong outputs.

LISTING 5.8 HDL Code for a Two-Input AND Gate with Strong Output—VHDL and Verilog

VHDL Two-Input AND Gate with Strong Output

```
library IEEE;
use IEEE.STD_LOGIC_1164.ALL;

entity and2Sgate is
    Port (y : out std_logic; a, b : in std_logic);
end and2Sgate;

architecture and_strong of and2Sgate is
```

```
component nmos
port (O1 : out std_logic; I1, I2 : in std_logic);
end component;

component pmos
port (O1 : out std_logic; I1, I2 : in std_logic);
end component;

for all : pmos use entity work.mos (pmos_behavioral);
for all : nmos use entity work.mos (nmos_behavioral);
constant vdd : std_logic := '1';
constant gnd : std_logic := '0';
signal s1, y1 : std_logic;
begin

--NAND
n1 : nmos port map (s1, gnd, b);
n2 : nmos port map (y1, s1, a);
p1 : pmos port map (y1, vdd, a);
p2 : pmos port map (y1, vdd, b);

--Invert
n3 : nmos port map (y, gnd, y1);
p3 : pmos port map (y, vdd, y1);

end and_strong;
```

Verilog Two-Input AND Gate with Strong Output

```
module and2Sgate (a, b, y);

input a, b;
output y;
supply1 vdd;
supply0 gnd;

//NAND
nmos (s1, gnd, a);
nmos (y1, s1, b);
pmos (y1, vdd, a);
pmos (y1, vdd, b);

//inverter
nmos (y, gnd, y1);
pmos (y, vdd, y1);
endmodule
```

EXAMPLE 5.7 Switch-Level Description of a Two-Input OR Gate with Strong Output

As was done in Listing 5.8, to produce a strong output, the OR gate is changed to an NOR and inverter. The switch-level logic of both NOR and inverter use NMOS switches to pull the output down to ground level, and NMOS switches to pull the output up to vdd. This generates strong outputs that are not degraded. Figure 5.9 shows the switch-level logic diagram of an OR gate constructed from the NOR gate and inverter.

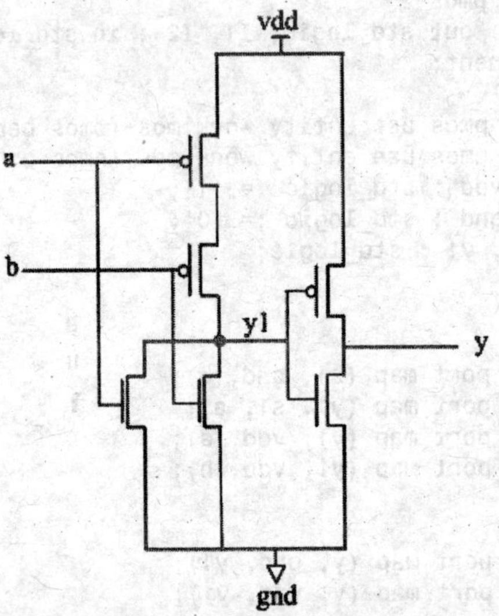

FIGURE 5.9 Switch-level logic diagram of an OR gate constructed from the NOR gate and Inverter.

Listing 5.9 shows the HDL code for an OR gate constructed from the NOR gate and inverter. The code is longer than that of Listing 5.5, but it should produce strong outputs.

LISTING 5.9 HDL Code of a Two-Input OR Gate with Strong Output—VHDL and Verilog

VHDL Two-Input OR Gate with Strong Output

```
library IEEE;
use IEEE.STD_LOGIC_1164.ALL;

entity OR2Sgate is
    Port (y : out std_logic; a, b : in std_logic);
end OR2Sgate;

architecture orgate_strong of OR2Sgate is

component nmos
port (O1 : out std_logic; I1, I2 : in std_logic);
end component;

component pmos
```

```
port (O1 : out std_logic; I1, I2 : in std_logic);
end component;

for all : pmos use entity work.mos (pmos_behavioral);
for all : nmos use entity work.mos (nmos_behavioral);
constant vdd : std_logic := '1';
constant gnd : std_logic := '0';
signal s1, y1 : std_logic;
begin

--NOR
n1 : nmos port map (y1, gnd, a);
n2 : nmos port map (y1, gnd, b);
p1 : pmos port map (s1, vdd, a);
p2 : pmos port map (y1, s1, b);

--Invert
n3 : nmos port map (y, gnd, y1);
p3 : pmos port map (y, vdd, y1);

end orgate_strong;
```

Verilog Two-Input OR Gate with Strong Output

```
module OR2Sgate (a, b, y);

input a, b;
output y;
supply1 vdd;
supply0 gnd;

//NOR
nmos (y1, gnd, a);
nmos (y1, gnd, b);
pmos (s1, vdd, a);
pmos (y1, s1, b);

//inverter
nmos (y, gnd, y1);
pmos (y, vdd, y1);
endmodule
```

EXAMPLE 5.8 Switch-Level Description of a Three-Input NAND Gate

Here, a three-input NAND gate is described. Table 5.8 shows the truth table of the three-input NAND gate.

As shown in Table 5.8, the output is 0 only when a, b, and c are 1. Table 5.2A, when extended to three switches, indicates the use of three NMOS switches connected in serial as the pull-down combination. For the pull-up combination, Table 5.2D, extended to three switches, needs three PMOS switches connected in parallel. Figure 5.10 shows the switch-level logic diagram for a three-input NAND gate.

TABLE 5.8 Truth Table for a Three-Input NAND Gate

Input			Output
a	b	c	y
0	0	0	1
1	0	0	1
0	1	0	1
1	1	0	1
1	0	1	1
1	0	1	1
1	1	0	1
1	1	1	0

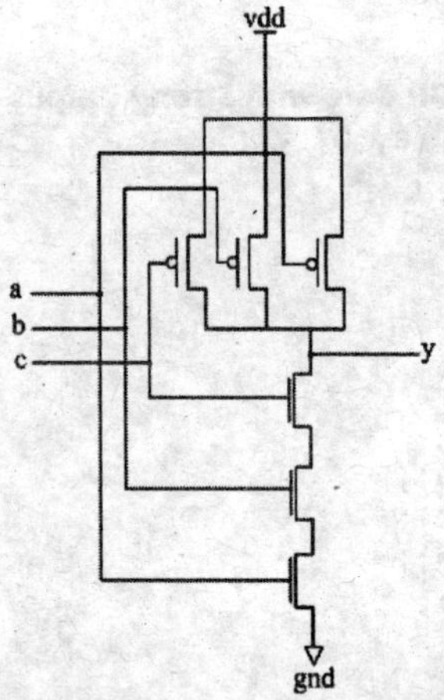

FIGURE 5.10 Switch-level logic diagram of a three-input NAND gate.

Listing 5.10 shows the HDL code for the three-input NAND gate, using `pmos` and `nmos` switches.

LISTING 5.10 HDL Code for a Three-Input NAND Gate—VHDL and Verilog

VHDL Three-Input NAND Gate Description

```
library IEEE;
use IEEE.STD_LOGIC_1164.ALL;
```

```
entity nand3gate is
    Port (y : out std_logic; a, b, c : in std_logic);
end nand3gate;

architecture nand3_switch of nand3gate is
component nmos
port (O1 : out std_logic; I1, I2 : in std_logic);
end component;

component pmos
port (O1 : out std_logic; I1, I2 : in std_logic);
end component;

for all : pmos use entity work.mos (pmos_behavioral);
for all : nmos use entity work.mos (nmos_behavioral);
constant vdd : std_logic := '1';
constant gnd : std_logic := '0';
signal s1, s2 : std_logic;
begin
n1 : nmos port map (s1, gnd, a);
n2 : nmos port map (s2, s1, b);
n3 : nmos port map (y, s2, c);

p1 : pmos port map (y, vdd, a);
p2 : pmos port map (y, vdd, b);
p3 : pmos port map (y, vdd, c);
end nand3_switch;
```

Verilog Three-Input NAND Gate Description

```
module nand3gate (a, b, c, y);
input a, b, c;
output y;
supply1 vdd;
supply0 gnd;

nmos (s1, gnd, a);
nmos (s2, s1, b);
nmos (y, s2, c);
pmos (y, vdd, a);
pmos (y, vdd, b);
pmos (y, vdd, c);

endmodule
```

EXAMPLE 5.9 Switch-Level Description of a Three-Input NOR Gate

In this Example, a three-input NOR gate is described, using switch-level description. Table 5.9 shows the truth table of the NOR gate.

Referring to Table 5.9, the NOR gate has an output of 1 only when a, b, and c are zeros. This is the opposite logic of NAND, so the serial combination of NMOS switches for the pull-down combination for the NAND is converted to a parallel combination of NMOS switches for the NOR gate. Similarly, the parallel combination of PMOS switches for the pull-up in the NAND gate is converted to a serial combination of PMOS switched in the NOR gate. Figure 5.11 shows the switch-level logic diagram of a three-input NOR gate.

TABLE 5.9 Truth Table for a Three-Input NOR Gate

Input			Output
a	b	c	y
0	0	0	1
1	0	0	0
0	1	0	0
1	1	0	0
0	0	1	0
1	0	1	0
0	1	0	0
1	1	1	0

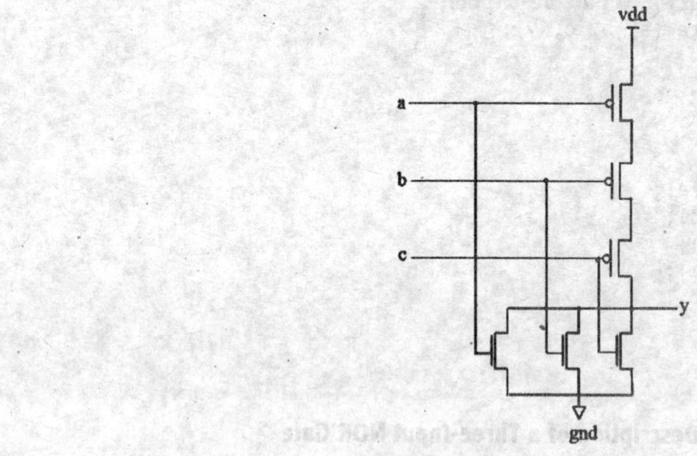

FIGURE 5.11 Switch-level logic diagram of an NOR gate.

Listing 5.11 shows the HDL code for the three-input NOR gate, using `pmos` and `nmos` switches.

LISTING 5.11 HDL Code for a Three-Input NOR Gate—VHDL and Verilog

VHDL Three-Input NOR Gate Description

```
library IEEE;
use IEEE.STD_LOGIC_1164.ALL;

entity nor3gate is
   Port (y : out std_logic; a, b, c : in std_logic);
end nor3gate;

architecture nor3_switch of nor3gate is

component nmos
port (O1 : out std_logic; I1, I2 : in std_logic);
end component;

component pmos
port (O1 : out std_logic; I1, I2 : in std_logic);
end component;

for all : pmos use entity work.mos (pmos_behavioral);
for all : nmos use entity work.mos (nmos_behavioral);
constant vdd : std_logic := '1';
constant gnd : std_logic := '0';
signal s1, s2 : std_logic;

begin
n1 : nmos port map (y, gnd, a);
n2 : nmos port map (y, gnd, b);
n3 : nmos port map (y, gnd, c);

p1: pmos port map (s1, vdd, a);
p2: pmos port map (s2, s1, b);
p3: pmos port map (y, s2, c);
end nor3_switch;
```

Verilog Three-Input NOR Gate Description

```
module nor3gate (a, b, c, y);

input a, b, c;
output y;
supply1 vdd;
supply0 gnd;
nmos (y, gnd, a);
nmos (y, gnd, b);
nmos (y, gnd, c);
pmos (s1, vdd, a);
pmos (s2, s1, b);
pmos (y, s2, c);

endmodule
```

EXAMPLE 5.10 Switch-Level Description of Simple Combinational Logic

This Example discusses the switch-level description of the logic presented by the Boolean function $y = \overline{abc + de}$. A straightforward approach would be to treat the logic as a three-input NAND gate—two two-input NAND gates and an inverter (see Figure 5.12). The number of switches (transistors) for this combination is $6+(2\times4)+2=16$.

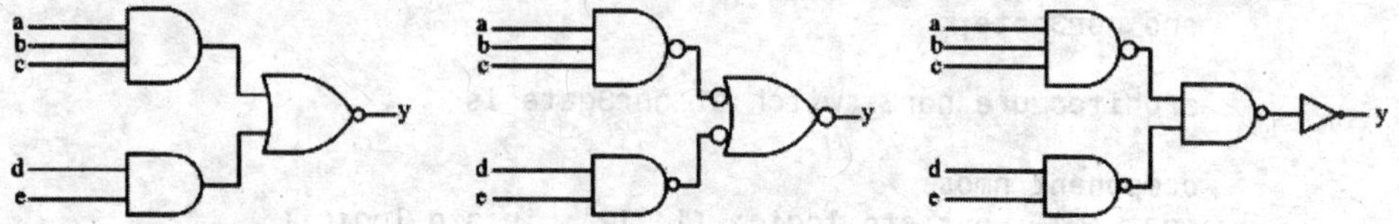

FIGURE 5.12 Gate-level logic diagram for $y = \overline{abc + de}$.

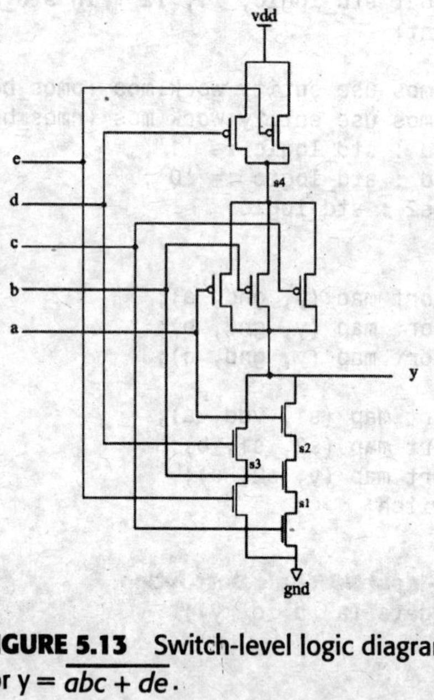

FIGURE 5.13 Switch-level logic diagram for $y = \overline{abc + de}$.

The number of transistors can be reduced by investigating the Boolean function. Note that y is pulled to zero only if abc = 1 or if de = 1. This means that the pull-down combination for abc is three NMOS switches driven by a, b, and c. The three switches are connected in serial. For the de, two serial NMOS switches are driven by d and e; the two switches are connected in parallel with the three NMOS switches. The pull-up combination is three PMOS switches driven by a, b, and c, and connected in parallel; the combination is connected in serial with another two PMOS switches driven by d and e, accounting for the ORing of abc with de. The total number of transistors is 10 in contrast to 16 for the straightforward approach. Figure 5.13 shows the switch-level logic diagram.

Listing 5.12 shows the HDL code for the logic, using `pmos` and `nmos` switches.

LISTING 5.12 HDL Code for the Logic $y = \overline{abc + de}$—VHDL and Verilog

VHDL $y = \overline{abc + de}$ Logic Description

```
library IEEE;
use IEEE.STD_LOGIC_1164.ALL;

entity simple_logic is
Port (y : out std_logic; a, b, c, d : in std_logic);
end simple_logic;

architecture ABC of simple_logic is
component nmos
port (O1 : out std_logic; I1, I2 : in std_logic);
end component;

component pmos
port (O1 : out std_logic; I1, I2 : in std_logic);
end component;
for all : pmos use entity work.mos (pmos_behavioral);
for all : nmos use entity work.mos (nmos_behavioral);
constant vdd : std_logic := '1';
constant gnd : std_logic := '0';
signal s1, s2, s3 : std_logic;

begin
n1 : nmos port map (s1, gnd, c);
n2 : nmos port map (s2, s1, b);
n3 : nmos port map (y, s2, a);
n4 : nmos port map (y, gnd, d);

p1 : pmos port map (y, s3, a);
p2 : pmos port map (y, s3, b);
p3 : pmos port map (y, s3, c);
p4 : pmos port map (s3, vdd, d);

end ABC;
```

Verilog $y = \overline{abc + de}$ Logic Description

```
module simple_logic (a, b, c, d, e, y);
input a, b, c, d, e;
output y;

supply1 vdd;
supply0 gnd;
```

```
nmos (s1, gnd, c);
nmos (s2, s1, b);
nmos (y, s2, a);
nmos (s3, gnd, e);
nmos (y, s3, d);

pmos (y, s4, a);
pmos (y, s4, b);
pmos (y, s4, c);

pmos (s4, vdd, d);
pmos (s4, vdd, e);

endmodule
```

EXAMPLE 5.11 Switch-Level Description of a XNOR Gate

To satisfy the requirement that NMOS switches pull down to ground (pass zero) and PMOS switches pull up (pass 1) to vdd, the XNOR gate is treated as the inverse of an XOR gate; so the Boolean function of the XNOR gate is:

$$y = \bar{a}\,\bar{b} + ab = \overline{(b\bar{a} + a\bar{b})} \tag{5.1}$$

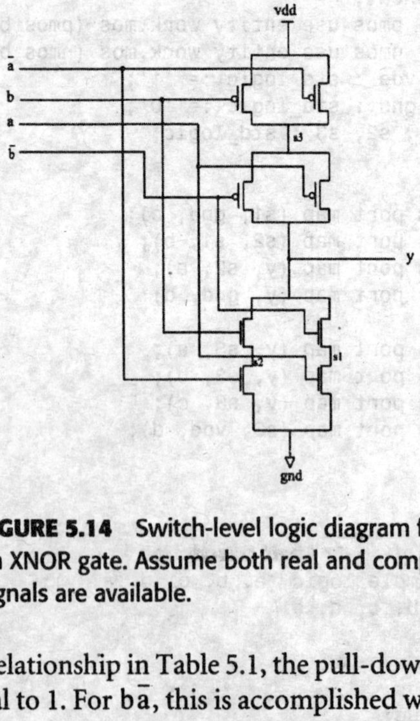

FIGURE 5.14 Switch-level logic diagram for an XNOR gate. Assume both real and complement signals are available.

According to the relationship in Table 5.1, the pull-down combination is active when $b\bar{a}$ or $a\bar{b}$ is equal to 1. For $b\bar{a}$, this is accomplished with two NMOS transistors (switches) connected in serial and driven by b and $\bar{a}$ (see Table 5.2A). The same is true for a $\bar{b}$; we need two transistors connected in serial. For the OR, the two serial transistors are connected in parallel (see Table 5.2C). For the pull-up combination, the serial and parallel combinations in the pull down are converted to parallel and serial, respectively. Figure 5.14 shows the transistor switch-level logic diagram of the XNOR gate.

Listing 5.13 shows the HDL code for the XNOR gate. Two inverters are used to generate the inverse of a and b. If the true and complement logic of a and b are available, then there is no need for the inverters.

LISTING 5.13 HDL Code for XNOR Gate–VHDL and Verilog

VHDL XNOR Gate Description

```
library IEEE;
use IEEE.STD_LOGIC_1164.ALL;

entity XOR_XNOR is
    Port (y : out std_logic; a, b : in std_logic);
end XOR_XNOR;

architecture XNORgate of XOR_XNOR is
component nmos
port (O1 : out std_logic; I1, I2 : in std_logic);
end component;

component pmos
port (O1 : out std_logic; I1, I2 : in std_logic);
end component;

for all : pmos use entity work.mos (pmos_behavioral);
for all : nmos use entity work.mos (nmos_behavioral);
constant vdd : std_logic := '1';
constant gnd : std_logic := '0';
signal abar, bbar, s1, s2, s3 : std_logic;
begin
--Invert a and b. If the complement of a and b are available,
--then there is no need for the following
--two pair (nmos and pmos) switches.

p1 : pmos port map (abar, vdd, a);
n1 : nmos port map (abar, gnd, a);
p2 : pmos port map (bbar, vdd, b);
n2 : nmos port map (bbar, gnd, b);

--Write the pull-down combination
n3 : nmos port map (s1, gnd, a);
n4 : nmos port map (y, s1, bbar);
n5 : nmos port map (s2, gnd, abar);
n6 : nmos port map (y, s2, b);

--Write the pull-up combination
```

```
p3 : pmos port map (y, s3, a);
p4 : pmos port map (y, s3, bbar);
p5 : pmos port map (s3, vdd, abar);
p6 : pmos port map (s3, vdd, b);

end XNORgate;
```

Verilog XNOR Gate Description

```
module XOR_XNOR (a, b, y);

input a, b;
output y;

supply1 vdd;
supply0 gnd;

/* Invert a and b. If the complement of a and b
   are available, then there is no need for the
   following two pair (nmos and pmos) switches */

pmos (abar, vdd, a);
nmos (abar, gnd, a);
pmos (bbar, vdd, b);
nmos (bbar, gnd, b);

// Write the pull-down combination
nmos (s1, gnd, a);
nmos (y, s1, bbar);
nmos (s2, gnd, abar);
nmos (y, s2, b);

// Write the pull-up combination
pmos (y, s3, a);
pmos (y, s3, bbar);
pmos (s3, vdd, abar);
pmos (s3, vdd, b);

endmodule
```

XOR/XNOR gates are very important, since they are the basic components in full adders. They have been also implemented in comparison circuits. Several publications can provide more information on reducing the number of transistors used in XOR or XNOR gates; see [Wang95] and [Weste03]. Figure 5.15 shows an XNOR gate with four transistors [Wang95]. Figure 5.15 is based on the fact that the output of the XNOR gate is equal to $\bar{b}$ if a = 0, or is equal to b if a = 1. Listing 5.14 shows the code for such an XNOR gate.

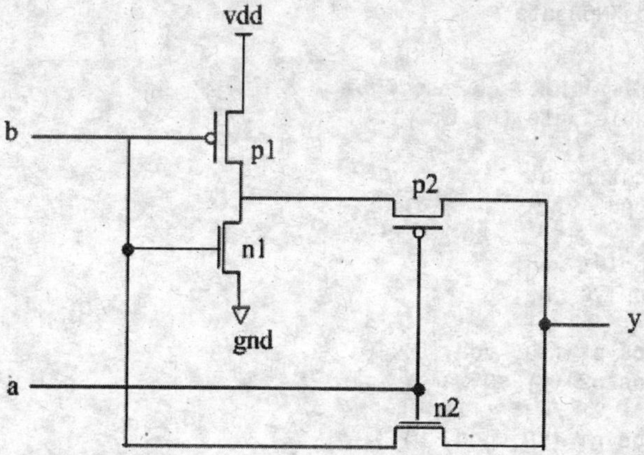

FIGURE 5.15 Switch-level logic diagram for an XNOR gate [Wang 95].

LISTING 5.14 HDL Code for an XNOR Gate—VHDL and Verilog

VHDL XNOR Gate Description

```
library IEEE;
use IEEE.STD_LOGIC_1164.ALL;

entity XNOR_degrade is
Port (y : out std_logic; a, b : in std_logic);
end XNOR_degrade;

architecture XNORgate of XNOR_degrade is
component nmos
port (O1 : out std_logic; I1, I2 : in std_logic);
end component;

component pmos
port (O1 : out std_logic; I1, I2 : in std_logic);
end component;

for all : pmos use entity work.mos (pmos_behavioral);
for all : nmos use entity work.mos (nmos_behavioral);
constant vdd : std_logic := '1';
constant gnd : std_logic := '0';
signal s0 : std_logic;

begin
p1 : pmos port map (s0, vdd, b);
p2 : pmos port map (y, s0, a);

n1 : nmos port map (s0, gnd, b);
n2 : nmos port map (y, b, a);
```

```
end XNORgate;
```

Verilog XNOR Gate Description

```
module gate (a, b, y);

input a, b;
output y;

supply1 vdd;
supply0 gnd;

pmos p1 (s0, vdd, b);
pmos p2 (y, s0, a);

nmos n1 (s0, gnd, b);
nmos n2 (y, b, a);

endmodule
```

EXAMPLE 5.12 Switch-Level Description of a 2x1 Multiplexer with Active High Enable

The Boolean function of such a multiplexer is shown in Equation 5.2.

$$y = E(a\ Sel + b\ \overline{Sel}) \tag{5.2}$$

E is the enable, a and b are the inputs, Sel is the select, and y is the output. If E = 0, the multiplexer is disabled and the output y is 0. If E = 1 and Sel = 1, the output y is a; if E = 1 and Sel = 0, the output y = b.

As in Listing 5.14, the output is inversed to satisfy the requirement that the NMOS switches pull down the output to ground level while the PMOS switches pull up y to vdd level. Accordingly, the truth table of the multiplexer is shown in Table 5.10.

TABLE 5.10 Truth Table for the Complement-Output Multiplexer

Input				Output
a	b	Sel	E	$\overline{y}$
x	x	x	0	1
0	0	0	1	1
1	0	0	1	1
0	1	0	1	0
1	1	0	1	0
0	0	1	1	1
1	0	1	1	0
0	1	1	1	1
1	1	1	1	0

From Table 5.10, note that $\overline{y}$ is 0 when Sel = 1 and a = 1, or when Sel = 0 and b = 1; so the pull-down combination is two NMOS switches in serial driven by a Sel connected in parallel, with two serial switches driven by b and $\overline{\text{Sel}}$. When E = 0, $\overline{y}$ = 1; this is a PMOS (pull-up) switch. The switch level of the multiplexer is shown in Figure 5.16.

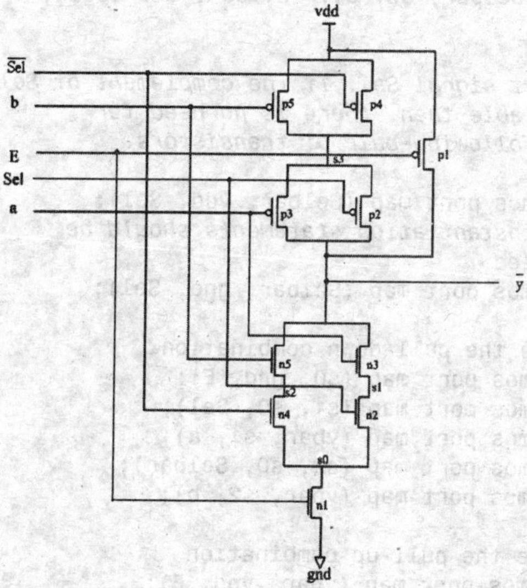

FIGURE 5.16 Switch-level logic diagram for a 2x1 multiplexer with active high enable and complement output. Assume $\overline{Sel}$ signal is available.

Listing 5.15 shows the HDL code for the multiplexer.

LISTING 5.15 HDL Code for a 2x1 Multiplexer with Active High Enable and Complement Output–VHDL and Verilog

VHDL 2x1 Multiplexer with Active High Enable and Complement Output

```
library IEEE;
use IEEE.STD_LOGIC_1164.ALL;

entity mux2x1 is
Port (a, b, Sel, E : in std_logic; ybar : out std_logic);
end mux2x1;

architecture mux2x1switch of mux2x1 is
component nmos
port (O1 : out std_logic; I1, I2 : in std_logic);
end component;
```

```
component pmos
port (O1 : out std_logic; I1, I2 : in std_logic);
end component;

for all : pmos use entity work.mos (pmos_behavioral);
for all : nmos use entity work.mos (nmos_behavioral);
constant vdd : std_logic := '1';
constant gnd : std_logic := '0';
signal Selbar, s0, s1, s2, s3 : std_logic;

begin
--Invert signal Sel. If the complement of Sel is
--available then, there is no need for
--the following pair of transistors.

v1 : pmos port map (Selbar, vdd, Sel);
--All instantiation statements should be
--labeled
v2 : nmos port map (Selbar, gnd, Sel);

--Write the pull-down combination
n1 : nmos port map (s0, gnd, E);
n2 : nmos port map (s1, s0, Sel);
n3 : nmos port map (ybar, s1, a);
n4 : nmos port map (s2, s0, Selbar);
n5 : nmos port map (ybar, s2, b);

--Write the pull-up combination
p1 : pmos port map (ybar, vdd, E);
p2 : pmos port map (ybar, s3, Sel);
p3 : pmos port map (ybar, s3, a);
p4 : pmos port map (s3, vdd, Selbar);
p5 : pmos port map (s3, vdd, b);

end mux2x1switch;
```

Verilog 2x1 Multiplexer with Active High Enable and Complement Output

```
module mux2x1 (a, b, Sel, E, ybar);

input a, b, Sel, E;
output ybar;

supply1 vdd;
supply0 gnd;

/* Invert signal Sel. If the complement of Sel
   is available then, there is no need for
   the following pair of transistors */

pmos (Selbar, vdd, Sel);
nmos (Selbar, gnd, Sel);
```

```
//Write the pull-down combination
nmos n1 (s0, gnd, E);
nmos n2 (s1, s0, Sel);
nmos n3 (ybar, s1, a);
nmos n4 (s2, s0, Selbar);
nmos n5 (ybar, s2, b);

//Write the pull-up combination
pmos p1 (ybar, vdd, E);
pmos p2 (ybar, s3, Sel);
pmos p3 (ybar, s3, a);
pmos p4 (s3, vdd, Selbar);
pmos p5 (s3, vdd, b);

endmodule
```

5.6 SWITCH-LEVEL DESCRIPTION OF SIMPLE SEQUENTIAL CIRCUITS

In Section 5.5, the switch-level description of combinational circuits was discussed. This chapter will describe some simple sequential circuits.

EXAMPLE 5.13 Switch-Level Description of an SR-Latch

The SR-latch was discussed in Chapter 4, "Structual Descriptions." and the gate-level logic diagram of the latch was shown in Figure 4.7. It is redrawn here for convenience in Figure 5.17.

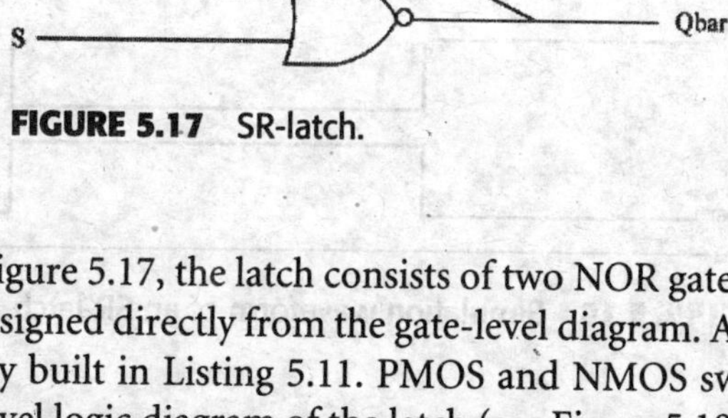

FIGURE 5.17 SR-latch.

As shown in Figure 5.17, the latch consists of two NOR gates. The switch-level logic diagram is designed directly from the gate-level diagram. A switch-level NOR gate was previously built in Listing 5.11. PMOS and NMOS switches are used to build the switch-level logic diagram of the latch (see Figure 5.18).

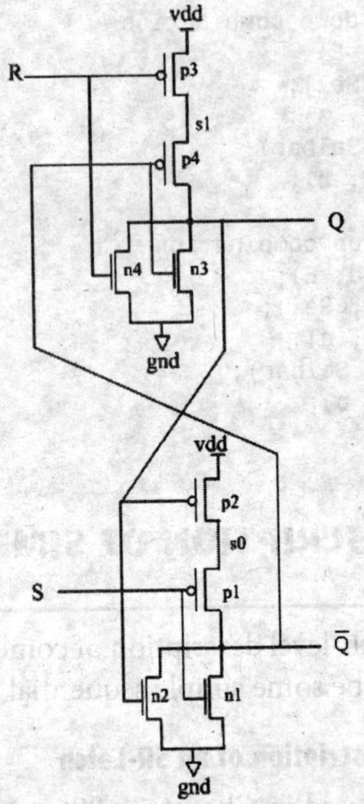

FIGURE 5.18 Switch-level logic diagram of an SR-latch.

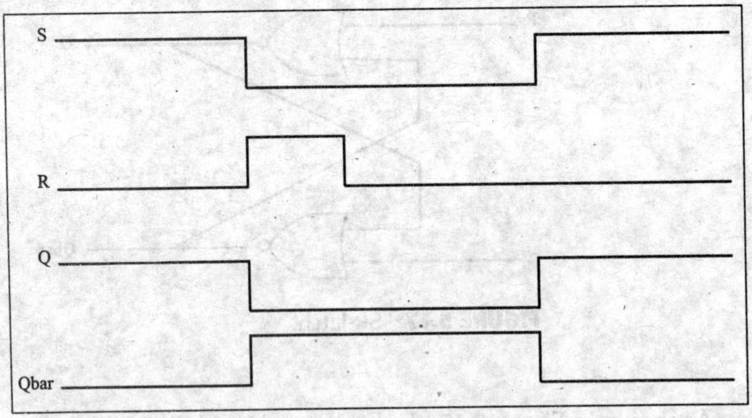

FIGURE 5.19 Simulation waveform of an SR-latch.

Listing 5.16 shows the HDL code of the latch. Since there are several transistors (switches), it is preferable to label the Verilog code for each transistor. For example, the Verilog code for switch n1 in Figure 5.18 is `nmos n1 (Qbar, gnd, S)`. The label `n1` in Verilog is optional, but because there are several transistors, each transistor has been labeled. In VHDL, the labeling of each instantiation statement is required. For example, the instantiation statement of transistor n1 is: `n1 : nmos port map (Qbar, gnd, S)`. Label `n1` is required. Figure 5.19 shows the simulation waveform of the multiplexer.

LISTING 5.16 HDL Code for an SR-Latch—VHDL and Verilog

VHDL SR-Latch Description

```
library IEEE;
use IEEE.STD_LOGIC_1164.ALL;

entity SR_Latch is
port (S, R : in std_logic; Q, Qbar : inout std_logic);
end SR_Latch;

architecture SR of SR_Latch is

component nmos
port (O1 : inout std_logic; I1, I2 : in std_logic);
--port O1 is selected here to be inout to match
--its use in the latch circuit
end component;

component pmos
port (O1 : inout std_logic; I1, I2 : in std_logic);
--port O1 is selected here to be inout
--to match its use in the latch circuit
end component;

for all : pmos use entity work.mos (pmos_behavioral);
for all : nmos use entity work.mos (nmos_behavioral);
--In this example only, the mode of Output port O1
--in the entity "mos" should
--be declared as inout instead of out.
constant vdd : std_logic := '1';
constant gnd : std_logic := '0';
signal s0, s1, s2 : std_logic;

begin

n1 : nmos port map (Qbar, gnd, S);
n2 : nmos port map (Qbar, gnd, Q);
p1 : pmos port map (s0, vdd, Q);
```

```
p2 : pmos port map (Qbar, s0, S);

n3 : nmos port map (Q, gnd, Qbar);
n4 : nmos port map (Q, gnd, R);
p3 : pmos port map (s1, vdd, R);
p4 : pmos port map (Q, s1, Qbar);

end SR;
```

Verilog SR-Latch Description

```
module SR_latch (S, R, Q, Qbar);
input S, R;
output Q, Qbar;
supply1 vdd;
supply0 gnd;

nmos n1 (Qbar, gnd, S);
nmos n2 (Qbar, gnd, Q);
pmos p1 (s0, vdd, Q);
pmos p2 (Qbar, s0, S);

nmos n3 (Q, gnd, Qbar);
nmos n4 (Q, gnd, R);
pmos p3 (s1, vdd, R);
pmos p4 (Q, s1, Qbar);

endmodule
```

5.6.1 CMOS Switches

In the previous sections, single switches (NMOS or PMOS) were discussed. It has been seen that for a strong signal, the NMOS switch should pass 0 and the PMOS should pass 1. Another family of MOS switches is the CMOS. As shown in Figure 5.20, the CMOS switch consists of two switches connected in parallel; one of the switches is NMOS and the other is PMOS. The gate controls of the two switches, gn and gp, are usually the true and the complement of the same signal. In this chapter, gn and gp are always the true and complement of the same signal. If gn is high (gp is low), the switch becomes conductive (output = input). If gn is low (gp is high), the switch becomes open. The main characteristic of the switch is that it can pass both strong 1 and strong 0.

Verilog has a built-in function to describe a CMOS switch. The following Verilog statement describes a CMOS switch with `input` and `output`, and gates `gn` for the NMOS switch and `gp` for the PMOS switch (see Figure 5.20).

```
cmos (output, input, gn, gp)
```

The basic VHDL package does not have a built-in code for CMOS switches, but it can be built as a macro consisting of the NMOS switch and PMOS switch described in Section 5.3.2. Listing 5.17 shows VHDL code for the CMOS switch shown in Figure 5.20.

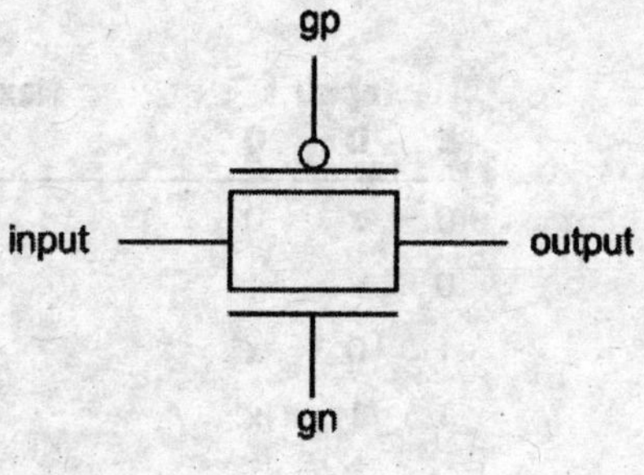

FIGURE 5.20 CMOS switch.

LISTING 5.17 VHDL Code for the CMOS Switch in Figure 5.20

```
library IEEE;
use IEEE.STD_LOGIC_1164.ALL;

entity CMOS is
port (output : out std_logic; input, gn, gp : in std_logic);
end CMOS;

architecture macro of CMOS is

--All switches presented here do not include any
--time parameters, such as
--rise time and fall times. They only mimic the
--logical functions of their
--Verilog counterparts.

component nmos
port (O1 : out std_logic; I1, I2 : in std_logic);
end component;

component pmos
port (O1 : out std_logic; I1, I2 : in std_logic);
end component;

for all : pmos use entity work.mos (pmos_behavioral);
for all : nmos use entity work.mos (nmos_behavioral);

begin
n1 : nmos port map (output, input, gn);
p1 : pmos port map (output, input, gp);

end macro;
```

EXAMPLE 5.14 Switch-Level Description of a D-Latch

The D-latch was covered in Chapter 2, "Data-Flow Descriptions." Table 5.11 shows the excitation table of the latch.

TABLE 5.11 Excitation Table for a D-Latch

Inputs E	D	Q	Next State Q+
0	x	0	0
0	x	1	1
1	0	x	0
1	1	x	1

The output follows D when the enable is high. When the enable is low, the output retains its previous value. The Boolean function of the output Q is:

$$Q = \bar{E}Q + ED \tag{5.3}$$

Two approaches are taken to find the switch-level logic diagram of the latch. The first approach used is the Boolean function, and NMOS and PMOS switches. The second approach uses CMOS switches.

Switch-Level Logic Diagram of a D-Latch Using PMOS and NMOS Switches

Equation 5.3 can be rewritten as:

$$\bar{Q} = \overline{(Q\bar{E} + ED)} \text{ and Q is the inverse of } \bar{Q}$$

Tables 5.2a–d are used to find the switch-level logic diagram. Figure 5.21 shows the switch-level logic diagram of the D-latch. Listing 5.18 shows the Verilog code for the latch.

LISTING 5.18 Verilog Code for a D-Latch Using NMOS and PMOS Switches

```
module D_latch (D, E, Q, Qbar);
input D, E;
output Q, Qbar;
supply1 vdd;
supply0 gnd;

pmos (Ebar, vdd, E);
nmos (Ebar, gnd, E);
```

```
nmos n1 (s0, gnd, D);
nmos n2 (Qbar, s0, E);
nmos n3 (s1, gnd, Q);
nmos n4 (Qbar, s1, Ebar);

pmos p1 (Qbar, s2, D);
pmos p2 (Qbar, s2, E);
pmos p3 (s2, vdd, Q);
pmos p4 (s2, vdd, Ebar);

endmodule
```

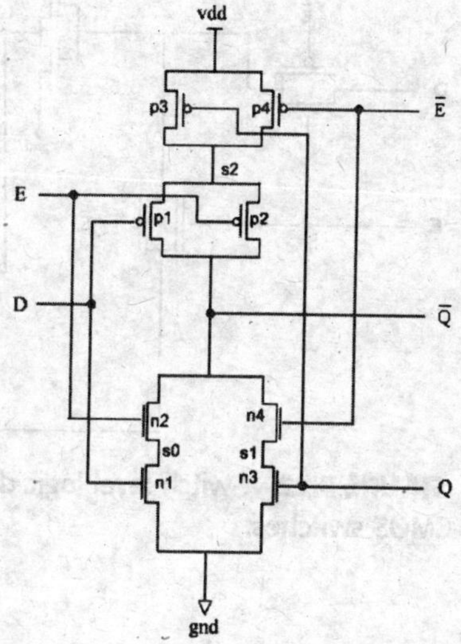

FIGURE 5.21 Switch-level logic diagram of a D-latch using PMOS and NMOS switches. Inverters between $\overline{Q}$ and Q, and between E and $\overline{E}$ are not shown.

Switch-Level Logic Diagram of a D-Latch Using CMOS Switches

Figure 5.22 shows the switch-level logic diagram of the D-latch. When enable (E) is high, CMOS switch c1 is closed, CMOS switch c2 is opened, and Q follows D. When E is low, CMOS switch c1 is opened, CMOS switch c2 is closed, and Q retains its previous value.

Listing 5.19 shows the HDL code for the D-latch. Due to the nature of signal Q where it is an input and output with more than one source (one cmos switch and an inverter), Q is declared as `inout`. Since there are three inverters, the inverter module discussed in Listing 5.3 is bound to the current module `D-Latch` rather than writing three individual inverters. In VHDL, use the statement:

```
for all : invert use entity work.inverter (Invert_switch);
```

to bind `inverter` to the current module `D_Latch`. In Verilog, we use the statement:

```
invert inv1 (Ebar, E);
```

which binds the module `invert` to the current module `D_Latch`.

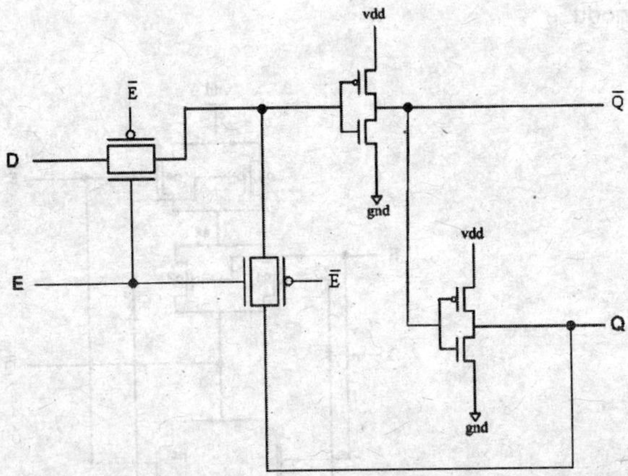

FIGURE 5.22 Switch-level logic diagram of a D-latch using CMOS switches.

LISTING 5.19 HDL Code for a D-Latch Using CMOS Switches–VHDL and Verilog

VHDL D-Latch Using CMOS Switches

```
library IEEE;
use IEEE.STD_LOGIC_1164.ALL;

entity D_Latch is
port (D, E : in std_logic; Q, Qbar : inout std_logic);
--Referring to Figure 5.22, signal Q is
--input and output and has multiple
--sources (the inverter and the CMOS switches,
--so Q has to be declared as
--inout. All other ports are also adjusted in
--the following components to be inout.

end D_Latch;

architecture DlatchCmos of D_Latch is
component CMOS
port (output : out std_logic; input, gn, gp : in std_logic);
```

```
end component;
component invert
Port (y : out std_logic; a : in std_logic );
end component;
for all : CMOS use entity work.CMOS (macro);
for all : invert use entity work.inverter( Invert_switch);
signal Ebar, s1 : std_logic;
begin
c1 : cmos port map (Q, D, E, Ebar);
c2 : cmos port map (Q, s1, Ebar, E);
inv1 : invert port map (Ebar, E);
inv2 : invert port map (Qbar, Q);
inv3 : invert port map (s1, Qbar);

end DlatchCmos;
```

Verilog D-Latch Using CMOS Switches

```
module D_latch (D, E, Q, Qbar);
input D, E;
output Q, Qbar;
cmos (Q, D, E, Ebar);
cmos (Q, s1, Ebar, E);
invert inv1 (Ebar, E);
invert inv2 (Qbar, Q);
invert inv3 (s1, Qbar);

endmodule

module invert (y, a);
input a;
output y;
supply1 vdd;
supply0 gnd;
pmos p1 (y, vdd, a);
nmos n1 (y, gnd, a);
endmodule
```

5.7 BIDIRECTIONAL SWITCHES

Bidirectional switches conduct in both ways—from drain to source and from source to drain. Their main use is as bidirectional buffers (busses). Three types of bidirectional switches are available in Verilog: `tran`, `tranif0`, and `tranif1`. Switch `tran` has no control; it conducts all the time. Switch `tranif1` conducts if `control` is 1; otherwise the nondriving signal (output) is put on high impedance. Switch `tranif0` conducts if `control` is 0; otherwise, the nonconducting signal (output) is put on high impedance. The Verilog code for the three switches is as follows:

```
tran (dataio1, dataio2);
trannif0 (dataio1, dataio2, control);
tranif1 (dataio1, dataio2, control);
```

VHDL does not have built-in switches, but we can build these switches (see Section 5.3.2).

Listing 5.20 shows the same Verilog code in Listing 5.11, but `tranif1` and `tranif0` are used instead of NMOS and PMOS switches.

LISTING 5.20 HDL Code for the Logic $y = \overline{abc + de}$–VHDL and Verilog

```
module simple_logic (a, b, c, d, e, y);
input a, b, c, d, e;
output y;

supply1 vdd;
supply0 gnd;

tranif1 (s1, gnd, c);
tranif1 (s2, s1, b);
tranif1 (y, s2, a);
tranif1 (s3, gnd, e);
tranif1 (y, s3, d);

tranif0 (y, s4, a);
tranif0 (y, s4, b);
tranif0 (y, s4, c);

tranif0 (s4, vdd, d);
tranif0 (s4, vdd, e);

endmodule
```

5.8 SUMMARY

In this chapter, HDL descriptions based on switches have been presented. The switches are built from perfect transistors. The transistor is either conducting to saturation or not conducting; this corresponds to two switch states: close and open, respectively. Switch-level is the lowest level of HDL description. Verilog has an extensive switch-level description Library. Standard VHDL does not have switch-level; if we use VHDL for switch-level description, packages have to built or imported from vendors.

VHDL switches have also been built as components (see Chapter 4). The power supply (vdd) and ground (gnd) in all systems covered in this chapter are the sources of the strongest 1s and 0s; `nmos` switches pass strong 0 and `pmos` switches pass strong 1. To produce strong output signals, nmos switches are employed as pull-down to ground networks, and `pmos` switches are employed as pull-up to vdd networks. Parallel and serial combinations of `pmos` and `nmos` switches have been implemented to describe combinational and sequential circuits. Other switches, such as `cmos`, `tran`, tranif0, and tranif1, constructed from parallel combinations of NMOS and PMOS switches, have been also been discussed.

Many publications are available on the Examples covered in this chapter. These publications may use innovative ways to reduce the number of transistors. The reader is encouraged to consult them (see References) if the main goal is to find a design with the minimum number of transistors. A summary of the statements covered in this chapter is shown in Table 5.12.

5.9 EXERCISES

In all the following questions, unless otherwise mentioned, choose the design that yields to strong outputs.

5.1 Derive the switch-level (transistor) logic of an XOR gate using a minimum number of transistors. Write and verify by simulation the VHDL code using PMOS and NMOS switches.

5.2 Without using the computer, inspect the Verilog code shown in Listing 5.21 and find the Boolean function of the output y. Translate the code to VHDL, and verify your code by simulating it.

LISTING 5.21 Verilog Code for Exercise 5.2

```
module Problem_2 (a, b, c, y);
input a, b, c;
output y;

supply1 vdd;
supply0 gnd;

pmos (d, vdd, c);
nmos (d, gnd, c);

cmos (y, a, c, d);
cmos (y, b, d, c);

endmodule
```

5.3 For the XNOR gate discussed in Listing 5.13, use NAND gates and inverters to design the XNOR gate. Write the switch-level Verilog code and verify your design. Contrast this approach with that of Listing 5.13 in terms of the total number of transistors needed.

5.4 Referring to Listing 5.15, construct the gate level of the multiplexer using NOR gates and inverters. Write the switch-level VHDL code and verify your design. What is the total number of transistors used in this gate-level design?

5.5 Design the switch level for an SR-latch from the Boolean function using the minimum number of switches. Compare the number of switches used with that of Listing 5.16. Write the VHDL code, and verify your design by simulation.

5.6 Write the VHDL code for Listing 5.18. Verify your code by simulation.

5.7 In Figure 5.22, the control E is active high. Modify the Figure to show an active low enable.

5.8 Repeat Listing 5.15, but use `tranif0` and `tranif1` instead of PMOS and NMOS switches.

5.10 REFERENCES

[Dillinger88] Dillinger, T. E., *VLSI Engineering*. Prentice Hall, Inc., 1988.

[Kang99] Kang, S. M. and Y. Leblebici, *CMOS Digital Integrated Circuits*, 2d ed. McGraw-Hill, Inc., 1999.

[Nelson95] Nelson V. P., H. T. Nagle, B. D. Carroll, and J. D. Irwin, *Digital Logic Circuit Analysis & Design*. Prentice Hall, 1995.

[Wang95] Wang, J., S. Fang, and W. Feng, "New Efficient Designs for XOR and XNOR Functions on the Transistor Level." *IEEE Journal of Solid State Circuits*, vol. 29, no. 7, pp. 780–786.

[Weste03] Weste, Neil H. E. and D. Harris, *CMOS VLSI Design*, 3d ed. Addison-Wesley, 2004.

6 Procedures, Tasks, and Functions

In This Chapter

- Understand the concept of procedures (VHDL), tasks (Verilog), and functions (both VHDL and Verilog).
- Review and understand how to convert between different types of data.
- Review signed vector multiplication.
- Understand a simple enzyme mechanism.

6.1 HIGHLIGHTS OF PROCEDURES, TASKS, AND FUNCTIONS

Facts

- Instead of writing the segment/construct every time it is used, a single call statement to a function, task, or a procedure that references this segment/construct is all that is needed.
- Procedures and tasks can have more than one input and more than one output. Functions have a single output, but can have more than one input.
- Procedures and functions in VHDL can be called only from within `process`. Tasks and functions in Verilog can be called only from within `always` or `initial`.

6.2 PROCEDURES AND TASKS

Procedures (VHDL) and tasks (Verilog) are similar to subroutines in other software languages, such as C. In many modules, a routine is repeatedly used, such as a multiplication algorithm, addition algorithm, or conversion between two numbering systems. Instead of writing these routines every time they are needed, the routines' codes can be stored as the body of a `procedure` (VHDL) or as the body of a `task` (Verilog). Whenever the routine needs to be executed, the procedure (task) is called by writing just one call statement. Section 6.2.1 discusses procedures, and Section 6.2.2 discusses tasks.

6.2.1 Procedures (VHDL)

Procedures are behavioral statements (see Chapter 3, "Behavioral Descriptions"). A procedure has two parts: the declaration and the body. The declaration includes the name of the procedure, the inputs to the procedure and their types, and the outputs of the procedure and their types. For example, the declaration:

```
procedure Booth (X, Y : in signed (3 downto 0);
    Z: out signed (7 downto 0)) is
```

declares a procedure by the name (identifier) `Booth`. The inputs are variables `X` and `Y`, each is 4-bits, and the type of the inputs is `signed`. The output is an 8-bit variable `Z`, and its type is `signed`. In the declaration statement, `procedure` and `is` are predefined words, and have to be inserted in the order shown. If the inputs or outputs are signals, they should be explicitly specified as follows:

```
procedure exmple (signal a : in std_logic ;
    signal y : out std_logic) is
```

The body of the procedure contains the behavioral statements that show the details of the procedure, mainly the relationship between the input(s) and the output(s). The body of the procedure cannot include the behavioral statement `process`. An example of a procedure is as follows:

```
procedure exmple (signal a : in std_logic; signal y : out std_logic) is
variable x : std_logic;
begin
x := a;
case x is

end case;
y <= x;
end exmple;
```

The procedure is called by a sequential statement that has to appear inside `process`. For example, the above procedure `exmple` is called as follows:

```
process (d, clk)
begin
......
exmple (d, z);
```

```
.........
End process
```

The input of the procedure a assumes the value of d. The type of a should match the type of d. After the procedure executes, the output of procedure y is passed to z. The type of z should match the type of y.

If a vector is an output or input of a procedure, it should not be constrained in length. Consider the declaration of procedure Vect_constr:

```
procedure Vect_constr (X : in std_logic_vector;
    Y : out std_logic_vector) is
```

The length of vectors X and Y should not be constrained (i.e., not specified).

VHDL has a large number of built-in procedures in its standard package. Other procedures can be imported from external packages. An example of a built-in procedure is open file (see Chapter 8, "Advanced HDL Descriptions").

6.2.2 Tasks (Verilog)

Tasks are Verilog subprograms. They can be implemented to execute specified routines repeatedly. The format in which the task is written can be divided into two parts: the declaration and the body of the task. In the declaration, the name of the task is specified, and the outputs and inputs of the task are listed. An example of task declaration is:

```
task addr;
output cc, dd;
input aa, bb;
```

addr is the name (identifier) of the task. The outputs are cc and dd, and the inputs are aa and bb. task is a predefined word. The body of the task shows the relationship between the outputs and the inputs. An example of the body of a task is:

```
begin
cc = aa ^ bb;
.............
end
endtask
```

The body of the task cannot include always or initial. A task must be called within the behavioral statement always or initial (see Chapter 3). An example of calling the task addr is as follows:

```
............
always @ (a, b)
begin
addr (c, d, a, b);
end
```

addr is the name of the task, and inputs a and b are passed to aa and bb. The outputs of the task cc and dd, after execution, are passed to c and d, respectively.

Verilog has a large number of built-in tasks included in its package.

6.2.3 Examples—Procedures and Tasks

The following Examples discuss procedures and tasks. Some of these Examples have been covered in Chapter 3. Here they are rewritten using procedure and task.

EXAMPLE 6.1 HDL Behavioral Description of a Full Adder Using Procedure and Task

In Chapter 4, "Structual Descriptions," a full adder was constructed from two half adders. Here we use the same concept to design a full adder from two half adders using behavioral description. The code for a half adder is written using procedure in VHDL or task in Verilog to construct the full adder. Figure 6.1 shows a block diagram of the full adder.

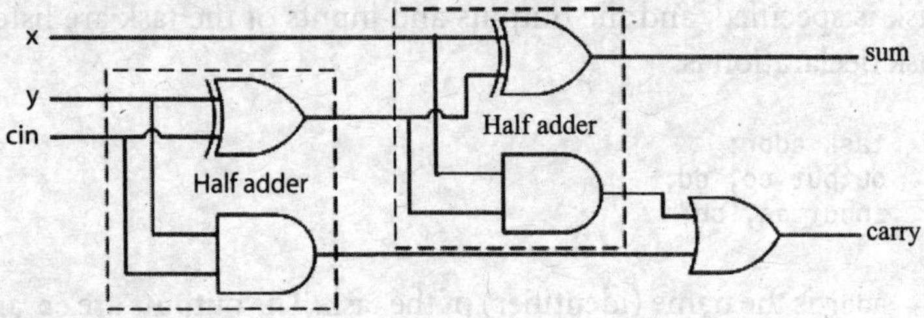

FIGURE 6.1 Block diagram of the full adder as two half adders.

Listing 6.1 shows the HDL code for the full adder using procedure (VHDL) and task (Verilog). Referring to the VHDL listing, the code for the half adder is written as a procedure:

```
procedure Haddr(sh, ch : out std_logic; ah, bh : in std_logic) is
begin
sh := ah xor bh;
ch := ah and bh;
end Haddr;
```

The name of the procedure is Haddr; the inputs are sh and ch, and the outputs are ah and bh. The type of the outputs and inputs is std_logic. The code of the procedure is based on the Boolean functions of the half adder. To call the procedure, it has to be inside `process`, since `procedure` is a behavioral (sequential) statement. To call the procedure `Haddr`:

```
Haddr (sum1, c1, y, cin);
```

where `Haddr` is the name of the procedure, and the values `y` and `cin` are passed to the inputs of the procedure `ah` and `bh`, respectively. After calculating the outputs (`sh` and `ch`), the procedure passes the value of those outputs to `sum1` and `c1`, respectively.

For the Verilog code, the task is:

```
task Haddr;
output sh, ch;
input ah, bh;
begin
    sh = ah ^ bh;
    ch = ah & bh;
end
endtask
```

The name of the task is `Haddr`, the inputs are `ah` and `bh`, and the outputs are `sh` and `ch`. The task code is based on the Boolean functions of the half adder. To call `task`, it has to be inside `always` or `initial`, since `task` is a behavioral (sequential) statement. Therefore, to call the task `Haddr`:

```
Haddr (sum1, c1, y, cin);
```

where `haddr` is the name of the task, and the values `y` and `cin` are passed to the inputs of the task `ah` and `bh`, respectively. After calculating the outputs (`sh` and `ch`), the task passes the value of the outputs to `sum1` and `c1`, respectively.

LISTING 6.1 HDL Description of a Full Adder Using `Procedure` and `Task`—VHDL and Verilog

VHDL Full Adder Using `Procedure`

```
library IEEE;
use IEEE.STD_LOGIC_1164.ALL;

entity full_add is
port (x, y, cin : in std_logic; sum, cout : out std_logic);
end full_add;

architecture two_halfs of full_add is
--The full adder is built from two half adders

procedure Haddr (sh, ch : out std_logic; ah, bh : in std_logic) is
```

```
--This procedure describes a half adder
begin
sh := ah xor bh;
ch := ah and bh;
end Haddr;

begin

addfull : process (x, y, cin)
variable sum1, c1, c2, tem1, tem2 : std_logic;
begin
    Haddr (sum1, c1, y, cin);
    Haddr (tem1, c2, sum1, x);
    –The above two statements are calls to the procedure Haddr
    tem2 := c1 or c2;
    sum <= tem1;
    cout <= tem2;
end process;

end two_halfs;
```

Verilog Full Adder Using Task

```
module Full_add (x, y, cin, sum, cout);
//The full adder is built from two half adders
input x, y, cin;
output sum, cout;
reg sum, sum1, c1, c2, cout;
always @ (x, y, cin)
begin

Haddr (sum1, c1, y, cin);
Haddr (sum, c2, sum1, x);
//The above two statements are calls to the task Haddr.
cout = c1 | c2;
end

task Haddr;
//This task describes the half adder
output sh, ch;
input ah, bh;
begin
    sh = ah ^ bh;
    ch = ah & bh;
end
endtask

endmodule
```

Notice that the half adder `procedure` (`task`) was executed twice, but the body of the `procedure` (`task`) was only written once.

EXAMPLE 6.2 HDL Description of an *N*-Bit Ripple-Carry Adder Using `Procedure` and `Task`

In Listing 4.18 of Chapter 4, the HDL structural description of a 3-bit ripple-carry adder was written. Here the behavioral code for an *N*-bit ripple-carry adder is written using `procedure` (VHDL) and `task` (Verilog). Listing 6.2 shows the HDL code of the adder. The procedure (task) `Faddr` describes a 1-bit full adder. To describe an *N*-bit adder, the procedure (task) is called *N* times.

LISTING 6.2 HDL Description of an *N*-Bit Ripple-Carry Adder Using `Procedure` and `Task`—VHDL and Verilog

VHDL N-Bit Ripple-Carry Adder Using `Procedure`

```
library IEEE;
use IEEE.STD_LOGIC_1164.ALL;

entity adder_ripple is
generic (N : integer := 3);
    port (x, y : in std_logic_vector (N downto 0);
        cin : in std_logic;
        sum : out std_logic_vector (N downto 0);
        cout : out std_logic);
end adder_ripple;

architecture adder of adder_ripple is
procedure Faddr (sf, cof : out std_logic;
        af, bf, cinf : in std_logic) is

--This procedure describes a full adder
begin

sf := af xor bf xor cinf;
cof := (af and bf) or (af and cinf) or (bf and cinf);
end Faddr;

begin
addrpl : process (x, y, cin)
variable c1, c2, tem1, tem2 : std_logic;
variable cint : std_logic_vector (N+1 downto 0);
variable sum1 : std_logic_vector (N downto 0);
begin
cint(0) := cin;
for i in 0 to N loop
    Faddr (sum1(i), cint(i+1), x(i), y(i), cint(i));
    --The above statement is a call to the procedure Faddr
end loop;
sum <= sum1;
cout <= cint(N+1);

end process;

end adder;
```

Verilog N-Bit Ripple-Carry Adder Using `Task`

```
module adder_ripple (x, y, cin, sum, cout);
parameter N = 3;
input [N:0] x, y;
input cin;
output [N:0] sum;
output cout;

reg [N+1:0] cint;
reg [N:0] sum;
reg cout;
integer i;
always @ (x, y, cin)
begin

    cint[0] = cin;
    for (i = 0; i <= N; i = i + 1)
    begin
        Faddr (sum[i], cint[i+1], x[i], y[i], cint[i]);
        //The above statement is a call to task Faddr
end

cout = cint[N+1];
end

task Faddr;
//The task describes a full adder
output sf, cof;
input af, bf, cinf;
begin

    sf = af ^ bf ^ cinf;
    cof = (af & bf) | (af & cinf) | (bf & cinf);
end
endtask

endmodule
```

EXAMPLE 6.3 Unsigned Binary Vector to Integer Conversion Using `Procedure` and `Task`

Since VHDL is a strict data type-oriented language, conversion between data types, such as integer and binary, is important. Verilog, however, is flexible when dealing with data types and allows computational operations between different types without any conversion. However, for the sake of instruction in how to use `task`, Verilog code will be used in some of the following conversion examples.

In Chapter 3, behavioral code was written for conversions between binary and integer data. For more information on converting between different number systems, refer to [Mano00] and [Nelson95]. Here procedure (task) is used to perform the conversion.

Listing 6.3 shows the HDL code for converting an unsigned binary vector to an integer. The conversion is based on accumulating the weighted sum of the binary bits. The code:

```
result := result + 2**i; --VHDL
int = int + 2**i          //Verilog
```

performs the accumulation. To create a global constant *N* that represents the number of binary bits:

```
generic (N : integer := 3); --VHDL
parameter N = 3;             //Verilog
```

is used for the binary to be converted. In Listing 6.3, $N = 3$ is used as an example; we can change the number of bits just by changing the value of *N*. The statement:

```
for i in bin'Range loop
```

has an index `i` with a range equal to that of `bin`. `Range` is a predefined attribute.

In addition to conversion, the procedure (task) outputs a flag (Z). Z = 1 if the value of the binary vector is zero, otherwise Z = 0.

LISTING 6.3 HDL Code for Converting an Unsigned Binary to an Integer Using `Procedure` and `Task`—VHDL and Verilog

VHDL: Converting an Unsigned Binary to an Integer Using `Procedure`

```
library ieee;
use ieee.std_logic_1164.all;
use ieee.numeric_std.all; --This Library is for type "unsigned"

entity Bin_Int is
generic (N : natural := 3);
    port (X_bin : unsigned (N downto 0);
        Y_int : out natural; Z : out std_logic);
        --Y is always positive
end Bin_Int;

architecture convert of Bin_Int is

procedure bti (bin : in unsigned; int : out natural;
    signal Z : out std_logic) is
--the procedure bti is to change binary to integer
--Flag Z is chosen to be a signal rather than a variable
--Since the binary vector is always positive,
--use type natural for the output of the procedure.
variable result : natural;
begin
```

```
result := 0;
for i in bin'Range loop

--bin'Range represents the range of the unsigned vector bin
--Range is a predefined attribute
    if bin(i) = '1' then
    result := result + 2**i;
    end if;
end loop;
int := result;
if (result = 0) then
    Z <= '1';
    else
    Z <= '0';
end if;
end bti;

begin
process (X_bin)
variable tem : natural;

begin
bti (X_bin, tem, Z);
Y_int <= tem;
end process;
end convert;
```

Verilog: Converting an Unsigned Binary to an Integer Using Task

```
module Bin_Int (X_bin, Y_int, Z);
parameter N = 3;
input [N:0] X_bin;
output integer Y_int;
output Z;
reg Z;
always @ (X_bin)
begin
    bti (Y_int, Z, N, X_bin);
end

task      bti;
parameter P = N;
output integer int;
output Z;
input N;
input [P:0] bin;
integer i, result;
begin
    int = 0;
//change binary to integer
    for (i = 0; i <= P; i = i + 1)
    begin
        if (bin[i] == 1)
```

```
            int = int + 2**i;
        end
        if (int == 0)
        Z = 1'b1;
        else
        Z = 1'b0;
    end
    endtask

    endmodule
```

The simulation output for Listing 6.3 is shown in Figure 6.2

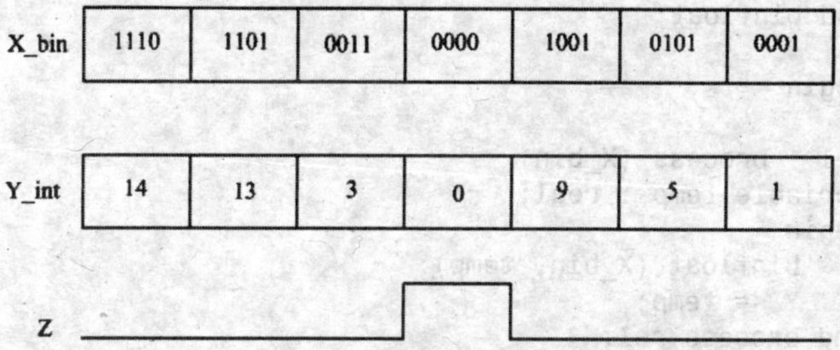

FIGURE 6.2 Simulation output for binary to integer conversion.

EXAMPLE 6.4 Fraction Binary to Real Conversion Using Procedure and Task

Here, a fraction binary represents a fixed point where the binary point is at the left of the most significant bit. Examples of such binary numbers are 0.11 (equivalent to $2^{-1} + 2^{-2} = 0.5 + 0.25 = 0.75$) and 0.001 (equivalent to $2^{-3} = 0.125$). Listing 6.4 shows the HDL code for converting the binary using `procedure` and `task` by multiplying each bit by its weight. The first, left-most bit has a weight of 2^{-1}; the next bit to the right has a weight of 2^{-2}, and so on.

LISTING 6.4 HDL Code for Converting a Fraction Binary to Real Using `Procedure` and `Task`—VHDL and Verilog

VHDL: Converting a Fraction Binary to Real Using `Procedure`

```
library ieee;
use ieee.std_logic_1164.all;

entity Bin_real is
generic (N : integer := 3);
port (X_bin : in std_logic_vector (0 to N); Y : out real);
end Bin_real;

architecture Bin_real of Bin_real is
```

```
procedure binfloat (a : in std_logic_vector; float : out real) is
variable flt : real;
begin

flt := 0.0;
rl : for i in N downto 0 loop

    if (a(i) = '1') then

        flt := flt + 1.0 / 2**(i+1);
        --The above statement multiplies each bit by its weight
    end if;
end loop rl;
float := flt;
end binfloat;

begin

rel : process (X_bin)
variable temp : real;
begin
    binfloat (X_bin, temp);
    Y <= temp;
end process rel;
end Bin_real;
```

Verilog: Converting a Fraction Binary to Real Using Task

```
module Bin_real (X_bin);
parameter N = 3;
input [N:0] X_bin;
real Z;

always @ (X_bin)
begin
    binfloat (X_bin, Z);
end

task binfloat;
parameter P = N;
input [0:P] a;
output real float;
integer i;
begin
    float = 0.0;
    for (i = 0; i <= P; i = i + 1)
    begin
        if (a[i] == 1)

        float = float + 1.0 / 2**(i+1);
        //The above statement multiplies each bit by its weight
    end
```

```
end
endtask

endmodule
```

The simulation output is shown in Figure 6.3.

X_bin	1000	0100	0010	0001	0101	1100
Z	0.5	0.25	0.125	0.0625	0.3125	0.75

FIGURE 6.3 Simulation output for fraction binary conversion to real.

EXAMPLE 6.5 Unsigned Integer to Binary Conversion Using `Procedure` and `Task`

In this Example, integer-type data is converted to binary-type data. As was done in Chapter 3, the integer is successively divided by 2 to find the equivalent binary. The `mod` function is used to find the remainder of the division by 2. Listing 6.5 shows the HDL code for converting an integer to binary using `procedure` and `task`. The code also checks to see if the integer is even or odd. The `even_flag` in Listing 6.5 equals 1 when the integer is even; if `even _flag` is 0, then the integer is odd.

LISTING 6.5 HDL Code for Converting an Unsigned Integer to Binary Using `Procedure` and `Task`—VHDL and Verilog

VHDL: Converting an Unsigned Integer to Binary Using `Procedure`

```
library IEEE;
use IEEE.STD_LOGIC_1164.ALL;

entity Int_Bin is
generic (N : integer := 3);
port (X_bin : out std_logic_vector (N downto 0);
    Y_int : in integer;
    flag_even : out std_logic);
end Int_Bin;

architecture convert of Int_Bin is

procedure itb (bin : out std_logic_vector;
    signal flag : out std_logic;
    N : in integer; int : inout integer) is

--The procedure itb is to convert the integer to binary
```

```
--The dimension of bin does not have to be specified
--at the above declaration statement; the procedure
--can determine the dimension of bin later in its body.

begin
if (int MOD 2 = 0) then
--The above statement checks int to see if it is even.
    flag <= '1';
    else
    flag <= '0';
end if;
for i in 0 to N loop

    if (int MOD 2 = 1) then
        bin (i) := '1';
        else
        bin (i) := '0';
    end if;

--perform integer division by 2
    int := int/2;
end loop;
end itb;

begin
process (Y_int)
variable tem : std_logic_vector (N downto 0);
variable tem_int : integer ;

begin
    tem_int := Y_int;
    itb (tem, flag_even, N, tem_int);
    X_bin <= tem;
end process;
end convert;
```

Verilog: Converting an Unsigned Integer to Binary Using Task

```
module Int_Bin (X_bin, flag_even, Y_int );

/*In general Verilog, in contrast to VHDL, does not
  strictly differentiate between integers and binaries;
  for example, if bin is declared as a binary of width 4,
  bin = bin/2 can be written, and the Verilog, but not
  VHDL, performs this division as if bin is integer.
  In the following, the corresponding VHDL program in
  Listing 6.5a is just translated to practice with
  the command task */

parameter N = 3;
output [N:0] X_bin;
output flag_even;
input [N:0] Y_int;
```

```
reg [N:0] X_bin;
reg flag_even;
always @ (Y_int)
begin
itb (Y_int, N, X_bin, flag_even);
end

task itb;
parameter P = N;
input integer int;
input N;
output [P:0] bin;
output flag;
integer j;
begin

if (int %2 == 0)
//The above statement checks int to see if it is even.
    flag = 1'b1;
    else
    flag = 1'b0;

for (j = 0; j <= P; j = j + 1)
    begin
        if (int %2 == 1)
        bin[j] = 1;
        else
        bin[j] = 0;
        int = int/2;
    end

end
endtask

endmodule
```

The simulation output of this conversion is shown in Figure 6.4.

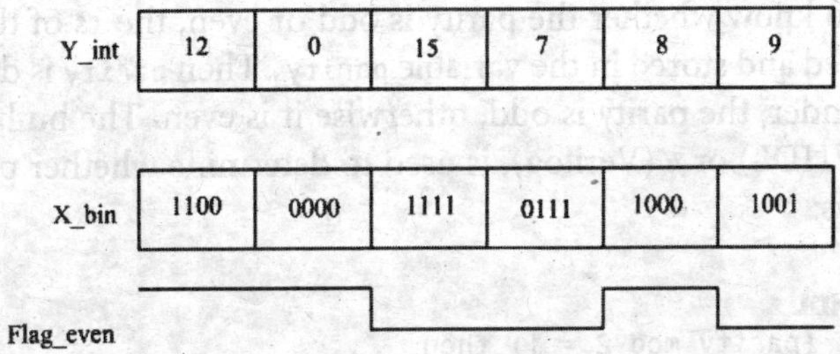

FIGURE 6.4 Simulation output for integer conversion to binary.

EXAMPLE 6.6 Signed Binary to Integer Conversion Using `Procedure` and `Task`

Here, a signed binary is considered; the value of the binary data can be negative or positive. As is common, the negative data is represented by its 2s complement. The most significant bit of the data is the sign bit—if it is 0, the number is positive; otherwise it is negative.

If the data is positive (the most significant bit is 0), then it is identical to unsigned data. For example, if 4-bit data is considered, 0101 is a positive number because its most significant bit is 0; the value of the number is 5. The data 1011 is a negative number; the value is –5. The decimal value of any negative number Y in the 2s complement format can be written as $Y' - 2^N$, where N is the number of bits of Y and Y' is equal to the decimal value of unsigned Y. For example if Y = 1011, then N = 4. Y' = 1011 unsigned = 11_d. So Y = 11 – 16 = –5.

Listing 6.6 shows the HDL code for converting from signed binary to integer using `procedure` (`task`). In addition to conversion, the procedure determines the parity (even or odd) of the input binary. Since code has previously been written for conversion from binary to integer (Listing 6.3), it is used here. If the binary data is positive, then it is the same code as in Listing 6.3. If the binary data is negative; its integer value is calculated as if it is unsigned, and then this integer value is corrected by subtracting 16 from it. Referring to the HDL code in Listing 6.6, the sign of the input `date` is tested for its most significant bit; if it is 1, we need to correct the integer value (`result`) as follows:

VHDL
```
if (binsg(M) = '1') then
result := result - 2**(M+1);
end if;
```

Verilog
```
if (bin [P] == 1)
int = int - 2**(P+1);
```

To know whether the parity is odd or even, the 1s of the input data are accumulated and stored in the variable `parity`. Then `parity` is divided by 2; if there is a remainder, the parity is odd, otherwise it is even. The built-in function modulus, `mod` (VHDL) or `%` (Verilog), is used to determine whether parity is odd or even, as follows:

VHDL
```
if (parity mod 2 = 1) then
--if parity is divisible by 2, then it is even,
--otherwise it is odd.
    even <= '0';
    else
```

```
    even <= '1';
end if;
```

Verilog

```
if ((parity % 2) == 1)
//if parity is divisible by 2, then it is even,
  otherwise it is odd.

even = 0;
else
even = 1;
```

The signal `even_parity` in Listing 6.6 identifies the parity of the input data. If the parity is even, then `even_parity` is 1, otherwise it is 0.

LISTING 6.6 HDL Code for Converting a Signed Binary to Integer Using `Procedure` and `Task`—VHDL and Verilog.

VHDL: Converting a Signed Binary to Integer Using `Procedure`

```
library ieee;
use ieee.std_logic_1164.all;
use ieee.numeric_std.all;

entity signed_btoIn is
generic (N : integer := 3);
port (X_bin : in signed (N downto 0); Y_int : out integer;
    even_parity : out std_logic );
end signed_btoIn;

architecture convert of signed_btoIn is

procedure sbti (binsg : in signed; M : in integer;
    int : out integer; signal even : out std_logic) is

--The procedure sbti is to change signed binary to integer and
--also to find whether the parity of the binary is odd or even.
--The dimension of "sbin" does not have to be specified
--at the declaration statement; it can be declared later
--in the body of the procedure.

variable result, parity : integer;
begin

result := 0;
for i in 0 to M loop
if binsg(i) = '1' then
result := result + 2**i;
parity := parity + 1;
end if;
end loop;
```

```
if (binsg(M) = '1') then
result := result - 2**(M+1);
end if;
int := result;

if (parity mod 2 = 1) then
    even <= '0';
    else
    even <= '1';
end if;

end sbti;

begin
process (X_bin)
variable tem : integer;

begin
    sbti (X_bin, N, tem, even_parity);
    Y_int <= tem;
end process;
end convert;
```

Verilog: Converting a Signed Binary to Integer Using `Task`

```
module signed_btoIn(X_bin, Y_int, even_parity);

/*In general, Verilog (in contrast to VHDL) does not
  strictly differentiate between integers and binaries;
  for example if bin is declared as binary of width 4,
  write bin = bin/2, and the Verilog (but not VHDL) will
  perform this division. In the following, just translate
  the corresponding VHDL counterpart program. */

parameter N = 3;
input signed [N:0] X_bin;
output integer Y_int;
output even_parity;
reg even_parity;

always @ (X_bin)
begin
    sbti (Y_int, even_parity, N, X_bin);
end

task sbti;
parameter P = N;
output integer int;
output even;
input N;
input [P:0] bin;
integer i;
reg parity;
```

```
begin

int = 0;
parity = 0;
//change binary to integer
for (i = 0; i <= P; i = i + 1)
    begin
        if (bin[i] == 1)
        begin
            int = int + 2**i;
            parity = parity + 1;
        end
    end

    if ((parity % 2) == 1)
    even = 0;
    else
    even = 1;

    if (bin [P] == 1)
    int = int - 2**(P+1);

end
endtask

endmodule
```

The simulation output of the conversion is shown in Figure 6.5.

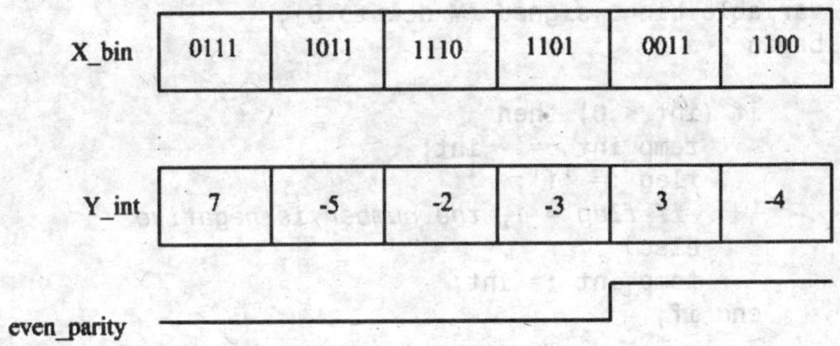

FIGURE 6.5 Simulation output for converting a signed binary to integer.

EXAMPLE 6.7 Integer to Signed Binary Conversion Using Procedure

In this Example, an integer is converted to signed binary (see Listing 6.7). We test the sign of the integer and negate it if it is negative, and then the same code as in Listing 6.3 is applied. We record the outcome of the sign test in the variable `flag`. After calculating the equivalent binary, its value is adjusted according to the flag. If the flag is 1, this means that the integer has been negated, so we negate the binary.

If the flag is 0, no action is taken. The conversion is written in procedure `sitb` and declared as:

```
procedure sitb (sbin : out signed; M, int : in integer) is
```

In the above declaration statement, the dimension of `sbin` does not have to be specified. The procedure can determine the dimension later on in its body.

LISTING 6.7 VHDL Code for Converting an Integer to Signed Binary Using `Procedure`

```
library IEEE;
use IEEE.STD_LOGIC_1164.ALL;
use ieee.numeric_std.all;

entity signed_IntToBin is
generic (N : integer := 3);
port (X_bin : out signed (N downto 0); Y_int : in integer);
end signed_IntToBin;

architecture convert of signed_IntToBin is
procedure sitb (sbin : out signed; M, int : in integer) is

--The procedure sitb is to convert integer into signed binary.
--The dimension of "sbin" does not have to be specified at the
--declaration statement; it can be declared later in the
--body of the procedure
variable temp_int : integer;
variable flag : std_logic;
variable bin : signed (M downto 0);
begin

    if (int < 0) then
        temp_int := - int;
        flag := '1';
        –if flag = 1, the number is negative
        else
        temp_int := int;
    end if;

    for i in 0 to M loop
        if (temp_int MOD 2 = 1) then
        bin (i) := '1';
        else
        bin (i) := '0';
        end if;
    –integer division by 2
    temp_int := temp_int/2;
    end loop;

    if (flag = '1') then
```

```
            sbin := - bin;
            else sbin := bin;
        end if;
        end sitb;

        begin
            process (Y_int)
            variable tem : signed (N downto 0);

            begin
                sitb(tem, N, Y_int);

                X_bin <= tem;
            end process;
    end convert;
```

EXAMPLE 6.8 Signed Vector Multiplication Using `Procedure` and `Task`

In this Example, vector multiplication is performed. Equation 6.1 shows vector multiplication where

$$d = a \times b \tag{6.1}$$

a is a row vector with three elements, and b is a column vector with three elements. Accordingly, d is a row vector with three elements. We can write Equation 6.1 as:

$$d = \begin{bmatrix} a0 & a1 & a2 \end{bmatrix} \times \begin{bmatrix} b0 \\ b1 \\ b2 \end{bmatrix} \tag{6.2}$$

From Equation 6.2:

$$d = a0\,b0 + a1\,b1 + a2\,b2 \tag{6.3}$$

In this example, all elements of Equation 6.3 are signed binary. To multiply two signed numbers, we use the Booth algorithm as discussed in Chapter 3. Listing 6.8 shows the HDL code for signed vector multiplication using `procedure (task)`. The inputs to the multiplication algorithm are written as:

```
port (a0, a1, a2, b0, b1, b2 : in signed (N downto 0);
    d : out signed (3*N downto 0));
```

If a large number of elements are being multiplied, the above code may not be practical because a large number of ports must be listed. In Chapter 7 ("Mixed-Type Descriptions"), the ports are listed as an array; this will shorten the code. The Booth algorithm is written as a procedure or task with the declaration:

VHDL
```
procedure booth (X, Y : in signed (3 downto 0);
    Z : out signed (7 downto 0))
```

Verilog
```
task booth;
input signed [3:0] X, Y;
output signed [7:0] Z;
```

where the inputs are X and Y, and the output is Z. The procedure (task) is restricted to 4x4 bits. We can generalize the procedure (task) to multiply any *N*x*N* bits (see Exercise 6.2). The three procedure (task) callings calculate the partial products a0b0, a1b1, and a2b2 as:

```
booth (a0, b0, tem0);
booth (a1, b1, tem1);
booth (a2, b2, tem2);
```

The partial products are stored in the 8-bit registers tem0, tem1, and tem2, respectively. To find the product d, add tem0 + tem1 + tem2; and according to Listing 6.8, the product is stored in 10-bit register d. By choosing 10 bits, any overflow is avoided that might occur after accumulating the partial products in register d. To calculate d in Verilog, simply write:

```
d = tem0 + tem1 + tem2;
```

In VHDL, since the language is strictly type and size oriented, the VHDL simulator may not perform the above operation, since d has a different size than tem0, tem1, and tem2. Several approaches can be taken to adjust the size. The approach here is to convert tem0, tem1, and tem2 to integers by using the procedure sbti, then add all integers and convert back to binary by using the procedure sitb. Another approach is to extend the sizes of tem0, tem1, and tem2 to 10 bits and then add (see Exercise 6.1).

LISTING 6.8 HDL Code for Signed Vector Multiplication Using Procedure and Task—VHDL and Verilog

VHDL: Signed Vector Multiplication Using Procedure
```
library IEEE;
use IEEE.STD_LOGIC_1164.ALL;
use ieee.numeric_std.all;

entity Vector_Booth is
generic (N : integer := 3);
port (a0, a1, a2, b0, b1, b2 : in signed (N downto 0);
    d : out signed (3*N downto 0));
```

```
end Vector_Booth;

architecture multiply of Vector_Booth is
procedure booth (X, Y : in signed (3 downto 0);
    Z : out signed (7 downto 0)) is
--Booth algorithm here is restricted to 4x4 bits.
--It can be adjusted to multiply any NxN bits.
variable temp : signed (1 downto 0);
    variable sum : signed (7 downto 0);
    variable E1 : unsigned (0 downto 0);
    variable Y1 : signed (3 downto 0);
begin

sum := "00000000"; E1 := "0";
    for i in 0 to 3 loop
    temp := X(i) & E1(0);
    Y1 := -Y;
    case temp is
        when "10" => sum (7 downto 4) :=
        sum (7 downto 4) + Y1;
        when "01" => sum (7 downto 4) :=
        sum (7 downto 4) + Y;
        when others => null;
    end case;
    sum := sum srl 1;
    sum (7) := sum(6);
    E1(0) := x(i);
    end loop;
    if (y = "1000") then

--If Y = 1000; then according to the code,
--Y1 = 1000 (-8 not 8 because Y1 is 4 bits only).
--The statement sum = -sum adjusts the answer.

    sum := -sum;
    end if;
    Z := sum;
    end booth;

procedure sitb (sbin : out signed; M, int : in integer) is
--The procedure sitb is to convert integer into signed binary.
--The dimension of "sbin" does not have to be specified
--at the declaration statement; it can be declared
--later in the body of the procedure.
variable temp_int : integer;
variable flag : std_logic;
variable bin : signed (M downto 0);
begin

if (int < 0) then
temp_int := -int;
flag := '1';
else
```

```
temp_int := int;
end if;

for i in 0 to M loop
if (temp_int MOD 2 = 1) then
bin (i) := '1';
else
bin (i) := '0';
end if;
temp_int := temp_int/2;
end loop;
if (flag = '1') then
sbin := -bin;
else
sbin := bin;
end if;
end sitb;

procedure sbti (binsg : in signed; M : in integer;
    int : out integer) is
--The procedure sbti is to change signed binary to integer.
--We do not have to specify the dimension of "sbin"
--at the declaration statement; it can be declared
--later in the body of the procedure.

variable result : integer;

begin

result := 0;
for i in 0 to M loop
if binsg(i) = '1' then
result := result + 2**i;
end if;
end loop;

if (binsg(M) = '1') then
result := result - 2**(M+1);
end if;
int := result;
end sbti;

begin
process (a0, b0, a1, b1, a2, b2)
variable tem0, tem1, tem2 : signed ((2*N + 1) downto 0);
variable d_temp : signed (3*N downto 0);
variable temi0, temi1, temi2, temtotal : integer;

begin
--Find the partial products a0b0, a1b1, a2b2
booth (a0, b0, tem0);
booth (a1, b1, tem1);
booth (a2, b2, tem2);
```

```
--Change the partial products to integers
sbti (tem0, (2*N+1), temi0);
sbti (tem1, (2*N+1), temi1);
sbti (tem2, (2*N+1), temi2);

--Find the total integer sum of partial products
temtotal := temi0 + temi1 + temi2;

--Change the integer to binary
sitb (d_temp, 3*N, temtotal);

d <= d_temp;
end process;
end multiply;
```

Verilog: Signed Vector Multiplication Using Task

```
module Vector_Booth (a0, a1, a2, b0, b1, b2, d);
parameter N = 3;
input signed [N:0] a0, a1, a2, b0, b1, b2;
output signed [3*N : 0] d;
reg signed [2*N+1 : 0] tem0, tem1, tem2;
reg signed [3*N : 0] d;
always @ (a0, b0, a1, b1, a2, b2)
begin
booth (a0, b0, tem0);
//booth is a task to multiply a0 x b0 = tem0

booth (a1, b1, tem1);
booth (a2, b2, tem2);
d = tem0 + tem1 + tem2;
end

task booth;
input signed [3:0] X, Y;
output signed [7:0] Z;
reg signed [7:0] Z;
reg [1:0] temp;
integer i;
reg E1;
reg [3:0] Y1;

begin
Z = 8'd0;
E1 = 1'd0;

for (i = 0; i < 4; i = i + 1)
begin
temp = {X[i], E1}; //This is catenation
Y1 = -Y; //Y1 is the 2' complement of Y
case (temp)
    2'd2 : Z [7:4] = Z [7:4] + Y1;
    2'd1 : Z [7:4] = Z [7:4] + Y;
```

```
        default : begin end
    endcase
    Z = Z >> 1; /*This is a logical shift of one position to
                   the right*/
    Z[7] = Z[6];
        /*The above two statements perform arithmetic shift
            where the sign of the number is preserved after
            the shift.*/
    E1 = X[i];

    end

        if (Y == 4'b1000) Z = -Z;

    /* If Y = 1000, then Y1 = 1000 (should be 8 not -8).
       This error is because Y1 is 4 bits only.
       The statement Z = -Z adjusts the value of Z. */

        end

    endtask
    endmodule
```

Figure 6.6 shows the output simulation of the vector multiplication.

a0	1001	1000	1000	1011
a1	0010	1000	1000	1111
a2	1011	1000	1000	0101
b0	0111	0111	1000	1110
b1	0010	0111	1000	1001
b2	0011	0111	1000	1000
d	1111000100	1101011000	0011000000	1111101001

FIGURE 6.6 Simulation output of vector multiplication.

EXAMPLE 6.9 Enzyme-Substrate Activity Using Procedure and Task

Enzymes are chemical molecules (generally proteins) that increase the speed of a reaction. The human body uses a large number of different enzymes to speed up various types of chemical reactions, such as those involving metabolism. Each enzyme is specific for a certain reactant, called a "substrate." For the substrate-enzyme complex to work, the enzyme must be capable of binding to the substrate; if the enzyme cannot bind to the substrate, the enzyme will not be active. The activity of the enzyme increases with the strength of binding. There are several theories that explain this binding, such as the key-lock mechanism. In this mechanism, the physical shape of the enzyme matches a groove on the substrate where it can bind. In Figure 6.7, the "(a) Strong" illustrates a potentially strong bond between the enzyme and substrate; "(b) Weak" shows a case where binding is almost impossible between the substrate and enzyme.

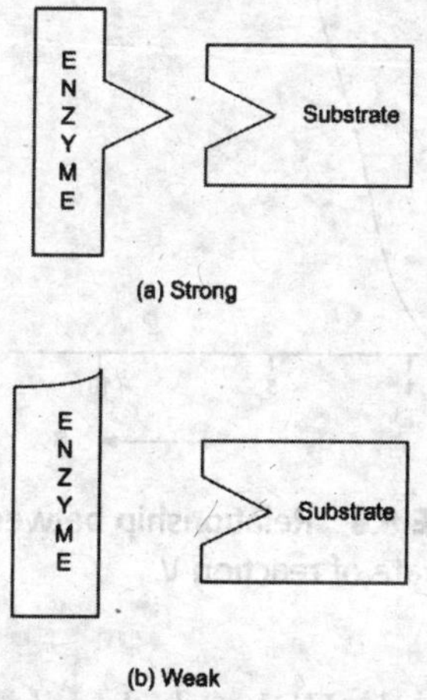

FIGURE 6.7 Binding between substrate and enzyme.

The binding strength between the substrate and the enzyme is measured by a parameter called the "dissociation constant M." If M is large, the binding or affinity between substrate and enzyme is weak, and vice versa. The rate of reaction between an enzyme with dissociation constant M and a substrate with concentration S is represented by Equation 6.4.

$$V = V_{max} \frac{S}{S + M} \tag{6.4}$$

where S is the concentration of the substance, V_{max} is the maximum possible rate of reaction when S >> M. Usually, V_{max} is assigned the value of 1 (100%); and accordingly, V is measured as a fraction or percentage. Figure 6.8 shows a graphical representation of Equation 6.4 for a dissociation constant of 3 units. Notice that if S = M, then V = $0.5V_{max}$; so M can be viewed as the concentration of substrate at which the rate of reaction is 50% of V_{max} . Figure 6.8 shows the relationship between the substrate concentration S and rate of reaction V.

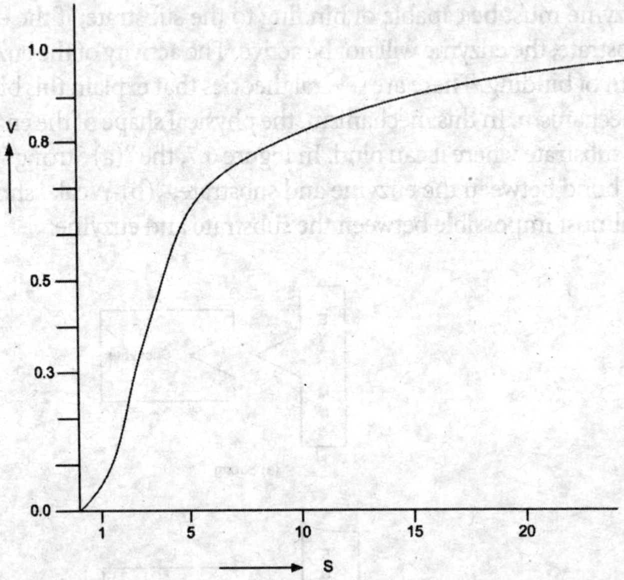

FIGURE 6.8 Relationship between the substrate concentration S and rate of reaction V.

Listing 6.9 shows the HDL code describing enzyme-substrate activity.

LISTING 6.9 HDL Description for Enzyme Activity Using `Procedure` and `Task`—VHDL and Verilog

VHDL: Enzyme Activity Using `Procedure`

```
library ieee;
use ieee.std_logic_1164.all;
use ieee.numeric_std.all;
use ieee.std_logic_arith.all;

--A description of enzyme-substrate binding mechanism.
--S= (Vmax *S)/(S + M) where S is the substrate concentration,
--M is the dissociation constant, and Vmax is the maximum
--rate of reaction. In this example, Vmax = 1.
--The inputs are S and M in binary (integer); the output v
--is in Q4 format. This means that v is always less than
```

```
--one, with the binary point placed to the left of the
--most significant bit. For example, if v = 1010, the decimal
--equivalent is .5 + .125 = 0.625.
--To calculate v, convert S and M to unsigned integers,
--find the real value of (S/(S + M)), convert this real
--value to Q4 by multiplying it with 2**4 = 16, and
--convert the integer to binary.

entity enzyme_beh is
    port (S : in std_logic_vector (3 downto 0);
        v : out std_logic_vector (3 downto 0);
        M : in std_logic_vector (3 downto 0));

end enzyme_beh;

architecture enzyme of enzyme_beh is
procedure bti (bin : in std_logic_vector; int : out integer) is

variable result : integer;
begin
result := 0;
    for i in 0 to 3 loop
    if bin(i) = '1' then
    result := result + 2**i;
    end if;
    end loop;
    int := result;
    end bti;
procedure itb (int : in integer; bin : out std_logic_vector) is
--the procedure itb is to change the integer to binary
variable temp : integer;

begin
temp := int;
for j in 0 to 3 loop
    if (temp MOD 2 = 1) then
    bin (j) := '1';
    else bin (j) := '0';
    end if;
    temp := temp/2;
    end loop;
end itb;
Procedure rti (r : in real; int : out integer) is

--This procedure converts a real value to an integer;
--the procedure is effective for small numbers <100.
```

```
--For very large numbers, the procedure is slow, since the
--execution time of the procedure is proportional to the
--value of the real number to be converted.

variable temp : real;
variable intg : integer := 0;
begin

temp := r;
while temp >= 0.5 loop
intg := intg + 1;
temp := r - 1.0 * intg ;
end loop;
int := intg;
end rti;

begin
P1 : process(S, M)
Variable S1, M1, v1 : integer;
Variable vr, vq4, vmax : real;
variable tem : std_logic_vector (3 downto 0);
begin
bti (S, s1); bti (M, m1);
vmax := 1.0;
vr := vmax*(1.0 *S1) / (S1 * 1.0 + M1 * 1.0);
vq4 := vr * 2**4;
rti (vq4, v1);
itb (v1, tem);
v <= tem;
end process P1;
end enzyme;
```

Verilog: Enzyme Activity Using Task

```
/* A description of enzyme-substrate binding mechanism.
   S= (Vmax *S)/(S + M), where S is the substrate
   concentration, M is the dissociation constant,
   and Vmax is the maximum rate of reaction. In this example,
   Vmax =1. The inputs are S and M in binary (integer);
   the output v is in Q4 format. This means that v is always
   less than 1, with the binary point placed to the left of
   the most significant bit. For example, if v = 1010, the
   decimal equivalent is .5 + .125 = 0.625. To calculate V,
   find the real value of (S /(S + M)), convert this real
   value to Q4 by multiplying it with 2**4 =16, and convert
   the integer to binary. */
```

```
module enzyme_beh (S, M, V);
input [3:0] S, M;
output [3:0] V;
integer vmax;
reg [3:0] V;
real vr;
always @ (S, M)
begin
vmax = 1;
vr = vmax * (1.0 * S) / (S * 1.0 + M * 1.0);
vr = vr * 2**4;
rti (vr, V);
end

task rti;
/* This task can be replaced by just one statement, v1= r.
   Verilog, in contrast to VHDL, can handle different
   types of the assignment statement. Verilog finds the
   equivalent integer value v1 for the real r. The task has
   been designed here only to match the VHDL procedure rti. */

input real r;
output [3:0] v1;
real temp;
begin
temp = r;
v1 = 4'b0000;
while (temp >= 0.5)
begin
   v1 = v1 + 1;
   temp = r - 1.0 * v1;
end
end
endtask
endmodule
```

Figure 6.9 shows the simulation output of the relationship between substrate concentration S and rate of reaction V for M = 3 units. Listing 6.9 simulates Equation 6.4—the relationship between the speed of reaction and concentrate of substrate. This same approach can be used to simulate other equations similar to Equation 6.4, such as the output of certain filters as a function of frequency, or a transistor collector's voltage as a function of collector current.

M	0011	0011	0011	0011	0011	0011
S	0001	0011	0111	1001	1011	1111
V	0100	1000	1011	1100	1101	1101
Vr	0.2500	0.500	0.700	0.75	0.785714	0.8333

FIGURE 6.9 Simulation output of the relationship between substrate concentration S and rate of reaction V for M = 3 units.

6.3 FUNCTIONS

Functions are behavioral statements. As is the case when calling procedures or tasks, functions must be called inside `process` (VHDL), or `always` or `initial` (Verilog). Functions take one or more inputs, and in contrast to `procedure` or `task`, they return only a single output value.

6.3.1 VHDL Functions

As with procedures, functions have a declaration and a body. An example of function declaration is:

```
function exp (a, b : in std_logic) return std_logic is
```

where `function` is a predefined word, `exp` is the user-selected name of the function, and `a` and `b` are the inputs. Only inputs are allowed in the function declaration. The function returns a single output with `return`, a predefined word. The function `exp` returns a variable of type std_logic, and `is` is a predefined word that has to be at the end of the declaration statement. The name of the output is not listed in the declaration; it is listed in the body of the function. The body of the function lists the relationship between the inputs and the output to be returned. All statements in the body of the function should be behavioral (sequential) statements, and `return` is used to point to the output of the function. An example of a function's declaration and body (VHDL) is shown in Listing 6.10.

LISTING 6.10 Example of a VHDL Function

```
library IEEE;
use IEEE.STD_LOGIC_1164.ALL;
entity Func_exm is
port (a1, b1 : in std_logic; d1 : out std_logic);
end Func_exm;

architecture Behavioral of Func_exm is
function exp (a, b : in std_logic) return std_logic is
variable d : std_logic;
begin
d := a xor b;
return d;
end function exp;

begin
process (a1, b1)
begin
d1 <= exp (a1, b1);
--The above statement is a function call
end process;
end Behavioral;
```

In Listing 6.10, the name of the function is `exm`; it has two inputs `a` and `b` of type `std_logic`. The type of the output to be returned is std_logic. The output to be returned is `d`. The function, as seen from its body, is performing an EXCLUSIVE-OR on the inputs `a` and `b`. To call the function, it should be written inside a `process`. The function is called by the following statement:

```
d1 <= exp (a1, b1);
```

The function call passes `a1` and `b1` to `a` and `b`, respectively, then calculates `a1` XOR `b1` and passes the output of the XOR to `d1`.

The standard VHDL package has many built-in functions; other functions can be imported from packages attached to the VHDL module. Some examples of built-in functions are: `mod`, which finds the modulo of X mod y; `abs`, which finds the absolute value of a signed number; `To_INTEGER`, which returns an integer value of a signed input; `and` `TO_SIGNED`, which takes an integer and returns its signed binary equivalent. The package ieee.numeric_std.all has a large number of built-in functions.

6.3.2 Verilog Functions

Functions in Verilog have a declaration statement and a body. In the declaration, the size (dimension), type, and name of the output are specified, as well as the names and sizes (dimensions) of the inputs. For example, the declaration statement:

```
function exp;
input a, b;
```

declares a function with a name (identifier) `exp`. The function has two inputs, `a` and `b`, and one output, `exp`. All inputs are 1-bit data; also the output is 1-bit data. The inputs and output can take 0, 1, x (don't care), or Z (high impedance). The body of the function follows the declaration, in which the relationship between the output and the inputs is stated. An example of a function and its call is shown in Listing 6.11. The function calculates exp = a XOR b.

LISTING 6.11 Verilog Function That Calculates exp = a XOR b

```
module Func_exm (a1, b1, d1);
input a1, b1;
output d1;
reg d1;

always @ (a1, b1)
begin

/*The following statement calls the function exp
  and stores the output in d1.*/

d1 = exp (a1, b1);
end

function exp ;
input a, b;
begin

exp = a ^ b;
end
endfunction

endmodule
```

In addition to user-defined functions, the standard Verilog package includes a large number of built-in functions, such as `modulus %`.

6.3.3 Function Examples

EXAMPLE 6.10 Function to Find the Greater of Two Signed Numbers

In this Example, the greater of two signed numbers, x and y, is determined. Each number is a signed binary of 4 bits, and `function` is called in the main module to find the greater of the two input numbers. The result is stored in z. Listing 6.12 shows the HDL code of this Example.

LISTING 6.12 HDL Function to Find the Greater of Two Signed Numbers—VHDL and Verilog

VHDL Function to Find the Greater of Two Signed Numbers

```
library IEEE;
use IEEE.STD_LOGIC_1164.ALL;
use ieee.numeric_std.all;

entity greater_2 is
port (x, y : in signed (3 downto 0); z : out signed (3 downto 0));
end greater_2;

architecture greater_2 of greater_2 is
function grt (a, b : signed (3 downto 0)) return signed is
--The above statement declares a function by the name grt.
--The inputs are 4-bit signed numbers.

variable temp : signed (3 downto 0);
begin
   if (a >= b) then
      temp := a;
      else
      temp := b;
   end if;
return temp;
end grt;

begin
process (x, y)
begin
   z <= grt (x, y); --This is a function call.
end process;

end greater_2;
```

Verilog Function to Find the Greater of Two Signed Numbers

```
module greater_2 (x, y, z);
input signed [3:0] x;
input signed [3:0] y;
output signed [3:0] z;
reg signed [3:0] z;

always @ (x, y)
```

```
begin
z = grt (x, y); //This is a function call.
end

function [3:0] grt;

/*The above statement declares a function by the name grt;
  grt is also the output of the function*/

input signed [3:0] a, b;
/*The above statement declares two inputs to the function;
  both are 4-bit signed numbers.*/

begin
if (a >= b)
grt = a;
else
grt = b;
end
endfunction

endmodule
```

Example 6.11 Function to Find the Floating Sum $y = \sum_{i=0}^{3}(-1)^i(x)^i$, $0 < x < 1$

In this Example, a function is written that accumulates the polynomial summation of x. The polynomial in this Example is of third degree. The numbers are positive fractions; they are represented as fixed-point numbers with Q4 formats. This means that the binary point is at the left of the most significant bit of the number, and the total number of bits is 4. For example, if the number is 1010, then its decimal value is $2^{-1} + 0 + 2^{-3} + 0 = 0.5 + 0.125 = 0.625$. The output y in this Example is assigned a Q16 format. To calculate y, we first convert x to real, then we calculate the real sum of $\sum_{i=0}^{3}(-1)^i(x)^i = 1 - x + x2 - x3$. To convert the sum to Q16, multiply the real sum by 2^{16}; this generates a real number. This real number is converted to an integer, and finally the integer is converted to binary. For example, if x = 1011, the following steps are executed:

Step 1: Convert x to real; 1011 is converted to 0.5 + 0.125 + 0.0625 = 0.6875.

Step 2: Multiply the real number in Step 1 by 2^{16}; $0.6875 \_ 2^{16} = 45056.0$.

Step 3: Convert the real in Step 2 to an integer; 45056.0 is converted to 45056.

Step 4: Convert the integer in Step 3 to a 16-bit binary; 45056 is converted to B000 (hex).

For more details about Q format and fixed-number representations, refer to [Ciletti02], [Hayes98], [Mano00], and [Nelson95].

Listing 6.13 shows the HDL code for calculating y. Referring to the VHDL, three procedures are built: `flt`, `rti`, and `itb`. The procedure `flt` converts `std_logic` to real. We need this procedure to convert the input x. The procedure `rti` converts the real value to an integer, and `itb` converts the integer to `std_logic`. The function `exp` implements the three procedures to calculate `y`. In VHDL, procedures are allowed to be written in the body of the function.

The Verilog code in Listing 6.13 consists of three functions: `float`, `rti`, and `exp`. In contrast to VHDL, Verilog does not allow tasks to be written in the body of the function. The function `float` converts binary numbers that represent fractions (Q4) to real numbers. The function `rti` converts real numbers to integers.

Since Verilog is not a very strict type-oriented language, we can rewrite `function rti` as:

```
function [15:0] rti;
input real r;

begin
    rti = r;
end
endfunction
```

The statement `rti = r;` has a left-hand `rti` of type integer and a right-hand side of `r` (real). Verilog allows this mixing of two types; it calculates the right-hand side as real, and when assigned to the left-hand side, the type is converted from real to integer.

LISTING 6.13 HDL Code for $y = \sum_{i=0}^{3}(-1)^i(x)^i$, $0 < x < 1$—VHDL and Verilog

---

VHDL Floating Sum Description

```
library IEEE;
use IEEE.STD_LOGIC_1164.ALL;
use IEEE.STD_LOGIC_ARITH.ALL;
use IEEE.STD_LOGIC_UNSIGNED.ALL;

entity segma is
port (x : in std_logic_vector (0 to 3);
    y : out std_logic_vector (15 downto 0));

end segma;

architecture segm_beh of segma is

procedure flt (a : in std_logic_vector (0 to 3); float : out real) is
```

```
--This function converts binary (fraction) to real
variable tem : real;
begin
   tem := 0.0;

   for i in 0 to 3 loop

      if (a(i) = '1') then

      tem := tem + 1.0 / (1.0 * 2**(i+1));
      end if;
   end loop;
float := tem;
end flt;

Procedure rti (r : in real; int : out integer) is
--This procedure converts real to integer
variable temp : real;
variable intg : integer := 0;
begin
temp := r;

while temp >= 0.5 loop
intg := intg + 1;
temp := r - 1.0 * intg;
end loop;
int := intg;
end rti;

procedure itb (bin : out std_logic_vector;
   N : in integer; int : in integer) is
variable temp_int : integer := int;
begin

   for i in 0 to N loop
      if (temp_int MOD 2 = 1) then
         bin(i) := '1';
         else bin(i) := '0';
      end if;
      temp_int := temp_int/2;
      end loop;
   end itb;

function exp (a : in std_logic_vector (0 to 3))
   return std_logic_vector is

variable z1 : real;
variable intgr : integer;
variable tem : std_logic_vector (15 downto 0);

begin
```

```
     flt (a, z1);
         z1 := 1.0 - z1 + z1 * z1 - z1 * z1 * z1;
         z1 := z1 * 2**16;
         rti (z1, intgr);
         itb (tem, 15, intgr);
         return tem;
     end exp;

begin

sg1 : process (x)
variable tem : std_logic_vector (15 downto 0);
begin

tem := exp(x);
y <= tem;
end process sg1;

end segm_beh;
```

Verilog Floating Sum Description

```
module segma (x, y);
input [0:3] x;
// x is a fraction in Q4 format, 0 < x < 1.
output [15:0] y;
reg [15:0] y;
always @ (x)
begin

    y = exp (x);

end

function real float;
//This function is to calculate the real value
//of a fraction in binary
input [0:3] a;

integer i;
begin

    float = 0.0;

        for (i = 0; i <= 3; i = i + 1)
        begin
            if (a[i] == 1)

            float = float + 1.0 / 2**(i+1);
        end

end
endfunction
```

```
function [15:0] rti;
input real r;

begin
    rti = r;
end
endfunction
function [15:0] exp;
input [0:3] a;
real z1;

begin

    z1 = float (a); //A call to function "float"
    z1 = 1.0 - z1 + z1**2 - z1**3;
    z1 = z1 * 2**16;
    exp = rti(z1);
end
endfunction

endmodule
```

The simulation output of Listing 6.13 is shown in Figure 6.10

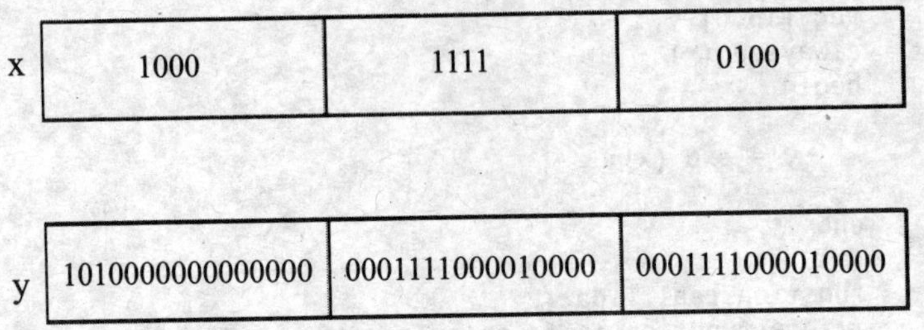

FIGURE 6.10 Simulation output of Listing 6.13.

6.4 SUMMARY

In this chapter, procedure (VHDL), task (Verilog), and function (both VHDL and Verilog) have been covered. Procedures, tasks, and functions can optimize the style of writing HDL code; they shorten the code. The procedure/task has a declaration statement and a body, and can have more than one input and more than one output. On the other hand, a function can have more than one input but only one output. VHDL allows procedure calls to be written inside functions; Verilog does not allow such calls. Table 6.1 shows the commands/components in VHDL and their counterparts (if any) in Verilog.

TABLE 6.1 VHDL versus Verilog

VHDL Command/Component	Verilog Counterport
`procedure`	`task`
`function`	`function`

6.5 EXERCISES

6.1 In Listing 6.6, negative binary numbers were converted to integers by reverse-negating them. Another approach is to find the integer value of any twos-complement number by detecting the beginning and end of strings of ones in the number (see Case Study 3.1). Apply this approach and write both the VHDL and Verilog codes for such a conversion. Verify your code by simulation and compare the two approaches.

6.2 In Listing 6.8, a VHDL Booth procedure was written that multiplies 4x4 bits. Modify the VHDL procedure so it can multiply any *NxN*. Verify your answer by simulation.

6.3 In Listing 6.8 (VHDL), `temtotal = tem0 + tem1 + tem2` was added by converting to integer, adding, and then changing back to binary. An alternate approach is to adjust the width of all partial products (after they are calculated) to be the same as `temtotal`, and then add. Perform this alternate approach and verify your results by simulation.

6.4 Derive the HDL code (both VHDL and Verilog) for the function y = e–x; 0 < x < 1. Express y in Q15 format.

6.5 Write a function to calculate the area of a sphere, given the radius.

6.6 REFERENCES

[Ciletti02] Ciletti, M. D., *Advanced Digital Design with The VERILOG HDL.* Prentice Hall, 2002.

[Hayes98] Hayes, J., *Computer Architecture and Organization,* 3d ed. McGraw Hill Companies, 1998.

[Mano00] Mano, M. M. and C. R. Kime, *Logic and Computer Design Fundamentals.* Prentice Hall, 2000.

[Nelson95] Nelson, V. P., H. T. Nagle, B. D. Carroll, and J. D. Irwin, *Digital Logic Circuit Analysis & Design. Prentice Hall,* 1995.

7 Mixed-Type Descriptions

In This Chapter

- Learn how to use different types (styles) of descriptions to write HDL modules.
- Learn which type or style of description to use for optimal writing style.
- Understand the concept of packages in VHDL and how to use them.
- Practice using real (floating) numbering systems.
- Practice user-defined types.
- Practice array use.
- Practice using finite sequential-state machines.
- Review and understand the steps needed to design and describe a basic computer.

In previous chapters, modules were written that focused on one type of description, such as data flow, behavioral, structural, or switch level. In this chapter, modules will use a mixture of more than one type of description. We call this style of writing, where different types of descriptions are used in the same module, "mixed-type descriptions." Modules representing complex systems are usually written using mixed-type descriptions.

7.1 WHY MIXED-TYPE DESCRIPTION?

Our definition of mixed-type description is that it is an HDL code that mixes different types of descriptions within the same module. In previous chapters, codes consisted mainly of one type, such as data flow (see Chapter 2, "Data-Flow Descriptions,"), behavioral (see Chapter 3, "Behavioral Descriptions"), structural (see Chapter 4, "Structural Descriptions"), or switch level (see Chapter 5, "Switch-Level Descriptions"). Here, we write our code using more than one type of description in the same module.

In fact, it is very common to write mixed descriptions, since each part of the system we model may be written best by a certain type of description. For example, consider a system that performs two operations: addition (Z = x + y) and division (Z = x / y). If we want to describe this system using HDL, we have few options. The first option is to use behavioral statements to model the addition and the division. This option is somewhat easy to write, since HDL has built-in addition and division functions. The behavioral statements are written inside `process` (VHDL) or `always` (Verilog) as:

```
Z := a + b; --VHDL          or      Z := x / y; --VHDL
Z = a + b;   //Verilog      or      Z = x / y;  //Verilog
```

As we know, the ultimate goal of VHDL or Verilog description is to synthesize (see Chapter 10 "Synthesis Basics") the description on electronic chips. If the behavioral description is used, we have no control over selecting the components or the methods used to implement the addition and division. The HDL package may contain addition or division algorithms not suitable for our needs. For example, the addition algorithm might need to be as fast as possible; to achieve this we have to use fast adders, such as carry–look ahead or carry-save adders. There is no guarantee that behavioral description implements these adders in its addition function. Most likely, it implements ripple-carry addition.

A second option is to use data-flow or structural description. These descriptions can also be implemented to describe the specific adder. It is, however, hard to implement descriptions of complex algorithms, such as division; the logic diagram of divisors is generally complex.

The third option is to use a mixture of two types of descriptions: structural or data-flow for addition, and behavioral for division. We refer to this description as mixed type.

Before considering examples of mixed-type description, we need to learn some tools and commands that are used to write mixed-type code. Section 7.2 discusses user-defined types, and Section 7.3 discusses packages and arrays.

7.2 VHDL USER-DEFINED TYPES

VHDL has an extensive set of predefined data types, such as `bit`, `std_logic`, `array`, and `natural` (see Chapter 1, "Introduction"). In some applications, we need to specify a type that is not available in the basic HDL package. Examples of such types are: weekdays, weather, or grades. These are user-defined types. To instantiate a user-defined type, the predefined word `type` is used. An example of instantiating a user-defined type is as follows:

```
type week_days is (mon, tues, wed, th, fr, sat, sun);
```

The above statement declares a user-defined type by the name of `week_days`, `type` is a predefined word; the elements or members of `week_days` are: `mon, tues, wed, th, fr, sat,` and `sun`. Another example of a user-defined type is:

```
type states is (S0, S1, S2, S3);
```

The above `type` statement declares a user-defined type by the name of `states`. The elements (members) of `states` are: `s0, s1, s2`, and `s3`. Another example of a user-defined type is:

```
type weather is (sunny, cloudy, rain, snow);
```

The above `type` statement declares a user-defined type by the name of `weather`, and the elements (members) of `weather` are: `sunny, cloudy, rain,` and `snow`. Another example of a user-defined type is:

```
type grades is (A, B, C, D, F, I);
```

The above `type` statement declares a user-defined type by the name of `grades`; the elements (members) of `grades` are: `A, B, C, D, F,` and `I`. Another example of a user-defined type is:

```
type decimal_numbers is ('0', '1', '2', '3', '4', '5');
```

The above statement declares a user-defined type by the name of `decimal_numbers`; the elements (members) of `decimal_numbers` are the integers: `'0', '1', '2', '3', '4',` and `'5'`. If the members of a type are digits, they should be written between two apostrophes, such as '5.'

The statement:

```
signal scores : grades;
```

declares `signal scores` as of type `grades`. This means that `signal scores` can be assigned a value of `A, B, C, D, F,` or `I`.

We can declare a subtype of a type by using the predefined word `subtype`, as shown below:

```
subtype failed is grades range D to I;
signal scores : failed;
```

where `failed` is a subtype of grades and has a range from `D` to `I`, `range` is a predefined attribute, so `signal scores` can be assigned a value of `D, F,` or `I`. Another example:

```
subtype values is integer range 10 to 100;
signal x : values;
```

Signal x can be assigned an integer value from 10 to 100. Remember from Chapter 1 that integer is a predefined type.

7.3 VHDL PACKAGES

Packages constitute an essential part of VHDL description. Packages allow the user to access built-in constructs. Packages may include type and subtype declarations, constant definitions, function and procedure, and component declarations. VHDL has default built-in packages that include predefined words, such as: bit, bit_vector, and integer. In addition to the defaults, the user can attach a variety of packages to the VHDL module.

Several packages have been seen in previous chapters; examples include packages authored by IEEE: ieee.std_logic_1164, ieee.std_logic_arith, ieee.numeric_std, ieee.std_logic_unsigned, and ieee.std_logic_signed. In addition to such built-in packages, the user can attach other packages to the VHDL module. A package consists of a declaration and a body. The declaration states the name (identifier) of the package, and the names (identifiers) of types, procedures, functions, and components. The body of the package contains the code for all the identifiers listed in the declaration. Listing 7.1 shows an example of a user-defined package.

LISTING 7.1 An Example of a VHDL Package

```
package conversions is
    Type wkdays is (mon, tue, wed, th, fr);
    Procedure convert (a : in bit; b : out integer);
    function incr (b : std_logic_vector) return std_logic_vector;
end conversions;

package body conversions is

Procedure convert (a : in bit; b : out integer) is
Begin
.......
End convert;
function incr (b : std_logic_vector) return std_logic_vector is
begin
...
end incr;

end conversions;
```

As shown in Listing 7.1, the name of the package is conversions; the package contains Type wkdays, Procedure convert, and function incr. The package body lists the code of the procedure `convert` and function `incr`. Listing 7.2 shows another package example. The name of the package is `codes`; the members are `add`, `mul`, `divide`, and `none`.

LISTING 7.2 An Example of a VHDL Package

```
library ieee;
use ieee.std_logic_1164.all;
package codes is
type op is (add, mul, divide, none);
end;
use work.codes;

entity ALUS2 is
    port (a, b : in std_logic_vector (3 downto 0);
        cin : in std_logic; opc : in op;
        z : out std_logic_vector (7 downto 0);
        cout : buffer std_logic);
end ALUS2;
```

To use this package in VHDL module, we write the statement `use work.codes;`. Notice that in the entity `ALUS2`, `opc` is declared as of type `op`; this means that `opc` can be assigned a value of `add`, `mul`, `divide`, or `none`.

7.3.1 Implementation of Arrays

As was seen in Chapter 1, arrays are a data type; all elements of the array should have the same type. The array can be single-dimensional or multidimensional. VHDL allows for multidimensional arrays, but Verilog only allows single-dimensional arrays. Arrays can be composed of signals, constants, or variables. This section covers arrays in detail, as well as several implementations.

7.3.1.1 Single-Dimensional Arrays

Single-dimensional arrays have single index. They are declared as follows:

VHDL Single-Dimensional Array

```
type datavector is array (3 downto 0) of wordarray;
subtype wordarray is std_logic_vector (1 downto 0);
```

The above two statements declare an array by the name of `datavector`; it has four elements; each element is 2 bits. An example of this array is:

("11", "10", "10", "01")

The value of each element of the array in decimal is:

```
datavector(0) = 1, datavector(1) = 2, datavector(2) = 2,
datavector(3) = 3.
```

Verilog Single-Dimensional Array

In Verilog, arrays are declared using the predefined word `reg`. An example of array declaration in Verilog is:

```
reg [1:0] datavector[0:3];
```

This declares an array by the name of `datavector`; it has four elements; each element is 2 bits. An example of this array is:

```
datavector[0] = 2'b01;
datavector[1] = 2'b10;
datavector[2] = 2'b10;
datavector[3] = 2'b11;
```

The following Examples cover array implementations.

EXAMPLE 7.1 Find the Greatest Among *N* Elements of an Array

Listing 7.3 shows the HDL code for finding the greatest element (`grtst`) of array `a`. We first initialize `grtst` with 0. Then `grtst` is compared with the first element of the array `a`. If the first element is greater than `grtst`, then we set `grtst` to be equal to the first element; otherwise, `grtst` is left unchanged. The same is done with the other elements.

LISTING 7.3 HDL Code for Finding the Greatest Element of an Array—VHDL and Verilog

VHDL: Finding the Greatest Element of an Array

```
library IEEE;
use IEEE.STD_LOGIC_1164.all;

--Build a package for an array
package array_pkg is
constant N : integer := 4;
--N+1 is the number of elements in the array.

constant M : integer := 3;
--M+1 is the number of bits of each element
--of the array.
subtype wordN is std_logic_vector (M downto 0);
type strng is array (N downto 0) of wordN;

end array_pkg;

library IEEE;
use IEEE.STD_LOGIC_1164.ALL;
```

```
use work.array_pkg.all;
--The above statement makes the package array_pkg visible in
--this module.
entity array1 is
    generic (N : integer :=4; M : integer := 3);

--N + 1 is the number of elements in the array; M = 1 is the
--number of bits of each element.

    Port (a : inout strng; z : out std_logic_vector (M downto 0));
end array1;

architecture max of array1 is

begin

com: process (a)
variable grtst : wordN;
begin

--enter the data of the array.
    a <= ("0110", "0111", "0010", "0011", "0001");

    grtst := "0000";

    lop1 : for i in 0 to N loop

    if (grtst <= a(i)) then
        grtst := a(i);
        report " grtst is less or equal than a";
    -- use the above report statement if you want to monitor the
    -- progress of the program

else
        report "grtst is greater than a";

        -- Use the above report statement to monitor the
        -- progress of the program
        end if;
        end loop lop1;

    z <= grtst;
end process com;

end max;
```

Verilog: Finding the Greatest Element of an Array

```
module array1 (start, grtst);
parameter N = 4;
parameter M = 3;
input start;
output [3:0] grtst;
```

```
reg [M:0] a[0:N];

/*The above statement is declaring an array of N + 1 elements;
  each element is M+1 bits. */

reg [3:0] grtst;
integer i;
always @ (start)
begin
a[0] = 4'b0110;
a[1] = 4'b0111;
a[2] = 4'b0010;
a[3] = 4'b0011;
a[4] = 4'b0001;
grtst = 4'b0000;

for (i = 0; i <= N; i= i +1)

    begin

        if (grtst <= a[i])
        begin
            grtst = a[i];
            $display (" grtst is less or equal than a");
// use the above statement to monitor the program
            end

        else
        $display (" grtst is greater than a");

// use the above statement to monitor the program

    end

end

endmodule
```

EXAMPLE 7.2 Multiplication of Two Signed *N*-Element Vectors Using Arrays

This Example describes the multiplication of two signed vectors. The two vectors have the dimension of $1 \times N$ and $N \times 1$. Chapter 6 discussed the multiplication of two three-element vectors; here, arrays are used to expand the multiplication to N elements. Listing 7.4 shows the description of two signed vectors of N elements. We use the Booth algorithm (see Chapter 3) and code from Chapter 6 ("Procedures, Tasks, and Functions") to multiply signed numbers in twos-complement format. The algorithm is written as `procedure` in VHDL or as `task` in Verilog.

In VHDL, we include the procedure in a package. The package `booth_pkg` is declared as:

```
package booth_pkg is
constant N : integer := 4;

constant M : integer := 3;

subtype wordN is signed (M downto 0);
type strng is array (N downto 0) of wordN;

procedure booth (X, Y : in signed (3 downto 0);
    Z : out signed (7 downto 0));

end booth_pkg;
```

The package `booth_pkg` includes the procedure `booth` and an array declaration. The array is declared as a user-defined type, `strng`, and a user-defined subtype, `wordN`. It has `N` + 1 elements; each element is `M` + 1 bits. In our example, we selected `N` = 4 and `M` = 3; so the array has five elements, and each element is 4 bits in signed (twos-complement) format.

In Verilog the array is declared as:

```
reg signed [M:0] b[0:N];
```

which is an array of `N` + 1 elements. Each element is `M` + 1 bits.

LISTING 7.4 Multiplication of Two Signed *N*-Element Vectors–VHDL and Verilog

VHDL: Multiplication of Two Signed N-Element Vectors

```
library IEEE;
use IEEE.STD_LOGIC_1164.all;
use ieee.numeric_std.all;

package booth_pkg is
constant N : integer := 4;
--N + 1 is the number of elements in the array.

constant M: integer := 3;
--M + 1 is the number of bits of each element
--of the array.

subtype wordN is signed (M downto 0);
type strng is array (N downto 0) of wordN;

procedure booth (X, Y : in signed (3 downto 0);
    Z : out signed (7 downto 0));

end booth_pkg;

package body booth_pkg is
```

```
procedure booth (X, Y : in signed (3 downto 0);
    Z : out signed (7 downto 0)) is
--Booth algorithm here is restricted to 4x4 bits.
--It can be adjusted to multiply any NxN bits.
variable temp : signed (1 downto 0);
    variable sum : signed (7 downto 0);
    variable E1 : unsigned (0 downto 0);
    variable Y1 : signed (3 downto 0);
begin

sum := "00000000"; E1 := "0";
    for i in 0 to 3 loop
    temp := X(i) & E1(0);
    Y1 := -Y;
    case temp is
        when "10" => sum (7 downto 4) :=
        sum (7 downto 4) + Y1;
        when "01" => sum (7 downto 4) :=
        sum (7 downto 4) + Y;
        when others => null;
    end case;
    sum := sum srl 1;
    sum(7) := sum(6);
    E1(0) := x(i);
    end loop;
    if (y = "1000") then
        sum := -sum;

        --If Y = 1000; then Y1 is calculated as 1000;
        --that is -8, not 8 as expected. This is because Y1 is
        --4 bits only. The statement sum = -sum corrects
        --this error.

        end if;
    Z := sum;
    end booth;

end booth_pkg;

--We start writing the multiplication algorithm using
--the package booth_pkg
library IEEE;
use IEEE.STD_LOGIC_1164.ALL;
use ieee.numeric_std.all;
use work.booth_pkg.all;

entity vecor_multply is
generic (N : integer := 4; M : integer := 3);
--N + 1 is the number of elements in the array; M + 1 is the
--number of bits of each element.
    Port (a, b : in strng; d : out signed (3*N downto 0));
end vecor_multply;
```

```
architecture multply of vecor_multply is

begin
process (a, b)
variable temp : signed (7 downto 0);
variable temp5 : signed (3*N downto 0) := "0000000000000";

begin

for i in 0 to 4 loop
booth(a(i), b(i), temp);

--accumulate the partial products in the product temp5
temp5 := temp5 + temp;
end loop;
d <= temp5;
end process;

end multply;
```

Verilog: Multiplication of Two Signed N-Element Vectors

```
module vecor_multply (start, d);
parameter N = 4;
parameter M = 3;
input start;
output signed [3*N:0] d;
reg signed [M:0] a[0:N];
reg signed [M:0] b[0:N];
reg signed [3*N:0] d;
reg signed [3*N:0] temp;
integer i;

always @ (start)
begin
    a[0] = 4'b1100;
    a[1] = 4'b0000;
    a[2] = 4'b1001;
    a[3] = 4'b0011;
    a[4] = 4'b1111;

    b[0] = 4'b1010;
    b[1] = 4'b0011;
    b[2] = 4'b0111;
    b[3] = 4'b1000;
    b[4] = 4'b1000;
    d = 0;
    for (i = 0; i <= N; i = i + 1)
        begin
            booth (a[i], b[i], temp);
            d = d + temp;
        end
end
```

```
task booth;
input signed [3:0] X, Y;
output signed [7:0] Z;
reg signed [7:0] Z;
reg [1:0] temp;
integer i;
reg E1;
reg [3:0] Y1;

begin
Z = 8'd0;
E1 = 1'd0;

for (i = 0; i < 4; i = i + 1)
    begin
        temp = {X[i], E1}; //This is catenation
        Y1 = -Y; //Y1 is the 2'complement of Y

            case (temp)
            2'd2 : Z[7:4] = Z[7:4] + Y1;
            2'd1 : Z[7:4] = Z[7:4] + Y;
            default : begin end

            endcase
        Z = Z >> 1;
        /*The above statement is a logical shift of
         one position to the right*/

        Z[7] = Z[6];
    /*The above two statements perform arithmetic shift where
      the sign of the number is preserved after the shift. */

    E1 = X[i];

    end

  if (Y == 4'b1000)

  /* If Y = 1000, then Y1 = 1000 (should be 8 not -8).
     This error is because Y1 is 4 bits only.
     The statement Z = -Z adjusts the value of Z. */

  Z = -Z;
  end

  endtask
  endmodule
```

Figure 7.1 shows the simulation output of the vector multiplication. Array a is written here in integer format for convenience:

$$a = \{-1\ 3\ -7\ 0\ -4\}$$

$$b = \{-8\ -8\ 7\ 3\ -6\}$$

$$\text{multiplying } a \times b = 8 - 24 - 49 + 0 + 24 = -41 = d$$

As shown in Figure 7.1, d has the correct value –41.

a	1111 0011 1001 0000 1100
b	1000 1000 0111 0011 1010
d	1111111010111

FIGURE 7.1 Simulation output of vector multiplication.

7.3.1.2 Two-Dimensional Arrays

VHDL allows for multidimensional arrays. Standard Verilog allows only single-dimensional arrays. In VHDL, two-dimensional arrays are described by using `type` statements. For example, the statements:

```
subtype wordg is integer;
type singl is array (2 downto 0) of wordg;
type doubl is array (1 downto 0) of singl;
```

describe a two-dimensional array. Each single-dimensional array has three elements, and each element is an integer. An example of a two-dimensional array is the array y:

$$y = ((10\ 5\ 6), (3\ -2\ 7))$$

The elements of the array y are:

y(0)(0) = 7 refers to element 0 of array 0

y(1)(1) = 5 refers to element 1 of array 1

y(2)(0) = 3 refers to element 2 of array 0

y(2)(1) = 10 refers to element 2 of array 0

EXAMPLE 7.3 Two-Dimensional Arrays

To practice multidimensional arrays, this Example considers a two-dimensional array. Listing 7.5 shows the VHDL description of a two-dimensional array. We use the package `twodm_array` to declare a two-dimensional array with five single arrays; each single array has five elements. The elements are of type `integer`.

LISTING 7.5 VHDL Two-Dimensional Array

```
library IEEE;
use IEEE.STD_LOGIC_1164.all;

--Build a package to declare the array
package twodm_array is

constant N : integer := 4;

--N+1 is the number of elements in the array.
--this is [N+1,N+1] matrix with N+1 rows and N+1 columns

subtype wordg is integer;
type strng1 is array (N downto 0) of wordg;
type strng2 is array (N downto 0) of strng1;

end twodm_array;

--use the package to describe a two-dimensional array
library IEEE;
use IEEE.STD_LOGIC_1164.ALL;
use work.twodm_array.all;
--The above statement instantiates the package twodm_array

entity two_array is
    Port (N, M : integer; z : out integer);
end two_array;

architecture Behavioral of two_array is

begin
com : process (N, M)
variable t : integer;
constant y : strng2 := ((7, 6, 5, 4, 3), (6, 7, 8, 9, 10),
    (30, 31, 32, 33, 34), (40, 41, 42, 43, 44),
    (50, 51, 52, 53, 54));
begin

t := y (N)(M);
--Look at the simulation output to identify the elements of the array
z <= t;
end process com;
end Behavioral;
```

Figure 7.2 shows the simulation output of Listing 7.5. From the simulation, we can see that:

y[0][0], the first element in the first array = 54

y[0][3], the fourth element of the first array = 51

y[2][4], the fifth element of the third array = 30

N	0	0	0	2	4	4
M	0	3	4	4	4	3
z	54	51	50	30	7	6

FIGURE 7.2 Simulation output of the array in Listing 7.5.

EXAMPLE 7.4 Matrix Addition

Here a VHDL code is written to add two matrices. The matrices have to have the same dimensions. The addition of the two matrices yields a matrix with the same dimension as the two matrices. Consider the addition of the two matrices:

$$\begin{bmatrix} 14 & -8 & 7 & 9 & 4 \\ 9 & 3 & -7 & -3 & 3 \\ 7 & -2 & -12 & 5 & 3 \\ 1 & 4 & -5 & 9 & 10 \\ 2 & 2 & -3 & 3 & -8 \end{bmatrix} + \begin{bmatrix} 4 & -7 & 3 & 9 & 14 \\ 4 & 6 & 9 & -18 & 6 \\ 3 & 5 & 7 & -8 & 6 \\ 3 & 1 & 7 & 8 & -4 \\ -9 & 3 & 2 & -11 & 5 \end{bmatrix}$$

The addition is done by adding, row by row. Listing 7.6 shows the VHDL description of the addition of two [5×5] matrices.

LISTING 7.6 VHDL Description: Addition of Two [5×5] Matrices

```
--First, write a package to declare a two-dimensional
--array with five elements
library IEEE;
use IEEE.STD_LOGIC_1164.all;
```

```
package twodm_array is

constant N : integer := 4;
--N+1 is the number of elements in the array.
--This is an NxN matrix with N rows and N columns.
subtype wordg is integer;
type strng1 is array (N downto 0) of wordg;
type strng2 is array (N downto 0) of strng1;

end twodm_array;

--Second, write the code for addition
library IEEE;
use IEEE.STD_LOGIC_1164.ALL;
use work.twodm_array.all;
entity matrices is
    Port (x, y : strng2; z : out strng2);
--strng2 type is 5x5 matrix
end matrices;

architecture sum of matrices is

begin
com : process (x, y)
variable t : integer := 0;
begin

for i in 0 to 4 loop
for j in 0 to 4 loop
t := x(i)(j) + y(i)(j);
z(i)(j) <= t;

end loop;

end loop;

end process com;
end sum;
```

After simulation of the above code, the first two rows of the sum matrix z are:

$$\{9\ {-21}\ 2\ 9\ 13\}\{18\ 18\ 10\ {-15}\ 18\}$$

with z(0,0) = 18, z(0,1) = –15, and z(1,3) = –21.

7.4 MIXED-TYPE DESCRIPTION EXAMPLES

This section presents some examples of mixed-type descriptions. The strategy is to use the type or style of description that best fits the needs of the system (or parts of the system) to be described. Structural or data-flow description may be the best fit for any part of the system that needs specific hardware architecture; and for any part of the system that is, for example, performing a complex arithmetic operation, and no specific hardware architecture is desired, behavioral description may be the best description type to use. If the system consists of transistors or transistor-based circuits, then switch-level description may be the best fit.

EXAMPLE 7.5 HDL Description of an Arithmetic-Logic Unit

The Arithmetic-Logic Unit (ALU) is one of the major units in a computer. The unit performs arithmetic operations such as addition, subtraction, and division, and logical operations such as AND, OR, and invert. The ALU in this Example has three inputs (see Figure 7.3), `a`, `b`, and `cin`. Inputs `a` and `b` are 4 bits, and `cin` is 1 bit. The output `z` is 6 bits. The unit can perform addition, multiplication, integer division, and no operation. To select one operation out of the available four, a 2-bit signal `opc` is implemented to select the desired operation. The selection is shown in Table 7.1.

In this Example, we want to have the addition implemented by carry–look ahead adders. Since the adders are look ahead, then the most convenient style of description is structural or data flow. Chapter 2 described these adders using data-flow description, so it is repeated here. As we know, data-flow description is usually implemented by writing the Boolean functions of the system. The multiplication and division, since no specific hardware structure is required, can be described by behavioral statements within a process. The multiplication operator (`*`) and the division operator (`/`) are used to perform the multiplication and division.

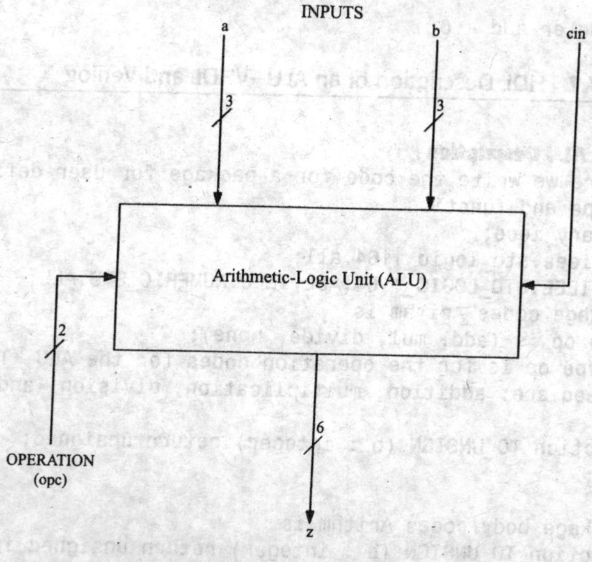

FIGURE 7.3 Block diagram of the arithmetic-logic unit.

TABLE 7.1 Operation Selection of the ALU

Operation Code (opc)	Operation
00	Addition
01	Multiplication
10	Integer Division
11	No Operation

Listing 7.7 shows the VHDL code for the ALU. The package `codes_Arithm` declares a user-defined type `op`; the elements of `op` are the operation codes for addition (`add`), multiplication (`mul`), division (`divide`), and no operation (`none`). The package also includes a user-defined function, `TO_UNSIGN`. The function converts from integer to unsigned. This function (or a similar one) may be available as built-in in some vendors' packages. Converting between integer and unsigned is needed because many VHDL simulators cannot perform the unsigned division z = a / b. VHDL can perform integer division.

Listing 7.7 also shows the Verilog code for the ALU. In Verilog, it is easy to perform addition, multiplication, and division on unsigned numbers; we do not have to convert values to integers to perform these operations. On the other hand, Verilog does not have as extensive user-defined type statements as does VHDL. We use the `parameter` statement to assign values to ALU operations. For example, to assign 00 to the addition operation code `add`, we write:

```
parameter add = 0;
```

LISTING 7.7 HDL Description of an ALU—VHDL and Verilog

VHDL ALU Description

```
--Here we write the code for a package for user-defined
--type and function.
library ieee;
use ieee.std_logic_1164.all;
use IEEE.STD_LOGIC_1164.ALL,IEEE.NUMERIC_STD.ALL;
package codes_Arithm is
type op is (add, mul, divide, none);
--type op is for the operation codes for the ALU. The operations we
--need are: addition, multiplication, division, and no operation

function TO_UNSIGN (b : integer) return unsigned;
end;

package body codes_Arithm is
function TO_UNSIGN (b : integer) return unsigned is
```

```
--The function converts integer numbers to unsigned. This function
--can be omitted if it is included in a vendor's package. The vendor's
--package, if available, should be attached.

variable temp : integer;
variable bin : unsigned (5 downto 0);
begin
temp := b;
for j in 0 to 5 loop

    if (temp MOD 2 = 1) then
    bin (j) := '1';
    else bin (j) := '0';
    end if;
    temp := temp/2;
    end loop;
    return bin;

end TO_UNSIGN;
end codes_Arithm;

--Now we write the code for the ALU
library IEEE;
use IEEE.STD_LOGIC_1164.ALL;
use ieee.numeric_std.all;
use work.codes_arithm.all;

--The above use statement is to make the user-
--defined package "codes_arithm.all" visible to this module.

entity ALU_mixed is

    port (a, b : in unsigned (2 downto 0); cin : in std_logic;
        opc : in op; z : out unsigned (5 downto 0));
--opc is of type "op"; type op is defined in the
--user-defined package "codes_arithm"
end ALU_mixed;

architecture ALU_mixed of ALU_mixed is
    signal c0, c1 : std_logic;
    signal p, g : unsigned (2 downto 0);
    signal temp1 : unsigned (5 downto 0);

begin

--The following is a data flow-description of a 3-bit look ahead
--adder. The sum is stored in the three least significant bits of
--temp1. The carry out is stored in temp1(3).

    g(0) <= a(0) and b(0);
    g(1) <= a(1) and b(1);
    g(2) <= a(2) and b(2);
```

```
        p(0) <= a(0) or b(0);
        p(1) <= a(1) or b(1);
        p(2) <= a(2) or b(2);
        c0 <= g(0) or (p(0) and cin);
        c1 <= g(1) or (p(1) and g(0)) or (p(1) and p(0) and cin);
        temp1(3) <= g(2) or (p(2) and g(1)) or (p(2) and p(1)
            and g(0)) or (p(2) and p(1) and p(0) and cin);

    --temp1(3) is the final carryout of the adders

        temp1(0) <= (p(0) xor g(0)) xor cin;
        temp1(1) <= (p(1) xor g(1)) xor c0;
        temp1(2) <= (p(2) xor g(2)) xor c1;
        temp1 (5 downto 4) <= "00";

    process (a, b, cin, opc, temp1)

    --The following is a behavioral description for the multiplication
    --and division functions of the ALU.

        variable temp : unsigned (5 downto 0);
        variable a1, a2, a3 : integer;
    begin
        a1 := TO_INTEGER (a);
        a2 := TO_INTEGER (b);
    --The predefined function "TO_INTEGER"
    --converts unsigned to integer.
    --The function is a member of the VHDL package IEEE.numeric.

        case opc is
            when mul =>
                a3 := a1 * a2;
                temp := TO_UNSIGN(a3);
    --The function "TO_UNSIGN" is a user-defined function
    --written in the user-defined package "codes_arithm."
            when divide =>
                a3 := a1 / a2;
                temp := TO_UNSIGN(a3);

            when add =>
                temp := temp1;
            when none =>
                null;

        end case;

    z <= temp;
    end process;

    end ALU_mixed;
```

Verilog ALU Description

```
module ALU_mixed (a, b, cin, opc, z);
parameter add = 0;
parameter mul = 1;
parameter divide = 2;
parameter nop = 3;
input [2:0] a, b;
input cin;
input [1:0] opc;
output [5:0] z;
reg [5:0] z;
wire [5:0] temp1;
wire [2:0] g, p;
wire c0, c1;

// The following is data-flow description
// for 3-bit look ahead adder
    assign g[0] = a[0] & b[0];
    assign g[1] = a[1] & b[1];
    assign g[2] = a[2] & b[2];
    assign p[0] = a[0] | b[0];
    assign p[1] = a[1] | b[1];
    assign p[2] = a[2] | b[2];
    assign c0 = g[0] | (p[0] & cin);
    assign c1 = g[1] | (p[1] & g[0]) | (p[1] & p[0] & cin);
    assign temp1[3] = g[2] | (p[2] & g[1]) | (p[2] & p[1]
        & g[0]) | (p[2] & p[1] & p[0] & cin);
    // temp1[3] is the final carryout of the adders

    assign temp1[0] = (p[0] ^ g[0]) ^ cin;
    assign temp1[1] = (p[1] ^ g[1]) ^ c0;
    assign temp1[2] = (p[2] ^ g[2]) ^ c1;

    assign temp1[5:4] = 2'b00;

    //The following is behavioral description

 always @ (a, b, cin, opc, temp1)
 begin

    case (opc)

        mul : z = a * b;
        add : z = temp1;
        divide : z = a / b;
        nop : z = z;
    endcase
 end

 endmodule
```

Figure 7.4 shows the simulation output of the ALU. Notice the integer division of 5 / 7 = 0.

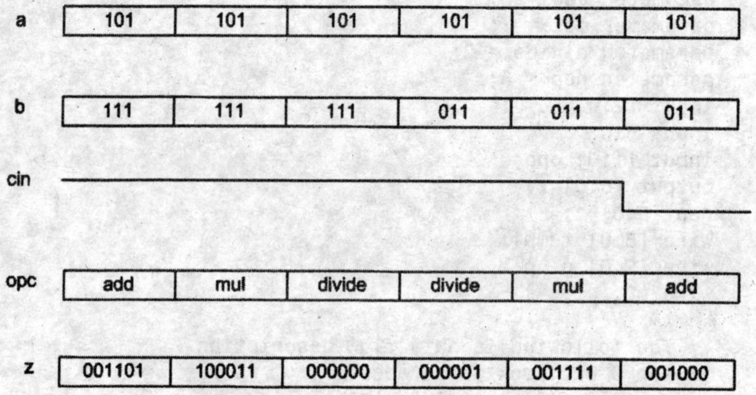

FIGURE 7.4 Simulation output of the ALU.

EXAMPLE 7.6 HDL Description of 16 ×8 SRAM

Chapter 4 described a static memory cell using structural description. In this Example, 16×8 SRAM is described. Since the description of this memory in structural style would be huge, and no specific logic is required, we use behavioral statements to describe the memory. Figure 7.5 shows a block diagram of the memory. The memory has 8-bit input data (Data_in), 8-bit output data (Data_out), 4-bit address bus (ABUS), a chip select (CS), and read/write signal (R_$\overline{\text{WR}}$).

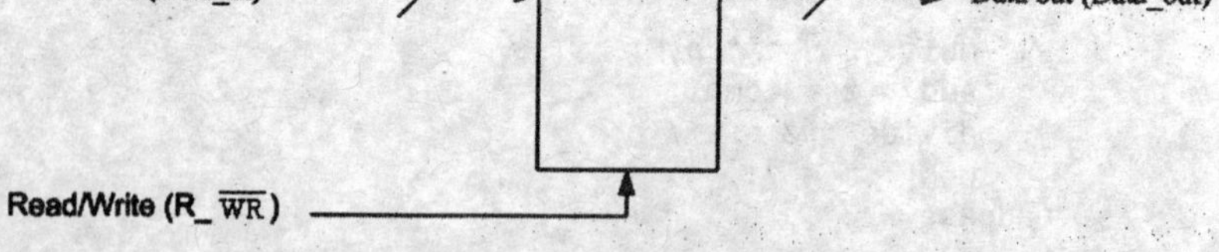

FIGURE 7.5 A block diagram of 16 x 8 static memory.

The function table of the memory is shown in Table 7.2. Listing 7. HDL code for the RAM.

TABLE 7.2 Function Table of SRAM

CS	R_$\overline{WR}$	Data_out	Memory function
0	x	Z (high impedance)	The memory is deselected.
1	1	M (ABUS)	This is a read; M refers to memory locations. Contents of a memory location pointed to by ABUS is placed in the output data.
1	0		This is a write cycle. Data in the Data_in are stored in M (ABUS).

Referring to Listing 7.8 VHDL, we use an array to represent the memory. Since the memory is 16×8 bits, an array of 16 elements is used, and each element is 8 bits. We write the array in a package `array_pkg`. Since the index of the array should be an integer, and the ABUS in the entity `memory16x8` is declared unsigned, the ABUS is converted from unsigned to integer using the predefined function `TO_INTEGER`.

In the Verilog version of Listing 7.8, an array is also used to represent the memory. The array is instantiated by the statement:

```
reg [7:0] Memory [0:15];
```

which describes an array by the name `Memory`; it has 16 words, and each word is 8 bits.

LISTING 7.8 HDL Description of 16 ×8 SRAM—VHDL and Verilog

VHDL 16×8 SRAM Description

```
library IEEE;
use IEEE.STD_LOGIC_1164.all;

--Build a package for an array
package array_pkg is
constant N : integer := 15;
--N+1 is the number of elements in the array.

constant M : integer := 7;
--M+1 is the number of bits of each element
--of the array.
subtype wordN is std_logic_vector (M downto 0);
type strng is array (N downto 0) of wordN;
```

```
end array_pkg;

library IEEE;
use IEEE.STD_LOGIC_1164.ALL;
use ieee.numeric_std.all;
use work.array_pkg.all;

entity memory16x8 is
generic (N : integer := 15; M : integer := 7);
--N+1 is the number of words in the memory; M+1 is the
--number of bits of each word.
    Port (Memory : inout strng; CS : in std_logic;
        ABUS : in unsigned (3 downto 0);
        Data_in : in std_logic_vector (7 downto 0);
        R_WRbar : in std_logic;
        Data_out : out std_logic_vector (7 downto 0));
end memory16x8;

architecture SRAM of memory16x8 is

begin

com : process (CS, ABUS, Data_in, R_WRbar)
variable A : integer range 0 to 15;
begin

if (CS = '1') then

A := TO_INTEGER (ABUS);
--TO_INTEGER is a built-in function

if (R_WRbar = '0') then

Memory (A) <= Data_in;
else

Data_out <= Memory(A);

end if;
else
Data_out <= "ZZZZZZZZ";
--The above statement describes high impedance.
end if;


end process com;

end SRAM;
```

Verilog 16 x 8 SRAM Description

```
module memory16x8 (CS, ABUS, Data_in, R_WRbar, Data_out);
input CS, R_WRbar;
input [3:0] ABUS;
input [7:0] Data_in;
output [7:0] Data_out;
reg [7:0] Data_out;
reg [7:0] Memory [0:15];

always @ (CS, ABUS, Data_in, R_WRbar)
begin

if (CS == 1'b1)
    begin

        if (R_WRbar == 1'b0)
        begin
            Memory [ABUS] = Data_in;
            end
            else
            Data_out = Memory [ABUS];
        end
    else
    Data_out = 8'bZZZZZZZZ;
//The above statement describes high impedance

end

endmodule
```

The simulation output of Listing 7.8 is shown in Figure 7.6. We write data in memory locations 0, 14, 15, and 8, and read the contents of two memory locations: 0 and 15; we find they have the same data that we wrote. The memory is deselected by pulling CS to zero, and the memory Data_out goes on high impedance, as expected.

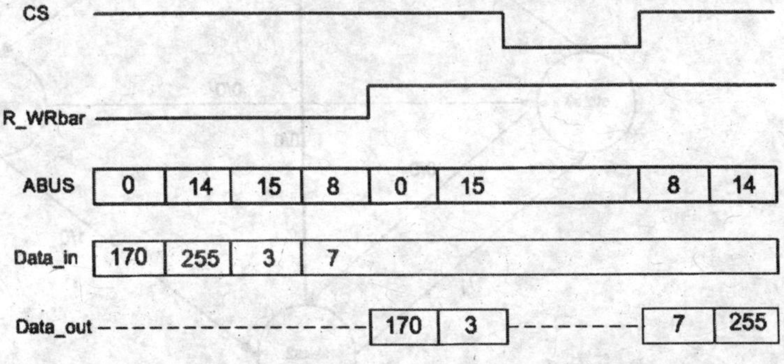

FIGURE 7.6 Simulation output of 16 x 8 static memory.

EXAMPLE 7.7 Description of a Finite Sequential-State Machine

State machines are very useful tools for designing systems because their operation can be described in time events or steps. The control unit of a computer is an example of such a system. (See Case Study 7.1, which will include information from this Example to write a mixed-type description of a basic computer.) The control unit generates different signals at certain time events. For example, when it boots up, a reset signal is needed to initialize components or registers in the computer. The control unit should generate this reset signal at the right time—that is, when operation starts. More details about computer control units can be found in [Hayes98], [Mano00], and [Nelson95].

In this Example, the control unit will be designed as a finite state machine. Chapter 4 illustrated finite state machines that were designed using structural description. Here, we design the machine by using behavioral description. The state diagram of the machine shows what signals need to be generated at each step and what the next step is. We will use the term "states" to refer to steps. Consider the state diagram shown in Figure 7.7.

The state machine in Figure 7.7 shows, for example, if the machine is in state0 and the input is 0, the machine stays in state0 and generates a signal of 1 at the output. If the input is 1, the machine generates a signal of 0 at the output, and transits to state1. Listing 7.9 lists the HDL code for the finite sequential-state machine shown in Figure 7.7.

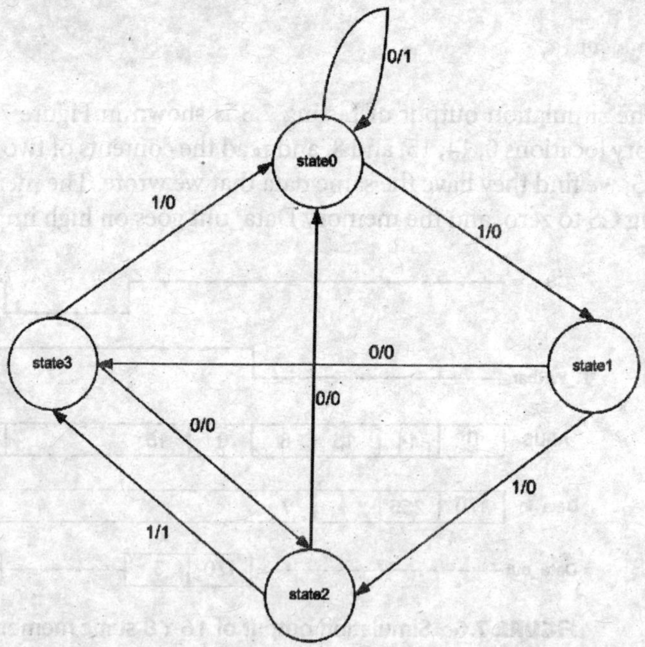

FIGURE 7.7 State diagram of a finite sequential-state machine.

LISTING 7.9 HDL Code for the State Machine in Figure 7.7—VHDL and Verilog

VHDL State Machine Description

```
library IEEE;
use IEEE.STD_LOGIC_1164.all;

--First we write a package that includes type "states."
package types is
type op is (add, mul, divide, none);
type states is (state0, state1, state2, state3);
end;

    --Now we use the package to write the code for the state machine.
library IEEE;
use IEEE.STD_LOGIC_1164.ALL;

use work.types.all;
entity state_machine is
    port (A, clk : in std_logic; pres_st : buffer states;
        Z : out std_logic);
end state_machine;

architecture st_behavioral of state_machine is

begin

FM : process (clk, pres_st, A)
variable present : states := state0;
begin
if (clk = '1' and clk'event) then
case pres_st is
    when state0 =>
        if A ='1' then
        present := state1;
        Z <= '0';
        else
        present := state0;
        Z <= '1';
        end if;
    when state1 =>
    if A ='1' then
        present := state2;
        Z <= '0';
        else
        present := state3;
        Z <= '0';
        end if;

    when state2 =>
        if A ='1' then
        present := state3;
        Z <= '1';
```

```
            else
            present := state0;
            Z <= '0';
        end if;

        when state3 =>
            if A ='1' then
            present := state0;
            Z <= '0';
            else
            present := state2;
            Z <= '0';
        end if;
    end case;
    pres_st <= present;
    end if;
    end process FM;
    end st_behavioral;
```

Verilog State Machine Description

```
`define state0 2'b00
`define state1 2'b01
`define state2 2'b10
`define state3 2'b11
// We could have declared these states as parameters.
// See Listing 7.7.

module state_machine (A, clk, pres_st, Z);

input A, clk;
output [1:0] pres_st;
output Z;
reg Z;

reg [1:0] present;
reg [1:0] pres_st;

initial
begin
    pres_st = 2'b00;
end
always @ (posedge clk)
begin

        case (pres_st)
        `state0 :
            begin
                if (A == 1)
                    begin
                        present = `state1;
                        Z = 1'b0;
                    end
```

```
                else
                begin
                    present = `state0;
                    Z = 1'b1;
                end

            end


        `state1 :
            begin
                if (A == 1)
                begin
                    present = `state2;
                    Z = 1'b0;
                    end
                else
                begin
                    present = `state3;
                    Z = 1'b0;
                    end

            end
            `state2 :
                begin
                    if (A == 1)
                    begin
                        present = `state3;
                        Z = 1'b1;
                        end
                    else
                    begin
                        present = `state0;
                        Z = 1'b0;
                        end

                end

                `state3 :
                    begin
                        if (A == 1)
                        begin
                            present = `state0;
                            Z = 1'b0;
                            end
                        else
                        begin
                            present = `state2;
                            Z = 1'b0;
                            end
```

```
                    end

endcase
pres_st = present;
end

endmodule
```

The simulation waveform is shown in Figure 7.8.

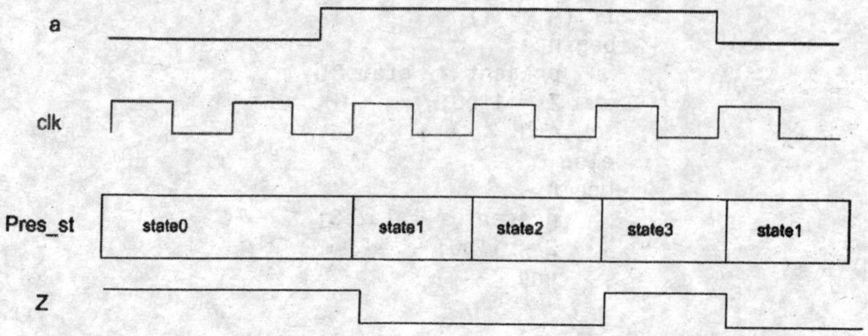

FIGURE 7.8 Simulation waveform of the state machine shown in Figure 7.7.

Case Study 7.1 HDL Description of a Basic Computer

In this Case Study, the HDL description for a basic computer will be written. In our computer, the CPU consists of ALU, registers, and a control unit. The ALU performs all arithmetic and logic operations (see Table 7.3). The registers inside the CPU store data, and communicate with the ALU and the memory. The memory here is 16 × 8 bits. Figure 7.9 shows the different computer registers.

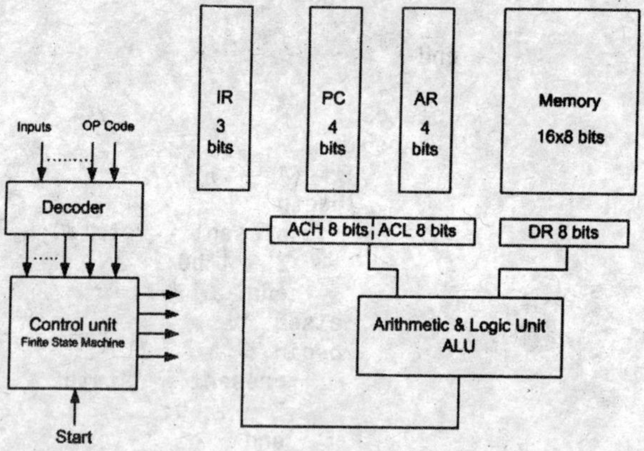

FIGURE 7.9 Registers in the basic computer.

Listed below are definitions of some of the components shown in Figure 7.9.

Program Counter (PC): Stores the address of the instruction to be executed. It is 4-bits wide.

Address Register (AR): Connected to the address bus of the memory, it supplies addresses to the memory. It is 4-bits wide. In our computer, AR is the only register that can provide addresses to the memory.

Data Register (DR): Connected to the data bus of the memory, it receives and stores data from the memory. It is 8-bits wide. In our computer, DR is the only register that can communicate with memory data bus.

Accumulator (AC): A general register that stores data, This register has two equal halves, low (ACL) and high (ACH), and each is 8 bits. The AC is 16-bits wide.

Instruction Register (IR): Stores 3-bit operation code (op code).

The control unit supervises all other units in the computer, providing timing and control signals. In our basic computer, all programs are stored in the memory. A program is a group of instructions and the data it is processing. The instruction is 8-bits wide (see Figure 7.10) and has two fields: operation code (op code) and address.

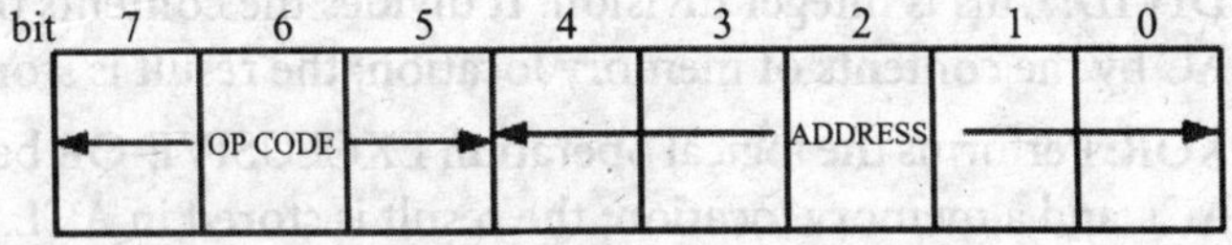

FIGURE 7.10 Basic computer instruction format.

The op code field determines the type of operation the computer should perform. The address determines the location of the operand in memory, and the operand is the data on which the operation is performed. In our computer, we have eight different instructions, so 3 bits are needed to decode the instruction operations. Table 7.3 shows a possible decoding for these operations.

TABLE 7.3 Operation Codes

Operation in Mnemonic	OP Code
HALT	000
ADD	001
MULT	010
DIVID	011
XOR	100 →

Operation in Mnemonic	OP Code
PRITY	101
NAND	110
CLA	111

The memory used here is 16×8 bits. To access this memory, a 4-bit address is needed. We will use 5 bits for the address; the extra bit is for any future expansion of the memory. So our instruction is 8-bit wide with 3 bits for the op code and 5 bits for the address. The following is a brief description of the instructions shown in Table 7.3.

HALT: Halts the computer by deactivating the master clock; all registers retain their current data.

ADD: This is an addition operation. The contents of the lower half of the Accumulator Register (ACL) are added to the contents of a memory location; the result is stored in ACL.

MULT: Multiply the contents of the lower half of the AC with an operand in the memory, and store the result in AC (both halves).

DIVID: This is integer division. It divides the contents of the lower half of the AC by the contents of memory location; the result is stored in ACL.

XOR: Performs the logical operation EXCLUSIVE-OR between the contents of ACL and a memory location; the result is stored in ACL.

PRITY: This is an even parity generator. The parity bit for the least significant 7 bits of ACL is calculated, and then the parity bit is inserted in the most significant bit of ACL.

NAND: Performs the logical operation NAND between the contents of ACL and a memory location; the result is stored in ACL.

CLA: Clears the contents of the ACL.

The memory location in all of the above instructions is determined by the address provided by the instruction, and is stored in the Address Register (AR). More details about basic computers can be found in [Hayes98], [Mano00], and [Nelson95]. Following are a couple of detailed instruction explanations.

ADD 7: This instruction adds the contents of the lower half of the accumulator to the contents of memory location 7; the result is stored in ACL.

DIVID 5: This instruction divides the contents of the lower half of the accumulator by the contents of memory location 5; the result is stored in ACL.

Our basic computer executes the instructions in two cycles: fetch and execute (see Figure 7.11). The control unit supplies all required signals necessary for operation of the two cycles. In the fetch cycle, the instruction is moved from the memory to the DR. The lower 4 bits (0 to 3) of DR are stored in AR; bits 5 to 7 of the DR are stored in IR. The PC is incremented to point at the next instruction to be fetched. The 3 bits of the IR is decoded into eight outputs by a 3×8 decoder. The output of the decoder determines the type of operation requested by the instruction. For example, if the least significant output of the decoder is active, then the operation requested belongs to the op code 000, which is HALT.

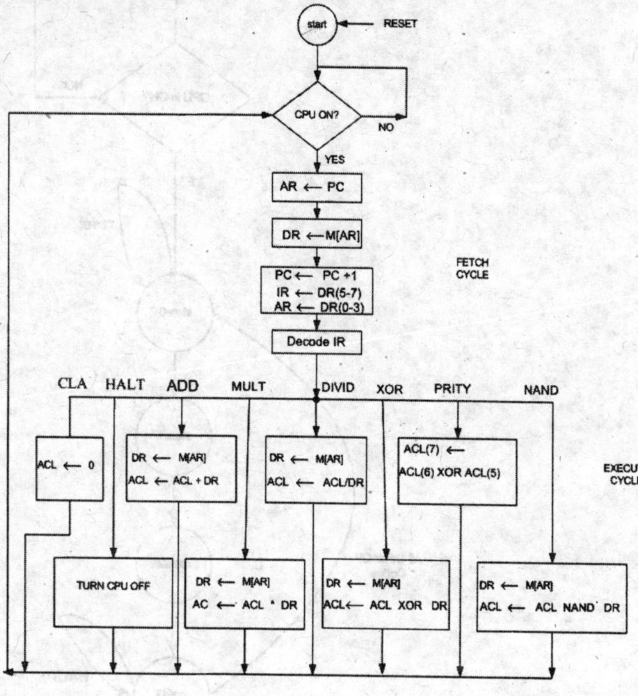

FIGURE 7.11 Fetch and execute cycles of the basic computer.

In the execute cycle, the computer executes the instruction that has been fetched. For example, if the instruction is ADD, then the execute cycle issues a memory read DR ← M [AR] to move the operand from the memory to the DR. M stands for memory. This movement is necessary, since the ALU can operate only on DR and AC, but not on data stored in memory. After moving the operand to DR, an ADD operation in the ALU is selected. Different ALU operations are selected according to control signals supplied by the control unit. The ALU executes the microoperation AC ← AC + DR. For the instruction PRITY, the execute cycle calculates the parity bit (bit 7 of the accumulator) as:

Parity (ACL(7)) = ACL(6) XOR ACL(5) XOR ACL(4) XOR ACL(3) XOR ACL(2) XOR ACL(1) XOR ACL(0)

As previously mentioned, the control unit oversees the fetch and execute cycle. We design the control unit as a finite sequential-state machine. Figure 7.12 shows the state diagram of the machine. The figure only shows transitions between states; it does not show outputs. The states state0, state1, and state2 are performing the three steps of the fetch cycle, while state3 performs the execute cycle (see Figure 7.11).

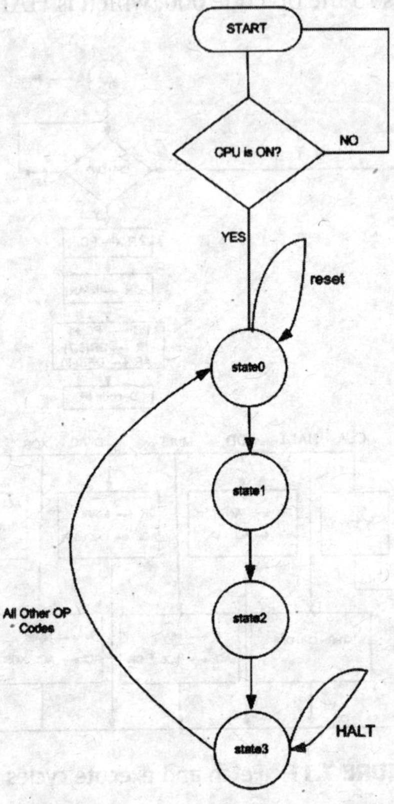

FIGURE 7.12 State diagram of the finite sequential-state machine.

To test the basic computer's operation, we store a program in memory. Table 7.4 shows the instructions of the program, with the op code written in mnemonic and the instructions written in hexadecimal. For example, the instruction:

1 ADD 9 29

is stored in memory location 1, the op code is ADD, and the address is 9. The instruction adds the contents of the accumulator (AC) to the contents of memory location 9; the result of addition is stored in the accumulator. The accumulator in our computer is always the default register. The binary value of the op code ADD is 001 (see Table 7.3). The instruction is 8-bits wide, so the binary representation of the instruction is 00101001, which is 29 in hexadecimal.

TABLE 7.4 Contents of Memory of the Basic Computer

Location in Hex	Instruction in Mnemonic or Data in Hex		Memory Contents (8 bits) in Hex
0	CLA		E0
1	ADD	9	29
2	XOR	A	8A
3	MULT	B	4B
4	DIVID	C	6C
5	XOR	D	8D
6	NAND	E	CE
7	PRITY		A0
8	HALT		00
9	C		0C
A	5		05
B	4		04
C	9		09
D	3		03
E	9		09
F	7		07

Listing 7.10 shows the HDL code for the basic computer program shown in Table 7.4. Referring to the VHDL listing, the package `Comp_Pkg` declares one dimensional array with 16 elements; each element is 8 bits. This array represents the memory of the computer. In the entity `computer_basic`, the signal `clk_master` simulates the master clock of the computer. The signal `ON_OFF` simulates an ON/OFF switch. The data-flow statement:

```
clk <= clk_master and ON_OFF;
```

simulates an AND gate. The signal `clk` simulates the clock signal of the CPU; if the switch is off, the clock signal to the CPU is inactive—and accordingly, the CPU is inactive. The statement

```
z(0) <= ACL(6) xor ACL (5) xor ACL (4)xor
        ACL (3)xor ACL (2)xor ACL (1)xor ACL (0);
```

generates an even parity bit. We selected to write this statement as data flow (outside always), because it is easier to write the Boolean as data-flow description, rather than the behavioral of this parity generator circuit. The statements:

```
ARI := TO_INTEGER(AR);
DR := Memory (ARI);
```

convert AR from unsigned to integer by the built-in function `TO_INTEGER`. This function is part of the package `ieee.numeric_std`. We convert to integer because the index of the array `ARI` has to be of type integer in VHDL.

Referring to the Verilog description, the memory is simulated by the statement:

```
reg [7:0] Memory [0:15];
```

which describes an array of 15 elements (words); each element is 8 bits. In contrast to VHDL, Verilog can accept an index of an array declared as bit_vector. For example, we can write:

```
DR = Memory [AR];
```

without specifying AR to be of type integer.

LISTING 7.10 HDL Code for the Basic Computer Memory Program (Table 7.4)—VHDL and Verilog

VHDL Basic Computer Memory Program

```
--Write the code for Package Comp_Pkg
library IEEE;
use IEEE.STD_LOGIC_1164.all;
use ieee.numeric_std.all;

package Comp_Pkg is
constant N: integer := 15;
--N+1 is the number of elements in the array.
constant M : integer := 7;
--M+1 is the number of bits of each element
--of the array.
```

```
subtype wordN is unsigned (M downto 0);
type strng is array (N downto 0) of wordN;

type states is (state0, state1, state2, state3);

end Comp_Pkg;

--Now write the code for the control unit
library IEEE;
use IEEE.STD_LOGIC_1164.ALL;
use IEEE.STD_LOGIC_UNSIGNED.ALL;
use ieee.numeric_std.all;
use work.Comp_Pkg. all;

entity computer_basic is

generic (N : integer := 15; M : integer := 7);
--N+1 is the number of words in the memory; M+1 is the
--number of bits of each word.

Port (Memory : inout strng; PC : buffer unsigned (3 downto 0);
    clk_master : std_logic;
    ACH : buffer unsigned (7 downto 0);
    ACL : buffer unsigned (7 downto 0);
    Reset : buffer std_logic; ON_OFF : in std_logic);

end computer_basic;

architecture Behavioral_comp of computer_basic is
signal z : unsigned (0 downto 0);
signal clk : std_logic;

begin

z(0) <= ACL(6) xor ACL(5) xor ACL(4) xor
    ACL(3) xor ACL(2) xor ACL(1) xor ACL(0);
--Z has to be in vector form to match ACL

clk <= clk_master and ON_OFF;

--The above two statements are data-flow description.
--The following is behavioral description.

cpu : process (Reset, PC, ACL, ACH, clk, Memory, z(0))
variable AR : unsigned (3 downto 0);
```

```
variable DR : unsigned (7 downto 0);
variable pres_st,  next_st : states;
variable ARI : integer range 0 to 16;
variable IR : unsigned (2 downto 0);
variable PR : unsigned (15 downto 0);

begin

if rising_edge (clk) then
if Reset = '1' then
pres_st := state0;
Reset <= '0';
PC <= "0000";
end if;

case pres_st is
when state0 =>
next_st := state1;
--This is fetch cycle
AR := PC;

when state1 =>
next_st := state2;
ARI := TO_INTEGER(AR);
--This is fetch cycle
DR := Memory (ARI);

when state2 =>
next_st := state3;
--This is fetch cycle
PC <= PC + 1;
IR := DR (7 downto 5);
AR := DR (3 downto 0);

when state3 =>
--This is execute cycle

case IR is
   when "111" =>
   --The op code is CLA
   ACL <= "00000000";
   next_st := state0;

   when "001" =>
   --The op code is ADD
   ARI := TO_INTEGER(AR);
```

```
DR := memory (ARI);
ACL <= ACL + DR;
next_st := state0;

when "010" =>
--The op code is MULT
ARI := TO_INTEGER(AR);
DR := memory (ARI);
PR := ACL * DR;
ACL <= PR (7 downto 0);
ACH <= PR (15 downto 8);
next_st := state0;

when "011" =>
--The op code is DIVID
ARI := TO_INTEGER(AR);
DR := memory (ARI);
ACL <= ACL / DR;
next_st := state0;

when "100" =>
--The op code is XOR
ARI := TO_INTEGER(AR);
DR := memory (ARI);
ACL <= ACL XOR DR;
next_st := state0;

when "110" =>
--The op code is NAND
ARI := TO_INTEGER(AR);
DR := memory (ARI);
ACL <= ACL NAND DR;
 next_st := state0;

when "101" =>
--The op code is PRITY
ACL(7) <= z(0);
 next_st := state0;

when "000" => null;
-- The op code is HALT
next_st := state3;

when others => null;
end case;
```

```
when others => null;
end case;
pres_st := next_st;
end if;
end process cpu;
end Behavioral_comp;
```

Verilog Basic Computer Memory Program

```
module computer_basic (PC, clk_master, ACH, ACL, Reset, ON_OFF);
parameter state0 = 2'b00;
parameter state1 = 2'b01;
parameter state2 = 2'b10;
parameter state3 = 2'b11;

output [3:0] PC;
input clk_master;
output Reset;
input ON_OFF;
output [7:0] ACH;
output [7:0] ACL;
reg [1:0] pres_st;
reg [1:0] next_st;
reg Reset;
reg [3:0] PC;
reg [3:0] AR;
reg [7:0] DR;
reg [2:0] IR;
reg [7:0] ACH;
reg [7:0] ACL;
reg [15:0] PR;
reg [7:0] Memory [0:15];

assign z = ACL[6] ^ ACL[5] ^ ACL[4]^
    ACL[3]^ ACL[2]^ ACL[1]^ ACL[0];

//The above statement can be written using the reduction XOR as:
//assign z = ^ ACL[6:0];

assign clk = clk_master & ON_OFF;

always @ (Reset, PC, ACL, ACH, posedge(clk), z, pres_st)
begin

    if (Reset == 1'b1)
        begin
        pres_st = state0;
```

```
    Reset = 1'b0;
    PC = 4'd0;
    Memory [0] = 8'hE0; Memory [1] = 8'h29;
    Memory [2] = 8'h8A; Memory [3] = 8'h4B;
    Memory [4] = 8'h6C; Memory [5] = 8'h8D;
    Memory [6] = 8'hCE; Memory [7] = 8'hA0;
    Memory [8] = 8'h00; Memory [9] = 8'h0C;
    Memory [10] = 8'h05; Memory [11] = 8'h04;
    Memory [12] = 8'h09; Memory [13] = 8'h03;
    Memory [14] = 8'h09;
    Memory [15] = 8'h07;

    end

case (pres_st)

state0 :
begin
    next_st = state1;
    AR = PC;
     end

state1 :
//This is fetch cycle
begin
    next_st = state2;
    DR = Memory [AR];
    end

    state2 :
    //This is fetch cycle
    begin
        next_st = state3;
        PC = PC + 1;
        IR = DR [7:5];
        AR = DR [3:0];
        end

    state3 :
    //This is execute cycle
    begin
        case (IR)
            3'd7 :
            //The op code is CLA
            begin
                ACL = 8'd0;
```

```
                next_st = state0;
                end

            3'd1 :
            //The op code is ADD
            begin
                DR = Memory [AR];
                ACL = ACL + DR;
                next_st = state0;
                end

            3'd2 :
            //The op code is MULT
            begin
                DR = Memory [AR];
                PR = ACL * DR;
                ACL = PR [7:0];
                ACH = PR [15:8];
                next_st = state0;
                end

            3'd3 :
            //The op code is DIVID
            begin
                DR = Memory [AR];
                ACL = ACL / DR;
                next_st = state0;
                end

            3'd4 :
            //The op code is XOR
            begin
                DR = Memory [AR];
                ACL = ACL ^ DR;
                next_st = state0;
                end

            3'd6 :
            //The op code is NAND
            begin
                DR = Memory [AR];
                ACL = ~(ACL & DR);
                next_st = state0;
                end

            3'd5 :
```

```
                //The op code is PRITY
                begin
                    ACL[7] = z;
                    next_st = state0;
                    end

                3'd0 :
                //The op code is HALT
                begin
                    next_st = state3;
                    end

                default :
                begin
                end

                endcase

        end

    default :
        begin
        end

    endcase
    pres_st = next_st;

end

endmodule
```

Figure 7.13 shows the simulation output of the accumulator register. To start simulation, reset is forced high and then unforced.

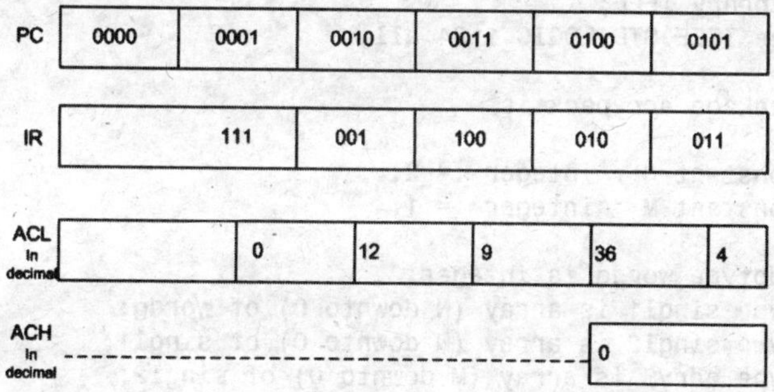

FIGURE 7.13 Simulation output of the accumulator register.

7.5 SUMMARY

This chapter discussed mixed-type descriptions, HDL code that includes more than one type of description in the same module. An example of mixed description is when we write a module using behavioral and data-flow statements. In some systems, one part can be best described by behavioral statements, and other parts of the system can be best described by data-flow description. Instead of writing a module with only behavioral or only data-flow, we write the module using both behavioral and data-flow descriptions; that is what is defined as mixed-type description.

An example to illustrate the mixed-type description is the ALU of a computer. Some operations of the ALU, such as division, are usually described by behavioral statements, since it is not easy to find the Boolean function or the hardware logic for them. Other operations, such as addition, may be described by data-flow or structural description, since it is usually easy to find the logic diagram of adders. In addition to mixed-type descriptions, packages and single/multidimensional arrays were covered. Packages are an essential construct in VHDL code. User-defined types, components, functions, and procedures can be written in a package, and made visible to a VHDL module by attaching (including) the package with the module. VHDL, in contrast to Verilog, allows for multidimensional arrays.

7.6 EXERCISES

7.1 Write the HDL code to find the value and the order of the smallest element in an array. The elements are 4-bit signed numbers. Simulate and verify your code.

7.2 Given an array of N elements, write the HDL code to organize the elements of the array in ascending order. All elements are integers.

7.3 Consider the code shown in Listing 7.11.

LISTING 7.11 Exercise 7.3

```
library IEEE;
use IEEE.STD_LOGIC_1164.all;

package arrypack is

constant N : integer := 2;
constant M : integer := 1;

subtype wordg is integer;
type singl1 is array (N downto 0) of wordg;
type singl2 is array (N downto 0) of singl1;
type arry3 is array (M downto 0) of singl2;
end arrypack;
```

```
library IEEE;
use IEEE.STD_LOGIC_1164.ALL;
use work.arrypack.all;

entity exercise is

    Port(N, M, P : integer; z : out integer);
end exercise;

architecture exercise of exercise is

begin
com : process (N, M, P)
variable t : integer;
constant y : arry3 := (((5, 4, 3), (8, 9, 10), (32, 33, 34)),
    ((42, 43, 44), (52, 53, 54), (-10, -7, -5)));
begin

t := y (N)(M)(P);
z <= t;
end process com;

end exercise;
```

a) What is the value of the following elements of y?
y (0,0,0), y (0,0,1), y (0,0,2), y (0,1,2), y (1,1,2), y (1,2,2)

b) If we change all `(N downto 0)` and `(M downto 0)` in package `arrypack` to `(0 to N)` and `(0 to M)`; what will be the values of the elements in part a?

7.4 Repeat Listing 7.8, but for a memory of 128_16. Store the following data in the corresponding memory locations:

Verify your storage by reading the data from the above locations.

7.5 For the state diagram shown in Figure 7.14, write a behavioral HDL program to simulate the state machine. Verify your answer by simulation.

7.6 For Case Study 7.1, increase the memory size to 32_16. Also, change all instructions so that the result of each instruction is stored in a memory location, rather than the accumulator. The address of this memory location is the same as the address provided in the instruction. For example, the instruction ADD 9 would mean addition of contents of AC to the contents of memory location 9, with storage of the result in memory location 9. Keep the size of all registers at 8 bits. Rewrite the VHDL code shown in Listing 7.10 and verify by simulation.

7.7 REFERENCES

[Hayes98] Hayes, J. P., *Computer Architecture and Organization*, 3d ed. McGraw Hill, 1998.

[Mano00] Mano, M. M. and C. R. Kime, *Logic and Computer Design Fundamentals*. Prentice Hall, 2000.

[Nelson95] Nelson V. P., H. T. Nagle, B. D. Carroll, and J. D. Irwin, *Digital Logic Circuit Analysis & Design*. Prentice Hall, 1995.

8 Advanced HDL Descriptions

In This Chapter

- Explore several advanced topics in HDL Description, such as file processing, character and string implementation, and the type `record`.
- Understand VHDL `Assert` and `Report` statements.
- Acquire a basic knowledge of artificial neural networks.

8.1 FILE PROCESSING

Files are valuable HDL description tools. For example, files can be used when dealing with a large amount of data that needs to be stored and accessed. Also, we may want to use files to display formatted output, such as reports. Files can be read or written. To read from or write to a file, it must be opened; and after reading or writing is finished, the file must be closed. A closed file cannot be accessed unless we open it. In Section 8.1.1, the VHDL file description is explored, and Section 8.1.2 discusses Verilog file descriptions.

8.1.1 VHDL File Processing

File processing can be slightly different from one HDL simulator to another. Appropriate packages have to be attached to the VHDL module. The reader is advised to consult his VHDL package and simulator for files-handling capability. This section will present complete examples of file description with the names of the appropriate packages. Files have to be declared by the predefined object type `file`. File declaration includes the predefined word `file` followed by (in this order) the port direction or mode of the file `(infile or outfile)`, a colon, and the subtype of the file. An example of file declaration is as follows:

```
file infile : text;
```

The above statement declares a file with mode `infile`, and the subtype of the file is `text`. The IEEE package `textio` should be used; see examples in the following sections. VHDL has built-in procedures for files-handling. These procedures include `file_open`, `readline`, `writeline`, `read`, `write`, and `file_close`. In the following sections, each of these procedures is briefly discussed.

File_open

This procedure opens the file; files cannot be accessed if not opened. The `file_open` procedure has the following declaration:

```
Procedure file_open (status : file_open_status, infile : File Type,
external_name : in string, open_kind : file_open_kind) is
```

The statement `status` enables the VHDL to keep track of the activities of the file (e.g., open, close, read, etc.); `infile` is the type (mode) of the file. We use `infile` for input files (their contents will be read) and `outfile` for output files (they will be written into). The `external_name` is the name of the file to be opened; the name has to be `in string` form, such as "rprt.txt" or "testfile.txt." The `open_kind` is the mode of opening the `read_mode` or `write_mode`. An example of implementing `file_open` is:

```
file_open (fstatus, infile, "testfile.txt", read_mode);
```

The above procedure opens a file by the name of `testfile.txt` for reading. The file is an input file (`infile`) with type `txt`. It is located in the same path as the procedure. For example, if the procedure is written in a module stored in directory C under a subdirectory VHDL_files, then testfile should be stored in subdirectory VHDL_files; otherwise, the path of testfile should be stated in the declaration of `file_open`. The file is then opened for reading.

The following procedure opens a text `outfile` by the name of `store.txt` for writing:

```
file_open (fstatus, outfile, "store.txt", write_mode);
```

File_close

`file_close` is a procedure to close an open file. For example:

```
file_close (infile);
```

closes the open file `infile`. The name and path of `infile` are specified in the procedure `file_open`. The following statement closes `outfile`:

```
file_close (outfile);
```

Readline

The predefined procedure `readline` reads a line from the file opened in read mode. An example of implementing this procedure is:

```
readline (infile, temp);
```

The above statement reads a line from `infile` and stores the line in variable temp. Variable temp has to be of a predefined type line. The name and type of infile should have been stated in the procedure `file_open`. Inside the file specified by `infile`, a carriage return is the separator between the lines. If `readline` is repeated before closing the file, another line is read. A carriage return indicates a new line.

Writeline

`writeline` is a predefined procedure that writes a line into an outfile that is open for write mode. An example of implementing this procedure is:

```
writeline (outfile, temp);
```

The above statement writes a line stored in the variable `temp` into the file `outfile`. Variable temp has to be of type `line`. The name and path of outfile should be specified in the procedure `file_open`. We can only write integers, real values, or characters to the outfile. If `writeline` is repeated before closing `outfile`, a new line is stored in `outfile`.

Read

`read` is a procedure to read an integer, a character, or a real value from a line in an infile that is open for read mode. For example, if `intg1` has been declared as of type integer, the statement:

```
read (temp, intg1);
```

performs a single read of an integer from line `temp` of the open file (for read mode) and stores the value of this integer in `intg1`. If we want to read a character or a real value, the variable `intg1` should be of type `character` or `real`, respectively. If `intg1` is a single value (not an array), each time the read operation is executed, a single word of the line is read and stored in `intg1`. If the read statement is repeated before closing of the file, the next word in the line is read and stored in `intg1`.

Write

The procedure `write` stores an integer, a character, or a real value from a line to an outfile that is open for `write_mode`. For example, if `intg1` has been declared as type `integer`, the statement

```
write (temp, intg1);
```

stores the integer `intg1` in the line `temp` of the open `outfile`, which is in `write mode`. If we want to write a character or a real value, the variable `intg1` should be of type `character` or `real`, respectively. Each time the write operation is executed, a single word is stored in the line. If the `write` statement is repeated before closing the file, a new value of `intg1` is stored in the line.

8.1.2 Verilog File Processing

Standard Verilog can handle several file operations. As in VHDL, before accessing a file, it must be opened. If the file is not open, it cannot be read from or written to. Accessing a file is accomplished through built-in tasks, such as: `$fopen`, `$fdisplay`, `$fmonitor`, and `$fclose`. Let us briefly investigate each of these tasks.

$Fopen

The task `$fopen` is used to open files. It is the counterpart of the VHDL procedure `file_open`. The format for opening a file is:

```
Channel = $fopen ("name of the file");
```

where `Channel` is a variable of type integer; it indicates the channel number. Verilog uses this channel number to track and identify which files are open. Verilog automatically assigns an integer value to each channel. For example, to open a text file named `testfile, we write:`

```
ch1 = $fopen ("testfile.txt");
```

and `ch1` becomes the indicator (identifier) of file `testfile.txt.`

$Fclose

The task `$fclose` closes a file indicated by the channel number. For example the task:

```
$fclose (ch1);
```

closes the file `testfile.txt.`

$Fdisplay

The task `$fdisplay` is the counterpart of `write` in VHDL. It can write variables, signals, or quoted strings. The format of `$fdisplay` is as follows:

```
$fdisplay (channel, V1, V2, V3, …);
```

Where V1, V2, V3, and so on are variables, signals, or quoted strings. For example, consider the following `$fdisplay` task:

```
$fdisplay (ch1, "item  description  quantity");
```

After executing the task, the file `testfile.txt` displays:

```
item   description   quantity
```

The number of spaces displayed in the file between each string is the same number of spaces inside the quotations.

$Fmonitor

Task `$fmonitor` has the following format:

```
$fmonitor (channel, V1, V2, V3, …);
```

The task monitors and records the values of V1, V2, V3, and so on. For example, consider the following `$fmonitor` task:

```
$fmonitor (ch1, "    %b", quantity);
```

The above task monitors the variable quantity and records its value in binary in the file `testfile.txt`, indicated by `ch1`; `%b` indicates binary format. If `quantity` = 7 in decimal, after execution of the above task, the file `testfile.txt` looks like:

```
item              description          quantity
                                         111
```

We can select a different format than the binary. Some other formats are as follows:

`%d`	Display in decimal
`%s`	Display strings
`%h`	Display in hex
`%o`	Display in octal
%c	Display ASCII character
`%f`	Display real numbers in decimal format

Escape characters may also used. Some of these characters are:

\n	Insert a blank line
\t	Insert tab
\\	Insert the character \
\"	Insert the character "
\	Insert the character %

8.2 EXAMPLES OF FILE PROCESSING

The following sections present and discuss some examples of file processing. Since VHDL and Verilog file processing are not very similar, their examples are discussed separately.

8.2.1 Examples of VHDL File Processing

The following examples will cover file processing in VHDL.

EXAMPLE 8.1 Reading a File Consisting of Integer Numbers

Assume that we store a text file by the name of `file_int.txt` in the same path as the VHDL module that accesses it (see Listing 8.1). The contents of the file are integers written in two lines (see Figure 8.1). The two lines are separated by a carriage return, and the integers are separated by a spaceband (the number of spacebands can be one or more than one).

```
12    –3    5
20
```

FIGURE 8.1 File `file_int.txt`.

In this Example, we want to multiply the first integer by 2, the second by 5, the third by 3, and the fourth by 4. The products are stored in the integer variables z, z1, z2, and z3 respectively.

To calculate the products, we need to open the file, read its contents, perform the multiplication, and close the file. Referring to Listing 8.1, the statement:

```
file_open (fstatus, infile, "file_int.txt", read_mode);
```

opens the `infile` `file_int.txt` for reading. The statement:

```
readline (infile, temp);
```

reads a line from the file `file_int.txt` and stores this line in a variable `temp` of type `line`. If the statement is repeated, `temp` acquires the next line. The statement:

```
read (temp, count);
```

reads a single integer from the line `temp` and stores the integer in the variable `count`. If the statement is repeated, `count` will acquire the next integer from the same line. The statement:

```
file_close (infile);
```

closes the file. No operation can be performed on the file as long as it is closed. If the file is opened again, `readline` reads the first line of the file.

LISTING 8.1 VHDL Code for Reading and Processing a Text File Containing Integers

```
library ieee;
use ieee.std_logic_1164.all;
use std.textio.all;

entity FREAD_INTG is
port (START : in std_logic;
z, z1, z2, z3 : out integer);
end FREAD_INTG;

architecture FILE_BEHAVIOR of FREAD_INTG is
begin

process (START)

--declare the infile as a text file
file infile : text;

--declare the variable fstatus (or any other variable name)
--as of type file_open_status
variable fstatus : file_open_status;
variable count : integer;

--declare variable temp as of type line
variable temp : line;

begin
--open the file file_int.txt in read mode
   file_open (fstatus, infile, "file_int.txt", read_mode);

--Read the first line of the file and store the line in temp
```

```
    readline (infile, temp);
-- temp now has the data: 12 -3 5

--Read the first integer (12) from the line temp and store it
--in the integer variable count.
    read (temp, count);

--count has the value of 12. Multiply by 2 and store in z
    z <= 2 * count;

--Read the second integer from the line temp and
--store it in count
    read (temp, count);
--count now has the value of -3

--Multiply by 5 and store in z1
    z1 <= 5 * count;

-- read the third integer in line temp and store it in count
    read (temp, count);

--Multiply by 3 and store in z2
    z2 <= 3 * count;

--Read the second line and store it in temp
    readline (infile, temp);
--temp has only the second line

--Read the first integer of the second line and store it in count
    read (temp, count);

--Multiply by 4 and store in z3
    z3 <= 4 * count;

--Close the infile
file_close (infile);
end process;

end FILE_BEHAVIOR;
```

After the code in Listing 8.1 executes, `z`, `z1`, `z2`, and `z3` take the following values:

$z = 24$, $z1 = -10$, $z2 = 15$, $z3 = 80$

EXAMPLE 8.2 Reading a File Consisting of Real Numbers

In this example a file by the name of `file_real.txt` is read. The contents of this file are real (float) numbers written in decimal format, such as 50.3 (see Figure 8.2). The contents are written in two lines separated by a carriage return. The numbers are separated by one or more spaces. Listing 8.2 shows the code for reading the file;

it is very similar to Listing 8.1. We open the file with `file_open` and read a line from the file using the procedure `readline`. After reading a line, one word is read at a time by invoking the procedure `read`. Each word is a real number; spaces are not read, but are recognized as separators between words.

–13.4	–5.654	.023
–55.32		

FIGURE 8.2 File `file_real.txt`.

LISTING 8.2 VHDL Code for Reading a Text File Containing Real Numbers

```
library ieee;
use ieee.std_logic_1164.all;
use std.textio.all;

entity FREAD_REAL is
port (START : in std_logic;
z, z1, z2, z3 : out real);
end FREAD_REAL;

architecture FILE_BEHAVIOR of FREAD_REAL is
begin

process (START)
file infile : text;
variable fstatus : file_open_status;
variable count : real;
--Variable count has to be of type real
variable temp : line;

begin
--Open the file
    file_open (fstatus, infile, "file_real.txt", read_mode);

--Read a line

    readline (infile, temp);

--Read one number and store it in real variable count
    read (temp, count);
--multiply by 2
z <= 2.0 * count;

--read another number
```

```
        read (temp, count);
    --multiply by 5
        z1 <= 5.0 * count;
        --read another number
            read (temp, count);
        --multiply by 3
            z2 <= 3.0 * count;

        --read another line
            readline (infile, temp);
            read (temp, count);
        --multiply by 4
            z3 <= 4.0 * count;
            file_close (infile);
    end process;

    end FILE_BEHAVIOR;
```

After the code in Listing 8.2 executes, `z`, `z1`, `z2`, and `z3` take the following values:

z = –26.8, z1 = –28.27, z2 = 0.069, z3 = –221.28

EXAMPLE 8.3 Reading a File Consisting of ASCII Characters

The file to be read is `file_chr.txt`, and the contents of this file are ASCII characters. ASCII characters can be digits (e.g., 0, 1, 2), letters of the alphabet (e.g., A, B, C), or special characters (e.g., ;, *, &, #). The spaceband is an ASCII character, and is read as a character. Listing 8.3 shows the code for reading the file `file_chr.txt`. The file has two lines (see Figure 8.3) separated by a carriage return. The first line has three characters, A5B, and the second line has one character, M. If the first line contains A B instead of A5B, it is still read as three characters—A, spaceband, and B.

Listing 8.3 shows the code for reading an ASCII file. We open the file with `file_open` and read a line from the file, using the procedure `readline`. After reading a line, one word at a time is read by invoking the procedure `read`; each word is a character, including spaces. The character is then stored in variable `count`; this variable has to be of type `character`.

```
A5B
M
```

FIGURE 8.3 File `file_chr.txt`.

LISTING 8.3 VHDL Code for Reading an ASCII File

```
library ieee;
use ieee.std_logic_1164.all;
use std.textio.all;

entity FREAD_character is
port (START : in std_logic;
    z, z1, z2, z3 : out character);
end FREAD_character;

architecture FILE_BEHAVIOR of FREAD_character is
begin

process (START)
file infile : text;
variable fstatus : file_open_status;
variable count : character;
--Variable count has to be of type character
variable temp : line;

begin
    file_open (fstatus, infile, "file_chr.txt", read_mode);

--read a line from the file
    readline (infile, temp);

--read a character from the line into count. Count has to be of
--type character
    read (temp, count);

--store the character in z
    z <= count;
    read (temp, count);
    z1 <= count;
    read (temp, count);
    z2 <= count;
    readline (infile, temp);
    read (temp, count);
    z3 <= count;
    file_close (infile);
end process;

end FILE_BEHAVIOR;
```

After the code in Listing 8.3 executes, `z`, `z1`, `z2`, and `z3` take the following values:

z = A, z1 = 5, z2 = B, z3 = M

In the previous Examples, we have been practicing with reading files. The following Examples cover writing into files. As mentioned, VHDL files can store integers, real values, and characters.

EXAMPLE 8.4 Writing Integers to a File

In this Example, we write to the text file `Wfile_int.txt`. Assume that the file is located in the same path as the VHDL module that accesses it (see Listing 8.4). Integers will be written to the file. Start by opening the file using the procedure `file_open`. We assemble the line that we want to write by using the procedure `write`, as follows:

```
write (temp, z);
```

The above statement stores the integer `z` in the line `temp`. Quoted characters can be stored in `temp` as follows:

```
write (temp, "This is an integer file");
```

Executing this statement results in storing the message "`This is an integer file`" in `temp`. And if the statement is repeated, another integer or character is stored in `temp`. We will store a space between each two integers. After all integers and characters have been stored in the line, the line is written to the file using the procedure:

```
writeline (outfile, temp);
```

The above procedure, `writeline`, writes the line `temp` to the outfile, `Wfile_int.txt`.

LISTING 8.4 VHDL Code for Writing Integers to a File

```
library ieee;
use ieee.std_logic_1164.all;
use std.textio.all;

entity FWRITE_INT is
port (START : in std_logic;
z, z1, z2, z3 : in integer);
end FWRITE_INT;

architecture FILE_BEHAVIOR of FWRITE_INT is
begin

process (START)
file outfile : text;
variable fstatus : file_open_status;
--declare temp as of type line
variable temp : line;

begin
    file_open (fstatus, outfile, "Wfile_int.txt", write_mode);
    --The generated file "Wfile_int.txt" is in
    --the same directory as this VHDL module
```

```
        --Insert the title of the file Wfile_int.txt.
        --Your simulator should support formatted text;
        --if not, remove all formatted statements " ".
        write (temp, "This is an integer file");

        --Write the line temp into the file
        writeline (outfile, temp);

        --store the first integer in line temp
        write (temp, z);

        --leave space between the integer numbers.
        write (temp, " ");
        write (temp, z1);

        --leave another space between the integer numbers.
        write (temp, " ");
        write (temp, z2);
        write (temp, " ");

        writeline (outfile, temp);
        --Insert the fourth integer value on a new line
        write (temp, z3);
        writeline (outfile, temp);
    file_close(outfile);

    end process;
    end FILE_BEHAVIOR;
```

After executing the code above, the outfile `Wfile_int.txt` is as shown in Figure 8.4.

```
This is an integer file
12    23    –56
–45
```

FIGURE 8.4 File `Wfile_int.txt`.

In the same way as was done in Listing 8.4, we can write characters or real numbers into an outfile.

Example 8.5 Reading a String of Characters into an Array

In previous Examples we read a single character from the file and stored it in a single variable count. In this Example, a string of characters will be read and the string stored in an array. To handle arrays, a package is built that contains an array of the characters. The package `array_pkg` is shown in Listing 8.5. We use `subtype wordchr` of type `character` and then write the array as type `string_chr`, which is an array of the subtype `wordchr`. So the array consists of $N + 1$ elements, and each element is type `character`.

LISTING 8.5 VHDL Code for Writing a Package Containing a String of Five Characters

```
library IEEE;
use IEEE.STD_LOGIC_1164.all;

package array_pkg is
constant N : integer := 4;
--N+1 is the number of elements in the array.
subtype wordChr is character;
type string_chr is array (N downto 0) of wordChr;

end array_pkg;
```

Now we want to read a string of characters from the file `string_chr` and store the string in an array. Listing 8.6 shows the code for reading a string from the file. A single word composed of five characters, "STORE," is stored in the file. We use the package written in Listing 8.5 to instantiate the array. In Listing 8.6, z is declared as type `string_chr`. This means that z is an array of five elements, (N down to 0) where $N = 4$; each element is a single character. We open the file, read the string, and store it in array `z`.

LISTING 8.6 VHDL Code for Reading a String of Characters into an Array

```
library ieee;
use ieee.std_logic_1164.all;
use std.textio.all;

--include the package with this module
use work.array_pkg.all;

entity FILE_CHARCTR is
port (START : in std_logic; z : out string_chr);

--string_char is included in the package array_pkg;
--Z is a 5-character array

end FILE_CHARCTR;

architecture FILE_BEHAVIOR of FILE_CHARCTR is
begin
```

```
process (START)
file infile : text;
variable fstatus : file_open_status;
variable count : string_chr;
variable temp : line;

begin
file_open (fstatus, infile, "myfile1.txt", read_mode);
readline (infile, temp);

read (temp, count);
--Variable count has been declared as an array of five elements,
--each element is a single character
z <= count;

file_close (infile);
end process;

end FILE_BEHAVIOR;
```

After code in Listing 8.6 executes, the signal z contains: "S" "T" "O" "R" "E."

Example 8.6 Finding the Word in a File with the Smallest ASCII Value

When we read an ASCII character, the VHDL package assigns the unique hexadecimal value for that character. Table 8.1 shows the hexadecimal values for several characters. Notice that A has the lowest hex value among the letters, while Z has the highest. In this Example, we want to find the word that has the lowest ASCII hex value.

TABLE 8.1 ASCII Character Hexadecimal Values

Character	Hex Value	Character	Hex Value
A	41	U	55
B	42	V	56
C	43	W	57
D	44	X	58
E	45	Y	59
F	46	Z	5A
G	47	0	30
H	48	1	31
I	49	2	32
J	4A	3	33
K	4B	4	34

→

Character	Hex Value	Character	Hex Value
L	4C	5	35
M	4D	6	36
N	4E	7	37
O	4F	8	38
P	50	9	39
Q	51	CARRIAGE RET	0D
R	52	SPACE	20
S	53	)	29
T	54	=	3D

The file that contains the word we want to find—the word with the smallest ASCII value (`f_smallest`)—is shown in Figure 8.5. The file consists of 11 words; each word has a maximum of five characters and is followed by carriage return. The file can have any number of words, but the last word must be "END."

```
STORE
STOP
ADD
ADA
SUB
MTPLY
LOAD
JUMP
HLT
COMPR
END
```

FIGURE 8.5 File `f_smallest`.

Listing 8.7 shows the VHDL code for finding the word with the lowest ASCII value. The smallest value will be stored in a character-type variable, `smallest`, and the variable is initialized with the highest possible ASCIII value—in our example, "ZZZZZ." We compare the value of `smallest` with each word. If the value of the word is less than the value of `smallest`, then `smallest` assumes the value of this word; otherwise, `smallest` retains its value. We continue this comparison until the last word in the file is encountered. The code tests each word to see if it is "END." If it is, then the program stops; if not, the program continues. The statement that checks for the word "END" in Listing 8.7 is a while-loop:

```
while (count /= ('E', 'N', 'D', ' ', ' ')) loop
```

The operator `/=` is the logic NOT EQUAL. The variable `count` has to be declared as type `character`. The above loop will continue running until the variable `count` is equal to END. The statement:

```
read (temp, count);
```

reads a character word from the line `temp`. Since `count` is declared as an array of characters (`string_chr`), then each time a word is read, its ASCII value corresponding to the characters of the word (see Table 8.1) is computed and stored in the variable `count`. This is how the VHDL determines that "ADD" is less than "AND."

LISTING 8.7 VHDL Code for Finding the Smallest ASCII Value

```
--The following package needs to be attached to the main module
library IEEE;
use IEEE.STD_LOGIC_1164.all;

package array_pkg is
constant N : integer := 4;
--N+1 is the number of elements in the array.
subtype wordChr is character;
type string_chr is array (N downto 0) of wordChr;

end array_pkg;

library ieee;
use ieee.std_logic_1164.all;
use std.textio.all;
use work.array_pkg.all;

--Now start writing the code to find the smallest
entity SMALLEST_CHRCTR is
    port (START : in std_logic; z : out string_chr);

end SMALLEST_CHRCTR;

architecture BEHAVIOR_SMALLEST of SMALLEST_CHRCTR is

begin

process (START)
file infile : text;
variable fstatus : file_open_status;
variable count, smallest :
    string_chr := ('z ', 'z ', 'z ', 'z ', 'z ');

--The above statement assigns initial values (Z's) to
```

```
--count and smallest.

variable temp : line;

begin
    file_open (fstatus, infile, "f_smallest.txt", read_mode);

    while (count /= ('E', 'N', 'D', ' ', ' ')) loop
    readline (infile, temp);

    read (temp, count);
        if (count < smallest) then
            smallest := count;
        end if;
    end loop;
z <= smallest;
file_close (infile);
end process;

end BEHAVIOR_SMALLEST;
```

After execution, the output z is equal to "ADA."

EXAMPLE 8.7 Identifying a Mnemonic Code and Its Integer Equivalent from a File

In many programming applications, the user writes the source code in mnemonic. The computer, without any assemblers or compilers, understands only machine language, which consists of zeros and ones. Assemblers and compilers translate from mnemonic to machine language. In this Example, we write the code for a simple assembler. An integer code is assigned to each mnemonic code. This assignment is user-selected. The mnemonic code and its integer value are stored in the file `cods.txt` (see Figure 8.6).

Mnemonic code	User-assigned integer code
HALT	0
ADD	1
XOR	4
MULT	2
DIVID	3
NAND	6
PRITY	5
CLA	7

FIGURE 8.6 File `cods.txt`.

Listing 8.8 is the VHDL code to find the integer code, given the mnemonic code. Referring to the Listing, the statement:

```
if (temp = assmbly_code) then
```

tests whether `temp` is equal to `assmbly_code`. We can do this comparison because `temp` and `assmbly_code` have been declared as arrays of characters.

LISTING 8.8 VHDL Code for Finding the Integer Code for a Mnemonic Code

```
--The following package needs to be attached to the main module
library IEEE;
use IEEE.STD_LOGIC_1164.all;

package array_pkg is
constant N : integer := 4;
--N+1 is the number of elements in the array.
subtype wordChr is character;
type string_chr is array (N downto 0) of wordChr;

end array_pkg;

--Start writing the code to find the assigned integer value
library ieee;
use ieee.std_logic_1164.all;
use std.textio.all;
use work.array_pkg.all;

entity OPCODES is
    port (assmbly_code : in string_chr; z : out string_chr;
        z1 : out integer);

end OPCODES;

architecture BEHAVIOR of OPCODES is

begin

process (assmbly_code)
file infile : text;

variable fstatus : file_open_status;
variable temp : string_chr := (' ', ' ', ' ', ' ', ' ');
variable tem_bin : integer;
variable regstr : line;

begin
file_open (fstatus, infile, "cods.txt", read_mode);

    for i in 0 to 8 loop
```

```
        --while loop could have been used instead of for loop. See
        --Exercise 8.3

        readline (infile, regstr);

        read (regstr, temp);
            if (temp = assmbly_code) then
            z <= temp;

            read (regstr, tem_bin);
            z1 <= tem_bin;

            exit;
                else if (i > 7)then
                report ("ERROR: CODE COULD NOT BE FOUND");
                z <= ('E', 'R', 'R', 'O', 'R');

            --assign -1 to z1 if an error occurs

                z1 <= -1;
                end if;
            end if;
    end loop;

    file_close(infile);

    end process;

    end BEHAVIOR;
```

EXAMPLE 8.8 VHDL Code of an Assembler

An assembly program is a group of instructions written in mnemonic code. The instructions usually contain four fields: label, operation code (opcode), address, and comments. In this Example, the instruction will have only two fields: opcode and address. The opcode determines the type of operation, such as addition, subtraction, or data movement.

Since the opcode in an assembly program is written in mnemonics, the operation for addition can be written as ADD. The address field determines the memory address of the operand. For example, the assembly code ADD 9 means the operation is addition, and the addition operation is adding the data (operand) in memory location address 9 to the contents of a CPU register (accumulator). The result of the addition is stored in the accumulator. For the CPU to understand the assembly instruction, we have to translate the contents of the instruction into machine language code, which consists of zeros and ones. The program that translates assembly code to machine code is called the "assembler" (see Figure 8.7).

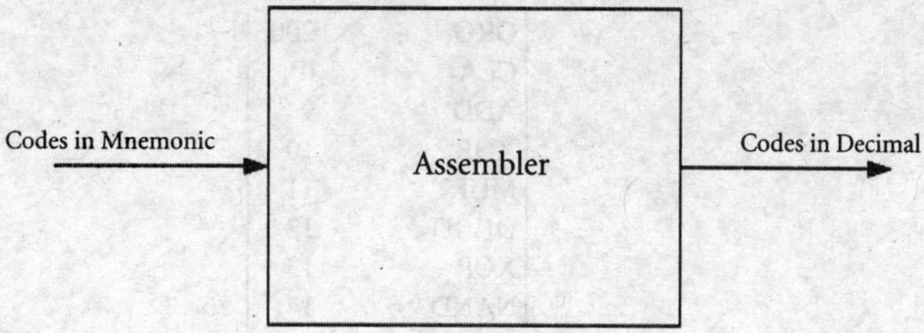

FIGURE 8.7 The input and output of an assembler.

Listing 8.9 shows the code for an assembler. The assembly program that we want to translate is written in the file `asm.txt` (see Figure 8.8). Integer opcodes are assigned to the mnemonic codes, as shown in Table 8.2. This assignment is arbitrary; we can assign any pattern of code to the mnemonic code as long as each code has a unique integer value. In this Example, the same code pattern is followed as in Figure 8.6. The mnemonic codes ORIG and END have no integer codes; they are called "pseudocodes." ORIG tells the assembler the starting memory location where the output of the assembler is stored. END tells the assembler where the last line of the assembly program is. Figure 8.9 shows the flowchart of our assembler.

TABLE 8.2 Integer Codes Assigned to Mnemonic Codes

Mnemonic Code	Assigned Integer Code
CLA	7
ADD	1
XOR	4
MULT	2
DIVID	3
NAND	6
PRITY	5
HALT	0

ORG	200
CLA	0
ADD	9
XOR	10
MULT	11
DIVID	12
XOR	13
NAND	14
PRITY	0
HALT	0
HLT	5
END	

FIGURE 8.8 File asm.txt.

The assembler first reads a line from the assembly file `asm.txt`. In Listing 8.9, the line is read by the read procedure `readline`:

```
readline (infile, regstr);
```

The infile is the file `asm.txt`. If we are reading the first line, then the contents of `regstr` would be:

```
ORIG  200
```

and `regstr` is read using the procedure `read`:

```
read (regstr, temp);
```

The above `read` stores one word (array of five characters) into `temp`. If this is the first line of `asm.txt`, then `temp` = "ORIG." As shown in Figure 8.9, the assembler tests the code to see what type it is. In the case of ORIG, we use the `if` statement as follows:

```
if (temp = ('O','R','I','G ',' ')) then

read (regstr, ctr);
```

If the code is "ORIG," then the same line is read again, which results in the value 200 stored in `ctr`. If the code of the first line is not "ORIG," an error is reported. After the first line is finished (see Figure 8.9), the subsequent lines are read, and the `case` statement used to determine the codes and the addresses. For example, the following statements:

```
when ('M','U','L','T',' ') => code := 2;
```

```
    write (regstw, code);
    write (regstw, "      ");
    write (regstw, addr);
    writeline (outfile, regstw);
```

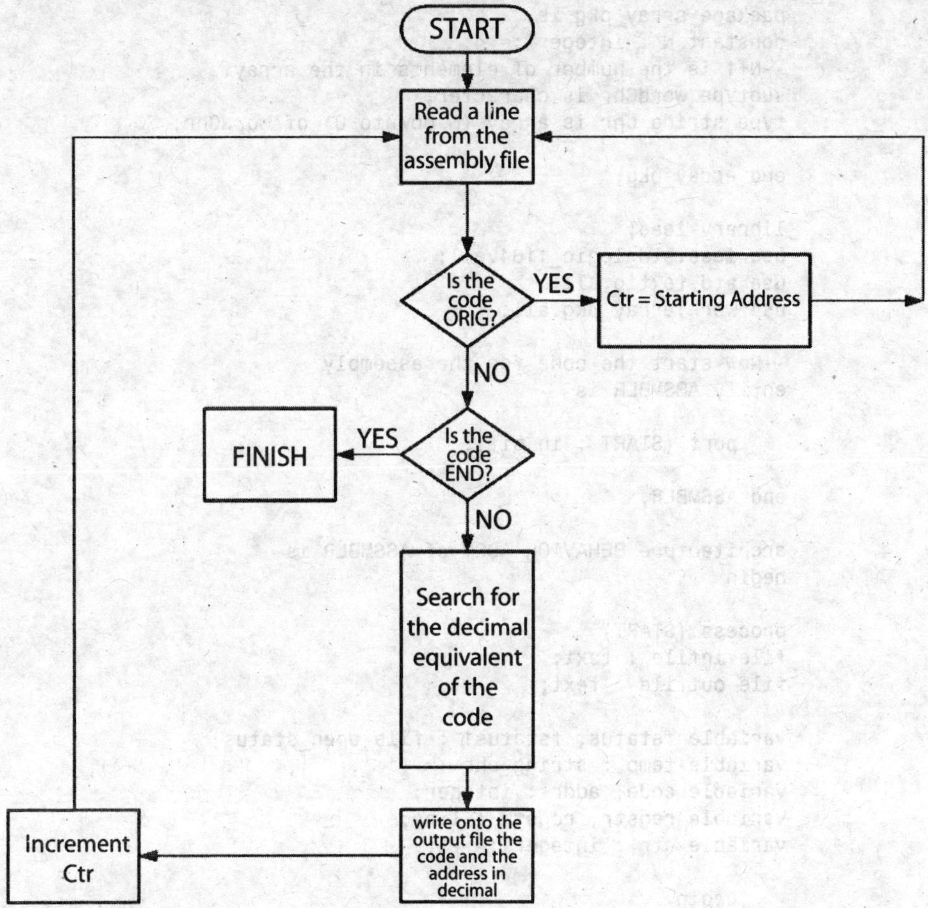

FIGURE 8.9 Flowchart of the assembler.

test the code to see if it is "MULT." If the code is "MULT," then we assign an integer for it equal to 2 (see Table 8.2), and we write the address part of the code into the outfile. In Listing 8.9, a for-loop is implemented to test all lines of the infile. Using for-loop means that we know exactly how many lines are in the infile; but while-loop could have been implemented to test all of the lines, regardless of the number of lines. This can be done by specifying an end-of-file word, such as "END," as the condition for terminating the while-loop (see Listing 8.7).

LISTING 8.9 VHDL Assembler Code

```
--The following package needs to be attached to the main module
library IEEE;
use IEEE.STD_LOGIC_1164.all;

package array_pkg is
constant N : integer := 4;
--N+1 is the number of elements in the array.
subtype wordChr is character;
type string_chr is array (N downto 0) of wordChr;

end array_pkg;

library ieee;
use ieee.std_logic_1164.all;
use std.textio.all;
use work.array_pkg.all;

--Now start the code for the assembly
entity ASSMBLR is

    port (START : in bit);

end ASSMBLR;

architecture BEHAVIOR_ASSM of ASSMBLR is
begin

process (START)
file infile : text;
file outfile : text;

variable fstatus, fstatus1 : file_open_status;
variable temp : string_chr := (' ', ' ', ' ', ' ', ' ');
variable code, addr : integer;
variable regstr, regstw : line;
variable ctr : integer := -1;

    begin
file_open (fstatus, infile, "asm.txt", read_mode);
file_open (fstatus1, outfile, "outf.txt", write_mode);

--Prepare the outfile where the results of the assembler
--are stored.

write (regstw, "Location                    Code Address");
writeline (outfile, regstw);

for i in 0 to 11 loop
--while-loop could have been used instead of for-loop.
```

```
readline (infile, regstr);

read (regstr, temp);

if (temp = ('O', 'R', 'I', 'G', ' ')) then

read (regstr, ctr);

elsif (ctr = -1)then

--If the code of the first line in the file is not ORIG
--report an error

write (regstw, " ERROR: FIRST OPCODE SHOULD BE ORIG");
writeline (outfile, regstw);
exit;

else
read (regstr, addr);
write (regstw, ctr);
write (regstw, "                              ");
ctr := ctr + 1;

case temp is

when ('H', 'A', 'L', 'T', ' ') =>
code := 0;
write (regstw, code);
write (regstw, "     ");
write (regstw, addr);
writeline (outfile, regstw);

when ('A', 'D', 'D', ' ', ' ') =>
code := 1;
write (regstw, code);
write (regstw, "     ");
write (regstw, addr);
writeline (outfile, regstw);

when ('M', 'U', 'L', 'T', ' ') =>
code := 2;
write (regstw, code);
write (regstw, "     ");
write (regstw, addr);
writeline (outfile, regstw);

when ('D', 'I', 'V', 'I', 'D') =>
code := 3;
write (regstw, code);
write (regstw, "     ");
write (regstw, addr);
writeline (outfile, regstw);
```

```
when ('X', 'O', 'R', ' ', ' ') =>
code := 4;
write (regstw, code);
write (regstw, "      ");
write (regstw, addr);
writeline (outfile, regstw);

when ('P', 'R', 'I', 'T', 'Y') =>
code := 5;
write (regstw, code);
write (regstw, " ");
write (regstw, addr);
writeline (outfile, regstw);

when ('N', 'A', 'N', 'D', ' ') =>
code := 6;
write (regstw, code);
write (regstw, "      ");
write (regstw, addr);
writeline (outfile, regstw);

when ('C', 'L', 'A', ' ', ' ') =>
code := 7;
write (regstw, code);
write (regstw, "      ");
write (regstw, addr);
writeline (outfile, regstw);

when ('E', 'N', 'D', ' ', ' ') =>
write (regstw, "END OF FILE ");
writeline (outfile, regstw);
exit;

when others =>
code := -20;
write (regstw, "ERROR ");
write (regstw, code);
writeline (outfile, regstw);
end case;

end if;

end loop;

file_close(infile);
file_close (outfile);

end process;

end BEHAVIOR_ASSM;
```

Figure 8.10 shows the outfile "outf.txt" after translating Figure 8.8. Notice that in Figure 8.8, the code "HALT" was intentionally miswritten as "HLT." Listing 8.9 spots this error and reports it in `outf.txt` (see Figure 8.10).

Location	Code	Address
200	7	0
201	1	9
202	4	10
203	2	11
204	3	12
205	4	13
206	6	14
207	5	0
208	0	0
209	ERROR	–20
210	END OF FILE	

FIGURE 8.10 Contents of file `outf.txt`.

Figure 8.11 shows the rewritten assembly program (Figure 8.8) and intentionally omits "ORIG" from the first line of code. According to Listing 8.9, this is an error.

CLA	0
ADD	9
XOR	10
MULT	11
DIVID	12
XOR	13
NAND	14
PRITY	0
HALT	0
HLT	5
END	

FIGURE 8.11 Variation of the infile `asm.txt`. ORIG is omitted.

Figure 8.12 shows the contents of the outfile according to the infile of Figure 8.11.

Location	Code Address
ERROR: FIRST OPCODE SHOULD BE ORIG	

FIGURE 8.12 Outfile `outf.text` for translating Figure 8.11.

8.2.2 Examples of Verilog File Processing

Verilog file processing is not as extensive as that of VHDL. As we have seen in Section 8.1.2, Verilog file processing is based on several built-in tasks, such as `$fopen`, `$fdisplay`, `$fmonitor`, and `$fclose`. All of these tasks are written inside `initial`. The following Example discusses file processing in Verilog.

EXAMPLE 8.9 Manipulating and Displaying Data in a Verilog File

In this Example, we consider a system with one 2-bit input, "a," and one 3-bit output, "b." Output b is related to input a as shown in Equation 8.1:

$$b = 2a \tag{8.1}$$

We want to record the value of the outputs as the inputs from a file named `file4.txt` change. This file is located in the same path as the Verilog module that accesses it. Listing 8.10 shows the Verilog code; we open the file using the task `$fopen` as follows:

```
ch1 = $fopen("file4.txt");
```

where `file4.txt` is the name of the file, and `ch1` is the indicator of the channel that keeps track of the opened file. We want to display the output b, so we write headings to the file. To write into the file, the task `$fdisplay` is used. For example, the following statement leaves two spaces, one blank line, then one tab, and writes the heading "This is file4.txt," and then leaves a blank line.

```
$fdisplay (ch1, " \n\tThis is file4.txt\n");
```

To monitor any signals, the task `$fmonitor` is used. This task monitors the value of the signal and prints this value onto the file. For example, the statement:

```
$fmonitor (ch1, " %d\t\t%d%b\n", a, b,
    b);
```

monitors the value of signals `a`, and `b`. These values are printed in `file4.txt` as follows: leave two spaces, print "a" in decimal, insert two tabs, print the value of "b" in decimal, leave 30 spaces, print the same value of "b" in binary.

LISTING 8.10 Verilog Code for Storing b = 2a in `file4.txt`

```
module file_test (a, b);
input [1:0] a;
output [2:0] b;
reg [2:0] b;
```

```
integer ch1;
always @ (a)
    begin

        b = 2 * a;
    end

initial
    begin
        ch1 = $fopen("file4.txt");
        $fdisplay (ch1, "\n\t\t\t    This is file4.txt \n");
        $fdisplay (ch1, " Input a in Decimal\t\tOutput b in
            Decimal\t\tOutput b in Binary\n ");
    /*The above statement when entered in the Verilog module
     should be entered in one line without carriage return */
        $fmonitor (ch1,"\t%d\t\t\t%d\t\t\t%b \n", a, b, b);
    end

endmodule
```

Figure 8.13 shows `file4.txt` after the code above executes.

This is `file4.txt`

Input a in Decimal	Output b in Decimal	Output b in Binary
0	0	000
1	2	010
2	4	100
3	6	110

FIGURE 8.13 `File4.txt` of Listing 8.10.

8.3 VHDL RECORD TYPE

Record type is a collection of elements, the elements of which can be of the same type or of different types. An example of `record` is shown in Listing 8.11. The `record` in Listing 8.11 includes elements of type `integer`, `weekdays`, and `weather`.

LISTING 8.11 Example of Record Type

```
Type weather is (rain, sunny, snow, cloudy);
Type weekdays is (Monday, Tuesday, Wednesday,
    Thursday, Friday, Saturday, Sunday);
Type forecast is
Record
```

```
Tempr : integer range -100 to 100;
Day : weekdays;
Cond : weather;
end record;
```

Another example of implementing `record` is shown in Listing 8.12. The user provides a certain day and a desired unit of temperature (Centigrade or Fahrenheit). The VHDL program outputs the current temperature and the forecast condition (e.g., rainy, cloudy, snowy, or sunny). Let's examine the following code from Listing 8.12:

```
process (Day_in)
variable temp : forecast;

begin

case Day_in is

when Monday =>
temp.cond := sunny;
if (unit_in = "CEN") then
temp.tempr := 35.6;
else
temp.tempr := 1.2 * 35.6 + 32.0;
end if;
```

The signal `Day_in` is declared as type `weekdays`; so possible values for this signal are `Monday`, `Tuesday`, `Wednesday`, `Thursday`, `Friday`, `Saturday`, or `Sunday`. The variable `temp` is declared as type `forecast`. This type is a `record`, so possible types for this variable are `real`, `string`, `weekdays`, or `cast`. To select one type out of these four types we write, for example, `temp.cond`; now `temp` is of type `cast` and can assume one of the values of this type (i.e., `rain`, `sunny`, `snow`, or `cloudy`).

LISTING 8.12 VHDL Code for an Example of Record

```
The following is the code of the package weather_fcst

package weather_fcst is
Type cast is (rain, sunny, snow, cloudy);
Type weekdays is (Monday, Tuesday, Wednesday,
    Thursday, Friday, Saturday, Sunday);
Type forecast is
Record
Tempr : real range -100.0 to 100.0;
unit : string (1 to 3);
Day : weekdays;
Cond : cast;
```

```
end record;
end package weather_fcst;

--Now we write the program
library ieee;
use ieee.std_logic_1164.all;
use std.textio.all;
use work.weather_fcst.all;

entity WEATHER_FRCST is
    port (Day_in : in weekdays; unit_in : in string (1 to 3);
        out_temperature : out real;
        out_unit : out string (1 to 3);
        out_day : out weekdays; out_cond : out cast);
-- Type string is a predefined

end WEATHER_FRCST;

--Now we write the code

architecture behavoir_record of WEATHER_FRCST is
begin
process (Day_in, unit_in)
variable temp : forecast ;

begin

case Day_in is

when Monday =>
temp.cond := sunny;
if (unit_in = "CEN") then
temp.tempr := 35.6;
elsif (unit_in = "FEH") then
temp.tempr := 1.2 * 35.6 + 32.0;
else
report ("invalid units");
end if;

when Tuesday =>
temp.cond := rain;

if (unit_in = "CEN") then
temp.tempr := 30.2;
elsif (unit_in = "FEH") then
temp.tempr := 1.2 * 30.2 + 32.0;
else
report ("invalid units");
end if;

when Wednesday =>
temp.cond := sunny;
```

```
if (unit_in = "CEN") then
temp.tempr := 37.2;
elsif (unit_in = "FEH") then
temp.tempr := 1.2 * 37.2 + 32.0;
else
report ("invalid units");
end if;

when Thursday =>
temp.cond := cloudy;
if (unit_in = "CEN") then
temp.tempr := 30.2;
elsif (unit_in = "FEH") then
temp.tempr := 1.2 * 30.2 + 32.0;
else
report ("invalid units");
end if;

when Friday =>
temp.cond := cloudy;
if (unit_in = "FEH") then
temp.tempr := 33.9;
elsif      (unit_in = "FEH") then

temp.tempr := 1.2 * 33.9 + 32.0;
else
report ("invalid units");
end if;

when Saturday =>
temp.cond := rain;
if (unit_in = "CEN") then
temp.tempr := 25.1;
elsif (unit_in = "FEH") then
temp.tempr := 1.2 * 25.1 + 32.0;
else
report ("invalid units");
end if;

when Sunday =>
temp.cond := rain;
if (unit_in = "FEH") then
temp.tempr := 27.1;
elsif (unit_in = "FEH") then
temp.tempr := 1.2 * 27.1 + 32.0;
else
report ("invalid units");
end if;

when others =>
temp.tempr := 99.99;
report ("ERROR-NOT VALID DAY");
```

```
end case;

out_temperature <= temp.tempr;
out_unit <= unit_in;
out_day <= Day_in;
out_cond <= temp.cond;
end process;
end behavoir_record;
```

The simulation output is shown in Figure 8.14.

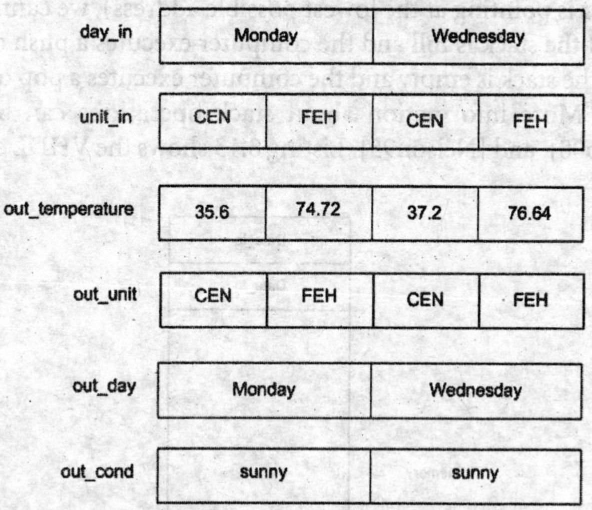

FIGURE 8.14 Simulation output of Listing 8.12.

EXAMPLE 8.10 Memory Stack Using Assert and Report Statements

Chapter 1, "Introduction," briefly discussed the statement `assert`. The format of this statement is:

```
assert (Boolean condition)
report " optional message display"
severity failure;
```

The severity level can be `note`, `warning`, `error`, or `failure`. The severity level `failure` is the highest priority; it causes the simulation to halt. This Example will implement the `assert` statement to design a memory stack.

The memory stack is part of the main memory. A special register called the "stack pointer" operates as an address pointer for the stack. The contents of the stack pointer are pointed at the top of the stack. The top of the stack does not necessary coincide with the physical top of the stack. The lowest address the stack pointer can assume is referred to as the bottom of the stack (see Figure 8.15). The stack has two major operations: push and pop. Push stores memory on top of the stack, and the stack pointer is incremented to point to the new top. Pop retrieves memory from the top of the stack, and the stack pointer is decremented to point at the new top of the stack.

Usually, the stack has two 1-bit flags to indicate whether the stack is full or empty. If the stack is full (i.e., the stack pointer is pointing at the highest possible address), we cannot execute a push operation. If the stack is empty (i.e., the stack pointer is pointing at the lowest possible address), we cannot execute a pop operation. If the stack is full and the computer executes a push operation, the full flag is set. If the stack is empty and the computer executes a pop operation, the empty flag is set. More information about stack operations can be found in [Hayes98], [Mano00], and [Nelson95]. Listing 8.13 shows the VHDL code for stack operation.

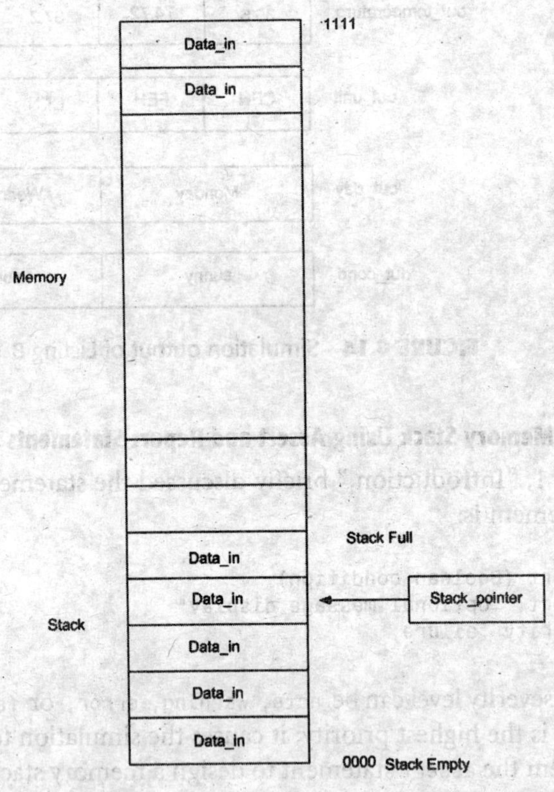

FIGURE 8.15 A block diagram of memory and the memory stack.

LISTING 8.13 VHDL Code for Stack Operation

```
library IEEE;
use IEEE.STD_LOGIC_1164.all;

library IEEE;
use IEEE.STD_LOGIC_1164.all;

package stack_pkg is
constant N : integer := 15;
constant M : integer := 3;
--N+1 is the number of elements in the array.
subtype Memoryword is std_logic_vector (M downto 0);
type Memory is array (N downto 0) of Memoryword;
--The above array represents a 16x4 bits memory

type stack is (push, pop, none);
--The above statement defines three members (push, pop, and none)
--of the user-defined type stack.

end stack_pkg;

library IEEE;
use IEEE.STD_LOGIC_1164.ALL;
use ieee.numeric_std.all;
use work.stack_pkg.all;

entity stck_asrt is
generic (N : integer := 15; M : integer := 3);
    Port (action : in stack; Data_in : in std_logic_vector
        (M downto 0); clk : in std_logic);
end stck_asrt;

architecture Behavioral of stck_asrt is

begin
stk : process (action, data_in, clk)
variable stack_pointer : integer := 0;
variable Mem_comp : Memory;
begin
if (rising_edge (clk)) then

case action is
when push =>
Mem_comp (stack_pointer) := data_in;
stack_pointer := stack_pointer + 1;
--if the operation is push, the stack pointer is incremented
--as shown above

assert (stack_pointer < 5)
report " stack is full-program halts"
severity Failure;
```

```
--The above three statements state that if the stack pointer is
--not less than 5, then the program halts and the message
--" stack is full-program halts" is displayed.

when pop =>
stack_pointer := stack_pointer - 1;
--If pop, the stack pointer is decremented

when others => null;
end case;

end if;
end process;

end Behavioral;
```

Figure 8.16 shows the simulation waveform for Listing 8.13.

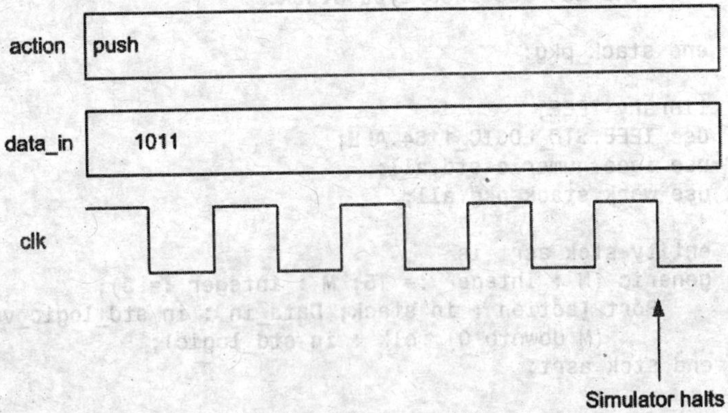

FIGURE 8.16 Simulation waveform of the stack in Listing 8.13.

Case Study 8.1 Simulation of Artificial Neural Networks

Artificial Neural Networks (ANNs) are simulated networks that mimic a simple biological nervous system. To understand how ANNs operate, let us review the operation of an extremely simple nervous system. The main cells in the nervous system are the neurons. A neuron is composed of three major parts: a soma (or body), an axon, and a dendrite (see Figure 8.17). The neuron receives signals from other neurons through its dendrites; so dendrites are the inputs.

The neuron sends signals to other neurons through its axons; so axons are the outputs of the neuron. The connection between the axons of one neuron to the dendrites or soma of another neuron is called a "synapse." The signals that a neuron sends to its neighbors can activate or excite the receiving neurons, or can deactivate or inhibit them. The signal that the neuron sends can be viewed as a spike. When the neuron sends this signal; we say the neuron is firing. The neuron sends this signal if it receives enough excitation signals from other neurons. A threshold electric level determines whether or not the excitation signals are high enough for firing. The neuron fires only when the weighted sum of these excitation signals is higher than the threshold. Each neuron asserts different weights on its neighbors.

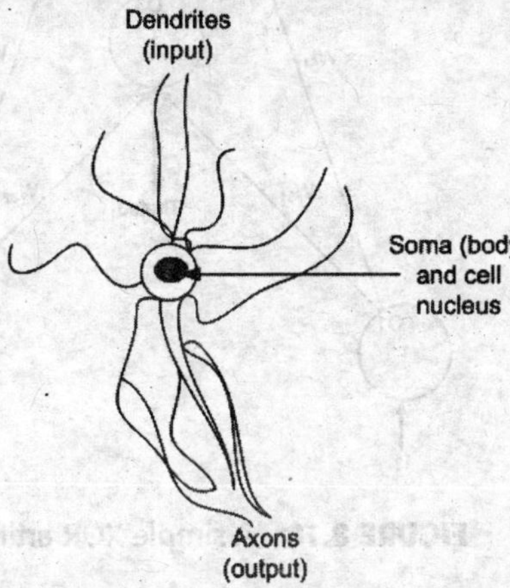

FIGURE 8.17 A biological neuron.

In the artificial neural network, a node simulates the neuron. Each node has an input and an output, and is connected to a group of other nodes. The assertion of each node on other nodes is measured by the weight of the connection. The networks are implemented in many applications, such as patter recognition and complex function generation. In this Case Study, we implement the network to generate a simple XOR function. Figure 8.18 shows a simple artificial neural network. The network consists of three layers: input, hidden, and output.

The input layer consists of two nodes, node1 and node2. The hidden layer consists of one node, node3; and the output layer consists of one node, node4. W_{ij} represents the weight between node j and node i. We want the network shown in Figure 8.18 to behave as an XOR gate. This means that the outputs and the inputs of our network should satisfy Table 8.3.

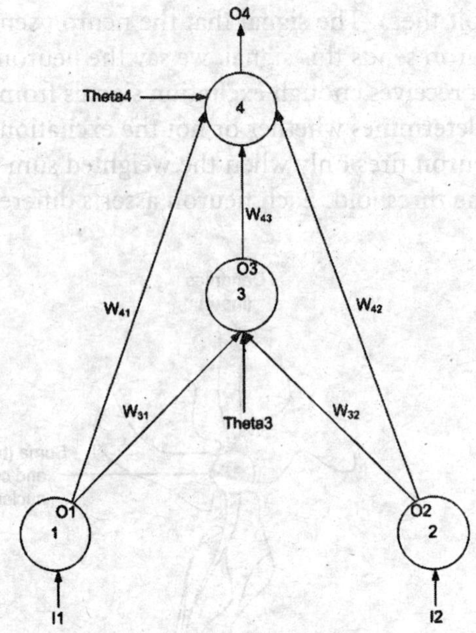

FIGURE 8.18 A simple XOR artificial neural network.

TABLE 8.3 Values of the Inputs and the Desired Outputs for an XOR Artificial Neural Network

I_1	I_2	Desired Output (O_4)
0	0	0
1	0	1
0	1	1
1	1	0

By adjusting the weights, we can force the network to behave as an XOR gate. Weight adjustment is called "training" the network. Network training is done in the following steps:

Step 1: Initialize the weights and assign random small values to the weights.

Step 2: Select an input with the desired output from Table 8.3.

Step 3: Calculate the output of each node, including the output node. For the input layer (nodes 1 and 2), the output is equal to the input O1 = I1, O2 = I2. For other nodes, the output is calculated as:

$$Oi = f\,(\text{weighted sum}) \tag{8.2}$$

where the weighted sum is the sum of each output of all nodes connected to the node i, multiplied by the weight. For example, for node 3, the weighted sum is:

$$\text{Weighted sum of node 3} = O_1W_{31} + O_2W_{32} + \text{Theta3} \times 1$$

Theta is called the "bias" or the "offset." The weight of all biases theta is equal to 1. The function f (see Equation 8.2) is called the "firing" function. In our example, we assume that f is a straight line, with saturation values in both positive and negative directions (see Figure 8.19). Many other firing functions are implemented in training of artificial neural networks. Some examples of these functions are sigmoid, linear, and relay (zero level or saturation level). More details on artificial neural networks can be found in [Hagan96] and [Haykin99].

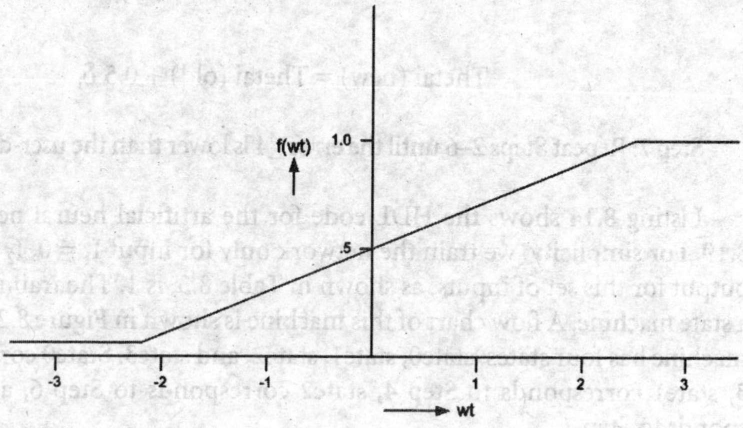

FIGURE 8.19 The firing function.

Step 4: The outputs of the network (node 4) calculated in Step 2 most likely are not equal to the desired output (see Table 8.3). The error resulted from the selection of weights in Step 1, which are calculated for the output node as:

$$\text{Error of node 4} = \delta_4 = (d - O_4)\, O_4\, (1 - O_4) \tag{8.3}$$

Since node 3 is not an output node, the error resulted from calculation of its output, which is different than the calculated output of node δ_4; see [Hagan96] and [Haykin99]. The node 3 error is calculated as:

$$\delta_3 = O_3\,(1 - O_3)\,(\delta_4\,W_{43}) \tag{8.4}$$

The term ($\delta 4\ W_{43}$) presents an error in all nodes connected to node 3 that are in a higher layer, adjusted by the weight of the connection. In our network, only one node (node 4) is connected to node 3 in the higher layer.

Step 5: Select another input and repeat Steps 3–4. Average the four δ4 errors and the four δ3 obtained from the four input sets. You can take the root mean square of the errors instead of the simple average.

Step 6: Now, start updating the weights with the new errors calculated in Step 5:

$$W_{4i}\,(\text{new}) = W_{4i}\,(\text{old}) + 0.5\,\delta_4 O_{i}\_i = 1, 3 \tag{8.5}$$

$$W_{3i}\,(\text{new}) = W_{2i}\,(\text{old}) + 0.5\,\delta_3 O_i\,\_i = 1, 2 \tag{8.6}$$

$$\text{Thetai (new)} = \text{Thetai (old)} + 0.5\,\delta_i \tag{8.7}$$

Step 7: Repeat Steps 2–6 until the error_4 is lower than the user-defined threshold.

Listing 8.14 shows the HDL code for the artificial neural network of Figure 8.19. For simplicity, we train the network only for input $I_1 = 0$, $I_2 = 1$. The desired output for this set of inputs, as shown in Table 8.3, is 1. The training is done using a state machine. A flow chart of this machine is shown in Figure 8.20. As shown, the machine has four states: state0, statel, state2, and state3. State0 corresponds to Step 3, statel corresponds to Step 4, state2 corresponds to Step 6, and state3 corresponds to Step 7.

LISTING 8.14 HDL Description of a Simple Artificial Neural Network

```
library IEEE;
use IEEE.STD_LOGIC_1164.all;
--Write a package to include user-selected type
package types is
type state_machine is (state0, state1, state2, state3);
end;

--Write the code for the state machine
library IEEE;
use IEEE.STD_LOGIC_1164.ALL;
use IEEE.STD_LOGIC_ARITH.ALL;
use ieee.numeric_std.all;
use work.types.all;
```

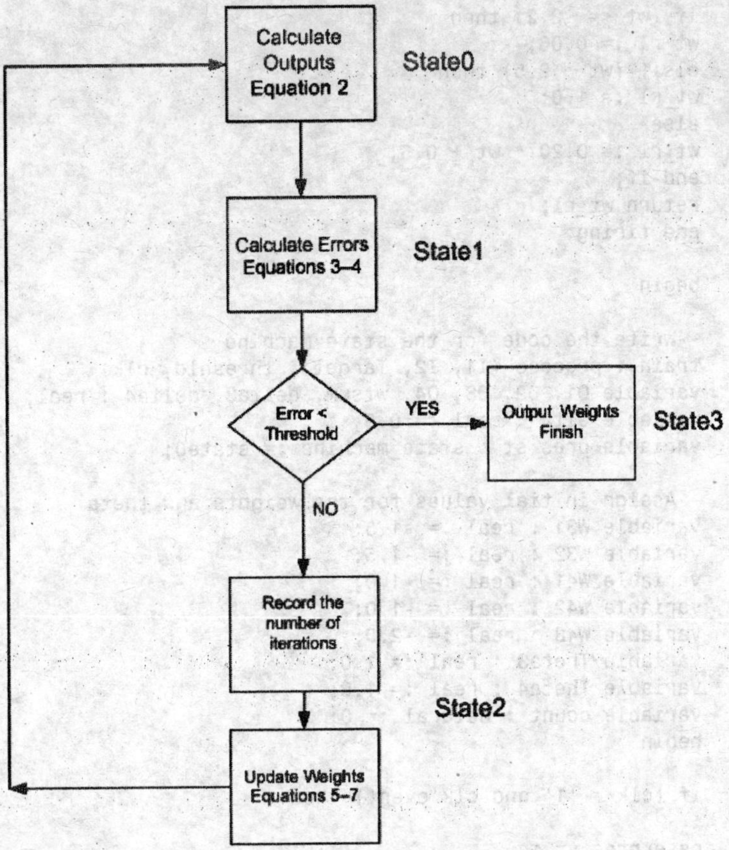

FIGURE 8.20 Flow chart of the state machine.

```
entity neural is

    port (clk : in std_logic; I1, I2, Target4, threshld : in real;
        W31_O, W32_O, W41_O, W42_O, W43_O, Theta3_O,
        Theta4_O : out real;
        output4 : out real; count_O : out natural);
--The weights could have been entered as an array
end neural;

architecture Behavioral of neural is
-- write the firing function
function firing (wt : in real) return real is
variable wt_rl : real;

begin
--The firing function here is a straight line with
--saturation levels at both the positive and negative ends
```

```
if (wt <= -2.2) then
wt_rl := 0.06;
elsif (wt > 2.5) then
wt_rl := 1.0;
else
wt_rl := 0.20 * wt + 0.5;
end if;
return wt_rl;
end firing;

begin

--Write the code for the state machine
train : process (I1, I2, Target4, threshld, clk)
variable O1, O2, O3, O4, wtsum, delta3, delta4 : real;
variable eita : real := 0.5;
variable pres_st : state_machine := state0;

--Assign initial values for the weights and theta
variable W31 : real := -1.5;
variable W32 : real := -1.5;
variable W41 : real := -1.0;
variable W42 : real := -1.0;
variable W43 : real := -2.0;
variable Theta3 : real := 1.0;
variable Theta4 : real := 1.0;
variable count : natural := 0;
begin

if (clk = '1' and clk'event) then

case pres_st is
    when state0 =>

--Calculate outputs from Equation 2
    O1 := I1;
    O2 := I2;

--Calculate the weighted sum
    wtsum := W31 * O1 + W32*O2 + Theta3;
--Apply the firing function
    O3 := firing (wtsum);

    wtsum := W41 * O1 + W42 * O2 + W43 * O3 + Theta4;

    O4 := firing (wtsum);

    pres_st := state1;

when state1 =>

--Calculate errors
```

```
            delta4 := (Target4 - O4)* O4 * (1.0 - O4);

            delta3 := O3 * (1.0 - O3) * (delta4 * W43);

            if (delta4 < threshld) then
        --The threshold is a user-selected value
            pres_st := state3;
            else
            pres_st := state2;
        --Record the number of iteration
            count := count + 1;
            count_O <= count;
            end if;

        when state2 =>
        --Update weights
            W41 := W41 + eita * delta4 * O1;
            W42 := W42 + eita * delta4 * O2;
            W43 := W43 + eita * delta4 * O3;
            Theta4 := Theta4 + eita * O4;

            W31 := W31 + eita * delta3 * O1;
            W32 := W32 + eita * delta3 * O2;
            Theta3 := Theta3 + eita * O3;

            pres_st := state0;

        when state3 =>
        --Finish; report results
            W41_O <= W41;
            W42_O <= W42;
            W43_O <= W43;
            W32_O <= W32;
            W31_O <= W31;
            Theta3_O <= Theta3;
            Theta4_O <= Theta4;
            output4 <= O4;
        end case;
        end if;
        end process train;

        end Behavioral;
        References
```

8.4 SUMMARY

In this chapter, some advanced descriptions were covered, including file processing in both VHDL and Verilog. We have seen that files have to be opened before they can be accessed. VHDL has an extensive variety of file-processing procedures, such as `file_open` to open files, `readline` to read a line from the file, `writeline` to write a line into the file, and `file_close` to close the file. Verilog has file-processing functions such as `$fopen` to open a file, `$fdisplay` to write data into the file, and `$fmonitor` to monitor an object in the file. The VHDL record type was covered, and we learned that `record` is a collection of types. Finally, artificial neural networks were discussed, as well as the complete VHDL code for their training.

8.5 EXERCISES

8.1 Write the following data in the VHDL text file, "exercise_ch8." In the file, keep the format and type of the data as it is shown below:

```
THIS IS THE FILE OF EXERCISE OF CHAPTER 8
Training data is 5 3.1 -2
Nodes   A, B, C, D
Test data 23 12    -5
END
```

8.2 Write the VHDL code to store the following words in a file called "greatest.txt." The words in the file should appear as follows:

```
ADD
STORE
MEMORY
ZEROS
SUB
STOP
```

Write the code (in the same module or new one) to find the word in the above file that has the greatest ASCII value; also, find its order (e.g., the order of the word "STORE" is 1).

8.3 Rewrite Listing 8.9 using a while-loop instead of a for-loop. Verify your code by simulation.

8.4 Modify the assembler code of Listing 8.9 to accept labels instead of explicit addresses. Verify your assembler with the program shown below. Notice that for the statement ADD Data1, Data1 is an address, and the value of this address is 208. Your code should find this address; do not manually substitute 208 for the address.

Label	Code	Address
	ORG	200
	CLA	0
	ADD	Data1
	XOR	Data2
	MULT	Data3
	XOR	Data2
	NAND	Data4
	PRITY	0
	HALT	0
Data1:	7	
Data2:	5	
Data3:	4	
Data4:	2	
	END	

8.5 Build a package with procedures to find the integer code given the mnemonic code.

8.6 Use Verilog file processing to compute and display the values of Y when X changes incrementally from 0 to 9. The relationship between X and Y is:

$$Y = X2 - 2X + 1$$

8.7 In Listing 8.12, we want to output our results to a file. Adjust your code, especially the user-defined types, to conform with the acceptable types that a VHDL file can handle. Rewrite the program and output your results to a text file named "Wthr_forcst." Each entry of the file should be preceded by a short explanation, such as "The Day is" or "The Temperature is."

8.8 For Listing 8.12, the following segment of code has been modified as shown below. The simulation output of the code after modification is not the same as in Figure 8.14. Can you spot the modification and explain why we are not getting the same output as in Listing 8.12?

LISTING 8.12 Modified

```
architecture behavoir_record of WEATHER_FRCST is
begin
process (Day_in)
variable temp : forecast;

begin

case Day_in is

when Monday =>
temp.cond := sunny;
if (unit_in = "CEN") then
temp.tempr := 35.6;
elsif       (unit_in = "FEH") then
temp.tempr := 1.2 * 35.6 + 32.0;
else
report ("invalid units");
end if;
```

8.9 In Listing 8.13, we wrote the code for a stack operation. An assertion was made on the condition when the stack is full. Use the `assert` statement with `report` to ensure that the stack cannot pop if it is empty. Simulate your code and verify.

8.10 Simulate the code shown in Listing 8.14 using a threshold of 10^{-8}. What are the final values of the weights, and how many cycles does it take the program to reach these final values?

8.11 In Case Study 8.1, a network was trained for the inputs $I_1 = 0, I_2 = 1$. Here, we want to train the network for all possible inputs. This can be done in the following steps:

Step 1. Initialize the weights as was done in the Case Study.

Step 2. Calculate the actual outputs for each input using the same set of weights.

Step 3. Calculate the errors separately for each of the four actual outputs. Each input set has its desired output. For example, the input set $I_1 = 1, I_2 = 1$ has a desired output of 0.

Step 4. Take the average of the four errors, and consider this average as the ERROR.

Step 5. Update the weights using the ERROR as was done in the Case Study.

Step 6 Repeat Steps 2-5 until the ERROR is lower than the threshold.

8.6 REFERENCES

[Hagan96] Hagan, M. T., H. B. Demuth, and M. Beale, *Neural Network Design*. ITP, Boston, 1996.

[Hayes98] Hayes, J. P., *Computer Architecture and Organization*, 3d ed. McGraw Hill, 1998.

[Haykin99] Haykin, S., *Neural Networks*, 2d ed. Prentice Hall, 1999.

[Mano00] Mano, M. M. and C. R. Kime, *Logic and Computer Design Fundamentals*. Prentice Hall, 2000.

[Nelson95] Nelson V. P., H. T. Nagle, B. D. Carroll, and J. D. Irwin, *Digital Logic Circuit Analysis & Design*. Prentice Hall, 1995.

9 Mixed-Language Descriptions

In This Chapter

- Understand the concept of mixed-language description.
- Learn the advantages of mixing between VHDL and Verilog modules.
- Learn how to invoke a Verilog module from a VHDL module.
- Learn how to invoke a VHDL module from a Verilog module.
- Learn the current limitations of mixed-language descriptions.

9.1 HIGHLIGHTS OF MIXED-LANGUAGE DESCRIPTION

Facts

- To write HDL code in mixed-language, the simulator used with the HDL package should be able to handle a mixed-language environment.
- In the mixed-language environment, both VHDL and Verilog module files are made visible to the simulator.
- In the mixed-language environment, both VHDL and Verilog Libraries are made visible to the simulator.
- At the present time, the mixed-language environment has many limitations; but the development of simulators that can handle mixed-language environments with minimal constraints is underway. One of these major constraints is that a VHDL module can only invoke the entire Verilog module; and a Verilog module can only invoke a VHDL entity. For example, we cannot invoke a VHDL procedure from a Verilog module.
- Mixed-language description can combine the advantages of both VHDL and Verilog in one module. For example, VHDL has more-extensive file operations than Verilog, including `write` and `read`. By writing mixed-language, we can use the VHDL file operations in a Verilog module.

9.2 HOW TO INVOKE ONE LANGUAGE FROM THE OTHER

As mentioned, when writing VHDL code, you can invoke (import) a Verilog module; if you are writing Verilog code, you can invoke (import) a VHDL entity. The process is similar in concept to invoking procedures, functions, tasks, and packages. For example, by instantiating a VHDL package in a Verilog module, the contents of this package are made visible to the module (see Section 9.2.1). Similarly, by invoking a Verilog module in a VHDL module, all information in the Verilog module is made visible to the VHDL module (see Section 9.2.2).

9.2.1 How to Invoke a VHDL Entity from a Verilog Module

In Verilog, `module` instantiates a module with the same name as the VHDL entity; the parameters of the module should match the type and port directions of the entity. VHDL ports that can be mapped to Verilog modules are: in, out, and inout; buffer is not allowed. Only the entire VHDL entity can be made visible to the Verilog module. Listing 9.1 shows an example of how to invoke a VHDL entity from a Verilog module.

LISTING 9.1 Invoking a VHDL Entity from a Verilog Module

```
//This is the Verilog module
module mixed (a, b, c, d);
input a, b;
output c, d;
...........
VHD_enty V1 (a, b, c, d);
/*The above module VHD_enty is the VHDL entity to be
invoked in this module*/
...........
endmodule

--This is the VHDL entity
library IEEE;
use IEEE.STD_LOGIC_1164.ALL;

entity VHD_enty is
    port (x, y : in std_logic; O1, O2 : out std_logic);
end VHD_enty;

architecture VHD_enty of VHD_enty is
begin
...........

end VHD_enty;
```

Referring to Listing 9.1, we wrote the following statement in the Verilog module:

```
VHD_enty V1 (a,b,c,d)
```

The simulator looks first in the Verilog module to see if there are any Verilog modules by the name of `VHD_enty`; If it could not find one, the simulator looks in the VHDL entities. When the simulator finds an entity with the name `VHD_enty`, it binds this entity to the Verilog module. In Listing 9.1, input `a` is passed to input port `x`; input `b` is passed to input `y`. The VHDL entity calculates the outputs `O1` and `O2`; these two outputs are passed to the Verilog outputs `c` and `d`, respectively. As you can see, invoking a VHDL module is very similar to invoking a function or a task.

9.2.2 How To Invoke a Verilog Module from a VHDL Module

In the VHDL module, we declare a component with the same name as the Verilog module we want to invoke (see Chapter 4, "Structural Descriptions"); the name and port modes of the component should be identical to the name and input/output modes of the Verilog module. Remember that Verilog is case sensitive, so be sure to match the case. Listing 9.2 shows an example of how to invoke a Verilog module from a VHDL module.

LISTING 9.2 Invoking a Verilog Module from a VHDL Module

```
--This is the VHDL Project

library IEEE;
use IEEE.STD_LOGIC_1164.ALL;

entity Ver_VHD is
      port (a, b : in std_logic; c : out std_logic);
end Ver_VHD;

architecture Ver_VHD of Ver_VHD is
component V_modl
    port (x, y : in std_logic; z : out std_logic);

-- The name of the Component V_modl should be
-- identical to the name of the
-- Verilog module; also, the ports should be
-- identical in name and mode
-- with the inputs and outputs of the Verilog module

end component;

.......
end Ver_VHD;

//This is the Verilog module
module V_modl (x, y, z);

    input x, y;
        output z;
```

```
endmodule
```

Referring to Listing 9.2, the component statement in the VHDL module:

```
component V_modl
    port (x, y : in std_logic; z : out std_logic);
end component;
```

declares a component by the name of `V_modl` with two input ports, `x` and `y`, and an output port `z`. The Verilog module `V_modl` has the same name (including the case) as the component and identical inputs and outputs. Accordingly, the Verilog module `V_modl` is bound to the VHDL component `V_modl`. If the Verilog module describes, for example, a two-input XOR gate, then in the VHDL module, component `V_modl` is a two-input XOR gate.

In the following, we cover complete examples of mixed-language descriptions.

9.3 MIXED-LANGUAGE DESCRIPTION EXAMPLES

This section presents mixed-language examples. Section 9.3.1 covers examples of invoking VHDL entities from Verilog modules, and Section 9.3.2 covers examples of invoking Verilog modules from VHDL modules.

9.3.1 Invoking a VHDL Entity from a Verilog Module

As previously mentioned, a VHDL entity is invoked in a Verilog module by instantiating the Verilog module with a name that is identical to the entity's name. No other construct should have the same name as the entity. In the following, we discuss complete examples.

EXAMPLE 9.1 Mixed-Language Description of a Full Adder

Here we construct a full adder from two half adders, as was done in Chapter 4. The logic diagram shown in Figure 4.6 is represented in Figure 9.1 for convenience. The code of the half adder is written in VHDL. We write a Verilog module to describe a full adder using the VHDL code of the half adder. Listing 9.3 shows mixed-language code for the full adder.

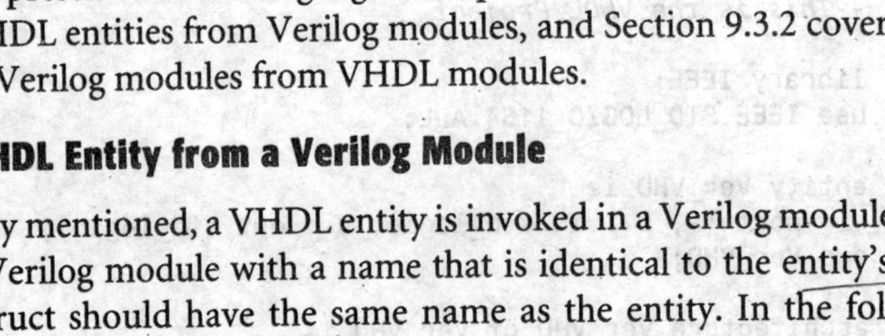

FIGURE 9.1 Full adder as two half adders.

LISTING 9.3 Mixed-Language Description of a Full Adder

```
--This is the Verilog module
module Full_Adder1 (x, y, cin, sum, carry);
    input x, y, cin;
    output sum, carry;
    wire c0, c1, s0;

HA H1 (y, cin, s0, c0);
HA H2 (x, s0, sum, c1);

// Description of HA is written in VHDL in the entity HA

    or (carry, c0, c1);
endmodule

library IEEE;
use ieee.std_logic_1164.all;
entity HA is

--For correct binding between this VHDL code and the above Verilog
--code, the entity has to be named HA

    port (a, b : in std_logic; s, c : out std_logic);
end HA;
architecture HA_Dtflw of HA is
begin
    s <= a xor b;
    c <= a and b;
end HA_Dtflw;
```

Referring to Listing 9.3, the Verilog statement:

```
HA H1 (y, cin, s0, c0);
```

invokes a module by the name of `HA`. Since there is no Verilog module by this name, the simulator looks at the VHDL modules attached to the Verilog modules. The simulator finds an entity by the name of `HA`; accordingly, this entity and its bound architecture(s) are made visible to the Verilog module. The architecture here is a data-flow description of a half adder. The inputs `y` and `cin` are passed to the input ports of `HA`, `a` and `b`. The VHDL entity calculates the outputs `s` and `c` as:

```
s <= a xor b; c <= a and b;
```

The outputs of the entity `s` and `c` are passed to the outputs of the module `HA`, `s0` and `c0`.

EXAMPLE 9.2 Mixed-Language Description of a 9-Bit Adder

In this example, we describe a 9-bit adder consisting of three adder slices; each adder slice is a 3-bit carry–look ahead adder. More details about adders can be found in [Hayes98], [Mano00], and [Nelson95]. Figure 9.2 shows a block diagram of the adder.

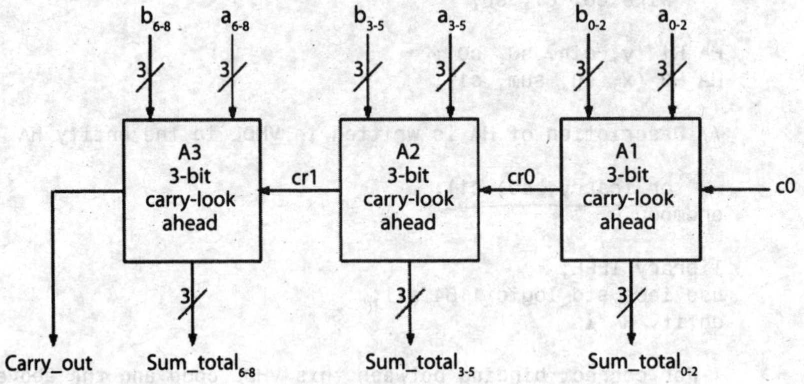

FIGURE 9.2 Block diagram of a 9-bit adder.

Listing 9.4 shows the mixed-language description of the 9-bit adder. The 3-bit carry–look ahead is described by a VHDL module, and the Verilog module invokes the VHDL entity three times. The VHDL entity `adders_RL` is a data-flow description of a 3-bit lookahead adder (see Chapter 2, "Data-Flow Description"). The delay propagation time in Listing 9.2 is taken as 0. In the Verilog module, we invoke the VHDL entity by the statement:

```
adders_RL A1 (a [2:0], b [2:0], c0, sum_total [2:0], cr0);
```

The above statement passes the inputs (a_2 a_1 a_0), (b_2 b_1 b_0), and `c0` to the input ports of the entity `adders_RL`, (x_2 x_1 x_0), (y_2 y_1 y_0), and cin. The entity calculates the 3-bit output (sum_2 sum_1 sum_0) and the 1-bit output `cout`. The outputs (sum_2 sum_1 sum_0) and `cout` are passed to the outputs of the Verilog module (sum_total_2 sum_total_1 sum_total_0), and `cr0`, respectively. Each time the VHDL entity is invoked, three bits are added, and the output is passed to the Verilog module. Invoking the VHDL entity generates a 9-bit adder.

LISTING 9.4 Mixed-Language Description of a 9-Bit Adder

```
module Nine_bitAdder (a, b, c0, sum_total, carry_out);
   input [8:0] a, b;
   input c0;
   output [8:0] sum_total;
```

```
    output carry_out;
    wire cr0, cr1;

    //Invoke the VHDL entity
    adders_RL A1 (a [2:0], b [2:0], c0, sum_total [2:0], cr0);
    adders_RL A2 (a [5:3], b [5:3], cr0, sum_total [5:3], cr1);
    adders_RL A3 (a [8:6], b [8:6], cr1,
        sum_total [8:6], carry_out);
    //adders_RL is the name of the VHDL entity
endmodule

library IEEE;
use IEEE.STD_LOGIC_1164.ALL;
-- This is a VHDL data-flow code for a 3-bit carry-lookahead adder
entity adders_RL is
port (x, y : in std_logic_vector (2 downto 0);
cin : in std_logic;
sum : out std_logic_vector (2 downto 0);
cout : out std_logic);

--The entity name is identical to that of the Verilog module.
--The input and output ports have the same mode as the inputs
--and outputs of the Verilog module.

end adders_RL;

architecture lkh_DtFl of adders_RL is

signal c0, c1 : std_logic;
signal p, g : std_logic_vector (2 downto 0);
constant delay_gt : time := 0 ns;
--The gate propagation delay here is equal to 0.
begin

g(0) <= x(0) and y(0) after delay_gt;
g(1) <= x(1) and y(1) after delay_gt;
g(2) <= x(2) and y(2) after delay_gt;
p(0) <= x(0) or y(0) after delay_gt;
p(1) <= x(1) or y(1) after delay_gt;
p(2) <= x(2) or y(2) after delay_gt;
c0 <= g(0) or (p(0) and cin) after 2 * delay_gt;

c1 <= g(1) or (p(1) and g(0)) or (p(1) and
    p(0) and cin) after 2 * delay_gt;
cout <= g(2) or (p(2) and g(1)) or (p(2) and p(1) and g(0)) or
    (p(2) and p(1) and p(0) and cin) after 2 * delay_gt;

sum(0) <= (p(0) xor g(0)) xor cin after delay_gt;
sum(1) <= (p(1) xor g(1)) xor c0 after delay_gt;
sum(2) <= (p(2) xor g(2)) xor c1 after delay_gt;
end lkh_DtFl;
```

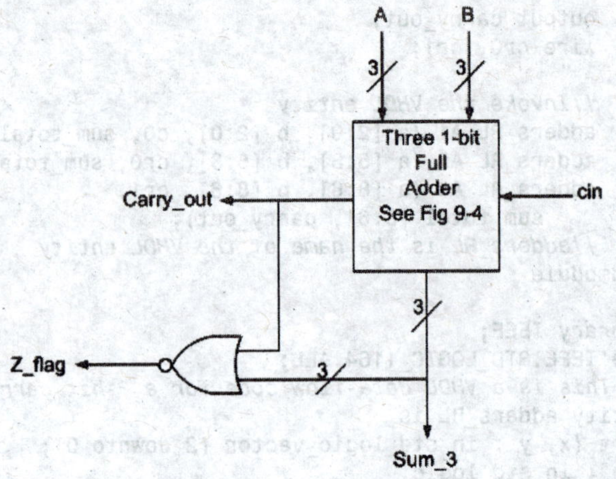

FIGURE 9.3 Block diagram of a 3-bit adder with a zero flag.

EXAMPLE 9.3 Mixed-Language Description of a 3-Bit Adder with Zero Flag

In this Example we write a mixed-language description of a 3-bit adder. The adder has a 1-bit flag. If the output of the adder is zero, the flag is set to 1; otherwise it is set to 0. Figure 9.3 shows the logic diagram of the adder. We implement a VHDL entity to describe the 1-bit adder, using structural description (see Chapter 4). The VHDL entity is invoked in the Verilog module three times.

Listing 9.5 shows the mixed-language description of the adder. The VHDL 1-bit adder is built from AND_OR_NOT gates (see Figure 9.4).

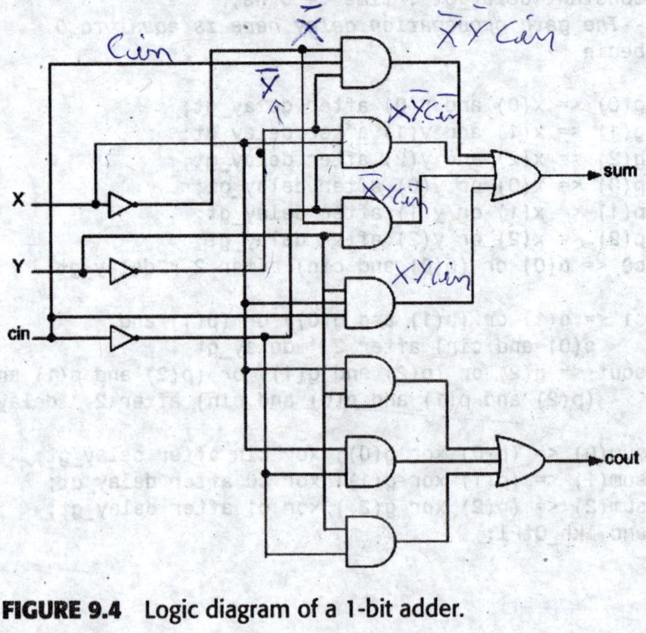

FIGURE 9.4 Logic diagram of a 1-bit adder.

The Verilog module:

```
full_add FA0 (A[0], B[0], cin, Sum_3[0], cr0);
```

invokes the VHDL entity `full_add`. This entity describes, in structural description, a 1-bit full adder. Invoking this entity three times from the Verilog module generates a 3-bit adder. The VHDL module looks very long due to the fact that standard VHDL, in contrast to Verilog, does not have built-in primitive gates.

LISTING 9.5 Mixed-Language Description of a 3-Bit Adder with a Zero Flag

```
module three_bitAdd (A, B, cin, Sum_3, Carry_out, Z_flag);
    input [2:0] A, B;
    input cin;
    output [2:0] Sum_3;
    output Carry_out;
    output Z_flag;
    wire cr0, cr1;

    full_add FA0 (A[0], B[0], cin, Sum_3[0], cr0);
    full_add FA1 (A[1], B[1], cr0, Sum_3[1], cr1);
    full_add FA2 (A[2], B[2], cr1, Sum_3[2], Carry_out);

--The above modules invoke the VHDL entity full_add

    assign Z_flag = ~(Sum_3[0] | Sum_3[1] | Sum_3[2] | Carry_out);
endmodule

library IEEE;
use IEEE.STD_LOGIC_1164.ALL;
entity full_add is
    Port (X, Y, cin : in std_logic; sum, cout : out std_logic);
--This is a 1-bit full adder component built from AND-OR-NOT
--gates; see Figure 9.4.
end full_add;

architecture beh_vhdl of full_add is
--Instantiate the components of a 1-bit adder;
--see Figure 9.4.
component inv
    port(I1 : in std_logic; O1 : out std_logic);
end component;
component and2
    port(I1, I2 : in std_logic; O1 : out std_logic);
end component;
component and3
    port(I1, I2, I3 : in std_logic; O1 : out std_logic);
end component;
component or3
    port(I1, I2, I3 : in std_logic; O1 : out std_logic);
```

```
end component;
component or4
    port(I1, I2, I3, I4 : in std_logic; O1 : out std_logic);
end component;
for all : inv use entity work.bind1 (inv_0);
for all : and2 use entity work.bind2 (and2_0);
for all : and3 use entity work.bind3 (and3_0);
for all : or3 use entity work.bind3 (or3_0);
for all : or4 use entity work.bind4 (or4_0);

--The above five "for" statements are to bind the inv, and3,
--and2, or3, and or4 with the architecture beh_vhdl.
--See Chapter 4, "Structural Descriptions."

    signal Xbar, Ybar, cinbar, s0, s1, s2,
        s3, s4, s5, s6 : std_logic;
begin
Iv1 : inv port map (X, Xbar);
Iv2 : inv port map (Y, Ybar);
Iv3 : inv port map (cin, cinbar);
A1 : and3 port map (X, Y, cin, s0);
A2 : and3 port map (Xbar, Y, cinbar, s1);
A3 : and3 port map (Xbar, Ybar, cin, s2);
A4 : and3 port map (X, Ybar, cinbar, s3);
A5 : and2 port map (X, cin, s4);
A6 : and2 port map (X, Y, s5);
A7 : and2 port map (Y, cin, s6);
O1 : or4 port map (s0, s1, s2, s3, sum);
O2 : or3 port map (s4, s5, s6, cout);
end beh_vhdl;

--The following is the behavioral description of the components
--instantiated in the entity full_add.
library IEEE;
use IEEE.STD_LOGIC_1164.ALL;
entity bind1 is
    port (I1 : in std_logic; O1 : out std_logic);
end bind1;
architecture inv_0 of bind1 is
begin
    O1 <= not I1;
end inv_0;

library IEEE;
use IEEE.STD_LOGIC_1164.ALL;

entity bind2 is
    port (I1, I2 : in std_logic; O1 : out std_logic);
end bind2;

architecture and2_0 of bind2 is
begin
O1 <= I1 and I2;
```

```
end and2_0;

architecture or2_0 of bind2 is
begin
O1 <= I1 or I2;
end or2_0;

library IEEE;
use IEEE.STD_LOGIC_1164.ALL;

entity bind3 is
    port (I1, I2, I3 : in std_logic; O1 : out std_logic);
end bind3;

architecture and3_0 of bind3 is
begin
    O1 <= I1 and I2 and I3;
end and3_0;

architecture or3_0 of bind3 is
begin
    O1 <= I1 or I2 or I3;
end or3_0;
library IEEE;
use IEEE.STD_LOGIC_1164.ALL;

entity bind4 is
    Port (I1, I2, I3, I4 : in std_logic; O1 : out std_logic);
end bind4;
architecture or4_0 of bind4 is
begin
    O1 <= I1 or I2 or I3 or I4;
end or4_0;
```

EXAMPLE 9.4 Mixed-Language Description of a Master-Slave D Flip-Flop

In Chapter 4, we wrote a structural description of a master-slave flip-flop. The flip-flop was built from two D-latches (see Figure 9.5).

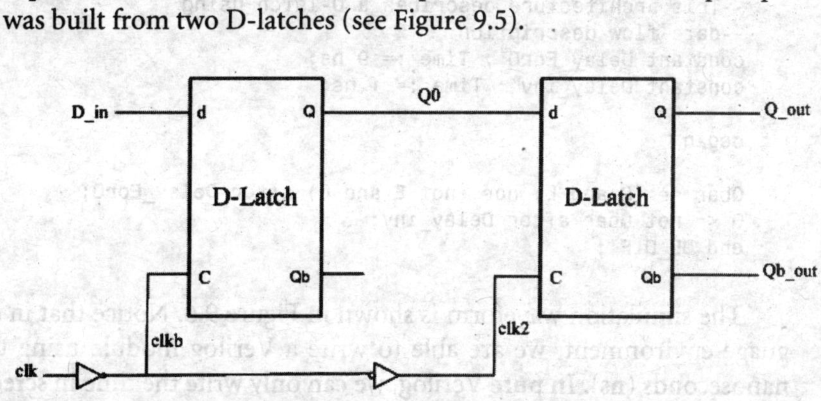

FIGURE 9.5 Logic diagram of master-slave D flip-flop.

In this Example, we write a mixed-language description of the flip-flop. Instead of structural description, VHDL data-flow description is used to simulate the D-latch (see Chapter 2). The master-slave flip-flop is described in a Verilog module. We invoke the VHDL entity to import the description of a D-latch. Listing 9.6 shows the mixed-language description of a master-slave flip-flop.

LISTING 9.6 Mixed-Language Description of a Master-Slave D Flip-Flop

```
//This is the Verilog module
module D_Master (D_in, clk, Q_out, Qb_out);
    input D_in, clk;
    output Q_out, Qb_out;
    wire Q0, Qb, clkb; // wire statement here can be omitted.
    assign clkb = ~ clk;
    assign clk2 = ~ clkb;
    D_Latch D0 (D_in, clkb, Q0, Qb);

//D_Latch is the name of a VHDL entity describing a D-Latch

    D_Latch D1 (Q0, clk2, Q_out, Qb_out);

endmodule

library IEEE;
use IEEE.STD_LOGIC_1164.ALL;

entity D_Latch is
--The entity has the same name as the calling Verilog module

port (D, E : in std_logic;
     Q, Qbar : buffer std_logic);

end D_Latch;

architecture DL_DtFl of D_Latch is
--This architecture describes a D-latch using
--data-flow description
constant Delay_EorD : Time := 9 ns;
constant Delay_inv : Time := 1 ns;

begin

Qbar <= (D and E) nor (not E and Q) after Delay_EorD;
Q <= not Qbar after Delay_inv;
end DL_DtFl;
```

The simulation waveform is shown in Figure 9.6. Notice that in a mixed-language environment, we are able to write a Verilog module using time units in nanoseconds (ns). In pure Verilog, we can only write the time in screen units.

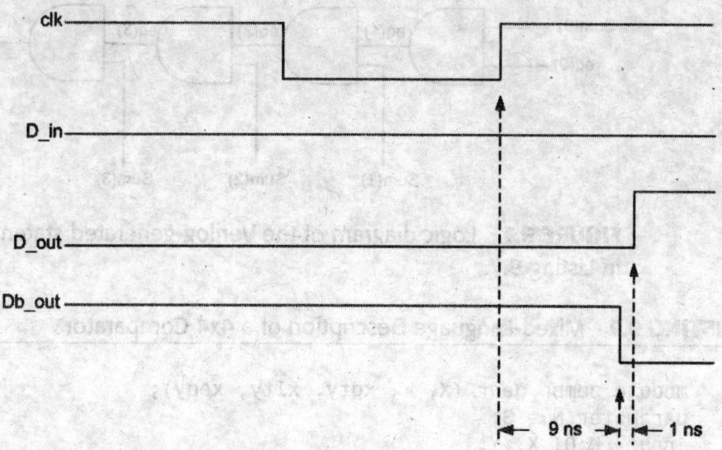

FIGURE 9.6 Simulation waveform of a master-slave D flip-flop.

EXAMPLE 9.5 Mixed-Language Description of a 4x4 Comparator

In Chapter 4, we wrote the HDL structural description of a 3x3 comparator. We built the comparator from three 1-bit adders (see Figure 4.14). This Example uses mixed-language description. We write a VHDL behavioral module (see Chapter 3, "Behavioral Descriptions") to describe a 1-bit full adder. A Verilog module invokes the VHDL module four times. Listing 9.7 shows the mixed-language description of 4x4 comparator. Consider the Verilog code:

```
generate

genvar i;
for (i = 0; i <= N; i = i + 1)
    begin : uC

    and (eq[i+1], sum[i], eq[i]);

end
endgenerate
```

If N = 3, the above Verilog code constitutes four two-input AND gates (see Figure 9.7). The input to each gate is sum(i) and eq(i); the output is eq(i+1). The output of the fourth AND gate, eq(4), is equal to 1 if, and only if, all sum(i), i = 1, 3 are equal to 1; otherwise it is equal to 0. If eq(4) = 1, this means that X = Y.

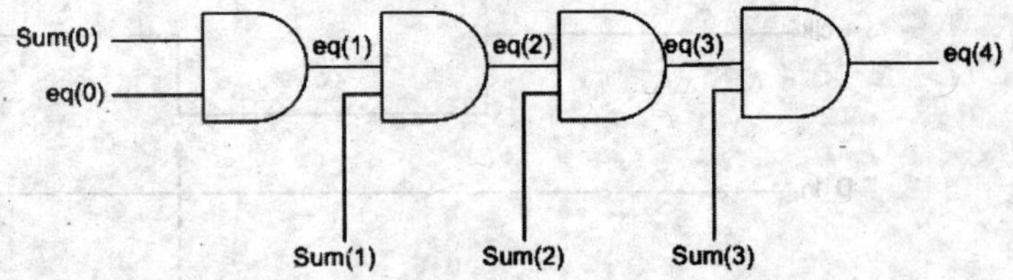

FIGURE 9.7 Logic diagram of the Verilog-generated statements in Listing 9.7.

LISTING 9.7 Mixed-Language Description of a 4x4 Comparator

```
module compr_genr (X, Y, xgty, xlty, xeqy);
parameter N = 3;
input [N:0] X, Y;
output xgty, xlty, xeqy;

wire [N:0] sum, Yb;
wire [N+1:0] carry, eq;
assign carry[0] = 1'b0;
assign eq[0] = 1'b1;
assign Yb = ~Y;

    FULL_ADDER FA (X[0], Yb[0], carry[0], sum[0], carry[1]);

-- The module FULL_ADDER has the same name
-- as the VHDL entity FULL_ADDER

    FULL_ADDER FA1 (X[1], Yb[1], carry[1], sum[1], carry[2]);
    FULL_ADDER FA2 (X[2], Yb[2], carry[2], sum[2], carry[3]);
    FULL_ADDER FA3 (X[3], Yb[3], carry[3], sum[3], carry[4]);

generate

genvar i;
for (i = 0; i <= N; i = i + 1)
    begin : uC

    and (eq[i+1], sum[i], eq[i]);

end
endgenerate

assign xgty = carry [N+1];
assign xeqy = eq [N+1];
nor (xlty, xeqy, xgty);
endmodule

library IEEE;
use IEEE.STD_LOGIC_1164.ALL;
entity FULL_ADDER is
```

```
    Port (A, B, cin : in std_logic; sum_1, cout : out std_logic);
end FULL_ADDER;

architecture beh_vhdl of FULL_ADDER is

--This architecture is a behavioral description of a full adder
begin

oneBit : process (A, B, cin)
    variable y : std_logic_vector (2 downto 0);
    begin
        Y := (A & B & Cin);
--The above statement is a concatenation of
--three bits A, B, and Cin

case y is
    when "000" => sum_1 <= '0'; cout <= '0';
    when "110" => sum_1 <= '0'; cout <= '1';
    when "101" => sum_1 <= '0'; cout <= '1';
    when "011" => sum_1 <= '0'; cout <= '1';
    when "111" => sum_1 <= '1'; cout <= '1';
    when others => sum_1 <= '1'; cout <= '0';
--Others here refer to 100, 001, 010

 end case;
    end process;
    end beh_vhdl;
```

9.3.2 Invoking a Verilog Module from a VHDL Module

As mentioned, we can instantiate a Verilog module from a VHDL module by instantiating a component in the VHDL module that has the same name and ports as the Verilog module. The Verilog module should be the only construct that has the same name as the component. Presently, this is the only way Verilog modules can be invoked from VHDL. In the following, we discuss several examples.

EXAMPLE 9.6 Instantiating an AND Gate from a VHDL Module

As was seen in Chapter 4, standard VHDL does not have built-in gates such as AND, OR, and XOR, unless the user attaches a vendor's package that contains a description of the gates. Standard Verilog, on the other hand, has built-in descriptions of primitive gates that we can take advantage of. Using mixed-language description, a Verilog module is invoked in the VHDL module, and the gates that we want to use are instantiated. Listing 9.8 shows a mixed-language description of instantiating an AND gate in a VHDL module. The description of the AND gate is provided by the Verilog module. Referring to Listing 9.8, the VHDL statements:

```
component and2
```

```
    port (x, y : in std_logic; z : out std_logic);

end component;
```

declares a component by the name of `and2`. The component has two input ports, `x` and `y`, and one output port, `z`. To link this component to a Verilog module, the module has to have the same name and ports as the component. The Verilog module is written as:

```
module and2 (x, y, z);
```

It has the same name and the same ports. So all Verilog statements pertaining to `x`, `y`, and `z` are visible to the VHDL module. In the Verilog module, we write:

```
assign z = x & y;
```

The above statement describes an AND relationship between `x`, `y`, and `z`.

LISTING 9.8 Mixed-Language Description of an AND Gate

```
library IEEE;
use IEEE.STD_LOGIC_1164.ALL;
use IEEE.STD_LOGIC_ARITH.ALL;

--This is the VHDL module

entity andgate is
    port (a, b : in std_logic; c : out std_logic);
end andgate;

architecture andgate of andgate is
component and2

--For correct binding with the Verilog module,
--the name of the component should be identical
--to that of the Verilog module.

    port (x, y : in std_logic; z : out std_logic);

--The name of the ports should be identical to the name
--of the inputs/outputs of the Verilog module.

end component;

begin
    g1 : and2 port map (a, b, c);
end andgate;
```

```
//This is the Verilog module
module and2 (x, y, z);

    input x, y;
    output z;
    assign z = x & y;

endmodule
```

TABLE 9.1 Excitation Table for a JK Flip-Flop

Clear	J	K	clk	q (Next State)
1	x	x	↑	q=0
0	0	0	↑	No change (hold), next = current
0	1	0	↑	1
0	0	1	↑	0
0	1	1	↑	Toggle (next state) = invert of (current state)

EXAMPLE 9.7 Mixed-Language Description of a JK Flip-Flop with a Clear

In this Example, we write a mixed-language description of a JK flip-flop. JK flip-flops were covered in Chapters 3 and 4. The excitation table of a JK flip-flop with a clear signal is shown in Table 9.1.

We declare the flip-flop as a VHDL component and then write a Verilog behavioral description of the flip-flop based on Table 9.1. The Verilog is linked to the VHDL component by giving the Verilog module the same name as the VHDL component. The ports of the component should be also the same as those of the Verilog module. Listing 9.9 shows the mixed-language description of the flip-flop. We declare the JK flip-flop as a component with the statement:

```
component jk_verilog
    port(j, k, ck, clear : in std_logic; q, qb : out std_logic);
end component;
```

and the above component is linked to a Verilog module by the statement:

```
module jk_verilog (j, k, ck, clear, q, qb);
```

The above module has the same name and ports as of the VHDL component `jk_verilog`. Accordingly, the relationship between the input and output ports described in the Verilog module is visible to the VHDL component. The Verilog module describes, in behavioral style, a JK flip-flop with an active high clear. Hence, the VHDL component `jk_verilog` is also a JK flip-flop with an active high clear.

LISTING 9.9 Mixed-Language Description of a JK Flip-Flop

```
library IEEE;
use IEEE.STD_LOGIC_1164.ALL;

entity JK_FF is
   Port (Jx, Kx, clk, clx : in std_logic; Qx, Qxbar : out std_logic);
end JK_FF;

architecture JK_FF of JK_FF is

--The JK flip flop is declared as a component
component jk_verilog
   port(j, k, ck, clear : in std_logic; q, qb : out std_logic);
end component;
begin

jk1 : jk_verilog port map (Jx, Kx, clk, clx, Qx, Qxbar);

end JK_FF;

module jk_verilog (j, k, ck, clear, q, qb);
// The module name jk_verilog matches
// the name of the VHDL components

input j, k, ck, clear;
output q, qb;
--The input and output ports match those of the
--VHDL component, jk_verilog

reg q, qb;
reg [1:0] JK;
always @ (posedge ck, clear)
begin
   if (clear == 1)
      begin
         q = 1'b0;
         qb = 1'b1;
      end
      else
         begin

            JK = {j, k};
            case (JK)
            2'd0 : q = q;
            2'd1 : q = 0;
            2'd2 : q = 1;
            2'd3 : q = ~q;
            endcase
            qb = ~q;
         end
 end
 endmodule
```

The simulation waveform of the JK flip-flop is shown in Figure 9.8.

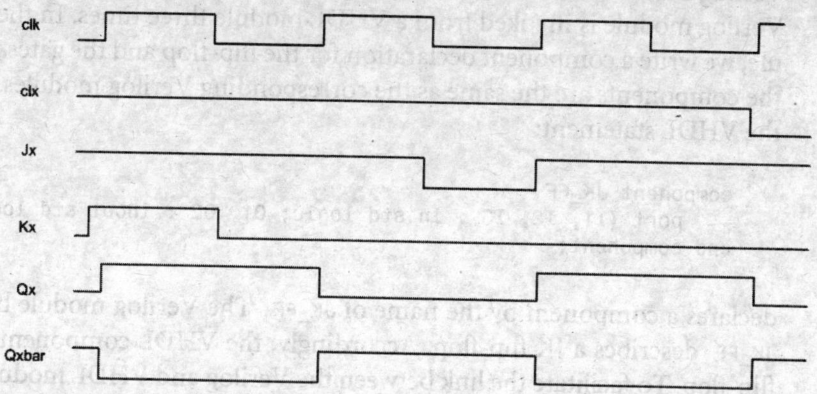

FIGURE 9.8 Simulation waveform of a JK flip-flop with an active high clear.

EXAMPLE 9.8 Mixed-Language Description of 3-Bit Synchronous Counter with Clear

This example was first covered in Chapter 4. Figure 4.20 shows the logic diagram of the counter, and Listing 4.21 shows the VHDL and the Verilog descriptions. In this Example, we want to write the counter code as mixed-language. For convenience, Figure 4.20 is presented again here as Figure 9.9. As shown, the counter consists of three JK flip-flops, and OR, AND, and INVERT gates.

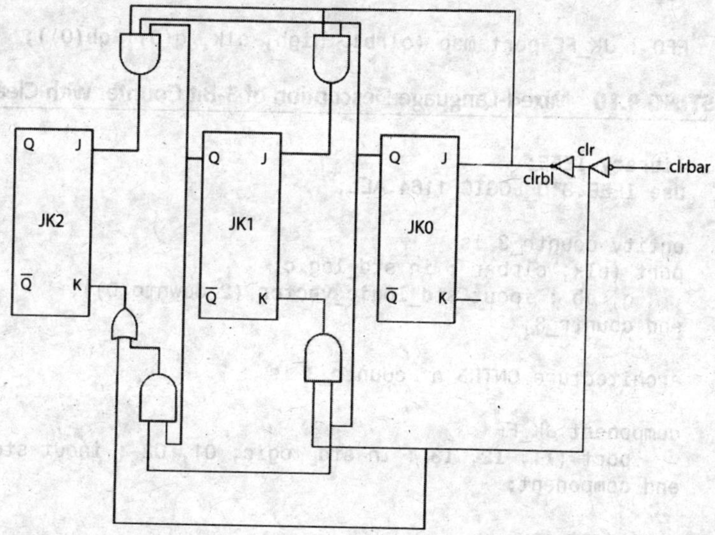

FIGURE 9.9 Three-bit synchronous counter with clear.

Listing 9.10 shows the mixed-language description of the counter. We write a Verilog module that describes a JK flip-flop, and an AND, OR, and INVERT. The Verilog module is invoked from a VHDL module three times. In the VHDL module, we write a component declaration for the flip-flop and the gates. The names of the components are the same as the corresponding Verilog modules. For example, the VHDL statement:

```
component JK_FF
    port (I1, I2, I3 : in std_logic; O1, O2 : inout std_logic);
end component;
```

declares a component by the name of `JK_FF`. The Verilog module by the name of `JK_FF` describes a JK flip-flop. Accordingly, the VHDL component `JK_FF` is a JK flip-flop. To facilitate the link between the Verilog and VHDL modules, we slightly modify the VHDL module from Listing 4.21, in which the instantiation statement for flip-flop `FF0` was written as:

```
FF0 : JK_FF port map (clrb1, '1', clk, q(0), qb(0));
```

The Verilog module can accept a signal, variable, or constant; but it cannot accept the value "1." So we declare a signal named `high` and assign it a value of "1," as follows:

```
high <= '1';

FF0 : JK_FF port map (clrb1, High, clk, q(0), qb(0));
```

LISTING 9.10 Mixed-Language Description of 3-Bit Counter with Clear

```
library IEEE;
use IEEE.STD_LOGIC_1164.ALL;

entity countr_3 is
port (clk, clrbar : in std_logic;
    q, qb : inout std_logic_vector (2 downto 0));
end countr_3;

architecture CNTR3 of countr_3 is

component JK_FF
    port (I1, I2, I3 : in std_logic; O1, O2 : inout std_logic);
end component;

component inv
    port (I1 : in std_logic; O1 : out std_logic);
end component;
```

```
component and2
    port (I1, I2 : in std_logic; O1 : out std_logic);
end component;

component or2
port (I1, I2 : in std_logic; O1 : out std_logic);
end component;

signal J1, K1, J2, K2, clr, clrb1, s1, high : std_logic;
begin

    high <= '1';

FF0 : JK_FF port map (clrb1, High, clk, q(0), qb(0));

A1 : and2 port map (clrb1, q(0), J1);
inv1 : inv port map (clr, clrb1);
inv2 : inv port map (clrbar, clr);

r1 : or2 port map (q(0), clr, K1);
FF1 : JK_FF port map (J1, K1, clk, q(1), qb(1));
A2 : and2 port map (q(0), q(1), s1);
A3 : and2 port map (clrb1, s1, J2);
r2 : or2 port map (s1, clr, K2);
FF2 : JK_FF port map (J2, K2, clk, q(2), qb(2));
end CNTR3 ;

module and2 (I1, I2, O1);
//This Verilog module represents an AND function

input I1, I2;
output O1;
assign O1 = I1 & I2;
endmodule

module inv (I1, O1);
//This Verilog module represents an INVERT function

input I1;
output O1;
assign O1 = ~I1;
endmodule

module or2 (I1, I2, O1);
//This Verilog module represents an OR function

input I1, I2;
output O1;
assign O1 = I1 | I2;
endmodule

module JK_FF (I1, I2, I3, O1, O2);
```

```
//This Verilog module represents a JK flip-flop.

input I1, I2, I3;
output O1, O2;

reg O1, O2;
reg [1:0] JK;
initial
    begin
    O1 = 1'b0;
    O2 = 1'b1;
    end
always @ (posedge I3)
begin

    JK = {I1, I2};
    case (JK)
    2'd0 : O1 = O1;
    2'd1 : O1 = 0;
    2'd2 : O1 = 1;
    2'd3 : O1 = ~O1;
    endcase
    O2 = ~O1;
end
endmodule
```

EXAMPLE 9.9 Mixed-Language Description of an *N*-Bit Counter with Ripple-Carry Out

In this Example, we discuss an *n*-bit asynchronous counter with a Ripple-Carry Out (RCO). Figure 9.10 shows the logic diagram of the counter. As shown, the ripple carry out is 1 when all Qs are 1s. In Chapter 4, asynchronous counters were discussed and described using the `generate` statement. Here we use mixed-language description to invoke a Verilog module from a VHDL module. Listing 9.11 shows the mixed-language description of the counter.

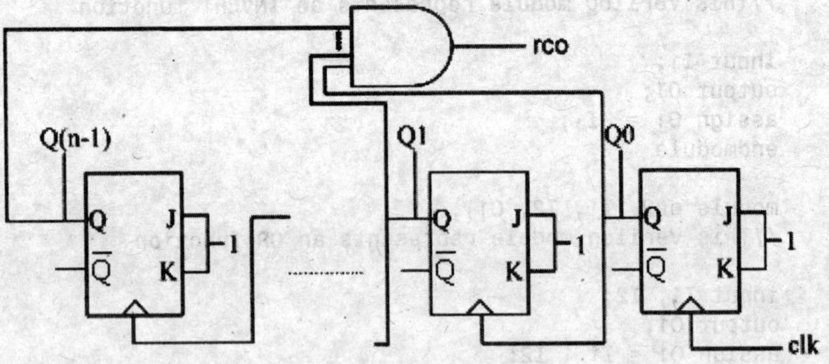

FIGURE 9.10 Logic diagram of an n-bit synchronous counter with ripple-carry out.

As shown in Figure 9.10, to construct the counter, we need *n*-JK flip-flops, and *n*-input and gates. Two Verilog modules, `jkff` and `andgate`, are implemented to describe a JK flip-flop and a three-input AND gate, respectively. The module `jkff` is written in behavioral description, and the module `andgate` is written in data-flow description.

LISTING 9.11 Mixed-Language Description of an *N*-Bit Asynchronous Counter

```
--This is a VHDL module
library IEEE;
use IEEE.STD_LOGIC_1164.ALL;

entity asynch_ctrMx is
Generic (N : integer := 3);

port (clk, clear : in std_logic;
     C, Cbar : out std_logic_vector (N-1 downto 0);
        rco : out std_logic);
end asynch_ctrMx;

architecture CT_strgnt of asynch_ctrMx is

component jkff is
--This is a JK flip-flop with a clear bound to Verilog module jkff

    port (j, k, clk, clear : in std_logic; q, qb : out std_logic);
end component;

component andgate is
--This is a three-input AND gate bound to Verilog module andgate

    port (I1, I2, I3 : in std_logic; O1 : out std_logic);
end component;

signal h, l : std_logic;
signal s : std_logic_vector (N downto 0);
signal s1 : std_logic_vector (N downto 0);
signal C_tem : std_logic_vector (N-1 downto 0);

begin
h <= '1';
l <= '0';
s <= (C_tem & clk);

-- s is the concatenation of Q and clk. We need this
-- concatenation to describe the clock of each JK flip-flop.

s1(0) <= not clear;

Gnlop : for i in (N - 1) downto 0 generate

G1 : jkff port map (h, h, s(i), clear, C_tem(i), Cbar(i));
```

```
end generate GnLop;
C <= C_tem;

rc_gen : for i in (N - 2) downto 0 generate

--This loop to determine the ripple carry-out
   rc : andgate port map (C_tem(i), C_tem(i+1), s1(i), s1(i+1));
   end generate rc_gen;
   rco <= s1(N-1);
end CT_strgnt;

module jkff (j, k, clk, clear, q, qb);
// This is a behavioral description of a JK flip-flop

input j, k, clk, clear;
output q, qb;
reg q, qb;
reg [1:0] JK;
always @ (posedge clk, clear)
begin
    if (clear == 1)
        begin
            q = 1'b0;
            qb = 1'b1;
        end
        else
            begin

                JK = {j,k};
                case (JK)
                2'd0 : q = q;
                2'd1 : q = 0;
                2'd2 : q = 1;
                2'd3 : q = ~q;
                endcase
                qb = ~q;
            end
end
endmodule

module andgate (I1, I2,I3, O1);
//This is a three-input AND gate
    input I1, I2, I3;
    output O1;
    assign O1 = (I1 & I2 & I3);
endmodule
```

The simulation waveform is shown in Figure 9.11.

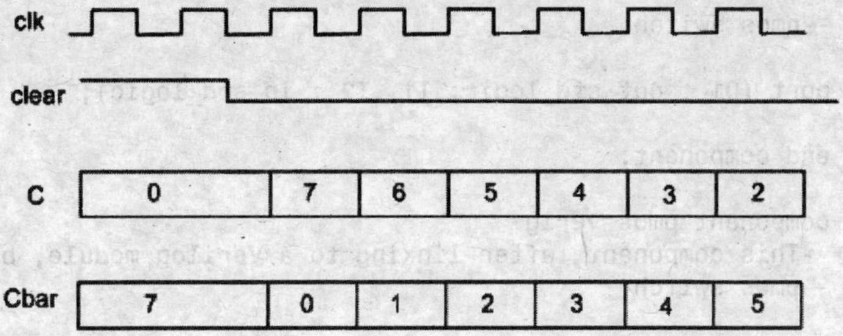

FIGURE 9.11 Simulation waveform for an n-bit asynchronous counter. The simulation pattern might be different than shown due to the presence of transient states (hazards).

EXAMPLE 9.10 Mixed-Language Description of a Switch-Level Multiplexer

In Chapter 5, "Switch-Label Descriptions," several combinational and sequential logics were described using VHDL or Verilog switch-level description. We have also seen that the basic VHDL package, in contrast to Verilog, does not have built-in switch-level primitives. Here, mixed-language description is used to describe a 2x1 multiplexer; a switch-level Verilog description is invoked from a VHDL module. By invoking Verilog modules, the VHDL module behaves as if it possesses built-in switch-level primitives. Listing 9.12 shows the mixed-language description of a 2x1 multiplexer. The statement:

```
component pmos_verlg
    port (O1 : out std_logic; I1, I2 : in std_logic);
end component;
```

declares a VHDL component by the name `pmos_verlg`. The name of the component is the same as the name of the Verilog module that uses the built-in primitive `pmos` to describe a `pmos` switch. In this way, the switch is made visible to the VHDL module.

LISTING 9.12 Mixed-Language Description of a 2x1 Multiplexer

```
--This is the VHDL module.
library IEEE;
use IEEE.STD_LOGIC_1164.ALL;

entity mux2x1_mxd is
Port (a, b, Sel, E : in std_logic; ybar : out std_logic);
end mux2x1_mxd;

architecture mux2x1switch of mux2x1_mxd is

component nmos_verlg
--This component, after linking to a Verilog module, behaves as an
```

```
--nmos switch

port (O1 : out std_logic; I1, I2 : in std_logic);

end component;

component pmos_verlg
--This component, after linking to a Verilog module, behaves as a
--pmos switch

    port (O1 : out std_logic; I1, I2 : in std_logic);
end component;

--constant vdd : std_logic := '1';
--constant gnd : std_logic := '0';

-- In Chapter 5 we wrote Vdd and gnd as constants.
-- Some VHDL/Verilog simulators do not transfer constants
-- between VHDL and Verilog. So we wrote them as signals.

signal vdd, gnd, Selbar, s0, s1, s2, s3 : std_logic;

begin
    vdd <= '1';
    gnd <= '0';

--Invert signal Sel. If the complement of Sel is available,
--then no need for the following pair of transistors.

v1 : pmos_verlg port map (Selbar, vdd, Sel);
v2 : nmos_verlg port map (Selbar, gnd, Sel);

--Write the pull-down combination
n1 : nmos_verlg port map (s0, gnd, E);
n2 : nmos_verlg port map (s1, s0, Sel);
n3 : nmos_verlg port map (ybar, s1, a);
n4 : nmos_verlg port map (s2, s0, Selbar);
n5 : nmos_verlg port map (ybar, s2, b);

--Write the pull-up combination
p1 : pmos_verlg port map (ybar, vdd, E);
p2 : pmos_verlg port map (ybar, s3, Sel);
p3 : pmos_verlg port map (ybar, s3, a);
p4 : pmos_verlg port map (s3, vdd, Selbar);
p5 : pmos_verlg port map (s3, vdd, b);

end mux2x1switch;

// This is the Verilog Module

module nmos_verlg (O1, I1, I2);
    input I1, I2;
    output O1;
```

```
nmos (O1, I1, I2);
endmodule

module pmos_verlg (O1, I1, I2);
    input I1, I2;
    output O1;
pmos (O1, I1, I2);
endmodule
```

EXAMPLE 9.11 Instantiating CASEX in VHDL

Chapter 3 covered the `casex` statement for both VHDL and Verilog. We have seen that `casex` ignores the "don't care" (x) in the values of the control expression. Consider the following `casex`:

```
casex (a)
    4'bxxx1 : b = 4'd1;
    4'bxx10 : b = 4'd2;
    ................
    endcase;
```

All x's are ignored; for example, `b` = 1 if, and only if, the least significant bit of `a` is 1, regardless of the value of the high-order bits of `a`. Another Verilog variation of `case` is the `casez` (see Chapter 3), where z is the high impedance. VHDL does not have an exact replica of `casex` or `casez`. With mixed-language description, we can instantiate a command similar to `casex` and `casez` in the VHDL module. Listing 9.13 shows a mixed-language description that instantiates a command by the name of `cas_x` in the VHDL module; this command performs the same function as the Verilog `casex`. Listing 9.13 represents a 4-bit priority encoder, which was discussed in Chapter 3. The truth table of the encoder is shown in Table 9.2.

TABLE 9.2 Truth Table for a 4-Bit Encoder

Input a	**Output b**
xxx1	1
xx10	2
x100	4
1000	8
Others	0

LISTING 9.13 Instantiating CASEX in a VHDL Module

```
library IEEE;
use IEEE.STD_LOGIC_1164.all;

entity P_encodr is
    Port (X : in std_logic_vector (3 downto 0);
        Y : out std_logic_vector (3 downto 0));
end P_encodr;

architecture P_encodr of P_encodr is

component cas_x
--The name of the component is identical to the name of the
--Verilog module

port (a : in std_logic_vector (3 downto 0);
    b : out std_logic_vector (3 downto 0));

end component;

begin

ax : cas_x port map (X, Y);

end P_encodr;

module cas_x (a, b);
    input [3:0] a;
    output [3:0] b;
    reg [3:0] b;
    always @ (a)
        begin
            casex (a)
            4'bxxx1 : b = 4'd1;
            4'bxx10 : b = 4'd2;
            4'bx100 : b = 4'd4;
            4'b1000 : b = 4'd8;
            default : b = 4'd0;

            endcase
        end

endmodule
```

EXAMPLE 9.12 Mixed-Language Description of a Low-Pass RC Filter

The function of an electronic filter is to block a certain frequency band in a signal. There are several types of simple filters, such as low pass, high pass, and band pass. Low-pass filters allow frequencies below a certain threshold (called the "cutoff frequency") to pass with or without minimal attenuation. All frequencies above the threshold are attenuated; frequencies close to the cutoff are less attenuation than those frequencies far from the cutoff. High-pass filters pass frequencies higher than the cutoff with or without minimal attenuation. Frequencies lower than the cutoff are attenuated; frequencies close to the cutoff are less attenuated than those signals far from the cutoff. More details about simple filters can be found in [Dorf04] and [Reed99].

Figure 9.12 shows a low-pass filter consisting of a resistance (R) connected in serial with a capacitance (C). The impedance of the capacitance is (1/jwC), where $w = 2\pi f$; f is the frequency, and $j = \sqrt{-1}$. The ratio of the output signal (Vo) to the input signal (Vi) is:

$$\frac{Vo}{Vi} = \frac{1/jwC}{R + 1/jwC} = \frac{1}{jwCR + 1} \qquad (9.1)$$

(Vo/Vi) is called the "transfer function" of the filter [H(w)]. The square of the amplitude of the transfer function can be written as:

$$[H(w)]^2 = \frac{1}{w^2CR + 1} \qquad (9.2)$$

$$\text{The cutoff frequency } w_c = (1/RC) \qquad (9.3)$$

Substitute Equation 9.3 into Equation 9.2, and we write $[H(w)]^2$ as:

$$[H(w)]^2 = \frac{1}{(w / w_c)^2 + 1} \qquad (9.4)$$

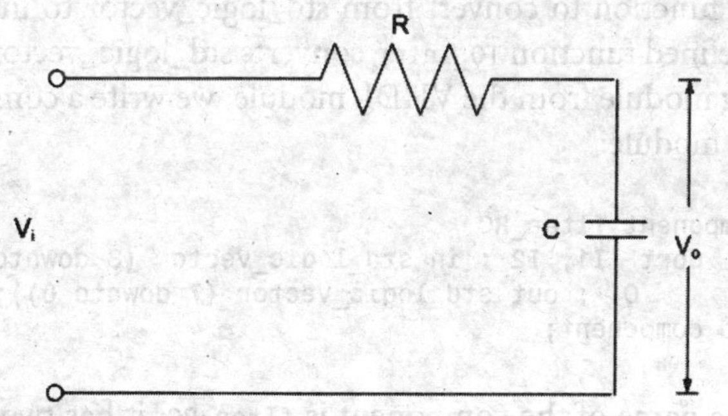

FIGURE 9.12 Simple low-pass RC filter.

We want to simulate Equation 9.4 using mixed-language description and output the value of $[H(w)]^2$ as it changes with w in a file. Since VHDL has extensive file operations, we implement the VHDL module to handle the file operations. The Verilog module will handle the calculations. Listing 9.14 shows the mixed-language description of a simple RC filter. In the VHDL module, the inputs and outputs are described as:

```
entity Filter_draw is
    Port (w, w_ctoff : in std_logic_vector (3 downto 0);
    Hw_vhd : out std_logic_vector (7 downto 0));
end Filter_draw;
```

As shown in the entity `Filter_draw`, the inputs and outputs are selected to be of type `std_logic_vector`. The output $[H(w)]^2$ in Equation 9.4 is represented by the signal `Hw_vhd`. The inputs w and w_c in Equation 9.4 are represented by `w` and `w_ctoff`. To simplify the description, all inputs and outputs are assumed to be integers. We could have selected the type of inputs and output in the entity to be integers, but here we want to practice converting from one type to another. Also, we want an easy link between the VHDL and Verilog ports, since integer ports are not allowed to be mapped from Verilog to VHDL. If the output `Hw_vhd` is calculated as in Equation 9.4, using integer division, the output would be zero for all values of w, since the numerator is always less than the denominator. Instead, we calculate Equation 9.4 as real division and then scale it up by multiplying it by 100. For example, if w = 3 units and the cutoff = 4 units, then from Equation 9.4:

$$\text{Real (Hw\_vhd)} = \frac{1}{(3/4)^2+1} = 0.64$$

After scaling up by 100, then `Hw_vhd` = 64

Since VHDL files accept only integers, real values, and characters, we write a VHDL function to convert from std_logic_vector to integer. In Listing 9.14, the user-defined function `TO_Intgr` converts std_logic_vector to integer. To invoke the Verilog module from the VHDL module, we write a component declaration in the VHDL module:

```
component flter_RC
    port (I1, I2 : in std_logic_vector (3 downto 0);
        O1 : out std_logic_vector (7 downto 0));
end component;
```

The name of the component is `flter_RC`; it has two input ports, `I1` and `I2` of type `std_logic_vector`, and one output port, `O1` of type `std_logic_vector`. To invoke the Verilog module, we declare the module as follows:

```
module flter_RC (I1, I2, O1);
input [3:0] I1, I2;
output [7:0] O1;
```

The above Verilog module has the same name and ports as the VHDL component; thus the module is visible to the VHDL module. In the Verilog module, we perform the real division $O1 = 1 / [(I1 / I2)^2 + 1]$. Since `I1` and `I2` are not declared as real, the division will be performed as integer, and O1 will be zero for all values of `I1` and `I2`. To avoid this, we multiply `I1` and `I2` by 1.0:

```
s1 = ((1.0 * I1) / (1.0 * I2)) ** 2;
S = 1.0 / (1.0 + s1);
```

`S` and `s1` are declared as real; the value of `S` is the real value of the division $1 / [(I1 / I2)^2 + 1]$. The output of the Verilog module, `O1`, is calculated by multiplying S by 100. This output is passed to the VHDL module. As can be seen, Verilog, in contrast to VHDL, is flexible in handling different data types. We would not have been able to easily perform the real division in VHDL. After calculating the output, it is entered into a text file. All of the data in `std_logic_vector` to be entered into the file must be converted to integers, since files cannot take the type `std_logic_vector`.

LISTING 9.14 Mixed-Language Description of a Simple RC Filter

```
library IEEE;
use IEEE.STD_LOGIC_1164.ALL;
use std.textio.all;
use ieee.numeric_std.all;

entity Filter_draw is
Port (w, w_ctoff : in std_logic_vector (3 downto 0);
    Hw_vhd : out std_logic_vector (7 downto 0));
end Filter_draw;

architecture Filter_draw of Filter_draw is

Function TO_Intgr (a : in std_logic_vector) return integer is
--This Function converts std_logic_vector type to integer
variable result : integer;

begin
    result := 0;
    lop1 : for i in a' range loop
    if a(i) = '1' then
    result := result + 2**i;
    end if;
    end loop;
return result;
end TO_Intgr;

component flter_RC
--The name of the component "flter_RC" is the same name as the
```

```
--Verilog module
    port (I1, I2 : in std_logic_vector (3 downto 0); O1 : out
        std_logic_vector (7 downto 0));
end component;
signal Hw_tmp : std_logic_vector (7 downto 0);
begin
dw : flter_RC port map (w, w_ctoff, Hw_tmp);

//output the data on a file
fl : process (w, w_ctoff, Hw_tmp)
file outfile : text;
variable fstatus : file_open_status;
variable temp : line;
variable Hw_int, w_int, w_ctoffintg : integer;

begin
--Files can take integer, real, or character;
--they cannot take std-logic-vector; so convert to integer.

Hw_int := TO_Intgr (Hw_tmp);
w_int := TO_Intgr (w);
w_ctoffintg := TO_Intgr (w_ctoff);
file_open (fstatus, outfile, "Wfile_int.txt", write_mode);
--The file name is Wfile_int.txt

--Write headings. Be sure the simulator supports formatted output.
--otherwise take out all formatted output statements
write (temp, "                                  This is a Simple
    R-C Low Pass Filter");

--The above statement, when entered in the VHDL module,
--should be entered in one line without carriage return */

writeline (outfile, temp);
write (temp, " ");
writeline (outfile, temp);
write (temp, " FREQUENCY
CUTOFF                  Amplitude Square");
--The above statement, when entered in the VHDL module,
--should be entered in one line without carriage return */

writeline (outfile, temp);
write (temp, "    ");

--write the values of the filter parameters
write (temp, w_int);
write (temp, "                    ");
write (temp, w_ctoffintg);
write (temp, "                              ");
write (temp, Hw_int);
writeline (outfile, temp);
```

```
file_close (outfile);
Hw_vhd <= Hw_tmp;
end process fl;
end Filter_draw;

// Next we write the Verilog module;
// the module performs a real division

module flter_RC (I1, I2, O1);

//The module performs the real division O1 = 1/[(I1/I2)**2 + 1]

input [3:0] I1, I2;
output [7:0] O1;
reg [7:0] O1;
real S, s1;
always @ (I1, I2)
begin
s1 = ((1.0*I1)/(1.0 * I2))**2 ;
//we multiply by 1.0 so the division is done in real format.

S = 1.0 / (1.0 + s1);
O1 = 100.00 * S;
end
endmodule
```

The File `Wfile_int.txt`, after simulation, is shown in Figure 9.13.

This is a Simple Low-Pass Filter		
FREQUENCY	CUTOFF	Amplitude Square*10
3	4	64

FIGURE 9.13 The File `Wfile_int.txt` after simulation.

9.4 LIMITATIONS OF MIXED-LANGUAGE DESCRIPTION

As previously mentioned, mixed-language description is at present rather limited. These limitations can be summarized as follows:

- Not all VHDL data types are supported in mixed-language description. Only `bit`, `bit_vector`, `std_logic`, `std_ulogic`, `std_logic_vector`, and `std_ulogic_vector` are supported.
- The VHDL port type `buffer` is not supported.
- Only a VHDL component construct can invoke a Verilog module. We cannot invoke a Verilog module from any other construct in the VHDL module.

- A Verilog module can only invoke a VHDL entity. It cannot invoke any other construct in the VHDL module, such as a procedure or function.

9.5 SUMMARY

This chapter discussed mixed-language descriptions-HDL code that includes constructs from both VHDL and Verilog. To be able to write in mixed-language style, the simulator should be able to handle mixed-language description. Presently, mixed-language description has some limitations. The main limitation is that in the VHDL module, only the entire Verilog module can be invoked; conversely, in the Verilog module, only the entire VHDL entity can be invoked. We have seen how to invoke/instantiate a VHDL entity from a Verilog module and how to invoke/instantiate a Verilog module from a VHDL component. To invoke a VHDL entity from a Verilog module, module statement is written in Verilog. The name of the module should be identical to the name of the entity, and the parameter types of the module should match the types of the ports of the entity. For example, the module statement:

```
HA H1 (y, cin, s0, c0);
```

written in a Verilog module invokes a VHDL entity named HA. In the Verilog module, no other module should have the name HA. On the other hand, invoking a Verilog module from VHDL is done by declaring a component in the VHDL module with the same name as the Verilog module. The component ports should have the same names and types as the ports of the Verilog module. For example, the VHDL component:

```
component V_modl
    port (x, y : in std_logic; z : out std_logic);
end component;
```

invokes a Verilog module named V_modl.

9.6 EXERCISES

9.1 Consider the code shown in Listing 9.15.

LISTING 9.15 Code for Exercise 9.1

```
module mixed (a, b, c, d);
input a, b;
output c, d;
lgic L1 (c, d, a, b)
endmodule
```

```
entity lgic is
    port (x, y : in std_logic; O1, O2 : buffer std_logic);
end lgic;

architecture lgic of lgic is
begin
O1 <= x and y;
O2 <= not x;
end lgic;
```

Without using a computer, find any error(s) in Listing 9.1. Correct the errors (if any), and write the values of `c` and `d` if `a` = 1 and `b` = 0. Verify your answer by simulating the program.

9.2 In Listing 9.4, set the gate delay to 8 ns. Simulate the adder with the new gate delay and measure the total delay. Analytically justify the delay that you measured.

9.3 In Listing 9.7, we wrote the Verilog module as behavioral description. Repeat Example 9.5, but use Verilog gate-level description instead of behavioral description. Verify your description by simulation.

9.4 In Listing 9.13, HDL code was written to instantiate the Verilog command `casex` in a VHDL module. Repeat the same steps to instantiate `casez` in a VHDL module. The truth table for `casez` is as shown in Table 9.3.

TABLE 9.3 Truth Table for `Casez`

Input a	**Output** b
zzz1	1
zz10	2
z100	4
1000	8
Others	0

9.5 In Example 9.12, we simulated a low-pass RC filter. Repeat the same steps for a high-pass RC filter.

9.7 REFERENCES

[Dorf04] Dorf, Svoboda, *Introduction to Electric Circuits*, 6th ed. John Wiley & Sons, Inc., New York, 2004.

[Hayes98] Hayes, J. P., *Computer Architecture and Organization*, 3rd ed. McGraw Hill, 1998.

[Mano00] Mano, M. M. and C. R. Kime, *Logic and Computer Design Fundamentals*, Prentice Hall, 2000.

[Nelson95] Nelson, V.P., H. T. Nagle, B. D. Carroll, and J. D. Irwin, *Digital Logic Circuit Analysis & Design*. Prentice Hall, 1995.

[Reed99] Reed, M. and R. Rohrer, *Applied Introductory Circuit Analysis for Electrical and Computer Engineers*. Prentice Hall, 1999.

10 Synthesis Basics

In This Chapter

- Understand the concept of synthesis.
- Learn how to map behavioral statements into logical gates and components.
- Learn how to verify your synthesis.
- Review and understand the fundamentals of digital-logic design for digital systems, such as adders, multiplexers, decoders, comparators, encoders, latches, flip-flops, counters, and memory cells.
- Understand the concept of sequential finite-state machines.

10.1 HIGHLIGHTS OF SYNTHESIS

This chapter will discuss the fundamentals of synthesis. Synthesis converts HDL behavioral code into logical gates or components. These logical gates and components can be downloaded into an electronic chip.

Facts

- Synthesis maps between the simulation (software) domain and the hardware domain.
- In this chapter, synthesis can be viewed as reverse engineering. The user is provided with the behavioral code and is asked to develop the logic diagram.
- Not all HDL statements can be mapped into the hardware domain. The hardware domain is limited to signals that can take zeros, ones, or that are left open. The hardware domain cannot differentiate, for example, between signals and variables, as does the simulation (software) domain.
- To successfully synthesize behavior code into a certain electronic chip, the mapping has to conform to the requirements and constrains imposed by the electronic chip vendor.

- Several synthesis packages are available on the market. These packages can take behavior code, map it, and produce a net list that is downloaded into the chip. In this chapter, we focus on learning how to synthesize the code manually, rather than on how to use the synthesizers.
- Two synthesizers may synthesize the same code using a different number of the same gates. This is due to the different approaches taken by the two synthesizers to map the code. Consider for example the VHDL statement y := 2x. One synthesizer might approach this statement as a shift to the left of x; another might approach it as a multiplication, and might use a multiplier, which usually results in more gates than the mere shift.
- General synthesis steps can be summarized (see Figure 10.1), as follows:

  Step 1: If the behavioral description of the system is available go to Step 3; otherwise, formulate a flowchart for the behavior of the system.

  Step 2: Use the flowchart to write a behavioral description of the system. Be sure to review the instructions of your synthesis tools to see if there are constraints on any of the behavioral statements you plan to use.

  Step 3: Simulate the behavioral code and verify that the simulation correctly describes the system.

  Step 4: Map the behavioral statements into components or logic gates (this chapter shows you how to do that). Be sure that the components used are acceptable to your synthesizer. A synthesizer can do this mapping step for you; however, synthesis optimization depends on the quality of synthesizer being using.

  Step 5: Write a structural or gate-level description of the components and logic gates of Step 3. Simulate the structural description, and verify that this simulation is similar to that of Step 3.

  Step 6: Use CAD tools to download the gates and components of Step 4 into the electronic chip—usually an FPGA chip.

  Step 7: Test the chip by inputting signals to the input pins of the chip, and observe the output from the output pins. This step is similar to the verification done in Step 5, except here we perform the test on real, physical signals.

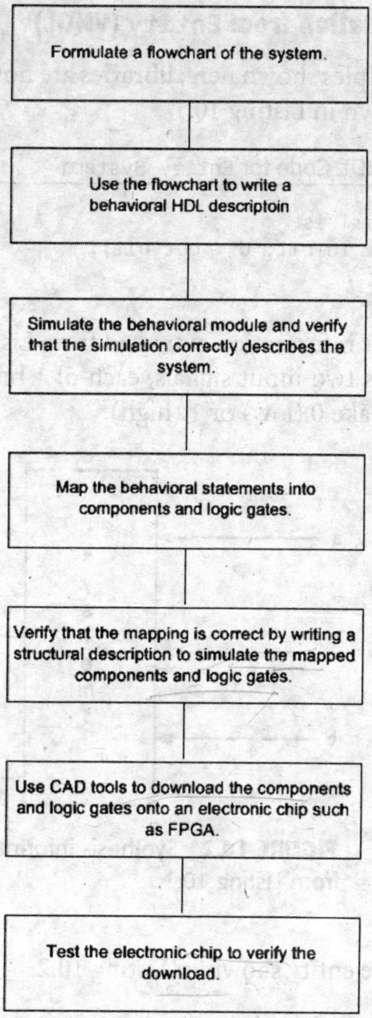

FIGURE 10.1 Synthesis steps.

10.2 SYNTHESIS INFORMATION FROM `Entity` AND `Module`

`Entity` (VHDL) or `Module` in (Verilog) provides information on the inputs and outputs, and their types. For all the following examples, unless otherwise explicitly stated, the digital hardware domain in which the HDL code is synthesized consists of binary signals; their values can be 0, 1, or tristate (open). The domain does not include analog or multilevel signals.

10.2.1 Synthesis Information from Entity (VHDL)

In all of the examples shown here; libraries are not shown in the code. Consider the VHDL code shown in Listing 10.1.

LISTING 10.1 VHDL Code for Entity System1

```
entity system1 is
port (a, b : in bit; d : out bit);
end system1;
```

The synthesis information extracted from Listing 10.1 is summarized in Figure 10.2; system1 has two input signals, each of 1 bit, and one output signal of 1 bit. Each signal can take 0 (low) or 1 (high).

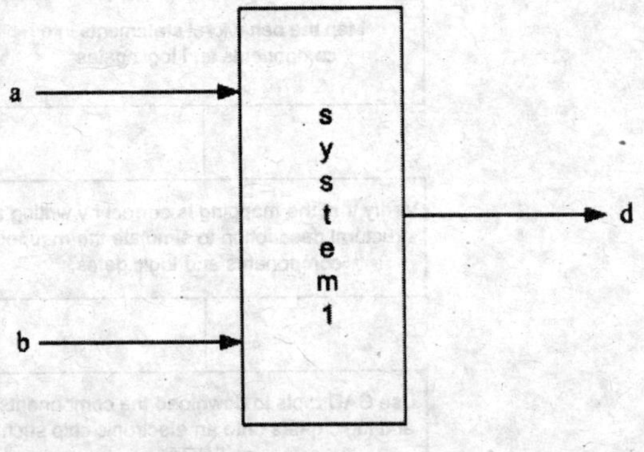

FIGURE 10.2 Synthesis information extracted from Listing 10.1.

Consider the entity shown in Listing 10.2.

LISTING 10.2 VHDL Code for Entity System2

```
entity system2 is
port (a, b : in std_logic; d : out std_logic);
end system2;
```

system2 also has two 1-bit input signals and one 1-bit output signal. However, because the type is std_logic, each signal can take 0 (low), 1 (high), or high impedance (open).

Consider the entity shown in Listing 10.3.

LISTING 10.3 VHDL Code for `Entity System3`

```
entity system3 is
port (a, b : in std_logic_vector (3 downto 0);
    d : out std_logic_vector (7 downto 0));
end entity system3;
```

`system3` has two 4-bit input signals and one 8-bit output signal. The input signals can be binary or left open. Figure 10.3 illustrates the information extracted from Listing 10.3.

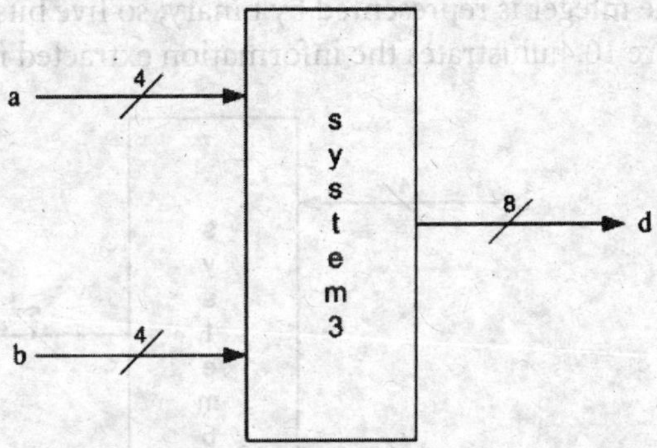

FIGURE 10.3 Synthesis information extracted from Listing 10.3.

Consider the entity shown in Listing 10.4.

LISTING 10.4 VHDL Code for `Entity System4`

```
entity system4 is
port (a, b : in signed (3 downto 0);
    d : out std_logic_vector (7 downto 0));
end entity system4;
```

`system4` has two 4-bit signals and one 8-bit signal. The input signal is binary; the output signal can be binary or high impedance.

Consider the entity shown in Listing 10.5.

LISTING 10.5 VHDL Code for `Entity System5`

```
entity system5 is
port (a, b : in unsigned (3 downto 0);
    d : out std_logic_vector (7 downto 0));
end entity system5;
```

Synthesis information extracted from Listing 10.5 is identical to that extracted from Listing 10.4. Now consider the entity shown in Listing 10.6.

LISTING 10.6 VHDL Code for `Entity System6`

```
entity system6 is
port (a, b : in unsigned (3 downto 0);
     d : out integer range -10 to 10);
end entity system6;
```

`system6` has two 4-bit input signals and one 5-bit output signal. In the hardware domain, the integer is represented by binary; so five bits is adequate for representing `d`. Figure 10.4 illustrates the information extracted from Listing 10.6.

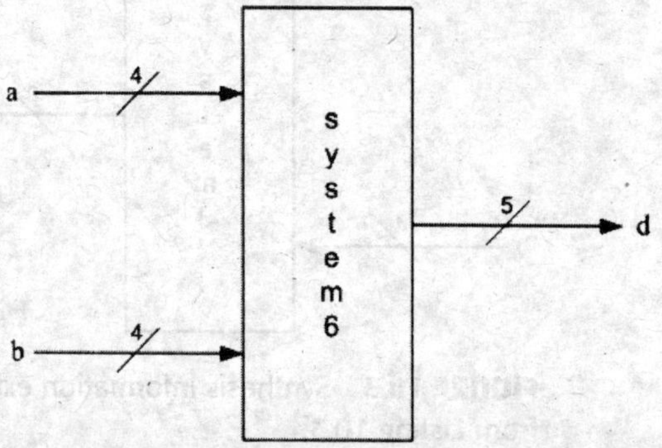

FIGURE 10.4 Synthesis information extracted from Listing 10.6.

Consider the entity in Listing 10.7.

LISTING 10.7 VHDL Code for `Entity System7`

```
entity system7 is
    generic (N : integer := 4; M : integer := 3);
        Port (a, b : in std_logic_vector (N downto 0);
            d : out std_logic_vector (M downto 0));
end system7;
```

Since `N` = 4 and `M` = 3, `system7` has two 5-bit input signals and one 4-bit output signal. All signals are in binary. `N` and `M` have no explicit hardware mapping. Figure 10.5 illustrates the synthesis information extracted from the code of Listing 10.7.

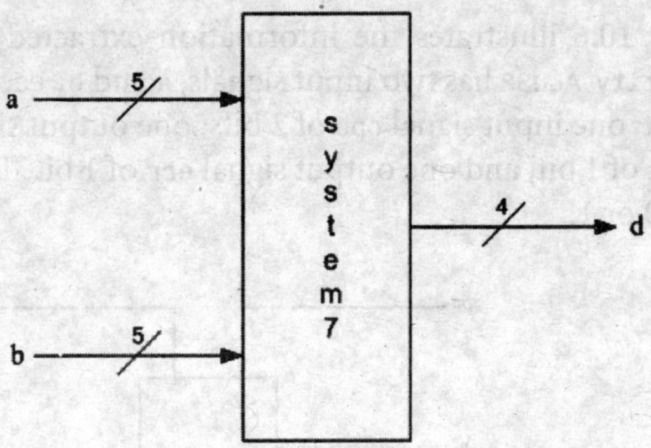

FIGURE 10.5 Synthesis information extracted from Listing 10.7.

Consider the entity in Listing 10.8.

LISTING 10.8 VHDL Code for `Entity ALUS2`

```
package codes is
type op is (add, mul, divide, none);
end;
use work.codes;

entity ALUS2 is
    port (a, b : in std_logic_vector (3 downto 0);
        cin : in std_logic; opc : in op;
        z : out std_logic_vector (7 downto 0);
        cout : out std_logic; err : out Boolean);
end ALUS2;
```

The package `codes` defines type `op`, and signal `opc` is of type `op`. In our digital hardware domain, we only have zeros and ones. Packages and Libraries have no explicit mapping into the hardware domain; they are simulation tools. To map the signal `opc` into the hardware domain, the signal is decoded. Since the signal can take one of four values (`add`, `mul`, `divide`, or `none`), we decode the signal using two bits. A possible decoding is as shown in Table 10.1. Any other 2-bit decoding can be used. For example, we may choose the binary for `add` to be 10 and 00 for `divide`.

TABLE 10.1 Decoding of Signal `opc`

Code	Binary Code
add	00
mul	01
divide	10
none	11

Figure 10.6 illustrates the information extracted from the Listing 10.8. As shown, `entity ALUS2` has two input signals, `a` and `b`, each of 4 bits; one input signal `cin` of 1 bit; one input signal `opc` of 2 bits; one output signal `z` of 8 bits; one output signal `cout` of 1 bit; and one output signal `err` of 1 bit. The Boolean type is mapped to binary 0 or 1.

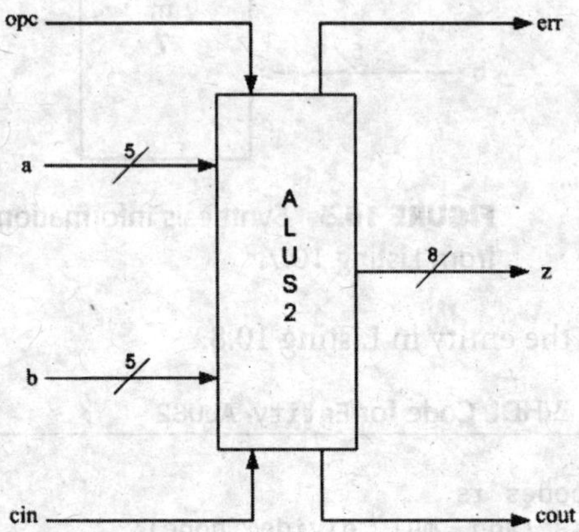

FIGURE 10.6 Synthesis information extracted from Listing 10.8.

Consider the entity and package shown in Listing 10.9.

LISTING 10.9 VHDL Code for `Entity Array1`

```
package array_pkg is
constant N : integer := 4;
constant M : integer := 3;
subtype wordN is std_logic_vector (M downto 0);
type strng is array (N downto 0) of wordN;
end array_pkg;

library IEEE;
use IEEE.STD_LOGIC_1164.ALL;
use IEEE.STD_LOGIC_ARITH.ALL;
use IEEE.STD_LOGIC_UNSIGNED.ALL;
use work.array_pkg.all;

entity array1 is
    generic (N : integer := 4; M : integer := 3);
        Port (a : in strng; z : out std_logic_vector (M downto 0));
end array1;
```

From the package, we observe that type `strng` is an array of five elements, and each element is 4 bits wide. So entity `array1` has five input signals, each of 4 bits; the output of `array1` is a 4-bit signal. Figure 10.7 illustrates the synthesis information extracted from the code of Listing 10.9.

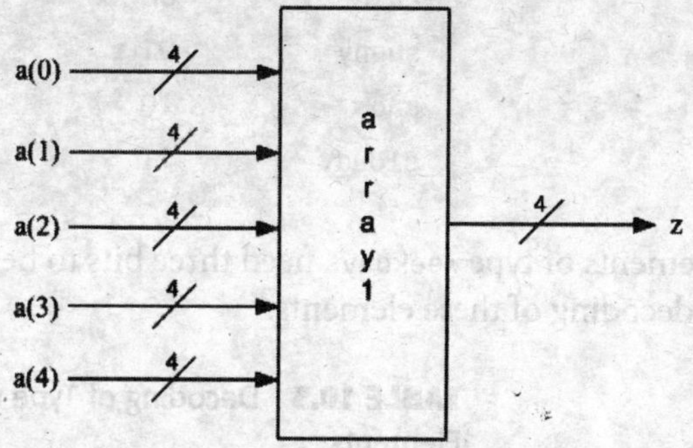

FIGURE 10.7 Synthesis information extracted from Listing 10.9.

Now consider the entity shown in Listing 10.10.

LISTING 10.10 VHDL Code for `Entity Weather_frcst`

```
package weather_fcst is
Type cast is (rain, sunny, snow, cloudy);
Type weekdays is (Monday, Tuesday, Wednesday,
    Thursday, Friday, Saturday, Sunday);
end package weather_fcst;

library ieee;
use ieee.std_logic_1164.all;
use std.textio.all;
use work.weather_fcst.all;

entity WEATHER_FRCST is
port (Day_in : in weekdays; out_temperature : out integer
    range -100 to 100; out_day : out weekdays;
    out_cond : out cast);

end WEATHER_FRCST;
```

Elements of type `cast` in package `weather_fcst` can be decoded by two bits, as shown in Table 10.2.

TABLE 10.2 Decoding Elements of Type `cast`

Code	Binary Code
`rain`	00
`sunny`	01
`snow`	10
`cloudy`	11

The elements of type `weekdays` need three bits to be decoded. Table 10.3 shows a possible decoding of these elements.

TABLE 10.3 Decoding of Type `weekdays` Elements

Code	Binary Code
`Monday`	000
`Tuesday`	001
`Wednesday`	010
`Thursday`	011
`Friday`	100
`Saturday`	101
`Sunday`	110

Accordingly, entity `WEATHER_FRCST` has one input signal, `Day_in`, which is 3 bits; an output signal `out_temperature` of 7 bits; an output signal `out_day` of 3 bits; and an output signal `out_cond` of 2 bits. Figure 10.8 illustrates the synthesis information extracted from the code of Listing 10.10.

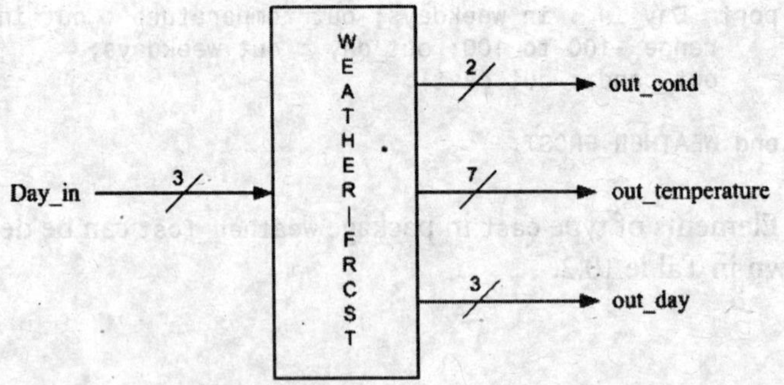

FIGURE 10.8 Synthesis information extracted from Listing 10.10.

Consider the code shown in Listing 10.11

LISTING 10.11 VHDL Code for `Entity Procs_Mchn`

```
library ieee;
use ieee.std_logic_1164.all;
package state_machine is
Type machine is (state0, state1, state2, state3);
Type st_machine is
record
state : machine;
weight : natural range 3 to 16;
Measr : std_logic_vector (5 downto 0);
end record;
end package state_machine;

library ieee;
use ieee.std_logic_1164.all;
use std.textio.all;
use work.state_machine.all;

entity Procs_Mchn is
port (S : in machine; Y : in st_machine;
    Z : out integer range -5 to 5);
end Procs_Mchn;
```

The entity `Procs_Mchn` has two inputs, `S` and `Y`, and one output, `Z`. Input `S` is of type `machine;` this type has four elements, so input `S` is mapped to two bits. Input `Y` is of type `st_machine`; this type is `record` (collection of different types). The `record` includes type `state`, which is mapped to a 2-bit signal; type `weight`, which is mapped to a 5-bit signal; and type `Measr`, which is mapped to a 6-bit signal. So signal `Y` is mapped to 6 bits (the largest out of 2, 5, and 6). Output `Z` is mapped to a 4-bit signal. Figure 10.9 shows the synthesis information extracted from the code of Listing 10.11.

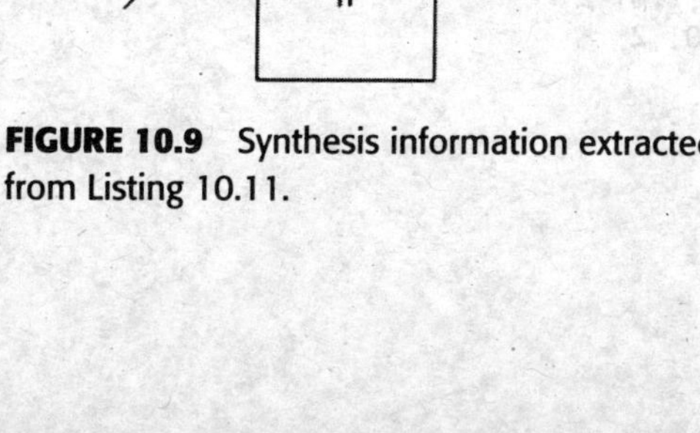

FIGURE 10.9 Synthesis information extracted from Listing 10.11.

10.2.2 Verilog Synthesis Information from Module Inputs/Outputs

Verilog, in contrast to VHDL, does not have a large variety of types. In the following, we discuss synthesis information that can be extracted from the inputs and outputs of a module. Consider the code shown in Listing 10.12.

LISTING 10.12 Verilog Code for Module System1v

```
module system1v (a, b, d);
input a, b;
output d;

endmodule
```

From Listing 10.12 we conclude that `system1v` has two input signals, `a` and `b`, each of 1 bit, and one output signal `d` of 1 bit. All signals can take 0, 1, or high impedance. Figure 10.10 shows the synthesis information extracted from Listing 10.12.

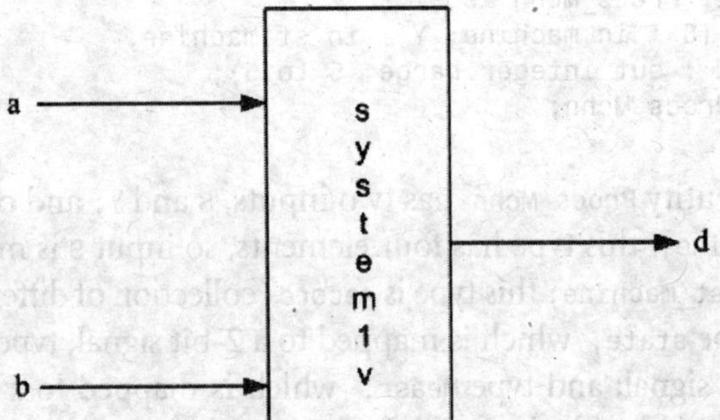

FIGURE 10.10 Synthesis information extracted from Listing 10.12

Consider the Verilog code shown in Listing 10.13.

LISTING 10.13 Verilog Code for Module System2v

```
module system2v (X, Y, Z);
input [3:0] X, Y;
output [7:0] Z;
reg [7:0] Z
........
endmodule
```

Listing 10.13 describes `system2v` with two input signals, `X` and `Y`, each of 4 bits, and one output signal `Z` of 8 bits. The statement `reg [7:0] Z;` does not convey any additional information to the hardware domain; its use is solely for simulation. Figure 10.11 illustrates the information extracted from Listing 10.13.

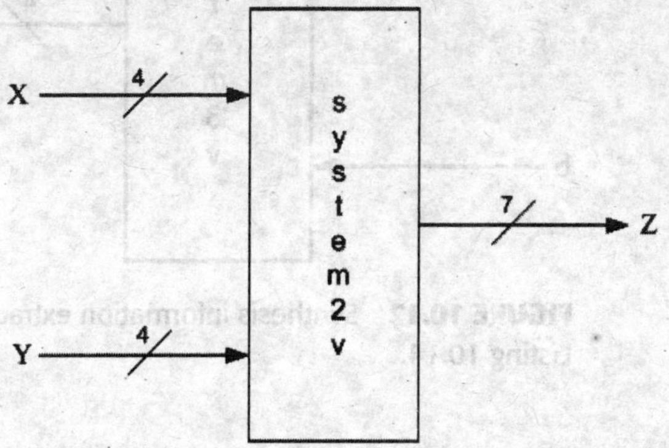

FIGURE 10.11 Synthesis information extracted from Listing 10.13.

Consider the code shown in Listing 10.14.

LISTING 10.14 Verilog Code for `Module System3v`

```
module system3v (a, b, c);
parameter N = 4;
parameter M = 3;
input [N:0] a;
output [M:0] c;
input b;
.........
endmodule
```

`Module system3v` has two input signals, `a` and `b`, and one output signal `c`. Input `a` is a 5-bit signal, input `b` is 1-bit, and output `c` is a 4-bit signal. `Parameter` has no explicit mapping in the hardware domain; it is just a simulation tool to instantiate `N` and `M`. Figure 10.12 illustrates the synthesis information extracted from Listing 10.14.

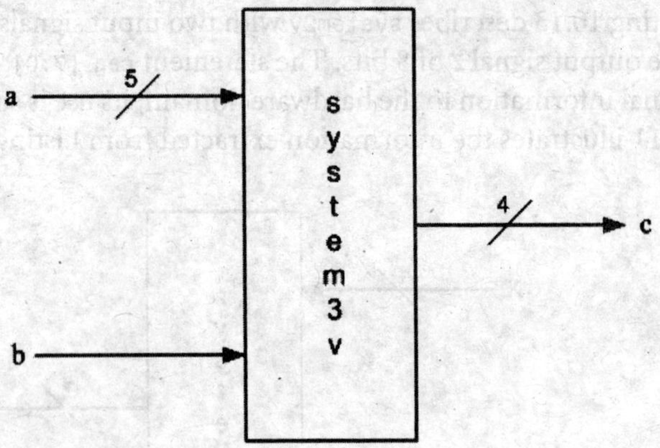

FIGURE 10.12 Synthesis information extracted from Listing 10.14.

Consider the code shown in Listing 10.15.

LISTING 10.15 Verilog Code for Module Array1v

```
module array1v (start, grtst);
parameter N = 4;
parameter M = 3;
input start;
output [3:0] grtst;
reg[M:0] a[0:N];

..............

endmodule
```

Module array1v has one 1-bit input signal (start) and one 4-bit output signal (grtst). The register a is an array of five elements, each of 4 bits. This register is mapped to five signals, each of 4 bits. Figure 10.13 illustrates the synthesis information extracted from Listing 10.15.

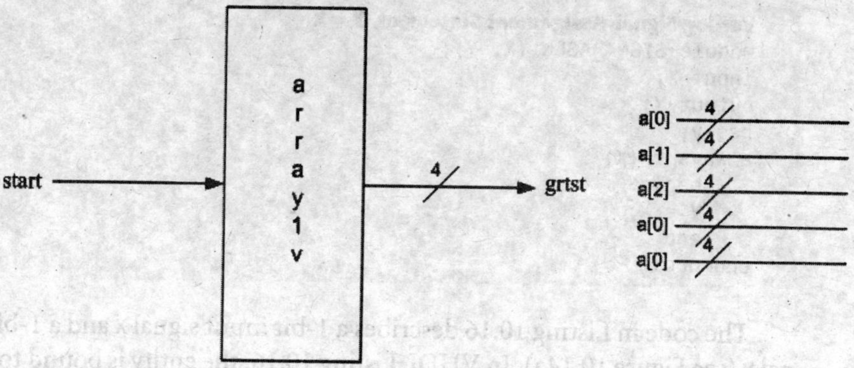

FIGURE 10.13 Synthesis information extracted from Listing 10.15.

10.3 MAPPING Process AND Always IN THE HARDWARE DOMAIN

`Process` (VHDL) and `always` (Verilog) are the major behavioral statements. These statements are frequently used to model systems with data storage, such as counters, registers, and CPUs. The first line in both statements declares, among other factors, the sensitivity list. This list determines the signals that activate `process` or `always`. The examples that follow deal with mapping behavioral code to gate or register level.

10.3.1 Mapping the Signal-Assignment Statement to Gate-Level

Consider the entity (module) shown in Listing 10.16.

LISTING 10.16 VHDL Code for a Signal-Assignment Statement, Y = X—VHDL and Verilog

VHDL Signal-Assignment Statement, Y = X

```
library ieee;
use ieee.std_logic_1164.all;

entity SIGNA_ASSN is
port (X : in bit; Y : out bit);
end SIGNA_ASSN;

architecture BEHAVIOR of SIGNA_ASSN is
begin

   P1 : process (X)
   begin
       Y <= X;
   end process P1;

end BEHAVIOR;
```

```
Verilog Signal-Assignment Statement, Y = X
module SIGNA_ASSN (X, Y);
input X;
output Y;
reg y;
always @ (X)
    begin
    Y = X;
    end
endmodule
```

The code in Listing 10.16 describes a 1-bit input signal `X` and a 1-bit output signal `Y` (see Figure 10.14a). In VHDL Listing 10.16, the entity is bound to architecture `BEHAVIOR`. The `process (always)` has `X` as the sensitivity list. The signal-assignment statement states that `Y = X`. In the hardware domain, this statement is mapped to a buffer. Other statements such as `begin`, `end`, and `architecture` have no hardware mapping. Figure 10.14b shows this mapping; if `X` changes, `Y` is updated. This mimics the process activation in Listing 10.16 when an event occurs on `X`.

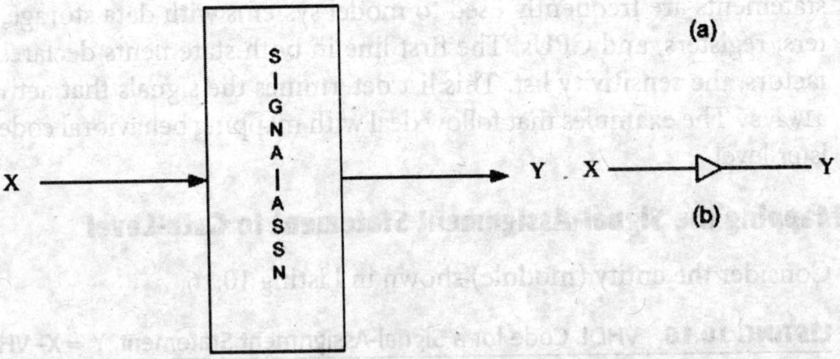

FIGURE 10.14 Gate-level synthesis of Listing 10.16. (a) Logic symbol. (b) Gate-level logic diagram.

Consider the entity (module) shown in Listing 10.17.

LISTING 10.17 VHDL Code for a Signal-Assignment Statement, Y = 2 * X + 3—VHDL and Verilog

```
VHDL Signal-Assignment Statement, Y = 2 * X + 3
library ieee;
use ieee.std_logic_1164.all;
use ieee.numeric_std.all;

entity sign_assn2 is
    port (X : in unsigned (1 downto 0);
```

```
        Y : out unsigned (3 downto 0));
end ASSN2;
architecture BEHAVIOR of sign_assn2 is
begin

P1 : process (X)
    begin
        Y <= 2 * X + 3;
    end process P1;

end BEHAVIOR;
```

Verilog Signal-Assignment Statement, Y = 2 * X + 3

```
module sign_assn2 (X, Y);
input [1:0] X;
output [3:0] Y;
reg [3:0] Y;
always @ (X)

    begin
        Y = 2 * X + 3;
    end
endmodule
```

Listing 10.17 shows an entity (`sign_assn2`) with one input `x` of 2 bits and one output `Y` of 4 bits (see Figure 10.15a). The architecture that is bound to the entity, and the Verilog module includes one process (`P1`) and one `always`, respectively. The `process` (`always`) contains one signal-assignment statement: `Y <= 2 * X + 3;` (VHDL); `Y = 2 * X + 3` (Verilog). To synthesize the code, we construct a truth table to find the logic diagram of `sign_assn2` and use gate-level synthesis. Table 10.4 shows the truth table of `sign_assn2`.

TABLE 10.4 Truth Table for Listing 10.17

Input X		Output Y			
X1	X0	Y3	Y2	Y1	Y0
0	0	0	0	1	1
0	1	0	1	0	1
1	0	0	1	1	1
1	1	1	0	0	1

From Table 10.4, we find:

$$Y(0) = 1$$

$$Y(1) = \overline{X(0)}$$

$$Y(2) = \overline{X(1)}\,X(0) + X(1)\,\overline{X(0)}$$

$$Y(3) = X(1)\,X(0)$$

Figure 10.15b shows the gate-level logic diagram of Listing 10.17.

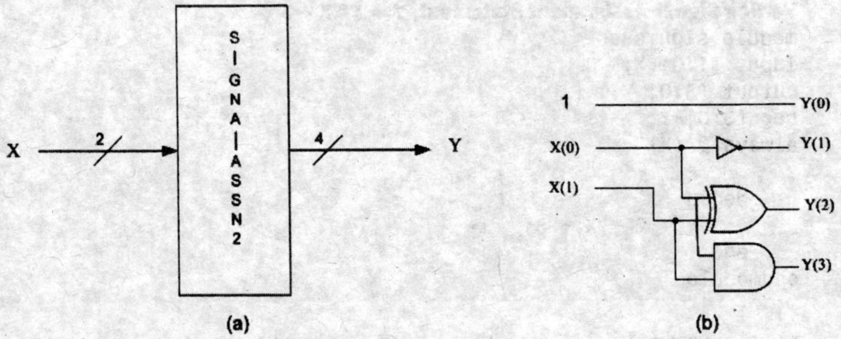

FIGURE 10.15 Gate-level synthesis of Listing 10.17. (a) Logic symbol. (b) Gate-level logic diagram.

To verify our synthesis, we write the structural code for the logic diagram shown in Figure 10.15b and then simulate it. If the simulation waveform is the same as the simulation waveform of Listing 10.17, then the synthesis is correct. The simulation waveform for Listing 10.17 is shown in Figure 10.16. The Verilog structural code is shown in Listing 10.18.

LISTING 10.18 Structural Verilog Code for the Logic Diagram in Figure 10.15b.

```
module sign_struc(X, Y);
input [1:0] X;
output [3:0] Y;
reg [3:0] Y;
always @ (X)
    begin
        Y[0] = 1'b1;
        Y[1] = ~ X[0];
        Y[2] = X[0] ^ X[1];
        Y[3] = X[1] & X[0];
    end

endmodule
```

After simulating the code in Listing 10.18, we find the simulation is identical to Figure 10.16. We conclude that the synthesis is correct.

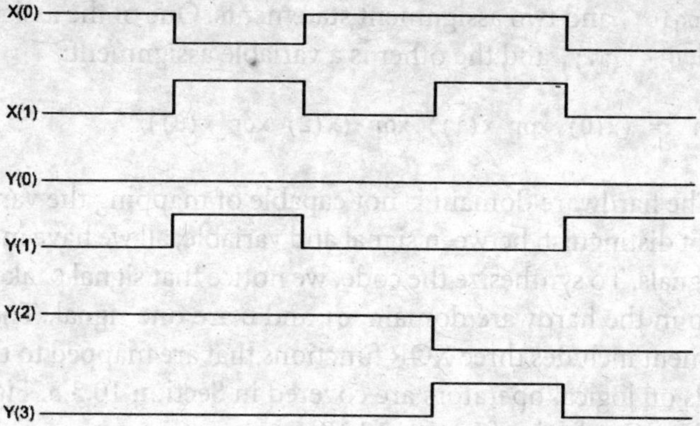

FIGURE 10.16 Simulation waveform for Listing 10.18.

10.3.2 Mapping the Variable-Assignment Statement to Gate-Level Synthesis

The variable-assignment statement is a VHDL statement. Verilog does not distinguish between signal- and variable-assignment statements. Consider the VHDL code shown in Listing 10.19.

LISTING 10.19 VHDL Variable-Assignment Statement

```
library ieee;
use ieee.std_logic_1164.all;

entity parity_even is
    port (x : in std_logic_vector (3 downto 0);
        C : out std_logic);
end parity_even;

architecture behav_prti of parity_even is
begin

P1 : process (x)
variable c1 : std_logic;
    begin
        c1 := (x(0) xor x(1)) xor (x(2) xor x(3));
        C <= c1;
    end process P1;
end behav_prti;
```

Listing 10.19 shows an entity with one 4-bit input and one 1-bit output (see Figure 10.17a). The architecture `behav_prti` is bound to the entity and consists of one process `(P1)`. The process contains one variable declaration, `variable c1 : std_logic;`, and two assignment statements. One of the assignment statements is a signal, `c <= c1;`, and the other is a variable assignment:

```
c1 := (x(0) xor x(1)) xor (x(2) xor x(3));
```

The hardware domain is not capable of mapping the variable declaration, and cannot distinguish between signal and variable; all we have in the hardware domain are signals. To synthesize the code, we notice that signal `c` takes the value of variable `c1`; so in the hardware domain, `c1` and `c` are one signal. The variable-assignment statement includes three XOR functions that are mapped to three XOR gates. More details on logical operators are covered in Section 10.3.3. Figure 10.17b shows the gate-level synthesis of Listing 10.19.

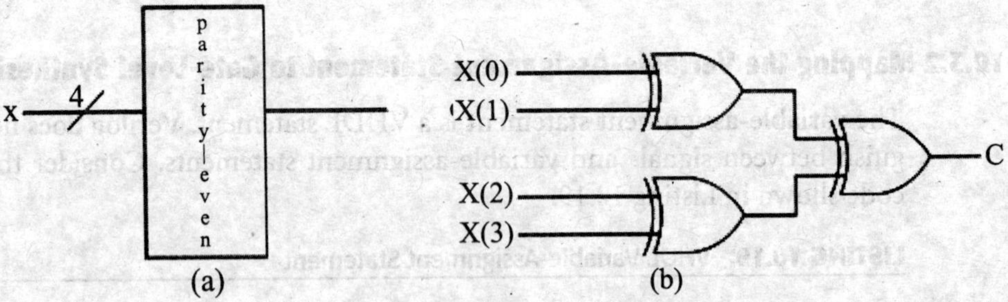

FIGURE 10.17 Gate-level synthesis of Listing 10.19. (a) Logic symbol. (b) Gate-level logic diagram.

10.3.3 Mapping Logical Operators

Mapping logical operators is relatively straightforward, because finding the gate counterpart of a logical operator is very easy. For example, the mapping of logical operator `and` (VHDL) or `&` (Verilog) is an AND gate. Table 10.5 shows the logical operators in VHDL and Verilog, and their gate-level mappings.

TABLE 10.5 Logical Operators and Their Gate-Level Mappings

Logical Operator		
VHDL	**Verilog**	**Gate-Level Mapping**
and	&	AND
or	|	OR
not	~	INVERTER
xor	^	XOR
xnor	^~	XNOR

To illustrate the mapping of logical operators, consider the code in Listing 10.20.

LISTING 10.20 Mapping Logical Operators—VHDL and Verilog

VHDL: Mapping Logical Operators

```
library IEEE;
use IEEE.STD_LOGIC_1164.ALL;

entity decod_var is
   port (a : in std_logic_vector (1 downto 0);
        D : out std_logic_vector (3 downto 0));
end decod_var;

architecture Behavioral of decod_var is

begin
dec : process (a)
variable a0bar, a1bar :   std_logic;
   begin
        a0bar := not a(0);
        a1bar := not a(1);
        D(0) <= not (a0bar and a1bar);
        D(1) <= not (a0bar and a(1));
        D(2) <= not (a(0) and a1bar);
        D(3) <= not (a(0) and a(1));
   end process dec;

end Behavioral;
```

Verilog: Mapping Logical Operators

```
module decod_var (a, D);
input [1:0] a;
output [3:0] D;
reg a0bar, a1bar;
reg [3:0] D;
always @ (a)
```

```
    begin
        a0bar = ~ a[0];
        a1bar = ~ a[1];
        D[0] = ~ (a0bar & a1bar);
        D[1] = ~ (a0bar & a[1]);
        D[2] = ~ (a[0] & a1bar);
        D[3] = ~ (a[0] & a[1]);
    end

endmodule
```

The statements:

```
a0bar := not a(0); -- VHDL
a0bar = ~ a[0];    // Verilog
```

represent an inverter. The input to the inverter is the least significant bit of the input `a`. The statements:

```
D[3] = ~ (a[0] & a[1]);            -- VHDL
D(3) <= not (a(0) and a(1)); // Verilog
```

represent a two-input NAND gate. The input is `a` and the output is the most significant bit of `D`.

Figure 10.18 shows the synthesis of the code in Listing 10.20.

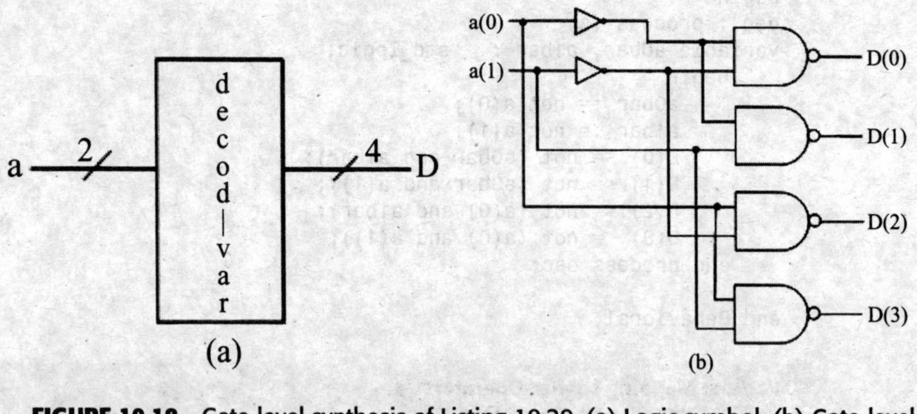

FIGURE 10.18 Gate-level synthesis of Listing 10.20. (a) Logic symbol. (b) Gate-level logic diagram.

10.3.4 Mapping the `If` Statement

Consider the HDL `if-else` statement shown in Listing 10.21.

LISTING 10.21 Example of `If-Else` Statement—VHDL and Verilog

VHDL `If-Else` Description

```
process (a, x)
begin
    if (a = '1') then
    Y <= X;
    else
    Y <= '0';
    end if;
end process;
```

Verilog `If-Else` Description

```
always @ (a, X)
begin
    if (a == 1'b1)
    Y = X;
    else
    Y = 1'b0;
end
```

The `if` statement in Listing 10.21 is synthesized by just an AND gate, as shown in Figure 10.19.

FIGURE 10.19 Gate-level synthesis of Listing 10.21.

Now consider the `if` statement shown in Listing 10.22.

LISTING 10.22 Example of Multiplexer `If-Else` Statement—VHDL and Verilog

VHDL Multiplexer `If-Else` Description

```
process (a, X, X1)
begin
    if (a = '1') then
    Y <= X;
    else
    Y <= X1;
    end if;
end process;
```

Verilog Multiplexer `If-Else` Description

```
always @ (a, X, X1)
begin
    if (a == 1'b1)
    Y = X;
    else
    Y = X1;
end
```

The `if` statement in Listing 10.22 represents a 2x1 multiplexer. Figure 10.20 shows the synthesis of Listing 10.22.

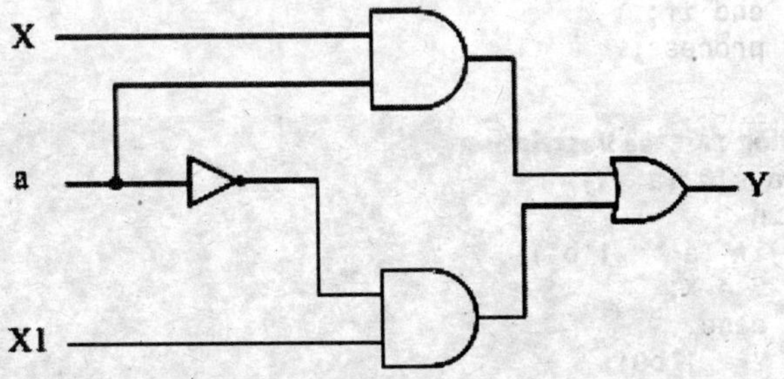

FIGURE 10.20 Gate-level synthesis of Listing 10.22.

Consider the `if` statement shown in Listing 10.23.

LISTING 10.23 Example of Comparison Using `If-Else` Statement—VHDL and Verilog

VHDL `If-Else` Statement

```
library IEEE;
use IEEE.STD_LOGIC_1164.ALL;

entity IF_st is
    port (a : in std_logic_vector (2 downto 0); Y : out Boolean);
end IF_st;

architecture IF_st of IF_st is
begin

IfB : process (a)
variable tem : Boolean;
begin
    if (a < "101") then
    tem := true;
    else
    tem := false;
    end if;
Y <= tem;
```

```
end process;
end IF_st;
```

Verilog If-Else Statement

```
module IF_st (a, Y);
input [2:0] a;
output Y;
reg Y;
always @ (a)
begin
if (a < 3'b101)
Y = 1'b1;
else
Y = 1'b0;
end
endmodule
```

To find the gate-level mapping of Listing 10.23, we construct a truth table (see Table 10.6).

TABLE 10.6 Truth Table for Listing 10.23

Input a			Output Y
a_2	a_1	a_0	Y
0	0	0	1
0	0	1	1
0	1	0	1
0	1	1	1
1	0	0	1
1	0	1	0
1	1	0	0
1	1	1	0

Figure 10.21 shows the K-map of Listing 10.23. From the figure, we find the Boolean function of Y:

$$Y = \overline{a(2)} + \overline{a(1)}\ \overline{a(0)}$$

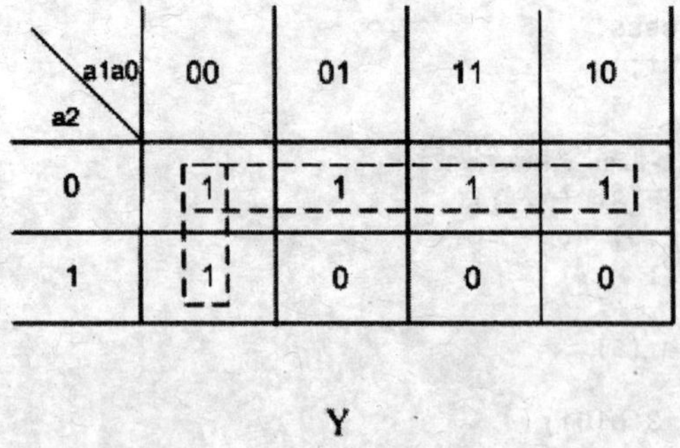

FIGURE 10.21 K-map for Listing 10.23.

From the Boolean function, we draw the gate-level synthesis for Listing 10.23, as shown in Figure 10.22.

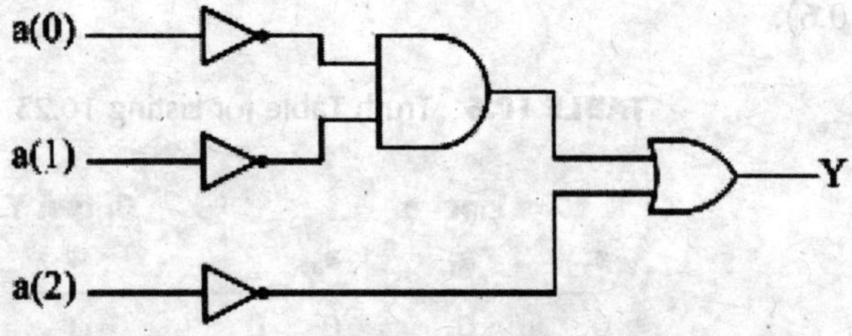

FIGURE 10.22 Gate-level synthesis of Listing 10.23.

Now consider the `elsif` (VHDL) and `else if` (Verilog) statements in Listing 10.24.

LISTING 10.24 Example of `Elseif` and `Else-If`—VHDL and Verilog

VHDL `Elseif` Description

```
library IEEE;
use IEEE.STD_LOGIC_1164.ALL;
use IEEE.STD_LOGIC_ARITH.ALL;

entity elseif is
port (BP : in natural range 0 to 7;
    ADH : out natural range 0 to 15);
    end;

architecture elseif of elseif is
    begin

    ADHP : process(BP)
        variable resADH : natural := 0;
```

```
        begin

            if BP <= 2 then resADH := 15;
            elsif BP >= 5 then resADH := 0;
            else
            resADH := BP * (-5) + 25;
            end if;

    ADH <= resADH;
    end process ADHP;
    end elseif;
```

Verilog `Else-If` Description

```
module elseif (BP, ADH);
input [2:0] BP;
output [3:0] ADH;
reg [3:0] ADH;
always @ (BP)
begin

    if (BP <= 2) ADH = 15;
        else if (BP >= 5) ADH = 0;
        else
        ADH = BP * (-5) + 25;
    end


endmodule
```

Notice that the variable `resADH` in Listing 10.24 (VHDL) is identical in value to the output `ADH`. Accordingly, `resADH` is not mapped into the hardware domain. To synthesize the code, we construct a truth table (see Table 10.7).

TABLE 10.7 Truth Table for Listing 10.24

BP 21 0	ADH 321 0
000	1111
001	1111
010	1111
011	1010
100	0101
101	0000
110	0000
111	0000

From Table 10.7, we construct K-maps to find ADH (see Figure 10.23).

Bp2 \ Bp1Bp0	00	01	11	10
0	1	1	0	1
1	1	0	0	0

ADH(0)

Bp2 \ Bp1Bp0	00	01	11	10
0	1	1	1	1
1	0	0	0	0

ADH(1)

FIGURE 10.23 K-maps of Table 10.7.

From the K-maps, we find:

$$ADH(0) = ADH(2) = \overline{Bp(1)}\,\overline{Bp(0)} + \overline{Bp(2)}\,\overline{Bp(1)} + \overline{Bp(2)}\,\overline{Bp(0)}.$$

$$ADH(1) = ADH(3) = \overline{Bp(2)}$$

Figure 10.24 shows the gate-level synthesis of Listing 10.24.

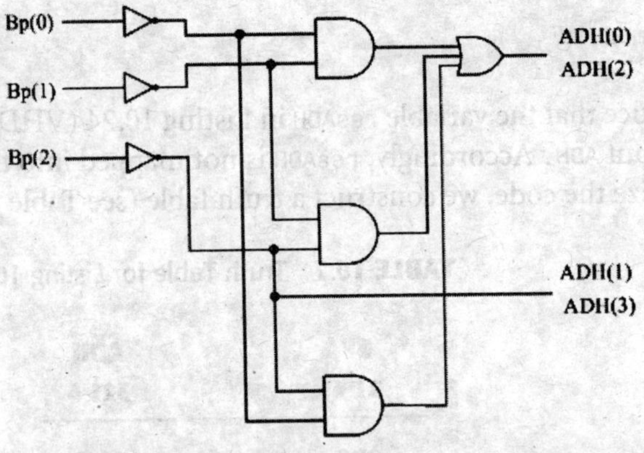

FIGURE 10.24 Gate-level synthesis of Listing 10.24.

Now consider the code in Listing 10.25.

LISTING 10.25 Example of `If` Statement with Storage—VHDL and Verilog

VHDL If Statement with Storage

```
library IEEE;
use IEEE.STD_LOGIC_1164.ALL;
```

```
entity If_store is
port (a, X : in std_logic; Y : out std_logic);
end If_store;

architecture If_store of If_store is

begin
    process (a, X)
    begin
        if (a = '1') then
        Y <= X;

        end if;
    end process;

end If_store;
```

Verilog `If` Statement with Storage

```
module If_store (a, X, Y);
input a, X;
output Y;
reg Y;
always @ (a, X)
    begin
        if (a == 1'b1)
        Y = X;

    end
endmodule
```

The `if` statement in Listing 10.25 is similar to that of Listing 10.22, except when a = 0. In Listing 10.22, the value of the output Y is explicitly stated when a = 0. In Listing 10.25, the code states that when a = 0, there should be no change in the values of any signals. This means that the value of all signals should be stored during the execution of the `if` statement. To store signals in the hardware domain we use latches or flip-flops. In Listing 10.25, we use signal a as a clock to a D-latch; the input to the latch is the signal X. If a = 0, then the output of the latch stays the same. If a = 1, then the output follows the input X. Figure 10.25 shows the mapping of Listing 10.25 to the hardware domain.

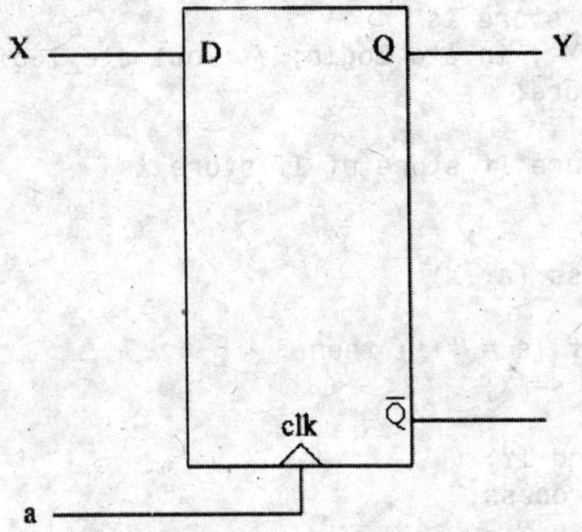

FIGURE 10.25 Synthesis of Listing 10.25.

Consider the code in Listing 10.26.

LISTING 10.26 `Else-If` Statement with Gate-Level Logic

```
package weather_fcst is
Type unit is (cent, half, offset);

end package weather_fcst;

library ieee;
use ieee.std_logic_1164.all;

use work.weather_fcst.all;
entity weather is
    port (a : in unit; tempr : in integer range 0 to 15;
        z : out integer range 0 to 15);
end weather;

architecture weather of weather is

begin

T : process (a, tempr)
variable z_tem : integer range 0 to 15;
    begin

        if ((tempr <= 7) and (a = cent)) then
        z_tem := tempr;

        elsif ((tempr <= 7) and (a = offset)) then
        z_tem := tempr + 4;

        elsif ((tempr <= 7) and (a = half)) then
        z_tem := tempr /2;
```

```
        else
        z_tem := 15;

        end if;

        z <= z_tem;
    end process T;

end weather;
```

From the entity (module), we can summarize the extracted information as follows:

- Input `a` is a 2-bit signal.
- Input `tempr` is a 4-bit signal.
- Output z is a 4-bit signal.

The code can be summarized as shown in Table 10.8.

TABLE 10.8 Summary of the Code in Listing 10.25

a	tempr	z
00 (cent)	0–7	z = tempr
01 (offset)	0–7	z = tempr + 4
10 (half)	0–7	z = tempr / 2
11	XX	z = 15
XX	>7	z = 15

If we want to construct a truth table, it will be 2 + 4 = 6-bit input and 4-bit output; this table will be huge and cannot be analyzed easily. Accordingly, the code in Listing 10.26 is analyzed logically. Input `a` can be the select lines of a multiplexer. The multiplexer has four inputs; each input is a 4-bit signal representing one of the four values `tempr`, `tempr+4`, `tempr/2`, and the constant 15. Figure 10.26 shows this analysis using Register Transfer Level (RTL) logic.

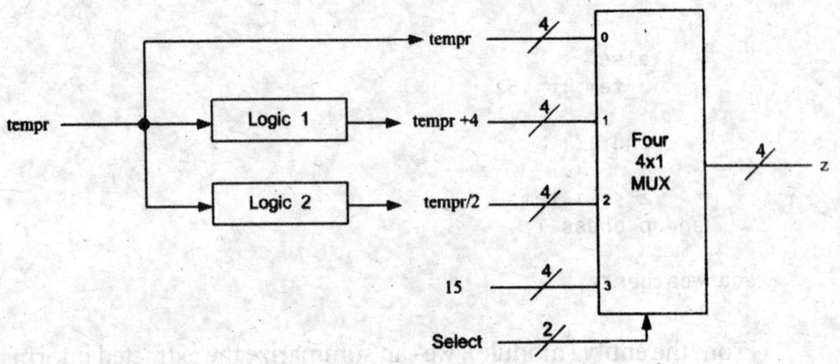

FIGURE 10.26 RTL synthesis of Listing 10.26.

To find the gate-level synthesis of Logic 1 in Figure 10.26, we construct a truth table as shown in Table 10.9.

TABLE 10.9 Truth Table for Logic 1

Tempr 3210	Tempr+4 3210
0000	0100
0001	0101
0010	0110
0011	0111
0100	1000
0101	1001
0110	1010
0111	1011
1000–1111	dddd

Inspecting Table 10.8, we can write tempr = 4 as follows:

$$\text{tempr+4}(0) = \text{tempr}(0)$$

$$\text{tempr+4}(1) = \text{tempr}(1)$$

$$\text{tempr+4}(2) = \overline{\text{tempr}(2)}$$

$$tempr+4(3) = tempr(2)$$

For logic 2, we do the same as for logic 1. Table 10.10 shows the truth table of logic 2.

TABLE 10.10 Truth Table for Logic 2

Tempr 3210	**Tempr/2** 3210
0000	0000
0001	0000
0010	0001
0011	0001
0100	0010
0101	0010
0110	0011
0111	0011
1000-1111	dddd

After inspecting Table 10.10, we can write:

$$tempr/2(0) = tempr(1)$$

$$tempr/2(1) = tempr(2)$$

$$tempr/2(2) = 0$$

$$tempr/2(3) = 0$$

For the Select in Figure 10.26, to satisfy the condition temp ≤ 7, tempr(3) must be equal to 0. Accommodating the values of a, we construct a truth table as shown in Table 10.11.

TABLE 10.11 Truth Table for Figure 10.26 Select

Tempr(3)	a(1)	a(0)	Select 10
0	0	0	00
0	0	1	01
0	1	0	10
0	1	1	11
1	0	0	11
1	0	1	11
1	1	0	11
1	1	1	11

Figure 10.27 shows the K-maps of Table 10.11. From the K-maps we write:

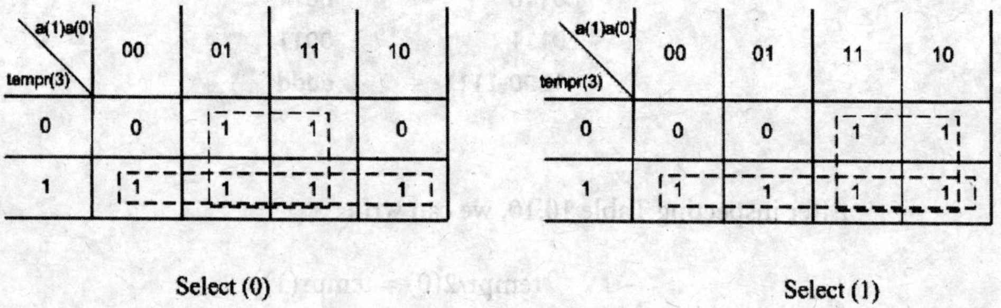

FIGURE 10.27 K-maps for Table 10.11.

$$Select(0) = temp(3) + a(0)$$

$$Select(1) = temp(3) + a(1)$$

Incorporating the gate-level logic of Logic 1, Logic 2, and Select in Figure 10.26, the synthesis diagram of Listing 10.26 is shown in Figure 10.28.

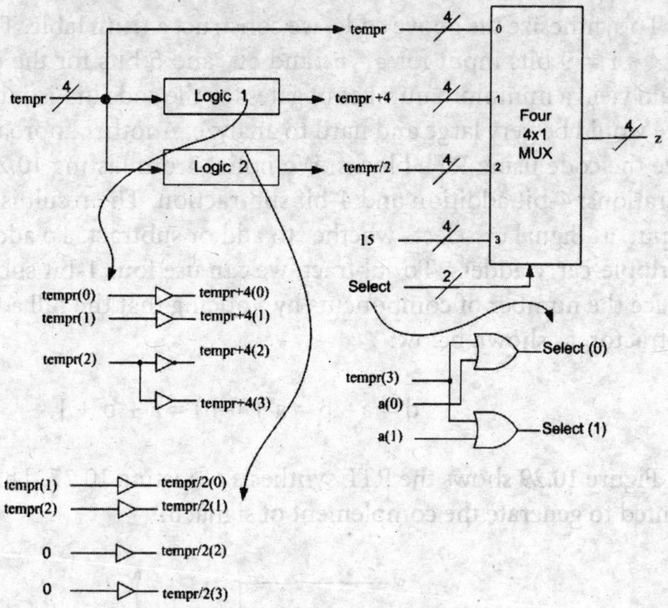

FIGURE 10.28 Synthesis of Listing 10.26.

10.3.5 Mapping the Case Statement

Mapping the `case` statement is very similar to mapping the `if` statement. We treat the `case` statement as a group of `if` statements. Consider the `case` statement in Listing 10.27.

LISTING 10.27 Example of Case Mapping

```
module case_nostr (a, b, ct, d);
input [3:0] a, b;
input ct;
output [4:0] d;
reg [4:0] d;
always @ (a, b, ct)
begin
case (ct)
1'b0 : d = a + b;

1'b1 : d = a - b;
endcase

end

endmodule
```

To synthesize the above code, we construct a truth table. This table would have 4 + 4 +1 = 9 bits input for `a`, `b`, and `ct`, and 5 bits for the output `d`. This table would yield a minimum number of gates for the code in Listing 10.27; however, the table would be very large and hard to analyze. Another approach is to logically analyze the code using RTL blocks. We notice from Listing 10.27 that there are two operations: 4-bit addition and 4-bit subtraction. The result is expressed in a 5-bit output, `d`. Signal `ct` selects whether to add or subtract. To add, we can use four 1-bit ripple-carry adders. To subtract, we can use four 1-bit subtractors, but we can reduce the number of components by noticing that the full adder can be used as a subtractor, as shown below:

$$d = a - b = a + (-b) = a + \bar{b} + 1$$

Figure 10.29 shows the RTL synthesis of Listing 10.27. The XOR gate is implemented to generate the complement of signal `b`.

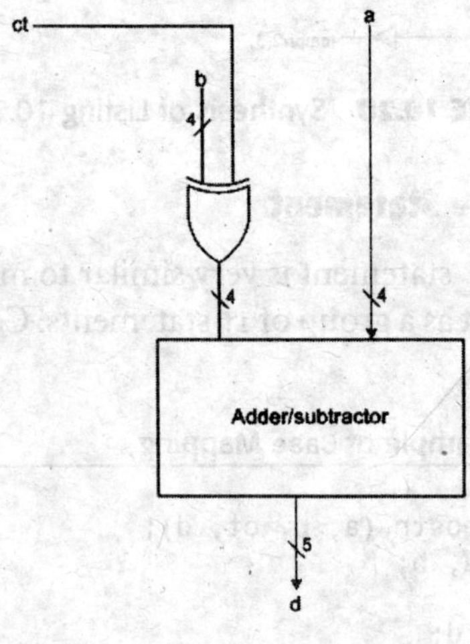

FIGURE 10.29 RTL synthesis of Listing 10.27.

Now, we slightly change the code of Listing 10.27 to that shown in Listing 10.28.

LISTING 10.28 Case Statement with Storage

```
module case_str (a, b, ct, d);
input [3:0] a, b;
input ct;
output [4:0] d;
reg [4:0] d;
always @ (a, b, ct)
```

```
begin
    case (ct)
        1'b0: d = a + b;

        1'b1: ; /*This is a blank statement with no operation
                  (null in VHDL)*/
    endcase
end

endmodule
```

The `case` in Listing 10.28 does not specify an action when `ct` = 1, so we have to use a latch to store the value of `d` when `ct` = 1. Figure 10.30 shows the RTL synthesis of Listing 10.28.

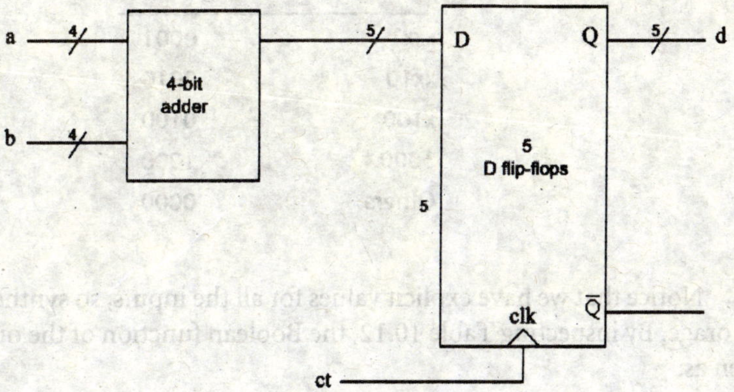

FIGURE 10.30 RTL synthesis of Listing 10.28.

As mentioned in Chapter 3, "Behavioral Descriptions," Verilog has a variation of the command `case`, `casex`. Listing 10.29 shows the Verilog code using `casex`.

LISTING 10.29 Verilog `Casex`

```
module Encoder_4 (IR, RA);
input [3:0] IR;
output [3:0] RA;

    reg [3:0] RA;
    always @ (IR)
        begin
            casex (IR)
                4'bxxx1 : RA = 4'd1;
                4'bxx10 : RA = 4'd2;
                4'bx100 : RA = 4'd4;
```

```
            4'b1000 : RA = 4'd8;
            default : RA = 4'd0;

        endcase
    end
endmodule
```

To synthesize the code in Listing 10.29, we build a truth table as shown in Table 10.12.

TABLE 10.12 Truth Table for the Code in Listing 10.29

Input IR	Output RA
xxx1	0001
xx10	0010
x100	0100
1000	1000
Others	0000

Notice that we have explicit values for all the inputs, so synthesis does not need storage. By inspecting Table 10.12, the Boolean function of the output can be written as:

$$RA(0) = IR(0)$$

$$RA(1) = \overline{IR(0)}\ IR(1)$$

$$RA(2) = \overline{IR(0)}\ \overline{IR(1)}\ IR(2)$$

$$RA(3) = \overline{IR(0)}\ \overline{IR(2)}\ \overline{IR(2)}\ IR(3)$$

Figure 10.31 shows the logic diagram of Listing 10.29.

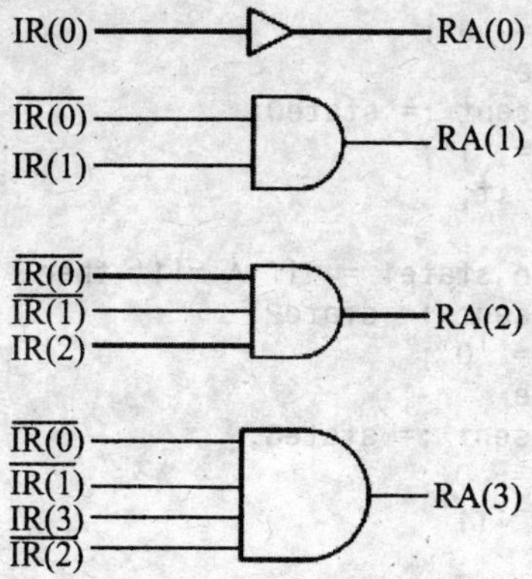

FIGURE 10.31 Logic diagram of Listing 10.29.

Now consider the code shown in Listing 10.30. This code is slightly different from that of Listing 7.9 (see Chapter 7, "Mixed-Type Descriptions").

LISTING 10.30 Example of Case with Storage

```
library IEEE;
use IEEE.STD_LOGIC_1164.all;
package types is
type states is (state0, state1, state2, state3);
end;

library IEEE;
use IEEE.STD_LOGIC_1164.ALL;

use work.types.all;
entity state_machine is
    port (A, clk : in std_logic; pres_st : buffer states;
        Z : out std_logic);
end state_machine;

architecture st_behavioral of state_machine is
begin

FM : process (clk, pres_st, A)
variable present : states := state0;
begin
if (clk = '1' and clk'event) then
--clock'event is an attribute to the signal clk; the above if Boolean
--expression means the positive edge of clk

    case pres_st is
        when state0 =>
        if A ='1' then
        present := state1;
```

```
        Z <= '0';
        else
        present := state0;
        Z <= '1';
        end if;

        when state1 => if A ='1' then
        present := state2;
        Z <= '0';
        else
        present := state3;
        Z <= '0';
        end if;

        when state2 => if A ='1' then
        present := state3;
        Z <= '1';
        else
        present := state0;
        Z <= '0';
        end if;

        when state3 => if A ='1' then
        present := state0;
        Z <= '1';
        else
        present := state2;
        Z <= '1';
        end if;
    end case;

pres_st <= present;
end if;
end process FM;
end st_behavioral;
```

In Listing 10.30, the package `types` declares user-select types `state0`, `state1`, `state2`, and `state3`. To decode these user-select types into the hardware domain we need 2 bits. So `state0` is decoded as 00, `state1` as 01, `state2` as 10, and `state3` as 11. The Libraries are software constructs that have no mapping into the hardware domain.

Now let us summarize the information collected from the entity. The name of the system or entity is `state-machine`. The system has a 1-bit input `A`, 1-bit input `clk`, 2-bit input/output states, and 1-bit output `Z`. Inspecting the architecture, we see it consists of `case` and `if` statements. Let us see if we need to use a storage element. Consider the `case` statement:

```
case pres_st is
    when state0 => if A ='1' then
```

```
present := state1;
Z <= '0';
else
present := state0;
Z <= '1';
end if;
```

In order to know which state to go to, we need to know the present state. For example, if the present is `state0`, then the next state can be `state1` or `state0`. The code implies that the current state must be recalled; so accordingly, we need storage elements to synthesize (recall) the code. The best approach here is to follow the same steps covered in Chapter 4, "Structural Description," for analyzing state machines. More details on state machines and related topics can be found in [Hayes98], [Katz05], [Mano00], and [Nelson95]. We write the excitation table of the machine and use D flip-flops. Table 10.13 shows the excitation table for Listing 10.30.

TABLE 10.13 Excitation Table for Listing 10.30

Present State Input			Next State		Output	D Flip-Flop	
Q1	Q0	A	Q1+	Q0+	Z	D1	D0
0	0	0	0	0	1	0	0
0	0	1	0	1	0	0	1
0	1	0	1	1	0	1	1
0	1	1	1	0	0	1	0
1	0	0	0	0	1	0	0
1	0	1	1	1	1	1	1
1	1	0	1	0	1	1	0
1	1	1	0	0	1	0	0

From Table 10.13, we construct K-maps to minimize the outputs. Figure 10.32 shows the K-maps.

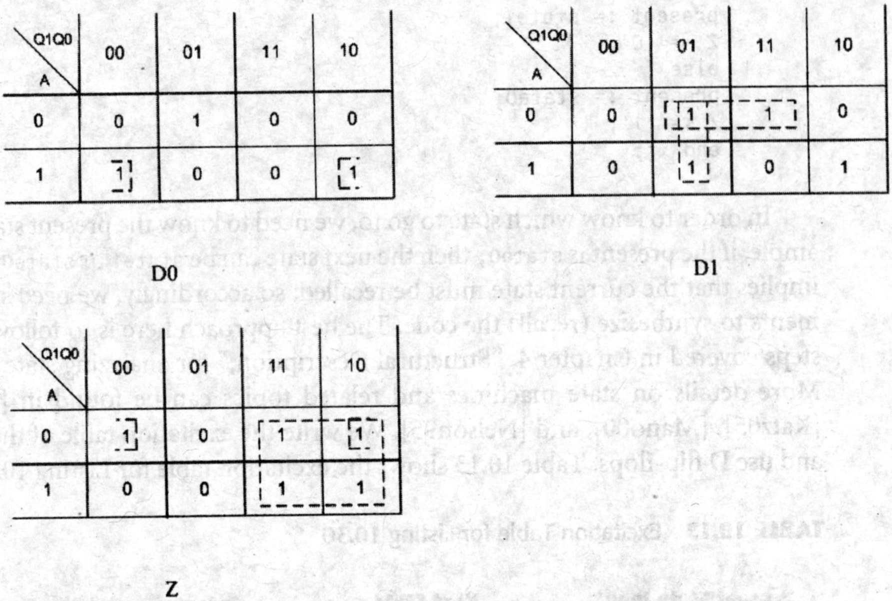

FIGURE 10.32 K-maps for Table 10.13.

From the K-maps, we find the Boolean function of the system as:

$$D0 = \overline{A}\,\overline{Q1}\,\overline{Q0} + A\overline{Q0}$$

$$D1 = Q0\,\overline{Q1} + \overline{A}Q0 + AQ1\overline{Q0}$$

$$Z = Q1 + \overline{A}\,\overline{Q0}$$

From the Boolean function, the logic diagram of the system is drawn. Figure 10.33 shows the logic diagram of Listing 10.30.

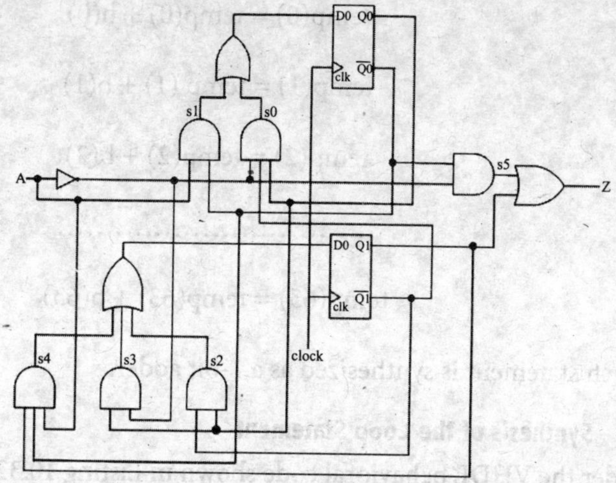

FIGURE 10.33 RTL logic diagram of Listing 10.30.

10.3.6 Mapping the Loop Statement

Loop in HDL description is an essential tool for behavioral modeling. It is, however, easier to code than it is to synthesize in the hardware domain. The problem is the repetition involved in the loop. For example, consider the VHDL `loop` statement shown in Listing 10.31.

LISTING 10.31 A For-Loop Statement—VHDL and Verilog

VHDL For-Loop Statement

```
for i in 0 to 63 loop
temp(i) := temp(i) + b(i);
end loop;
```

Verilog For-Loop Statement

```
for i = 0; i <= 63; i = i + 1
    begin
    temp[i] = temp[i] + b[i];
    end
```

As shown in Listing 10.31, the loop repeats the statement `temp(i) = temp(i) + b(i)` 64 times. This statement can be synthesized using adders. Each time the statement repeats, the index of the operands to be added is incremented. So the three lines of code in Listing 10.31 result in 64 adders. The straightforward approach to synthesizing a loop is to expand the loop into statements and synthesize each statement individually. For example, the loop in Listing 10.31 can be logically written as:

$$temp(0) = temp(0) + b(0)$$

$$temp(1) = temp\ (1) + b(1)$$

$$temp(2) = temp(2) + b(2)$$

....

$$temp(63) = temp(63) + b(63)$$

Each statement is synthesized as a 1-bit adder.

EXAMPLE 10.1 Synthesis of the Loop Statement

Consider the VHDL behavioral code shown in Listing 10.32.

LISTING 10.32 VHDL Code Includes For-Loop

```
library IEEE;
use IEEE.STD_LOGIC_1164.ALL;

entity listing10_32 is

port (a : in std_logic_vector (3 downto 0);
    c : in integer range 0 to 15;
    b : out std_logic_vector (3 downto 0));

    end listing10_32;
    architecture listing10_32 of listing10_32 is
    begin
    shfl : process (a, c)
    variable result, j : integer;
    variable temp : std_logic_vector (3 downto 0);
    begin

        result := 0;
        lop1 : for i in 0 to 3 loop
            if a(i) = '1' then
            result := result + 2**i;
            end if;
        end loop;
            if result > c then
            lop2 : for i in 0 to 3 loop
                j := (i + 2) mod 4;
                temp (j) := a(i);
            end loop;
                else
```

```
            lop3 : for i in 0 to 3 loop
                j := (i + 1) mod 4;
                temp (j) := a(i);
            end loop;

        end if;
    b <= temp;
end process shfl;

end listing10_32;
```

The code in Listing 10.32 describes a system with one 4-bit input a, one integer input c, and a 4-bit output b. In the hardware domain, there are only bits; so the integer c, since its range is from 0 to 15, is represented by 4 bits. If you are using a vendor's synthesizer, be sure to specify the integer range; otherwise, the synthesizer, since it does not know the range, will allocate more than 32 bits for the integer. Figure 10.34 summarizes the information retrieved from the entity.

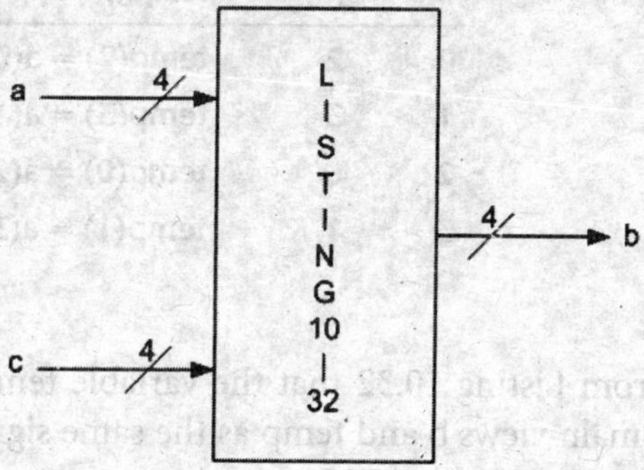

FIGURE 10.34 Information retrieved from entity listing10_32.

The simulation output of the system described by Listing 10.32 is shown in Figure 10.35. From the figure, we see that the system shuffles input a with two shuffling patterns, depending on whether a is greater than c or not.

The code in Listing 10.32 included a process labeled shfl. The process has an if statement and three for-loops: lop1, lop2, and lop3. The first for-loop, lop1, converts the std_logic_vector a to an integer. This conversion is ignored by the hardware domain; the main goal of this conversion is so that a can be compared with the integer c. The hardware views the variable result and a as the same signal. The if statement that starts with:

```
if result > c then
```

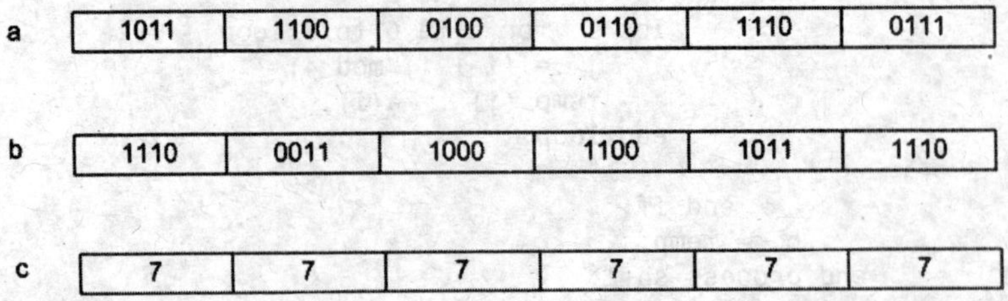

FIGURE 10.35 Simulation output of Listing 10.32.

is complete; if `result > c`, then loop `lop2` is executed. Otherwise, loop `lop3` is executed. Accordingly, latches are not needed to synthesize this `if` statement. For loop `lop2`, we expand the loop as shown in Table 10.14.

TABLE 10.14 Expanding the Loop `lop2`

i	j	temp(j) = a(i)
0	2	temp(2) = a(0)
1	3	temp(3) = a(1)
2	0	temp(0) = a(2)
3	1	temp(1) = a(3)

Notice from Listing 10.32 that the variable temp is identical to signal b; the hardware domain views b and temp as the same signal. For loop `lop3`, we expand the loop as shown in Table 10.15.

TABLE 10.15 Expanding Loop `lop3`

i	j	temp(j) = a(i)
0	1	temp(1) = a(0)
1	2	temp(2) = a(1)
2	3	temp(3) = a(2)
3	0	temp(0) = a(3)

From Tables 10.14 and 10.15, we conclude that the logic diagram of the system consists of a 4-bit magnitude comparator and four 2x1 multiplexers (see Figure 10.36). The 4-bit comparator can be built from 4-bit adders (see Chapter 4).

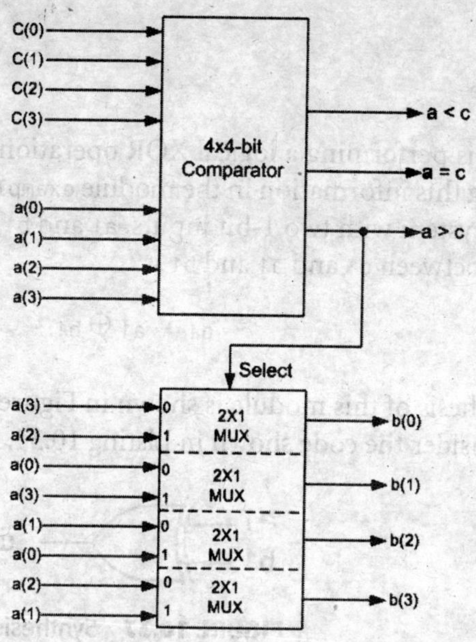

FIGURE 10.36 RTL synthesis of Listing 10.32.

10.3.7 Mapping Procedure or Task

As mentioned in Chapter 6, "Procedures, Tasks, and Functions," procedures, tasks, and functions are code constructs that optimize HDL module writing. In the hardware domain, we do not have a logic for procedures or tasks, they are incorporated in the entity or the module that calls them. Consider the Verilog code for task shown in Listing 10.33.

LISTING 10.33 A Verilog Example of a Task

```
module example_task (a1, b1, d1);
input a1, b1;
output d1;
reg d1;
always @ (a1, b1)
begin

xor_synth (d1, a1, b1);
end

task xor_synth;
output d;
input a, b;
begin
d = a ^ b;
end
```

```
endtask

endmodule
```

The task is performing a logical XOR operation on two operands, a and b. By incorporating this information in the module example_task, we can summarize the module as a system with two 1-bit inputs, a1 and b1, and one 1-bit output, d1. The relationship between d1 and a1 and b1 is:

$$d1 = a1 \oplus b1.$$

The synthesis of this module is shown in Figure 10.37.

Now consider the code shown in Listing 10.34.

FIGURE 10.37 Synthesis of Listing 10.33.

LISTING 10.34 An Example of a Procedure

```
library IEEE;
use IEEE.STD_LOGIC_1164.ALL;

entity Int_Bin is
generic (N : integer := 3);
port (X_bin : out std_logic_vector (N downto 0);
    Y_int : in integer;
    flag_even : out std_logic);
end Int_Bin;

architecture convert of Int_Bin is

procedure itb (bin : out std_logic_vector;
    signal flag : out std_logic;

N : in integer; int : inout integer) is

begin
if (int MOD 2 = 0) then
    flag <= '1';
    else
    flag <= '0';
end if;
for i in 0 to N loop
```

```
        if (int MOD 2 = 1) then
        bin (i) := '1';
        else
        bin (i) := '0';
        end if;

        int := int / 2;
    end loop;
    end itb;

    begin
    process (Y_int)
    variable tem : std_logic_vector (N downto 0);
    variable tem_int : integer;

    begin
        tem_int := Y_int;
        itb (tem, flag_even, N, tem_int);
        X_bin <= tem;
    end process;
    end convert;
```

Let's analyze the procedure `itb`. This procedure has two outputs (`flag` and `bin`), one input (`N`) and one inout (`int`). In the hardware domain, there is no distinction between variables and signals; all are signals. Also, type integer has to be converted to binary. The signal flag checks to see if signal `int` is divisible by 2 (even) or not (odd). This is done by the statements:

```
if (int MOD 2 = 0) then
    flag <= '1';
    else
    flag <= '0';
end if;
```

The procedure also includes a for-loop:

```
for i in 0 to N loop

    if (int MOD 2 = 1) then
        bin (i) := '1';
        else
        bin (i) := '0';
    end if;

    int := int / 2;
end loop;
```

The loop is converting type integer `int` to binary `bin`. This conversion is not mapped to the hardware domain. As mentioned above, all signals in the hardware domain are binary; we cannot have an integer signal in the hardware domain. So for our synthesis, the procedure is performing a test to see whether the signal is even or odd.

Now let's analyze the entity `Int_Bin`. The entity has two outputs: a 4-bit signal `X_bin` (since `N` = 3) and a 1-bit signal `flag_even`. The entity has one input of type integer, `Y_int`. The entity has one process:

```
process (Y_int)
variable tem : std_logic_vector (N downto 0);
variable tem_int : integer;

begin
    tem_int := Y_int;
    itb (tem, flag_even, N, tem_int);
    X_bin <= tem;
end process;
```

FIGURE 10.38 Synthesis of Listing 10.34.

The process is calling the procedure `itb`; the integer `Y_int` is converted to binary `X_bin`, and `flag_even` is assigned a value 1 if `Y_int` is even or 0 if it is odd. To find the hardware logic of `flag_even`, we notice that if any binary number is even, then the least significant bit is 0, otherwise the number is odd. So, `flag_even` = $\overline{X\_bin(0)}$. That is all there is to the synthesis of Listing 10.34. Figure 10.38 shows the synthesis of Listing 10.34; it is just a single inverter.

10.3.8 Mapping the Function Statement

Functions, like procedures, are simulation constructs; they optimize the HDL module writing style. Consider the Verilog code shown in Listing 10.35.

LISTING 10.35 Verilog Example of a `Function`

```
module Func_synth (a1, b1, d1);
input a1, b1;
output d1;
reg d1;

always @ (a1, b1)
begin


d1 = andopr (a1, b1);
end
```

```
function andopr;
input a, b;
begin

andopr = a ^ b;
end
endfunction

endmodule
```

In the hardware domain, there is no distinction between the main module and a function; we look to see what the function is performing, and then we incorporate this information in the entity or module where the function is being called. For

FIGURE 10.39 Synthesis of Listing 10.35.

example, in Listing 10.35, we see that the function `andopr` is performing an AND logical operation on two operands. The result is a single operand. In the module `Func_synth`, this function is called to perform an AND operation on the two inputs of the module, `a1` and `b1`; the result is stored in the output of the module `d1`. So Listing 10.35 is synthesized as shown in Figure 10.39; it has an AND gate with two 1-bit inputs, `a1` and `b1`, and a 1-bit output, `d1`.

Another example of function synthesis is shown in Listing 10.36.

LISTING 10.36 Example of Function Synthesis

```
module Function_Synth2 (x, y);

input [2:0] x;
output [3:0] y;
reg [3:0] y;

always @ (x)
begin
y = fn (x);
end

function [3:0] fn;
input [2:0] a;
begin

if (a <= 4)

fn = 2 * a + 5;
```

```
end
endfunction

endmodule
```

The function in Listing 10.36 has one 3-bit input a and one 4-bit output fn. If the value of the input is less or equal to 4, the output is calculated as fn = 2 * a + 5. If the input is greater than 4, the function does not change the previous value of the output. Incorporating the function into the module Function_Synth2, we summarize the module as representing a system with one 3-bit input x and one 4-bit output y. If x is less or equal to 4, y = 2 * a + 5. If x is greater than 4, y retains its previous value. This means that latches must be used to retain the previous value.

Figure 10.40 shows the simulation output of the module Function_Synth2. As is shown, if x is greater than 4, y retains its previous value. To synthesize this module, we use four high-level triggered D-latches, since output y is 4 bits. If x is from 0 to 4, these latches should be transparent; if x is from 5 to 7, these latches should be inactive. We design a signal clk connected to the clock of the latches; if x is from 0 to 4, the clk is high; otherwise it is low. Table 10.16 shows the truth table of signal clk.

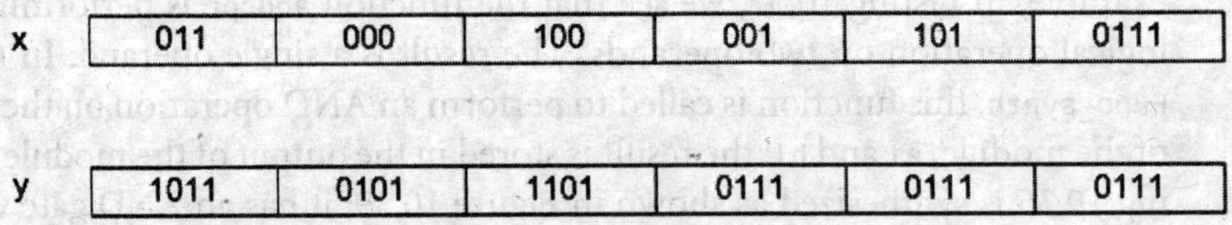

FIGURE 10.40 Simulation output of Listing 10.36.

TABLE 10.16 Truth Table for Signal clk

x(2)	x(1)	x(0)	clk
0	0	0	1
0	0	1	1
0	1	0	1
0	1	1	1
1	0	0	1
1	0	1	0
1	1	0	0
1	1	1	0

From Table 10.16, the signal clk can be written as:

$$clk = \overline{x(2)} + \overline{x(0)}\ \overline{x(1)}$$

The truth table of output y when clk is high is shown in Table 10.17.

By inspecting Table 10.17, we find:

TABLE 10.17 Truth Table for Output y When clk is High

x(2)	x(1)	x(0)	y(3)	y(2)	y(1)	y(0)
0	0	0	0	1	0	1
0	0	1	0	1	1	1
0	1	0	1	0	0	1
0	1	1	1	0	1	1
1	0	0	1	1	0	1
1	0	1	d	d	d	d
1	1	0	d	d	d	d
1	1	1	d	d	d	d

$$y(0) = 1$$

$$y(1) = x(0)$$

$$y(2) = \overline{x(1)}$$

$$y(3) = x(1) + x(2)$$

Figure 10.41 shows the synthesis of Listing 10.36.

As shown in Figure 10.41, the main components of the synthesis are latches. These latches are for storing the previous values of y. If we can modify the `if` statement in Listing 10.36 to make it complete, we may avoid the use of the four latches in Figure 10.41 (see Exercise 10.8).

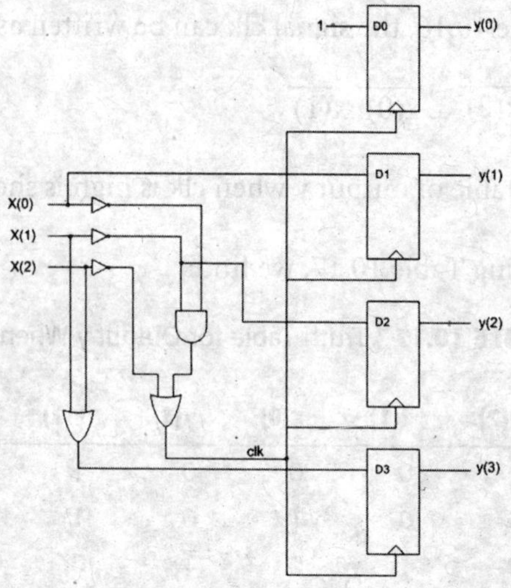

FIGURE 10.41 Synthesis of Listing 10.36.

10.4 SUMMARY

This chapter covered the fundamentals of hardware synthesis. We looked at synthesis as reverse engineering; HDL code has synthesized it into gates and latches. The steps of synthesizing any system can be summarized as follows:

1. Formulate the flowchart of the system.
2. Write the behavioral code of the system.
3. Simulate the behavioral code to verify the code.
4. Map the behavioral statements into hardware components and gates.
5. Write the structural code for the components and gates.
6. Simulate the structural code and compare it with the behavioral simulation to verify the mapping.
7. Download the components and gates into an electronic chip.
8. Test the chip to verify that the download represents the system.

We saw that the hardware domain is very limited in comparison to the simulation domain. For example, the hardware domain cannot distinguish between VHDL variables and signals. We learned how to map behavioral statements, such as `if`, `case`, and `for-loop`. Any signal that needs to retain a value must be mapped using latches. Procedures, tasks, and functions are simulation tools; they do not have explicit hardware mappings. The operations they perform should be incorporated in the entity or in the module to be synthesized. Integers should be declared, if possible, with a range; this reduces the number of bits the synthesizer allocates for the integer. If the range is not specified; the synthesizer allocates at least 32 bits for integers.

10.5 EXERCISES

10.1 Synthesize the code in Listing 10.37, simulate it, write the structural description, and verify it.

LISTING 10.37 Code for Exercise 10.1

```
library IEEE;
use IEEE.STD_LOGIC_1164.ALL;
use ieee.numeric_std.all;

entity IF_sgned is
port (a : in signed (3 downto 0); Y : out Boolean);
end IF_sgned;

architecture IF_sgned of IF_sgned is

begin

IfB : process (a)
variable tem : Boolean;
begin
if (a < "1100") then
tem := true;
else
tem := false;
end if;
Y <= tem;
end process;
end IF_sgned;
```

10.2 Synthesize the code in Listing 10.38. Simulate it, write the structural description, and verify it.

LISTING 10.38 Code for Exercise 10.2

```
module elseif2 (inp, outp);
input [3:0] inp;
output [2:0] outp;
reg [2:0] outp;
always @ (inp)
begin

    if (inp[0] == 1'b1)
    outp = 3'd7;
    else if (inp[1] == 1'b1)
```

```
        outp = 3'd6;
        else if (inp[2] == 1'b1)
        outp = 3'd5;
        else
        outp = 3'd0;
    end

    endmodule
```

10.3 Verify the synthesis of Listing 10.26 by writing gate-level structural VHDL code for Figure 10.26. Simulate the code and verify that the simulation output is the same as that for Listing 10.26.

10.4 For the code in Listing10.26, change the following lines:

```
    else
        z_tem := 15;

        end if;
```

to just

```
        end if;
```

Synthesize the new code using multiplexers, gates, and flip-flops (if needed).

10.5 Simulate the VHDL behavioral code of Listing 10.30. Write the VHDL structural description of the logic diagram shown in Figure 10.32 and simulate it. Verify that the two simulations are identical.

10.6 Synthesize the behavioral code shown in Listing 10.39 using RTL.

LISTING 10.39 Code for Exercise 10.6

```
library IEEE;
use IEEE.STD_LOGIC_1164.ALL;

entity exercise is

port (a : in std_logic_vector (3 downto 0);
    c : in integer range 0 to 15;
    b : out std_logic_vector (3 downto 0));

    end exercise;
    architecture exercise of exercise is
    begin
    shfl : process (a, c)
    variable result, j : integer;
```

```
        variable temp : std_logic_vector (3 downto 0);
    begin

        result := 0;
        lop1 : for i in 0 to 3 loop
            if a(i) = '1' then
            result := result + 2**i;
            end if;
            end loop;
            if result > c then
            lop2 : for i in 0 to 3 loop
                j := (i + 3) mod 4;
                temp (j) := a(i);
                end loop;

            end if;
    b <= temp;
    end process shfl;

end exercise;
```

10.7 For Figure 10.41, write the structural code for the logic shown in the figure, simulate it and verify that the figure is the synthesis of Listing 10.36.

10.8 We want to realize Figure 10.41 on a programmable device, such as an FPGA. Use the synthesis tools (provided in most cases with the HDL package) to synthesize the code of Listing 10.36. Compare the outcome of the synthesizer with Figure 41 and report the differences. Now, use the tools provided in your HDL package to download the design into an FPGA or compatible chip. Use the same test signals to compare the software's simulation and the hardware's. Report the differences and suggest how to minimize these differences.

10.9 In Listing 10.36, if statement inside function `fn` is written as:

```
function [3:0] fn;
input [2:0] a;
begin

if (a <= 4)

fn = 2 * a + 5;
end
endfunction

endmodule
```

then it is likely that the code is intended to say that if a is greater than 4, then the value of `fn` is unimportant. If this is true, can you modify the function's code to avoid using the four latches? Redraw the synthesis of your code.

10.6 REFERENCES

[Hayes98] Hayes, J. P., *Computer Architecture and Organization*, 3rd ed. McGraw Hill, 1998.

[Katz05] Katz, B., *Digital Design from Gates to Intelligent Machines.* Charles River Media, 2005.

[Mano00] Mano, M. M. and C. R. Kime, *Logic and Computer Design Fundamentals.* Prentice Hall, 2000.

[Nelson95] Nelson V. P., H. T. Nagle, B. D. Carroll, and J. D. Irwin, *Digital Logic Circuit Analysis & Design.* Prentice Hall, 1995.

Appendix

A Creating a Project in Xilinx 7.1® Using VHDL or Verilog

In the following, we show the steps necessary to create a project using Xilinx ISE 1.7i Webpack. Although these steps are for ISE 1.7i, the same concepts here can be applied to other versions or to other vendors' products. These steps are for beginners. To find out more about this Webpack, go to: *http://www.xilinx.com/ise/logic_design_prod/webpack.htm.*

1. Double-click on the Xilinx Project Navigator icon. From the toolbar, select File > New Project. A dialog box will open (see Figure A.1).

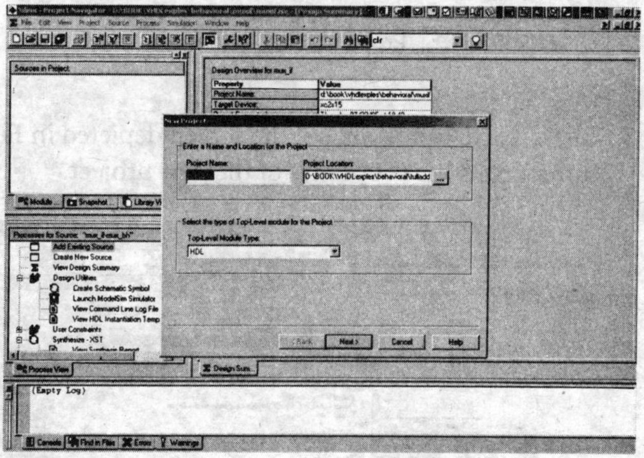

FIGURE A.1 New Project dialog box.

2. In the New Project dialog box, type the desired location in the Project Location field, or browse to the directory under which you want to create your new project directory using the browse (...) button next to the Project Location field.

3. Enter the name of the project. In Figure A.1; the name entered is "fulladder."
4. Click "Next" (see Figure A.2) and enter the appropriate information. In Figure A.2, the language is selected to be VHDL, and the simulator is ModelSim™. The device is the chip where the HDL program, if desired, is downloaded after synthesis. If the desired language is Verilog, then select Verilog instead of VHDL.

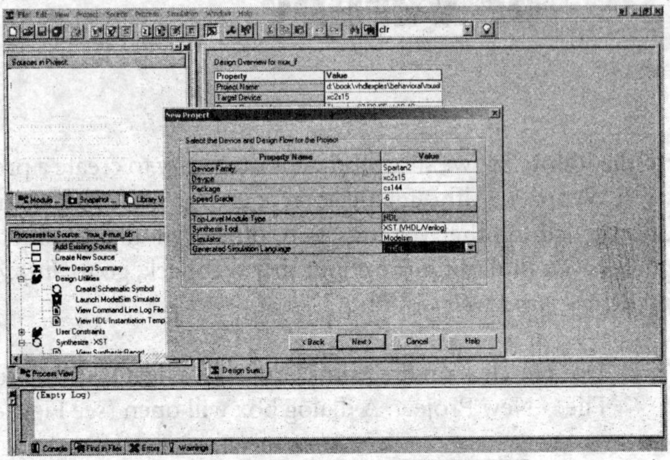

FIGURE A.2 Project dialog box.

5. Click "Next" until you see the screen depicted in Figure A.3. This window summarizes the properties of the new project.

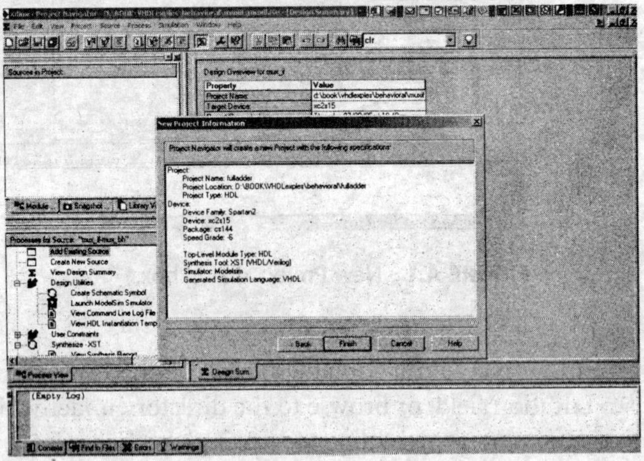

FIGURE A.3 Summary of entries to the project "fulladder."

6. Click "Finish" (see Figure A.4). The screen now shows the name of the project and the device.

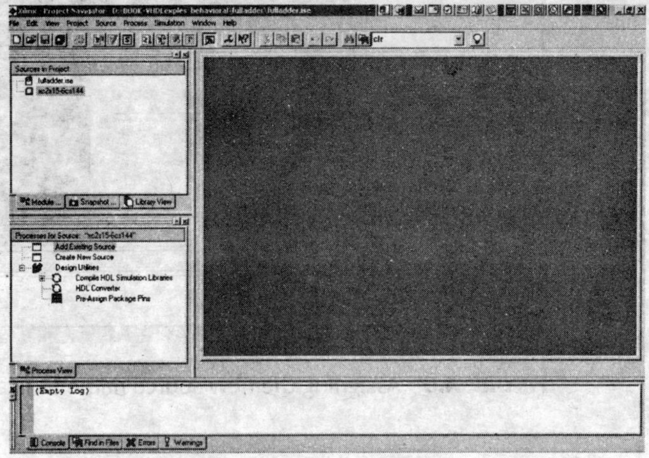

FIGURE A.4 Simulation screen after clicking "Finish."

7. Attach the HDL module to your project. Click "Project" and select "New Source" (see Figure A.5).

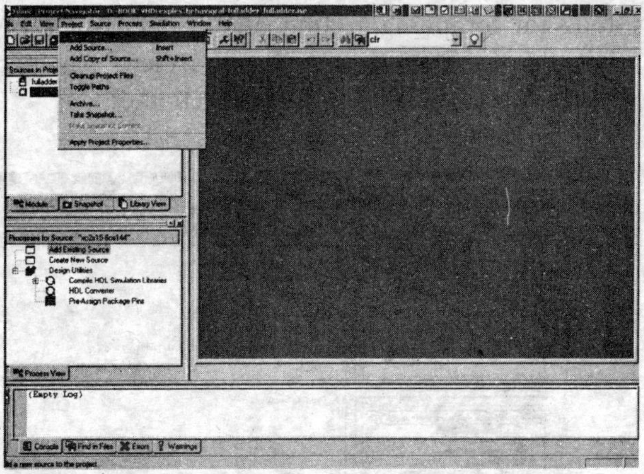

FIGURE A.5 Attaching a new source to the project.

8. Since we are writing a VHDL module, select "VHDL Module" and enter its name (Figure A.6). It is preferable to leave the location as it is so that the module and the project are stored in the same directory. If writing Verilog, select "Verilog Module."

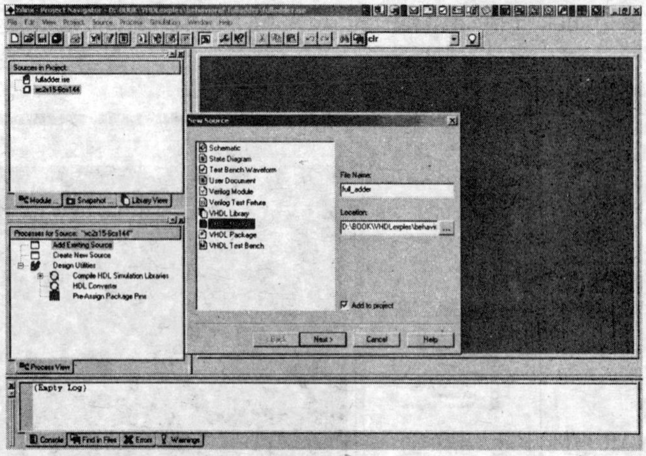

FIGURE A.6 Assigning the new source name and language.

9. Keep clicking "Next" until you can click "Finish." You will then have the windows shown in Figure A.7. The screen section of "Sources in Project" shows the name of the project and the VHDL module. The right-hand section of the screen shows a template for the VHDL module. Erase any comments or Libraries that you do not need in your module. Referring to the left-hand side of Figure A.7, the "Processes for Source" panel shows the tools for compiling, testing, and synthesizing the VHDL module. On the bottom of the screen, the "Process View" panel accesses selected tools to display reports (logs) on various activities.

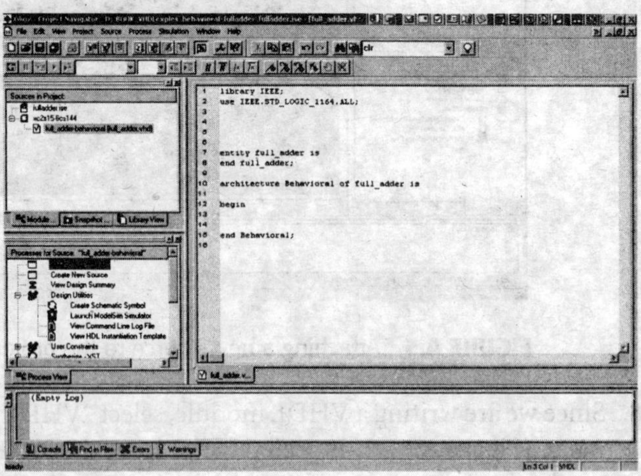

FIGURE A.7 The project and module screen.

10. Enter the VHDL module (see Figure A.8). "Copy," "Cut," and "Paste" can be accessed via "Edit" on the toolbar. After you finish writing the module, click "Save."

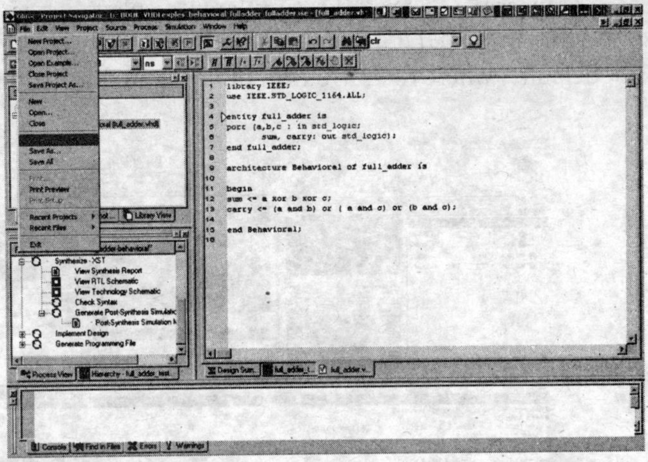

FIGURE A.8 Saving the module.

11. Check the syntax of the VHDL program by clicking on "Check Syntax" (see Figure A.9). Be sure that the file "full_adder" is selected, as shown in Figure A.9. The compiler displays a report in the "Process View" section of the screen. If there are any compilation errors, they will be listed in this report.

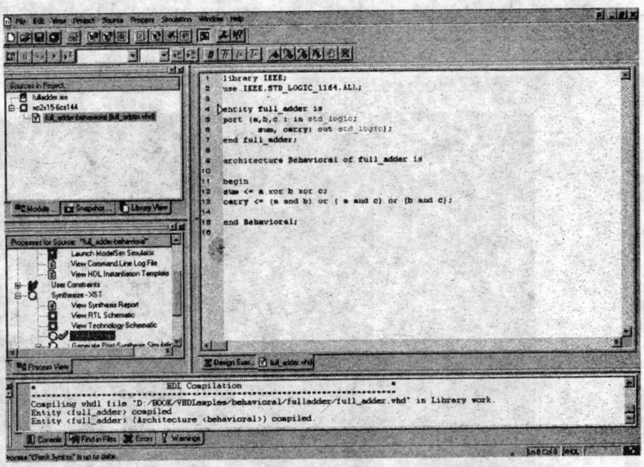

FIGURE A.9 Checking the syntax of the HDL module.

12. Double-click on "Launch ModelSim Simulator" located in the "Processes in Source" section of the screen. Figure A.10 shows the screen after double-clicking. The figure includes two screens, the main screen under the name "Transcript," where the simulator displays its activities, including any errors in the HDL module; and waveform screen under the name "wave-default," where the waveform of the simulation is displayed.

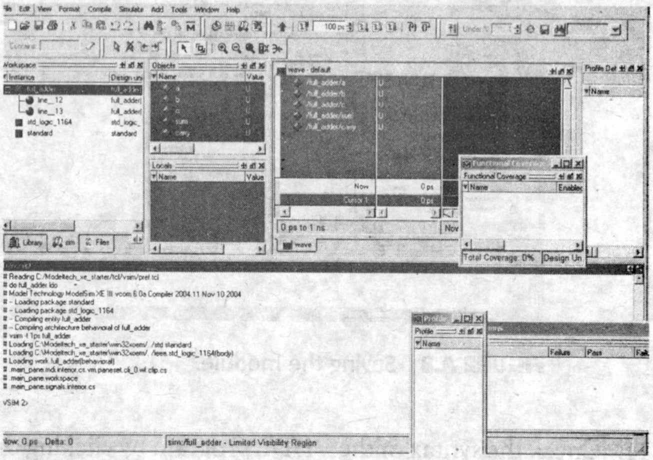

FIGURE A.10 Simulation Screen.

13. Select the waveform screen by clicking the "+" button in the upper-right corner of the "wave-default" screen. Figure A.11 shows the waveform screen.

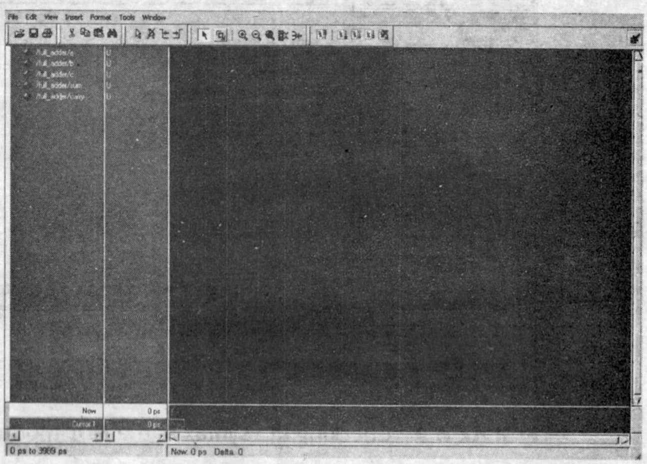

FIGURE A.11 Waveform screen.

14. Now we want to assign signals to the inputs of the full adder (a, b, c). This is done by selecting the signal on the waveform screen and right-clicking the mouse. Click "Clock" on the dialog box, and the "Define Clock" window will open (see Figure A.12). Select a period of 400 ps for the clock. Do the same for signal b, but select a clock with period of 200 ps.

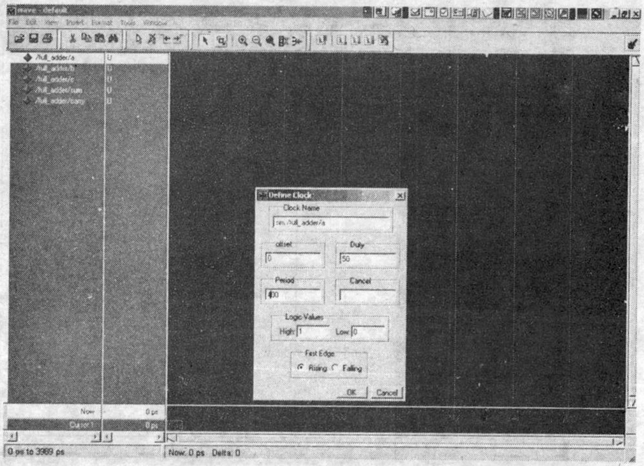

FIGURE A.12 Assigning a clock signal of period 400 ps to signal a.

15. For signal c, we want to assign a value of 1. This is done by selecting "/full_adder/c" in the waveform window, right-clicking, and selecting "Force" from the dialog box. Figure A.13 shows how to assign a value of 1 to signal c.

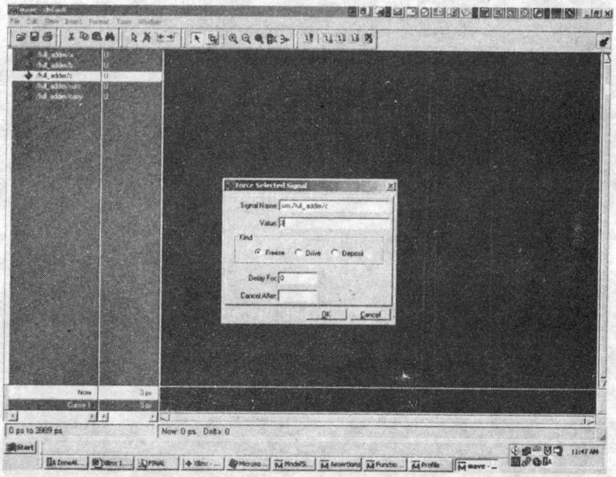

FIGURE A.13 Assigning a value of 1 to signal c.

16. Click the "Run" button located on the toolbar of the "wave-default" screen (↓). The screen will display the waveform of the output signals (sum and carry), as shown in Figure A.14. By inspecting the waveform, we find that it represents a full adder; at any value of a, b, and c, sum and carry represent the sum and carry after adding a + b + c.

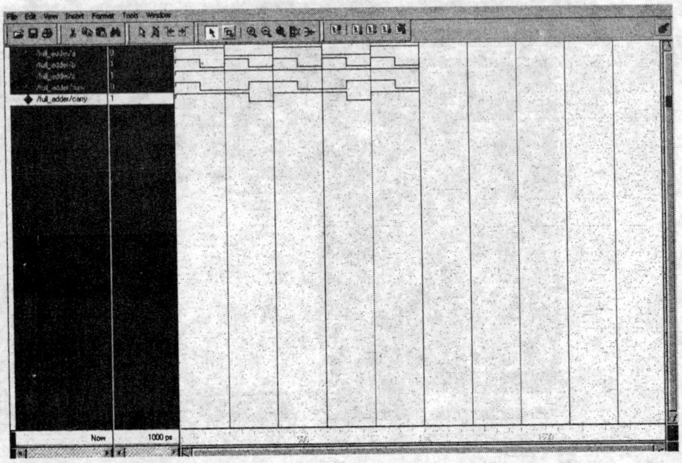

FIGURE A.14 Simulation waveform of a full adder.

Appendix

B Summary of HDL Commands

The following list summarizes the major commands for both VHDL and Verilog.

I. GENERAL ORGANIZATION

VHDL

```
library IEEE;
use IEEE.STD_LOGIC_1164.ALL;
entity indx is
port(I1, I2 : in std_logic;
I3 : bit_vector (5 downto 0);
    O1 : buffer bit);
end;
architecture anyname of indx is
signal s1 : std_logic;
begin
s1 <= I1;
P1 : process (I1)
variable s2 : std_logic;
begin
if (I1 ='0') then
s2 := I1;
else
s2 := I2;
end if;
end process P1;
end anyname;
```

Verilog

```
module indx(I1, I2, I3, O1);
output O1;
input I1, I2;
input [5:0] I3;

wire s1;
reg s2;
assign s1 = I1;
always @ (I1)
begin

if (I1 == 0)
s2 = I1;
else
s2 = I2;
end
endmodule
```

II. GATE-LEVEL DESCRIPTION

VHDL

```
architecture gt_lvl of
        entity_name is
component andgate2
port (I1, I2 : bit;
      O1 : out bit);
end component;
component orgate3
port (I1, I2, I3 : bit;
      O1 : out bit);
end component;
for all : andgate2
use entity work.
name_entity (name_architecture);
for all : andgate3
use entity work.
name_entity (name_architecture);

begin
--instantiation statements

a1 : andgate2
port map (x, y, z);
a2 : andgate3
port map (x1, y1, y2, z);
end gt_lvl ;
```

Verilog

```
and (z, x, y);

and(z, x1, y1, y2, z);
```

III. SWITCH-LEVEL DESCRIPTION

VHDL

No built-in

switch level statements

Verilog

```
nmos n1 (drain, source,
  gate);
pmos n1 (drain, source,
  gate);
cmos (output, input, gn, gp);
tran (dataio1, dataio2);
trannif0 (dataio1, dataio2,
   control);
tranif1 (dataio1, dataio2,
control);
```

IV. OPERATORS

VHDL	Verilog
Arithmetic	
+, -, *, /, mod, **, (&)	+, -, *, /, %, **, {,}
Relational	
=, /=, <, <=, >, >=	==, !=, <, <=, >, >=, ===, !==
Shift	
sll, slr, sla, sra, rol, ror	<<, >>
Logical	
AND, OR, NAND, NOR, XOR, XNOR, NOT	&, |, ~(&), ~(|), ^, ~^, ~

V. SEQUENTIAL STATEMENTS

IF Statement

VHDL

```
if (Boolean Expression) then
    statements;
    else
    statements;
    end if;
        begin
            statements;
        end
```

Verilog

```
if(Boolean Expression)
begin
    statements;
end
else
```

Else-If Statement

VHDL

```
if (Boolean Expression1) then
statements;
elsif (Boolean expression2) then
    statements;
        else
    statements;
end if;
```

Verilog

```
if (Boolean Expression1)
begin
    statements;
end
else if (Boolean expression2)
begin
    statements;
end
else
begin
    statements;
end
```

Case Statement

```
case (control-expression) is
    when test value => statements;

    when test value => statements;

    when test value => statements;

    when others => statements;

end case;
```

```
case (control-expression)
    test value1 : begin
statements; end
    test value2 : begin
statements; end
    test value3 : begin
statements; end
    default : begin
statements; end
endcase
```

For-Loop Statement

```
for i in 0 to N loop
1)
    statements;
end loop;
```

```
for (i = 0; i <= N; i = i +

begin
    statements;
end
```

```
for i in N downto 0 loop
1)
    statements;
end loop;
```

```
for (i = N; i >= 0; i = i -

begin
    statements;
end
```

While-Loop Statement

```
while (i < x)loop
    statements;
end loop;
```

```
while (i < x)
begin
    statements;
end
```

Verilog Repeat

```
repeat (N)
begin
statements;
end
```

Verilog Forever

```
initial
begin
clk = 1'b0;
forever #20 clk = ~clk;
end
```

Procedure Example

```
procedure Haddr (sh, ch :
out bit; ah, bh : in bit) is
```

Task Example

```
task Haddr;
output sh, ch;
input ah, bh;
```

```
begin
sh := ah xor bh;
ch := ah and bh;
end Haddr;
```

```
begin
sh = ah ^ bh;
ch = ah & bh;
end
endtask
```

Function Example

```
function exp (a, b : in std_logic)
    return std_logic is
variable d : std_logic;
begin
d := a xor b;
return d;
end function exp;
```

```
function exp
input a, b;
begin
exp = a ^ b;
end
endfunction
```

VI. MISCELLANEOUS

VHDL

Verilog

Generate Statement

```
L1 : for i in 0 to N generate
--instantiation statements
v1 : inv port map (Y(i), Yb(i));
--other concurrent statements
end generate;
end
```

```
generate
genvar i;
for (i =0; i <= N; i = i + 1)
begin : u
not (Yb[i], Y[i]);
//other structural statements
endgenerate
```

Generic

```
Generic (N : integer := 3);
```

Parameter

```
parameter N = 3;
```

Concatenation

```
s <= (Q & clk);
```

```
assign s = {Q, clk};
```

VHDL Type Example

```
type grades is (A, B, C, D, F, I);
```

VHDL Package Example

```
package conversions is
    type wkdays is (mon, tue, wed);
    procedure convert (a : in bit;
        b : out integer);
    function incr (b : std_logic_vector)
        return std_logic_vector;
end conversions;
```

```
package body conversions is

Procedure convert (a : in bit;
b : out integer) is
Begin
    .......
End convert;
function incr (b : std_logic_vector)
return std_logic_vector is
begin
    ...
 end incr;

 end conversions;
```

Report

```
report "message";
```

Display

```
$display ("message");
```

Arrays

Single Array of Four Elements, Each Element is 2 Bits

```
type datavector is array
    (3 downto 0) of wordarray;
subtype wordarray is
    std_logic_vector (1 downto 0);
```

```
reg [1:0] datavector [0:3];
```

VHDL Two-Dimensional Array, Each Single-Dimensional Array Has Three Elements of Type Integer

```
subtype wordg is integer;
type singl is array (2 downto 0) of wordg;
type doubl is array (1 downto 0) of singl;
```

VII. MIXED LANGUAGE

VHDL

Invoking a Verilog Module from A VHDL Component

```
library IEEE;
use IEEE.STD_LOGIC_1164.ALL;
entity Ver_VHD is
    port (a, b : in std_logic;
        c : out std_logic);
end Ver_VHD;
is the VHDL entity to be
component V_modl
    port (x, y : in std_logic;
```

Verilog

Invoking a VHDL Module from A Verilog Module

```
module mixed (a, b, c, d);
input a, b;
output c, d;
...........
VHD_enty V1 (a, b, c, d);
/*The above module VHD_enty
                  ...........
endmodule
```

```
        z : out std_logic);

--The name of the Component V_modl
--should be identical to the name
--of the Verilog module.

end component;

.......
end Ver_VHD;
```

Appendix

C About the CD-ROM

The CD-ROM included with *HDL Programming Fundamentals* includes all of the code from the various Examples and Listings found in the book.

CD-ROM FOLDERS

Code: Contains all the code from the Listings and Examples in the book, by chapter. To use the code, copy and paste it into the project navigator screen of the HDL simulator.

Figures: Includes all of the figures from the book, by chapter.

OVERALL SYSTEM REQUIREMENTS

- Windows NT®, Windows® 2000, or Windows® XP.
- VHDL and Verilog Simulator Package. Read the simulator's specifications to find its system requirements. To run mixed-language examples, the simulator should be able to handle mixed-language code.

Index

Numbers

Symbols

E

F

O

P

R